Decent, Safe and
Sanitary Dwellings

ALSO BY JAMES P. HUBBARD

The United States and the End of British Colonial Rule in Africa, 1941–1968 (McFarland, 2011)

Decent, Safe and Sanitary Dwellings

The National Conversation About Public Housing, 1932–1973

JAMES P. HUBBARD

McFarland & Company, Inc., Publishers
Jefferson, North Carolina

LIBRARY OF CONGRESS CATALOGUING-IN-PUBLICATION DATA

Names: Hubbard, James P. (James Patrick), 1945– author.
Title: Decent, safe and sanitary dwellings : the national conversation about public housing, 1932–1973 / James P. Hubbard.
Description: Jefferson, North Carolina : McFarland & Company, Inc., Publishers, 2018 | Includes bibliographical references and index.
Identifiers: LCCN 2018023808 | ISBN 9781476674483 (softcover : acid free paper) ∞
Subjects: LCSH: Public housing—United States—History—20th century. | Housing policy—United States—History—20th century.
Classification: LCC HD7288.78.U5 H83 2018 | DDC 363.50973/0904— dc23
LC record available at https://lccn.loc.gov/2018023808

BRITISH LIBRARY CATALOGUING DATA ARE AVAILABLE

ISBN (print) 978-1-4766-7448-3
ISBN (ebook) 978-1-4766-3336-7

© 2018 James P. Hubbard. All rights reserved

No part of this book may be reproduced or transmitted in any form or by any means, electronic or mechanical, including photocopying or recording, or by any information storage and retrieval system, without permission in writing from the publisher.

Front cover photograph of slum housing, November 1935, by Carl Mydans (Library of Congress); *background* aerial view of Williamsburg Houses, Brooklyn, New York, 1939 (Library of Congress)

Printed in the United States of America

McFarland & Company, Inc., Publishers
  Box 611, Jefferson, North Carolina 28640
  www.mcfarlandpub.com

Table of Contents

Preface 1

♦ CHAPTER ONE ♦
Competing Visions 3

♦ CHAPTER TWO ♦
The 1937 Housing Act 42

♦ CHAPTER THREE ♦
The 1949 Housing Act 64

♦ CHAPTER FOUR ♦
After the 1949 Act 101

♦ CHAPTER FIVE ♦
Buildings 132

♦ CHAPTER SIX ♦
Tenants 159

♦ CHAPTER SEVEN ♦
African Americans 185

♦ CHAPTER EIGHT ♦
Final Judgments 221

Conclusions 237
Chapter Notes 245
Bibliography 269
Index 283

Preface

In 1937, the Congress passed the Housing Act of 1937 whose goal was to produce "decent, safe and sanitary dwellings" for low-income families. Thirty-six years later, President Richard Nixon halted the program authorized by the Housing Act, claiming that it had turned the federal government into the "biggest slumlord in history." According to Nixon, the government had built some of the worst housing in America. Many projects were "monstrous, depressing places—run down, overcrowded, crime-ridden." Nixon's statement could be offered as an example of hyperbole since the federal government was not the landlord in any public housing developments. It is more significant, however, in that it marked the end of national conversation about public housing, that is, government-funded, -built and -managed rental housing for families.[1]

What follows is an account of that conversation from about 1932, when housing became a national issue, through 1973, when Nixon brought the public housing program to a close. The aim is to use the debates about public housing to illuminate the history of both the United States and public housing.

I have tried to capture what people wrote and said about public housing in public, in journals and before congressional committees. I have taken public statements at face value and not considered private correspondence or other views into behind-the-scenes events. Similarly, I have concentrated on materials readily available to a wide public and paid less attention to writing available to smaller audiences, such as real estate industry newsletters.

Describing debates about public housing involved, to an extent, describing public housing itself: what was built, how it was managed, who lived there. Doing so proved more difficult than I had imagined. Debates about public housing proved notoriously short on facts and, therefore, contemporaneous accounts provide only so much information. Since 1973, historians have explored public housing, some to good effect. I have relied heavily on their efforts. Nevertheless, we still know little about the details of federal and local housing authority policies, about how local policies were put into practice, and, most striking, about the people who lived in public housing. Even within the debates about public housing, tenant voices are rarely heard. They figure only marginally in historical accounts. It does not help, of course, that public housing was dispersed across the country, in a myriad of housing projects managed by hundreds of local housing authorities. New York, Chicago, St. Louis, Philadelphia and Boston account for the bulk of, but by no means all, public housing. And we don't have thorough accounts of public housing in all those cities. I did not try to remedy the situation and write a history of public housing. I simply made the best use of what information was available. It provides a framework for the debate, but a robust account, or perhaps accounts, of public housing remains to be written.

Mine is not a totally disinterested account. Housing, especially for the least prosperous third, or even half of the American population, remains problematic. Awareness of the problems caused by the mismatch between incomes and housing costs has grown in recent years. I am optimistic enough to believe that a clear account of earlier debates about housing can contribute to solutions.

CHAPTER ONE

Competing Visions

The Great Depression made housing a hot topic. During the prosperous 1920s, writers of various persuasions worried about the state of American housing and imagined alternatives, but had little impact. The collapse of home construction in the wake of the 1929 stock market crash gave housing new urgency. Construction workers needed jobs and stimulating home construction seemed a likely step towards economic revival. With government intervention now thinkable, Americans for the first time seriously considered public housing, that is, non-private rental housing and, more narrowly, rental housing funded, built and managed by government agencies. For some, public housing was consistent with their earlier ideas. For others, concerned principally about slums, public housing represented a departure from a past emphasis on regulation as the means to eliminate bad housing. For everyone, it was a concept that needed further definition and refinement. Who should public housing serve? What sort of housing should it be? Who should pay for it? These and other questions needed answers.

Hoover Commission

Thanks to Herbert Hoover, we have a picture of mainstream American thinking about housing in the early 1930s. In December 1931, President Hoover convened a conference on home building and home ownership. Headed by Secretary of Commerce Robert Lamont and Secretary of the Interior Ray Wilbur, the conference involved a planning committee of 30 members and more than two dozen working committees. Participants included prominent architects and planners, representatives of the real estate industry, housing experts, a labor union leader, and other influential Americans. The 11 volumes produced by the conference portrayed the problems that afflicted housing in the United States and the solutions deemed acceptable by influential and well-placed Americans.

In the foreword to one volume, Secretary of Interior Wilbur wrote that the housing conditions of wage earning Americans, with few exceptions, were characterized by ugliness, poor sanitation and overcrowding. Such conditions affected millions of Americans and the slums and blighted areas of American cities and towns were an economic and social liability and disgrace. No nation, he argued, could afford to permit conditions of unwholesome daily living if only because of the colossal expenditures on poor relief and social service needed to ameliorate them. Wilbur accepted that efforts at amelioration were required but added that when prevention was possible, cure was a costly expedient.[1]

Elsewhere, the conference argued that the nation needed clear housing standards; not minimum standards; not just enough air to avoid asphyxiation, or enough light to permit life or enough space to find shelter. The standards proposed suggest the problems the conference saw in American housing.[2]

The conference held that a housing unit should have adequate light. A multiple unit dwelling should be no more than two rooms in depth. There should be no courts or light shafts. Rooms should open only on the street or on large yards or gardens with no opposite wall nearer than the height of the building.[3]

There should be adequate provision for privacy for each member of the family. Each child and older person should have a place where he could be undisturbed and quiet. Each family member should have a sleeping room. Every apartment should have its own toilet and bathroom. Rooms should be generous in size; a living room should contain at least 180 square feet. In single-family homes, ceilings should be 8½ feet high; in apartments, nine feet.[4]

The neighborhood surrounding a home should, as far as possible, have charm and distinctiveness and be free from ugliness and monotony and other conditions that tended to depress or humiliate the family. It should be primarily residential. It should be free from "moral nuisances" such as disorderly houses, centers of liquor traffic and gambling houses. Reflecting the thinking of planners like Clarence Perry, the conference saw new development in terms of neighborhoods. New developments should be developed along organic lines in self-contained communities.[5]

Perry's idea of neighborhood units included at least six principles.

Residential developments should house the population served by an elementary school. Arterial streets should define the neighborhood's boundaries. The neighborhood should include parks and recreation spaces. The elementary school and other community facilities should be centrally located. Shops to serve the neighborhood should be located on the periphery, preferably at traffic junctions and near shops serving other neighborhoods. The neighborhood's internal street system should be sized to the projected traffic and should be designed to discourage through traffic. Perry believed these principles applied to neighborhoods regardless of the type of structures. He produced plans for apartment house projects as well as single-family developments.[6]

The conference thought that the single-family detached house should be norm. It reported a "startling" trend away from such homes in favor of larger multiple dwellings. This tendency was unfortunate, it argued. Some, the conference noted, thought that it threatened American institutions. The "passing of the home" created a lack of space, order, privacy and comfort that accounted for "many tendencies" in present-day America, the conference wrote.[7]

Consistent with the home ownership promotion programs sponsored by Herbert Hoover during the 1920s, the conference also thought home ownership should be the norm. Families competent to own a home should be able to do so with a minimum of risk and at a cost that did not starve their budget for other essentials. Renting was acceptable only where the cost of financing and maintenance and taxes was too high or where "labor mobility" was needed. Families should have to pay no more than 20 percent of their income for housing. Conceding that some families were too large or too poor to be able to secure housing for 20 percent of their income, the conference thought that new methods for financing home purchases should be developed, that attracted more capital, involved lower interest rates and offered longer periods for amortization.[8]

The conference acknowledged that the private real estate industry had not produced decent homes at affordable prices for many families. The conference thought the failure to serve large numbers of families originated in a fragmented, tradition-bound construction industry, dominated by small firms each building a few houses a year using old methods. Expensive financing methods, reliance on small-scale efforts, inadequate planning, excessive labor costs were also parts of the problem.

Large-scale housing corporations were the conference's solution. The automobile industry was the model, large corporations that used new methods to produce goods for even low-income families. The conference imagined that such large housing corporations could invest in research and development of new materials and methods; achieve economies of scale; produce better designs and plans; negotiate more favorable labor agreements; and manage the construction process more effectively. Large housing corporations would be equipped to cooperate with government, industry, labor, finance and the courts to deal with housing issues. The conference saw precedents for large-scale developments in the Sunnyside (New York) and Radburn (New Jersey) projects built by the private City Housing Corporation, and in New York City projects funded by the Metropolitan Life Insurance Company and by the Amalgamated Clothing Workers.[9]

The conference maintained that, besides building better housing, the United States needed to rid itself of slums and blighted areas. According to the conference, blighted areas were those that had become an economic liability to the community. Slums were residential areas where the houses and conditions of life were a "squalid and wretched character" and which had therefore become a social liability to the community. Some slums generated profits for landlords and therefore were not an economic liability in one sense, but their economic strength made them a greater threat to the community. Slums cost the community considerable sums, for relief, for public health services, and for fire and police protection but did not generate commensurate tax revenues.[10]

According to the conference, slums had various causes. The poor quality of housing stemmed from aging and obsolescence, from outdated planning and site design, from failures to regulate housing properly and from public neglect generally. Slum neighborhoods suffered from the presence of businesses and industry, of dirt and noise. Slum dwellers were poor; some shiftless and ignorant.[11]

The conference described how it thought cities should rehabilitate the physical aspects of the slums. Cities needed legal authority to demolish houses that were hazardous to health, safety or morals, while compensating the owners fairly. Structurally sound houses would be reconditioned. The city would re-plan and re-zone the cleared areas consistent with a city's master plan. If necessary, the city would add needed public facilities, streets, parks or transportation. Private developers could then rebuild the area to the proper standards and the city would enact measures to prevent development of other slums.[12]

The conference thought that responsibility for eliminating slums and building better housing rested with the business community and existing government agencies. At the same time, the conference conceded that the private sector and local governments had made negligible progress and that traditional methods were unlikely to produce the needed investments. The committee estimated that decent housing for 10 percent of the population, the families earning just less than the top third of all earners, would cost $5.5 billion. The conference listed possible financing methods—government-built housing, limited dividend corporations with government subsidies, public-private partnerships, privately-financed corporations, tax exemptions, cooperative housing, housing for municipal workers, and investments by philanthropists. Of these, it preferred limited dividend corporations, private corporations that agreed to limit their profits in order to produce cheaper housing.[13]

Limited dividend corporations, while not unknown in the United States, would not create themselves, the conference wrote. Businessmen would need to appreciate that reviving the construction industry was in the nation's best interests. Investors would need to be convinced that the government would cooperate and that limited dividend corporations were needed and could operate on a businesslike basis. To stimulate their creation, the conference proposed a national housing agency, tied to the federal government, but headed by an independent board of leading citizens. The national housing agency would stimulate states and cities to carry out the conference's other recommendations.[14]

The conference was sufficiently pessimistic about the private sector's ability and willingness to produce decent affordable housing that it raised the specter of government-built housing. If business, financial and industrial groups did not take on the task, the conference warned, American cities would turn to European methods and subsidize housing or even build and operate housing themselves. This was an all or nothing proposition. Once government entered the housing field, private companies would withdraw, believing that they could not compete with subsidized housing.[15]

The conference's focus was on houses and only secondarily on the people who lived in them. Faced with the argument that some people could not afford to live anywhere but slums, the conference argued that families displaced by slum clearance would be able to find acceptable housing elsewhere. As private companies rebuilt the slums with better and more expensive housing, more affluent people would move in and vacate older houses. Displaced families would find housing in the vacated dwellings. Believing that families living in substandard housing were needy in some sense, the conference argued that better housing conditions would help restore family welfare and earning capacity. The conference held that housing for slum families could somehow be adapted to their "needs and limitations" and that they could be educated in better housekeeping standards.[16]

The conference's reports focused on slum housing, its economic impact on the community and the steps needed to eliminate slums. Its final report also included a paper by Manuel Elmer, head of the sociology department at the University of Pittsburgh, that added a harsh portrayal of slum dwellers. According to Elmer, the slum was more than an economic condition. It was a social phenomenon in which attitudes, ideas, ideals and practices played important roles. Slums lacked the social forces that created a community. The slum lacked the capacity for concerted action. Normal family life was absent. Gangsters, corrupt politicians, gamblers and "human vultures" took the place of constructive leaders.[17]

In Elmer's view, some families living in the slums were relatively successful but could not or would not leave. Many of the rest were unsuccessful people who for one reason or another had "drifted down to the disintegrated areas." In the slums one could also find colonies of immigrants who chose to live there to maintain the "village life" they had been accustomed to. Finally there were the "queer, the unadjusted, the radical and the Bohemian." For some, living in the slum was a transitional stage, but each wave of people passing through left a "residue of poverty-stricken, socially unadjusted, maladjusted defectives and delinquents." Such slum dwellers posed a risk. The slum sent them out to carry "slum patterns" to other groups and in this way other blighted areas became slums.[18]

The conference reports were works of prose. Numbers were strikingly absent. In 1931, the United States collected little data about housing or about incomes. The mention of housing for 10 percent of the population costing $5.5 billion is one of the few attempts to deal in quantities. Moreover, size is relative. Sunnyside Gardens, one of the large-scale projects mentioned, included 1,200 units, a substantial size for the time, but in 1930 New York City had a population of about 7.5 million.

Housing in the Early 1930s

Surveys conducted by the Roosevelt administration from 1934 to 1936 gave the United States housing situation greater definition. The Civil Works Administration conducted a survey of 64 cities in 1934 and the Works Progress Administration sponsored other surveys through 1936. In all, the surveys covered 203 cities, including about eight million housing units and about 40 percent of the urban population.[19]

The surveys did not employ a single definition of substandard housing. Instead they tracked the presence of toilets and baths, the condition

Slum housing, Milwaukee, Wisconsin, 1936 (Library of Congress).

of buildings, the degree of overcrowding and the presence of "extra" families, families in addition to the primary family occupying the home. On all measures, the surveys identified significant problems. Fifteen percent of houses lacked private indoor flush toilets; 20 percent lacked private bathtubs or showers. Sixteen percent of all houses outside New York City were in need of major repairs or were unfit for use. Overcrowding was widespread. Seventeen percent of houses held more than one person per room and 5 percent of all families were living as extra families. Eight percent of all units were vacant; a third of these were unfit for use or in need of major repairs.

Owner-occupied housing differed significantly from rented housing. Outside of New York City, about 40 percent of houses were owner-occupied. Half of these houses were mortgaged. Owner-occupied houses were more likely to have private toilets and baths. Eighty percent of owner-occupiers had been in their homes for more than five years; only 18 percent of renters had been in their homes that long. Forty percent of renters had been in their homes less than a year.

The surveys documented that housing in New York City was exceptional. More than 80 percent of urban homes outside New York City were single-family homes. In New York City only 43 percent were. Outside New York City, only 5 percent of residential structures were intended to house more than one family and only 2 percent could be classified as apartments. In the rest of the country, 18 percent of housing units were in multi-family structures (intended to house three or more families); in New York City, 67 percent of housing units were.

The Residential Security Maps prepared by another New Deal agency, the Home Owners Loan Corporation (HOLC), in the middle 1930s provide still more information about housing in the United States. The HOLC's mission was to shore up the residential housing market by refinancing delinquent and defaulted mortgages. Since refinancing involved assessment of a borrower's ability both to repay the mortgage and to sell the property, the HOLC prepared maps to assess the current and future desirability of neighborhoods.[20]

The HOLC first used factors related to the housing: the demand for sale and rental, the age and quality of the structures, the topography, the sufficiency of public utilities and the accessibility of public facilities, like churches, schools and stores. To these material factors, the HOLC added the social status of the population. Social status involved, first, the income and occupation of the homeowners. The occupations recorded included, in status order: executives, professionals, white-collar workers, factory workers, and domestics. The HOLC reviewers also added identity to the status hierarchy. The maps recorded the presence of African Americans and the foreign-born in each neighborhood. At the top of HOLC's four-step grading scale were neighborhoods of the newest and best houses occupied by wealthy white executives. At the bottom were neighborhoods with the oldest, least attractive houses occupied by laborers and domestics, often African Americans. The HOLC maps do not use the terms "slums" or "blighted areas" but the presumption is that many neighborhoods in the lowest grade would qualify.

Housing quality and the availability of mortgage financing were the most important determinates in the HOLC's neighborhood grades. Consistent with the data produced by the real property surveys, nearly two-thirds of neighborhoods fell into the lower two grades and only 10 percent in the top grade. Old, low-quality housing was common across the United States. The presence of African Americans or the foreign-born in a neighborhood lowered a neighborhood's grade. In Chicago, every neighborhood that included African Americans fell into the bottom two grades, usually the bottom grade. At the same time, many other neighborhoods received similar grades. In Chicago, Cleveland and St. Louis, 68 percent of the neighborhoods in the bottom two grades had no African American inhabitants.[21]

The HOLC maps incorporate an understanding of neighborhoods and of neighborhood change or succession. The key assumption was that the social status and identity of a neighborhood's inhabitants should be homogenous. People wanted to live surrounded by people like themselves. A primary risk to a neighborhood's rating or desirability was the "infiltration" of "lower grade" populations. Lower grade meant those earning less or in lower status occupations or with different ethnic or racial identities, often African Americans and the foreign-born. The HOLC and later the Federal Housing Administration (FHA) considered it prudent for property deeds to include restrictions on sales to lower status groups, especially African Americans, the foreign-born and various other identifiable ethnic or religious groups. Infiltration might occur for various reasons, but the principal cause was the structures' aging and increasing obsolescence. As the more affluent abandoned older homes for newer, more attractive homes, lower status groups took their place. A neighborhood's desirability would decline because the quality of its houses and the social status of its inhabitants had changed. In other contexts, the real estate industry talked about this in terms of real estate "filtering down."

The HOLC maps are important for several reasons. They document, in part, how federal agencies implemented their housing programs. The private real estate industry developed the concepts incorporated in the maps and the maps, therefore, also demonstrate the considerable degree to which the federal housing agencies carried out the real estate industry's agenda. The concepts behind the maps were useful to the real estate industry to the degree that they portrayed accurately how Americans, especially American homeowners, thought about housing and behaved in the housing market. In the early 1930s, it is safe to conclude, therefore, that American homeowners wanted to live in a neighborhood populated by people like themselves and that they worried about other sorts of people moving in. It is also clear that maintaining the hierarchy of neighborhoods was central to the real estate industry's way of thinking as well as to the thinking of American homeowners.

The emergence of suburbs around U.S. cities was another manifestation of such thinking. Beginning in the late 19th century, better-off Americans protected themselves and their neighborhoods from infiltration by migrating to the suburbs outside the cities and creating their own, usually small, municipalities. Such towns characterized places like Nassau and Westchester counties outside New York City or Delaware County

Slum housing, Washington, D.C., 1935 (Library of Congress).

outside Philadelphia. By controlling planning and zoning, suburban jurisdictions could also control the kinds of houses built and the kinds of people who could move in.

Edith Wood

The Hoover conference's reports showed the influence of Edith Elmer Wood. Wood graduated from Smith College in 1890, married a naval officer, wrote fiction and was involved in anti-tuberculosis work in Puerto Rico. In 1919, she earned a Ph.D. from Columbia and published her dissertation, *The Housing of the Unskilled Wage Earner*. From 1917 until 1929, she was the chairperson of the National Committee on Housing of the American Association of University Women. In 1931, she published her principal work, *Recent Trends in American Housing*.

Wood thought that the housing industry in the United States served the needs of no more than a third of the population in normal times. In her view, one-third of the population lived in good houses in the 1920s.

At the height of the Depression, Wood thought that this number might be as small as 20 percent. The middle third, or perhaps during the Depression, the middle half, lived in older, less convenient houses in less attractive, ill-planned neighborhoods. The bottom third lived in the oldest and worst cast-off houses. In 1935, Wood estimated that nine or ten million of the lowest income families lived in housing that was so inadequate that it endangered their health, safety or morals. The upper third had their needs met because they could afford to buy or build a home. Even if they rented, landlords recognized that they could move elsewhere and acted accordingly. Everyone else had to settle for whatever older housing they could afford. Most below the top third were renters; they could not count on landlords to keep their properties in good repair. Wood thought that inadequate housing was not confined to the big city slums; one could find bad housing in a qualitative sense in all types of cities.[22]

Wood thought that housing was too expensive for most American families. According to Wood's analysis, land, materials, financing and profit each accounted for a quarter of the costs. Land, particularly in central locations, could be expensive. Various groups had studied how to use less expensive materials and more efficient construction methods, but their efforts had achieved very little. The cost of money effected every stage of the construction process; builders and buyers were at the mercy of speculative lenders. Speculative builders and real estate dealers had to have their profits as well.[23]

Although Wood thought that the crux of the housing problem was "modern industrial civilization," she thought the solution lay with cheaper housing. According to Wood, the U.S. economic system left two-thirds of the population unable to afford decent housing. The usual workings of supply and demand did not operate because most people lacked sufficient income. Wood was skeptical that changing the distribution of income or raising wages was possible or wise. Reducing the cost of housing was easier. It disturbed the existing order less. She thought the U.S. should follow the "conservatively progressive" examples of European countries, like England, France and Germany.[24]

For Wood, overcrowding was a critical housing problem. She thought that any home that had more inhabitants than rooms was crowded and any home with more than two persons per room was overcrowded. Overcrowding was unhealthy, she contended. Wood often cited a 1925 study by the U.S. Children's Bureau that found that infant mortality was significantly higher in overcrowded homes. Wood thought that, overcrowding, combined with the "noise of city tenements," created nervous strain.

Overcrowding led to immorality. "When privacy is impossible and where old and young are herded together like animals, the inhibitions of civilization melt away." According to Wood, overcrowding contributed to other social problems. Adolescents escaped to the street and then to the dance halls and poolrooms. "Alcoholism, desertion and juvenile delinquency come next and the disintegration of the family is complete."[25]

The link between slum conditions and social problems, Wood conceded, was not simple and straightforward. Citing Clifford Shaw's 1929 study *Delinquency Areas*, she wrote that there might not be a causal link between bad housing and delinquency. A third factor like poverty might be at work. "It is bad associates rather than bad bricks and mortar that incite to delinquency," she wrote, adding that it was the lack of adequate rooms and yards that pushed young people onto the streets where they might find bad associates.[26]

For Wood, other aspects of bad housing were also problematic. She thought a lack of sunlight promoted rickets and tuberculosis. Dampness caused rheumatism. Poor sanitation created an environment where typhoid and hookworm could flourish. Stagnant water bred mosquitoes that spread malaria. Shabbiness and dilapidation produced depression and inferiority complexes. In the extreme, slum conditions provoked hatred of society and radicalism.[27]

Proper housing was, in Wood's view, a single-family detached house. A house with its own garden was the best place to raise children. In smaller cities where land values were not excessive, the only people who should live in apartments were "celibates, childless couples and elderly people" with grown children. Newly married couples might live in apartments, but only until they had children. In cities with more expensive land, even in New York City, moving to the suburbs or outlying districts was entirely possible.[28]

In the best case, Wood thought families should own their homes. Some families could not afford their own homes, however. Others needed to be able to move to where there was work. Nevertheless, owner-occupied houses tended to be better built and they offered non-material benefits. Wood thought they provided a sense of permanence, good training in thrift, and a good environment for raising children. Anything the government could do to promote homeownership was worth doing.[29]

Since the existing housing market did not produce affordable homes for most American families, perhaps as many as two-thirds, Wood proposed that housing for the un-served populations become a community responsibility like water and sewers or schools and libraries. Housing should become a public utility for all those who could not afford private housing. Wood was content to leave the private real estate industry alone where it could produce acceptable houses. She thought only extreme radicals, as in Soviet Russia or socialist Vienna, sought to eliminate private sector housing. For the lowest third of the population, public agencies would provide housing on a non-profit or subsidized basis. For parts of the middle third, limited dividend companies might do the same. Wood thought that the real estate industry, other than owners of old properties, had no reason to object since these were not markets it served or could hope to serve. This new approach to housing was not family relief, Wood argued. Nor was it intended for people on relief or who might be on relief. It was intended for the laboring classes who could not afford privately built housing.[30]

Slums should be eliminated, Wood argued. They created unwholesome conditions and put health, morals and welfare at risk. Slums were a financial burden to cities. Like many in the 1930s, Wood assumed that the United States was nearing a period of stable population. Cities, she thought, could not afford to provide public services to peripheral areas where the population was growing and inner areas where the population was dwindling. Redeveloping slum areas would generate higher tax revenues. Nevertheless, Wood argued that the first priority in slum clearance should be rehousing the current population, perhaps on the same site. Nevertheless, Wood was skeptical about the prospects for successful slum clearance. While various European countries had produced considerable standard housing at low cost, she thought none of them had managed to clear their slums. She hoped the United States could do better, but she had her doubts.[31]

Wood's wariness extended to the politics of housing. She thought that the real estate industry had discredited the housing the federal government built for war workers during the First World War. After the war, the United States, unlike most of Europe, had returned housing entirely to the private sector. Wood believed that working people could have secured better housing. Vague ideas, the absence of an organized campaign, and a preference for seeking higher wages made that impossible. Wood saw tenant organizing in New York City and the embrace of the housing issue by all mayoral candidates in the 1929 New York City elections as signs that public opinion could be marshaled behind better housing. If badly housed people could decide what they wanted and how to get it, they had enough votes to bring it about. At the same time, skillful propaganda from the real estate industry could just as easily turn them against any new programs.[32]

Community Planners

During the 1920s, a group of architects, planners and writers in New York City coalesced into a semi-formal group called the Regional Planning Association of America. They were interested in urban and housing issues, especially broad developments across urban regions. Besides meeting to discuss urban issues, they were involved in the planning and design of two communities, Sunnyside Gardens in the borough of Queens in New York City and Radburn, in suburban New Jersey. The developments were intended to provide superior housing and communities to ordinary Americans. Sunnyside included row houses and low-rise apartment houses and incorporated considerable, by New York City standards, open space. Radburn featured detached, row and apartment houses. While Sunnyside conformed to New York City's street grid, Radburn featured an innovative approach to streets, separating foot and auto traffic. Radburn also made use of gardens and open space. When the Regional Planning Association of America dissolved in the early 1930s, some of its members formed the Housing Study Guild and continued to work on housing issues.[33]

At least four members of the Association were prominent in the 1930s housing debate. Edith Wood was a member. Alfred Mayer and Henry Wright were architects; Wright, along with Clarence Stein, designed Sunnyside Gardens. Lewis Mumford was an intellectual jack-of-all-trades. Largely self-educated, he produced works about literature, architecture, history and society. Beginning in 1910, he produced a steady flow of articles for publications like *The Nation, New Republic* and *New Masses*. In 1931, he became *The New Yorker*'s architecture critic, producing a column entitled *The Sky Line*.

Wright, Mayer and Mumford agreed with Edith Wood that most Americans could not afford decent housing. Without substantial subsidies or changes in the distribution of income, two-thirds of Americans would have to settle for ill-designed, ill-built, over-priced housing. "No dodge of architecture or mass production" could provide housing cheap enough for most workers to purchase, Mumford wrote.[34]

The system short-changed even the families who had bought homes since the First World War. The community planners argued that the new homeowners were little different from renters. They held title to the property, but assumed all the risk and, should they lose their jobs, would lose their investment as well. Promoting home ownership without promoting secure incomes was "romantic folly." According to Mumford, Hoover's efforts to promote home ownership had saddled homeowners with houses that did not meet their needs and burdened cities with excessive costs. Mayer was critical of the early efforts of the Federal Housing Administration created by the Housing Act of 1934. He thought that the FHA was trying to go back to the methods and conditions of the 1920s.[35]

All three writers had had tried to produce good low-cost houses without subsidies. Despite building on vacant land and employing new planning and construction methods, neither Sunnyside Gardens nor Radburn were within the means of most Americans. Writing in 1938, Mumford observed that communities built on the periphery of urban regions, if workers were the sole inhabitants, could not afford the public services and utilities provided by cities. To generate enough tax revenue, he thought new communities had to include middle-class and wealthy homeowners.[36]

The community planners believed that the larger problem was the absence of planning across urban regions. Like nearly all housing advocates in the 1930s, Wright, Mayer and Mumford were talking about the New York region and only secondarily about other American cities. They thought that New York City and the surrounding suburbs were full of low-grade houses, scattered across the landscape without any discernible plan. Private builders had built and sold a few homes at a time, making no attempt to create the basis for communities. The cheap houses they built and the unattractive neighborhoods they created were primed to degenerate into blighted areas and eventually into slums. Development had sprawled into the outer boroughs and then beyond the city's boundaries. Land had been subdivided, streets built and public utilities added long before there was any need. The city's finances are endangered because it had to pay for improvements before outlying areas yielded significant tax revenue. Because, even in the outer boroughs, land had been divided into small parcels, assembling enough land to plan and build a large-scale community was expensive and time consuming.[37]

Although the tenements of areas like the Lower East Side were problems, Mumford and his associates thought vast areas of Brooklyn, the Bronx and Queens were already blighted or headed in that direction. The small frame houses on small lots built in the 1920s in areas like Flatbush in Brooklyn, or Astoria and Long Island City in Queens, were the problem. Similar areas could be found in Philadelphia, Chicago, Detroit and St. Louis. In what Mumford called an "orgy" of house building and home ownership, private builders had erected houses that were inferior to the housing constructed by the government in Camden, New Jersey or Bridgeport, Connecticut, during the First World War or even to houses built before the war. Mumford argued that the era of prosperity from 1922 to

1929 had produced a steady decline in the quality of American housing. Builders eager for profits had built poor housing and no one had tried to create real communities.[38]

Everyone, Mayer wrote, was entitled to a safe, sanitary place to live, with plenty of light and air. They needed access to proper open spaces and recreational areas safe for children. To absorb increasing leisure time, there should be organized efforts to create community life. Creating a neighborhood was just as important as building the right kind of housing. The structures should be row houses and low-rise (two- or three-story) apartment houses. Within the urban region, residential communities should be linked conveniently with each other and with business and industrial areas. The trip to work should not be long and dreary. Roads and transportation facilities would need to be revamped. Unlike the loosely-organized, sprawling suburban development that had begun, the a properly planned region would feature "fairly compact and carefully related community organization." In the best case, cities would replace old neighborhoods in their outlying areas with new planned communities. They would improve housing and communities while avoiding the cost of new streets and public utilities. Wright thought that there was enough vacant or cheap land in eastern Queens and northern Brooklyn to build new communities of 10,000 to 50,000 people.[39]

The community planners thought "big." Mumford wrote that if a critic could not afford the luxury of a comprehensive and exhaustive view of a problem, where would such views come from? He wrote about planning "in four dimensions." The government would need to embrace a "gigantic" program of urban reconstruction and community planning. It would need to embrace change; it would need to be frank that it was replacing the old with the new. Strong national leadership would be needed, an independent agency responsible for all types of housing, with expert staff and the authority and funding to get things done. The effort should depend on public efforts and public ownership of land used for community development. Individual projects needed to be large scale, directed by large-scale organizations. The small builder and the individualistic approach to planning and building would be things of the past. Only large-scale efforts could achieve economies or create communities. The newest technology and building methods would be the norm.[40]

In 1935, Mayer suggested that the housing problem could not be solved under capitalism. Only a program based on "an untrammeled capacity to produce" could succeed. He added that he was not willing to wait until capitalism collapsed. In the meantime, the most feasible approach left the private sector to do what it could while the government funded low-rent housing for everyone else. Limited dividend corporations might be able to serve some middle- and low-income families.[41]

Wright and Mumford's writings were apolitical, but Mayer expended some words on how a big, new housing program could come about. Mayer thought that architects and city planners understood the issues, but didn't know how to popularize their solutions. Those who sought to improve slum conditions, "social workers" in Mayer's terminology, cared about the issues but did not understand them. Slum dwellers were silent; Mayer thought they did not know what good housing was. The two political parties would go only as far as public pressure pushed them. The building trades were interested, but mainly in increased employment. They would not insist on the right kind of housing. The push had to come from elsewhere: certainly the more radical unions, maybe other unions, the Unemployed Councils organized by the Communist party, perhaps "Negro" organizations or neighborhood groups. Perhaps these groups could push the Roosevelt administration into action.[42]

Mayer also addressed the question of overall need and cost. He cited an estimated need of 14 million new dwelling units, including 6.5 million for low-income families, built over ten years. He thought the cost would be $6.5 billion a year or $65 billion in total. The U.S. had not produced that many new houses a year in the past, but Mayer thought the economy had spare capacity. He imagined that part of the cost would be in the forms of loans and would ultimately be repaid. He wondered whether savings banks and insurance companies might be required to invest some of their cash in new housing.[43]

United States housing was at a critical juncture, according to Mayer and Mumford. People were now aware of the housing problem and some wanted to address it. Faulty efforts at the outset could discredit the push for better housing. In the early stages, some "pretty sad schemes" would be proposed. Minimum standards or housing just a little better than the current stock should not be acceptable. Nevertheless, now was the time to act; waiting for perfection could endanger the entire effort. If the economy revived and the families who had moved in with relatives or friends looked for housing of their own, demand would soar. If nothing had changed, if community planning was not underway, with new standards and techniques and lower rents, the situation would revert to pre–1929 conditions, with bad construction and high prices.[44]

These three writers were sure about what they did not want included in a new housing program and that was slum clearance. Here they disagreed with Edith Wood who thought that demonstration projects in the slums were the way to start. Mumford, Wright and Mayer vehemently disagreed. They thought that advocates for slum clearance were in a rush to do something and had not thought through the consequences. They believed that slum clearance was a concession to private real estate interests and would do little for low-income workers.[45]

The community planners were certain that land in slum areas, especially in Manhattan, was over-valued. The capacity of slum housing to generate profits inflated land values. Speculators had bought properties in anticipation of redevelopment. To an extent, the New York City government, and other city governments, had an interest in high land values since they underpinned higher taxes. Slum land was subdivided into small parcels and, therefore, involved many owners. Buying slum land, even through eminent domain, was expensive and time consuming. Once the condemnation process started, some owners might raise their asking price. In 1928, Wright had surveyed Manhattan real estate for the New York Housing Board and confirmed earlier studies. No land in Manhattan was cheap enough to support low-rent housing.[46]

Building low-rent housing on cleared slum land was a mistake, the community planners argued. Because the cost of acquiring the land was high, rents would be too high for most slum dwellers. To lower rents, large subsidies would be required. That alone would push city governments away from low-rent housing and toward middle- or high-income housing. High land costs would motivate housing authorities to increase the number of housing units on a site and to lower housing standards. High densities would lead to construction of apartment houses of more than three or four stories and would necessitate elevators. The community planners thought that living in high-rise apartments was unhealthy. Providing adequate light and air was difficult in tall apartment houses and they did not create a safe environment for children. Mumford considered most Manhattan real estate inadequate, including fashionable apartment houses on Park Avenue. He opposed adopting them as the template for the new housing. High densities and low standards would produce unattractive, uninviting neighborhoods that would push families out of central districts, rather than revive the city by creating new, better neighborhoods.[47]

The community planners wanted to get rid of slums, but preferred an indirect approach. Their first step would be to build new, cheaper housing on vacant or cheap land elsewhere in the city. The new housing would draw families out of the slums. Since the community planners also assumed that the population was not likely to grow, they thought the slums would then be depopulated; property values would decline and slum properties could be acquired and redeveloped at a reasonable cost. They assumed that the more central locations were most suitable for housing that only middle- or high-income families could afford. While the city was building new housing for slum dwellers, it would replace housing in blighted areas, especially in the outer boroughs, with new planned communities. In the end, the city would be rebuilt; the slums eliminated, and new slums prevented.[48]

Razing slum housing without providing alternative housing would make the situation worse. It would force low-income families to seek other private housing, most likely in other slum or blighted areas and would increase overcrowding. By increasing the demand for slum housing it would increase the value of slum properties and make future slum clearance that much more difficult and expensive. Building small "model" projects would have the same effect. Unless they had at least the same density as the housing they replaced, they would push some families into other slum housing.[49]

Catherine Bauer

Catherine Bauer graduated from Vassar in 1926, interested in art and architecture. She traveled in Europe, lived in New York City, and met Lewis Mumford. Under Mumford's influence, Bauer's focus shifted from architecture to housing. She worked with Mumford and other members of the Regional Planning Association of America and served as its executive secretary. In 1934 she published *Modern Housing*, a book-length exposition of housing problems and their solutions.[50]

The housing Bauer preferred resembled the community planners' ideals. The fundamental unit for planning, construction and living was the neighborhood. The end result was to have "some sort of organic form." She credited Patrick Geddes, the Scottish intellectual, with recognizing that housing was more than shelter. It involved recreation and social life and had to be inseparable from a neighborhood. Within properly designed neighborhoods, housing units were to have plenty of light and air. No building would be more than two rooms deep; none more than four stories high. Housing would be safe and sanitary. It would offer every member of the family privacy and access to open spaces.[51]

To the mix, Bauer added "modern" architecture. In *Modern Housing* and journal articles, she cited housing developments built in the 1920s in

Europe, especially in Frankfurt, Germany, as models to be emulated. Typically they were low apartment buildings surrounded by substantial open space and located on the edge of cities. She saw them as new building forms, combining new materials and standards with a modern aesthetic sensibility. She talked about precision, simplicity and economy and about the buildings forming an organic whole instead of an infinite series of competitive structures. Bauer thought that these European developments represented an intelligent approach to standardization and to mass production.[52]

Housing in the United States was worse than that in Europe, in Bauer's estimation. Urban housing, especially in New York City, for rich and poor, included the "grimmest type of construction to be found anywhere." On the Lower East Side and on Park Avenue, one found "ugly, contorted formless buildings" and "deep apartments betokening interior, windowless rooms." Even as new houses in the United States had become more expensive, they served the real needs of individuals and families less well. Often they were so badly laid out and constructed that they were destined to create blighted areas. Bauer criticized "sprawling, speculative suburbs" as well as skyscrapers, which she thought created congestion. At the heart of the problem was the fact that the private sector could not produce houses that most Americans could afford. In 1935 testimony to a Senate committee, she argued that only 20 percent of American families could afford new houses. All other families were forced "willy-nilly in a handed down dwelling" often in blighted neighborhood or a slum.[53]

In 1935, Bauer argued that the country would need as many as eight million new homes in the next ten years, 14 million if it wanted to replace all the unfit dwellings. The United States real estate industry was unlikely to produce enough houses, even if they were second-rate. The greatest boom in residential construction in United States history, between 1920 and 1930, had produced no more than 6.5 million new homes.[54]

Home ownership was not the answer, in Bauer's view. Buying a house when you could lose your job or be forced to move elsewhere in search of work was akin to buying stock on margin without additional resources. Government efforts to promote home ownership represented a misplaced emphasis on a comparatively unimportant factor; it was "romantic wish fulfillment." Real estate interests had pushed the ideal of home ownership so much that ordinary Americans, despite the clear evidence of foreclosures and eviction, continued to approach housing as "petty capitalists" rather than as workers and consumers. A house of one's own remained the vague symbol of "respectable security and sudden riches."[55]

According to Bauer, government housing policy through the middle 1930s was inadequate. The New Deal's first forays into housing were aimed at increasing employment, not at housing. They had since become ensnarled in so many issues that they might produce only deadlock. They might just boil down to a half-hearted desire to tear down some of the more spectacular slums without "hurting anyone's feelings and changing anything important." Bauer told the Senate that many Americans still thought that housing policy involved only slum dwellers, a special and limited group. Housing policy was a "new frill of reform" promoted by social workers and unemployed architects. They thought that housing problems were temporary; an economic recovery would resolve them. Bauer argued otherwise. Housing problems touched every consumer and wage earner. The entire real estate industry had to be reorganized. A housing movement would incorporate redistributing incomes, "puncturing" land values, relocating industry and people and reforming municipal finance.[56]

The federal government needed to intervene in housing, but federal action would not be sufficient. Bauer argued that better housing for low-income families required federal subsidies. The federal government also needed to push states and localities to enact housing legislation and to carry out demonstration projects, particularly in areas where local housing authorities were unlikely to act. Immediate responsibility for the new housing, however, needed to reside elsewhere, with local public housing authorities, and even more important, with limited dividend corporations and housing cooperatives. Only then would a broad, democratic housing movement be possible.[57]

Bauer could sound more radical than she was. Bauer did not flinch when challenged that better housing for all Americans could cost more than $60 billion. She argued that the unwillingness of 19th century reformers to challenge conventional economic and social thought had prevented them from solving housing problems. Because they would not countenance either subsidies or general wage increases, they could not supply decent housing to the underprivileged. Elsewhere she wrote that the housing she advocated, "modern housing," was antithetical with much of the framework of contemporary western society. Her notions about housing, she claimed, were not consistent with "capitalism, inviolate private property, entrenched nationalism, class distinction or governments" intent on preserving old interests. Nevertheless she did not consider her ideas "socialist" or use the term. She argued that housing programs of German cities like Frankfurt were not socialism. They were instead "municipal capitalism" in that they charged economic prices and might make profits. She preferred the housing work of German social democrats to that of Austrian socialists. She was not committed to government ownership; she imagined cooperative housing associations as a key part of the future. Her ideas left room for the private real estate industry to continue to build housing for the more affluent.[58]

Bauer was explicit that better housing would not come to the United States without organized political demand from workers and consumers. Too many housing advocates were politically naïve, she thought. They criticized the real estate industry but still expected it to support different housing policies. She observed that the notion that Washington would solve all the housing problems was as impossibly un–American as "the reddest of red revolutions." In Europe, research into housing problems had promoted a general sense that past methods had failed and that they could and should be replaced. Nevertheless, only when citizens demanded a housing program for themselves, not for "some vague, hypothetical slum dwellers," but for themselves and their families, did European efforts move forward. Even though the United States lacked some elements found in Europe, in particular a tradition of government paternalism or involvement in city development, Bauer believed that the United States could achieve "modern housing" once workers and consumers took a hand in the solution.[59]

Labor Unions

Bauer was not content with theorizing. In 1933, she became executive secretary of the Labor Housing Conference, established by the Pennsylvania Federation of Labor to lobby for housing reform. Working with Oscar Stonorov, an architect, and John Edelman, a union organizer for Philadelphia textile workers, she pushed labor unions across the country to create housing committees. With their support, she lobbied in Washington for housing legislation that would incorporate her ideas.

Bauer's effort had some success. Unions across the country created housing committees. The American Federation of Labor (AFL) passed resolutions supporting government low-cost housing at its 1935 and 1936 conventions. Representatives of the AFL and other unions testified for low-cost housing legislation. AFL president William Green announced that the legislation proposed in 1937 was labor's bill and its number one legislative priority.[60]

Stimulating the economy was a high priority for the labor witnesses at congressional hearings, a higher priority than any particular form of housing. J.W. Williams, from the AFL building trades department, offered support for any legislation that improved housing and put his members back to work. While Green offered support for specific legislative measures, he argued that government intervention into housing was essential to reducing unemployment in construction industry. Private efforts, even with assistance from new federal agencies like the Home Loan Bank Board, would not be enough. Government support for the private real estate industry was welcome, but not sufficient.[61]

Federal art project public housing poster, 1936 (Library of Congress).

Labor witnesses talked about a large low-cost housing program, not a program limited to the poorest. Green stressed that a housing shortage was coming. To eliminate slum housing and match the anticipated growth in households, the United States needed to build more than 13 million new homes by 1945. Production in 1936 had been less than a third of average annual production between 1923 and 1929. The AFL resolution called for decent housing for all American families. The mine workers' representative envisioned housing for the "average wage earner" even if the lowest paid got priority. John Edelman, testifying for the hosiery workers' union, specified that the activities of local housing authorities should go beyond the "lowest rental group." The building trades' representative pointed out that even well-paid union construction workers could rarely afford the houses they built for private developers.[62]

National Public Housing Conference

When Bauer, Mumford and their colleagues referred to "social workers," they were referring to the National Public Housing Conference and its associates. In 1931, a group of prominent New Yorkers organized themselves to agitate for better housing. First called the Public Housing Conference and then (in 1932) the National Public Housing Conference, the organization derived from the Subcommittee on Housing of the City Affairs Committee, a government watchdog group started by Norman Thomas and others. The City Affairs Committee opposed Tammany Hall's control of New York City government and established committees to monitor city departments.

Among the founding members of the National Public Housing Conference were Helen Alfred, Louis Pink, Ira Robbins and Mary Simkhovitch. Robbins and Pink had been legal advisors to the New York State Board of Housing, established in the 1920s. Edith Wood, Lewis Mumford and Clarence Stein were early members, but the organization's positions most often reflected the views of Simkhovitch, Alfred and other "social workers." During the 1930s, the conference and its leaders cooperated with other national organizations interested in social issues, such as the American Association of Social Workers, the National Federation of Settlements, the National Women's Trade Union League and the National Council of Catholic Charities.

Simkhovitch was the key figure. Born in Massachusetts, she studied at Boston University, Radcliffe, Columbia and the University of Berlin. While in Berlin, she met Vladimir Simkhovitch, a Russian economist who went on to teach at Columbia through the early 1940s. Mary Simkhovitch was involved in the settlement work in Boston and then in New York. In 1902, she and others founded Greenwich House, a settlement in Greenwich Village. Simkhovitch became a prominent figure in the settlement house movement in New York City and across the country. She participated in good government campaigns in New York including campaigns to improve housing. Her early efforts focused on the problems created by overcrowding. Her work in civic affairs brought her into contact with influential New Yorkers, including Eleanor Roosevelt and Senator Robert Wagner (D–New York).

The creation of the National Public Housing Conference marked a shift on the part of Simkhovitch and other New York housing reformers. Like similar activists across the country, they had favored regulation as the solution to bad housing. Health and building codes enforced through inspections were the preferred tools. The construction, sale and rental of housing were the responsibility of the private housing market, in their view. At most, state and local governments should use laws and regulations to curb the worse abuses. By 1931, however, they accepted that greater government intervention was needed.

The change of heart owed something to private sector failures. It also had something to do with New York politics. Housing was a prominent and contentious issue in New York City, especially in Manhattan and the adjoining areas filled with tenements and other apartment houses. Particularly after the First World War, tenants had organized themselves to resist rent increases and evictions; in response, landlords had formed their own groups. Although tenant organizations were less active and less radical in the 1920s, they remained a factor in city politics. During the 1920s city and state governments had enacted housing legislation. In the 1929 mayoral election, all three major candidates included housing measures in their platforms. The Tammany Hall Democrat, Jimmy Walker, argued for slum clearance. Fiorello LaGuardia, the Republican reformer, favored enlarged activity by the State Board of Housing. Norman Thomas, the Socialist candidate, pushed for "municipal housing."[63]

The conference accepted Edith Wood's analysis of housing costs and family incomes. Housing produced by the private sector was too expensive for most American families, to buy or to rent. Even in good times, the majority of workers did not earn enough to rent decent apartments. The government needed to do something.

By the middle 1930s, new data were available to support this view. In 1934, the Brookings Institution published in *America's Capacity to Consume* what data were available about family incomes. Because the Brookings study used pre–1929 data, from before the economic collapse, its figures seemed that much more impressive. Based on these data, the conference claimed that, at a time when newly constructed apartments in large cities cost $12 per month per room, more than two-thirds of American families could not afford to spend more than $6.25 per month per room. At the height of American prosperity, in 1929, as many as half of American households earned less than $1,535 a year.[64]

Although the National Public Housing Conference's leaders thought that the private sector had failed, they were not hostile to the private real estate industry. They accepted that the government should stimulate and assist the private sector to meet as much of the demand for housing as it could. Because the private sector did not serve low-income families and probably could not, the conference contended that government-funded housing would not compete with the private market. To ensure that public housing did not compete with private housing, applicants and tenants in public housing should be subject to income limits. That way, occupants of more expensive private housing could not move into public housing. The conference argued that, since public housing was likely to be funded by borrowing, it would be financed by private capital. Public housing bonds could become a "large and promising outlet for surplus funds."[65]

Slums were at the heart of the conference's program. The conference argued that not only were many Americans forced to live in crowded, substandard housing, but also that crime and disease seemed to coincide with the worst housing. Conference leaders, like Rabbi Edward Israel and Monsignor John O'Grady, Secretary of the National Council of Catholic Charities, testified before congressional committees that bad housing seemed to breed crime. The areas with the worst housing also had high rates of infant mortality and tuberculosis. The link between bad housing and crime or disease was not clear, but conference leaders argued that efforts to curb crime and cure disease could not succeed without better housing.[66]

Slums were costly. Efforts, in cities like Cleveland, to tie municipal costs to neighborhoods suggested that slum neighborhoods consumed municipal services that cost more than the tax revenue they generated. Apparently fighting crime and disease in the slums cost more than elsewhere. Slums seemed to produce less tax revenue. Advocates like Ernest Bohn, a Cleveland city official, saw slum clearance and public housing as steps towards bolstering the cities' finances. The social workers agreed.[67]

For the conference, clearing the slums and rehousing the inhabitants were the answers. The government ought to pursue them apart from its other activities to improve housing. It would take a long time, but local governments needed to tear down and replace slum housing. Helen Alfred, conference secretary, argued that slum dwellers needed to be rehoused on the same sites. Building better housing elsewhere, in garden cities or satellite towns, to drain away the slums' population would not work. It had not worked in Britain, she claimed. Slum clearance and rehousing had to be separate from other government housing programs. Slum clearance and rehousing were fundamentally different, in method and purpose, from other housing programs.[68]

It would take federal subsidies to clear the slums and rehouse slum dwellers. Labor unions and cooperatives had built low-cost housing in Europe, but, in the view of conference leaders, they were unlikely to do so in the United States. Private charities and government relief programs were feeding and clothing families, but providing money to families to rent private housing would be difficult to administer and would treat millions of Americans as if they were paupers. Raising incomes would close the gap between wages and rents, but increasing incomes broadly would be much more difficult in the United States than building better, cheaper housing. Building large-scale projects using new methods and materials could lower costs; so could access to cheaper money and exemption from local property taxes. Nonetheless such measures by themselves would leave rents beyond the reach of many American families. The federal government needed to subsidize construction and operation further if the majority of low-income families were to be served.[69]

Conference leaders were certain that public housing needed to be managed and controlled at the local level. Federal funds were essential and the federal government might establish standards and methods. The federal government had already expanded its reach into what had been local responsibilities, like relief. Nevertheless, local bodies should design the housing program, acquire the lands, and construct the housing. Even intervention by state governments was not a good idea. In the best case, the local bodies would be controlled, not by representatives of the real estate industry or even architects, but by community organizers, educators, clergy, labor leaders and politicians.[70]

The push for local control stemmed, in large part, from the conference's New York City roots. The conference's key members lived and worked in New York. New York's tenements were America's archetypical substandard, crowded housing; the Lower East Side its archetypical slum. By 1934, New York City has its own housing authority. In January 1934, Fiorello LaGuardia, the newly elected mayor, established the New York City Housing Authority with Louis Pink and Mary Simkhovitch among its five members. Within a year, the New York authority had built its first housing project, First Houses, without federal assistance. Once the federal Public Works Administration (PWA) announced plans to construct two projects in the city, Harlem River Houses and Williamsburg Houses, a fierce struggle for control of the projects ensued between the New York housing authority and LaGuardia, on the one hand, and the PWA and Secretary of the Interior Harold Ickes, on the other.

The conference's program, centered on slum clearance, threatened the status quo far less than the community planners' ideas. Replacing bad housing in the slums with better housing would have little or no impact on other neighborhoods or disturb the hierarchy of neighborhoods, particularly if most of the original inhabitants were rehoused on the same sites. On the other hand, regional planning and new, large, planned communities built on vacant land were fundamental changes to American urban patterns. Creating what in effect were new neighborhoods might not necessarily impact existing neighborhoods but, if the new communities were planned, funded, and built by the government, the real estate industry's role would be diminished. In addition, the vacant, relatively inexpensive land around cities was a resource the real estate industry wanted to keep for itself.

New Housing

Most observers in the 1930s accepted that public housing would have to be economically constructed. If the public was to support government-subsidized housing, "every reasonable economy" had to be made. Some writers put the solution in negative terms. Public housing would have to do without landscaped gardens, or fully fireproof buildings, or the "flashy gee-gaws" that private builders used to lure customers. Others took more positive approaches. They imagined that one could start with the "activities and functions" of a "normal family of low income," presumably different from those of a middle-class family, and from them design a healthy, safe housing unit. You could not simply take a middle-class house and make it smaller and include less equipment. Public housing would be designed for use, not profit, to meet basic needs over the long term. Once it was certain that public housing met "minimum standards," one could search for cost savings. "Simple, spacious, and sturdy" structures would be needed.[71]

Frank Watson, writing in 1935, questioned what he called the "social implications" of the housing built by European governments, the "honeycomb type structures" found in places like Vienna. He argued that apartment houses were not conducive to satisfactory family life. Housing provided at government expense was apt to undermine a sense of individual responsibility and to promote dependency. He thought that government housing in Europe often did not go to the tenants who most needed it. In any case, choosing tenants based on income was likely to create a "dangerous class consciousness."[72]

If public housing were to serve those who could not afford private housing, it was widely assumed that a limit on the incomes of applicants and tenants would be needed. Since it was also assumed that the new housing would be more attractive than much existing housing, families who could afford private housing might apply to live there. Steps to screen them out would be needed; a limit on incomes seemed a practical tool. Some families who might prove disruptive, the "socially pathological," would also apply. It was assumed that they too would be screened out. Commentators were generally optimistic on this score. The demand for the new housing would be great and the supply small, at least at first. Housing managers could afford to be selective.[73]

Coleman Woodbury, Director of the National Association of Housing Officials, argued against establishing an income limit in a federal statute. A national standard could prove mischievous. Incomes for poor families varied across the country, as did building costs. Incomes changed. What would housing managers do when a family's income increased above the limit or decreased to the point that it could not afford the rent? How would a family's income be computed? Would children's wages be included? Housing needs varied. A rent that could provide a childless couple with adequate housing might yield overcrowding for a family of five. Tying public housing rents to what families had previously paid would penalize African American families and others who had had to pay especially high rents. Woodbury worried that setting a limit on incomes would produce "colonies or segregated areas" of poor families. He argued that public housing developments could include housing for more well-to-do families, constructed by private builders.[74]

Some writers assumed that public housing would provide more than housing. Despite efforts to screen out the socially undesirable, some families would struggle to adjust to their new surroundings. Housing managers would furnish "education and guidance." The most enthusiastic promoters added the notion that the new housing could produce a new spirit, a new atmosphere. Nathan Straus claimed that Hillside Homes, his New York development, represented the "rebirth" of "the enjoyment of home surroundings" and a "dignified self-respecting sense of citizenship" that had been lost in the slums. The tenants had been liberated to live the "kind of lives all American city dwellers would like to live."[75]

Lavanburg Homes

Existing philanthropic and limited dividend projects provided examples of how public housing might work. Fred Lavanburg, a well-to-do manufacturer, funded the Lavanburg Homes, on the Lower East Side in 1927. He involved an advisory committee that included Clarence Stein, Clarence Perry and Lillian Wald, another prominent member of the New York settlement movement. The building was a six-story walk-up, with 113 apartments, with one, two or three bedrooms. In *The Diary of a Housing Manager* (1938), Abraham Goldfield described how it functioned.[76]

Lavanburg's aim was to serve poor families with children by providing decent housing at affordable rents. The advisory committee thought it undesirable to have the tenants labeled as dependent and downplayed the charitable character of the enterprise. Nonetheless, nearly half the initial 1,130 applicants were rejected for having incomes that were too high. After visits to applicants' homes, review of their applications, and checks with the Social Service Exchange, a clearing house for private agencies providing social services, the staff rejected another nearly 400 families because they had badly kept homes, had no children or only grown children, lived in decent housing, or for other reasons. In 1928, nearly all the income earners were manual workers; about three-quarters earned less than $40 a week. Even before the Depression, about 8 percent were supported by charitable agencies. The aim was to serve "normal" families, not families needing other services. Nonetheless, when Goldfield checked with the Social Service Exchange, he discovered that nearly a third of the tenants had received services from social agencies. Goldfield promoted social and educational activities among the tenants "from a preventive point of view." When families had problems, he referred them to the appropriate social agency.[77]

Lavanburg's initial policy was that tenants who earned a great deal above the average income would be asked to leave and free up an apartment for another deserving family. With the start of the Depression, lowered incomes were more commonly the issue. In 1931, management agreed not to evict tenants for failure to pay rent and to adjust rents on a case-by-case basis. In the face of agitation from a tenants council in 1935, management agreed to forgive the accumulated rent arrears and to continue adjusting rents.[78]

Goldfield thought children were the biggest challenge in managing the building. In 1928, the 113 apartments housed 547 people, 329 of them children. The children were noisy. Until a curfew was imposed, they and their friends from the neighborhood played in the courtyard until all hours. Children running and playing in the hallways added to wear and tear and made keeping the building clean more difficult. Goldfield worked hard to create play spaces in the basement and on the roof.[79]

National Association of Housing Officials

The National Association of Housing Officials emerged from a national conference on slum clearance held in Cleveland in 1933. Supported by funds from the Rockefeller Foundation, the association brought city and state officials concerned with housing in contact with other architects, planners and activists. In 1934, it sponsored a tour of the United States by several European housing experts and convened a meeting in Baltimore of Americans concerned about housing. The meeting produced a document entitled, "A Housing Program for the United States." Among the 83 signatories were Catherine Bauer, Monsignor John O'Grady, Langdon Post, Mary Simkhovitch, and Edith Wood.[80]

The report reflected agreement on certain notions. The private sector could not provide decent housing for low-income families. Housing had to be a public responsibility and provided as a public service. The federal government should set standards, encourage the states to enact appropriate legislation, and, most important, provide financial assistance. State governments had a role to play, but housing was a local matter. Local governments or local agencies associated with them should be responsible for providing and maintaining housing for low-income families. If only because housing needed to be coordinated with city and regional planning, local responsibility and interest had to be encouraged.[81]

Government agencies could reduce housing costs and the rents charged to tenants. In construction, they could employ better designs, new materials and more efficient methods. Housing authorities might have access to cheaper credit and longer amortization periods. Long-term public ownership might minimize the risks associated with vacancies or demographic changes. Such measures would open up decent housing for many families not now served by the private sector. To serve families unable to afford even this new low-cost housing, the federal government should provide subsidies, either a one-time contribution toward capital costs or periodic grants. The report acknowledged that the program would have moved beyond housing finance into the sphere of social services.[82]

Helping tenants, the report made clear, could not come at the expense of the new housing's financial stability. Rents had to be collected; substantial rent arrears could not be tolerated. The housing program could not undo poverty; public assistance or social insurance should do that. Poor tenants should get enough financial assistance so that they could pay their rent. Otherwise housing managers should be able to evict them.[83]

The report dodged the issue of where public housing should be built. Although slum clearance and low-cost housing were parts of a complete housing program, they were different. The report accepted that slums were not usually the most economical place to build low-cost housing. If housing had to be built on cleared slum sites, the government needed to provide larger subsidies or the owners of slum properties had to absorb a loss. Otherwise, choosing between central, usually slum, sites and outlying locations would depend on local conditions. Decision-makers should weigh the advantages and disadvantages carefully. One could not rely on abstract principles or focus on only one factor, such as land costs. Factors like access to work or stores, opportunities for outdoor recreation, construction costs, land costs, and the kind of houses built all played a role. The report acknowledged that, although the new housing could not wait for construction of "satellite" communities, they were the best places to demonstrate improved planning and building.[84]

The housing to be built depended on local conditions and "habits of life." Combining several types on the same site might be the most economical solution and might allow a healthy variety of buildings and families. Some general principles applied. Every adult needed at least 500 cubic feet of living space; two children counted as an adult. Single family, detached houses were seldom the most economical. They made sense only where land was cheap or where large garden plots could supplement a family's diet. Attached houses and three-story apartment buildings were economical and could allow the individual gardens the report considered essential. Even increasing densities beyond the ideal, perhaps 12 houses to the acre, was preferable to building higher apartment buildings. Only when attached houses with small gardens were not possible did taller apartment structures make sense, and then only with ample open space.[85]

Did bad tenants make bad dwellings? Or did bad dwellings make bad tenants? The report began with an assertion that European experience showed that most slum dwellers would respond to new conditions. Nonetheless, better housing was not sufficient, especially where tenants "have been accustomed to a low standard of living conditions." Public housing needed different management from private housing. The new housing's economic success was not enough; it needed to secure the "maximum social return" for the community. Managers and staff had to exercise a "helpful social influence." The report cited the methods developed by the British housing activist, Octavia Hill; they involved female rent collectors who monitored and advised tenants. Whether public housing should employ its own social workers depended on the size of the project, the tenants' capacity to organize themselves, and the existence of other social agencies.[86]

A 1935 report prepared for the housing officials' organization returned to the question of managing tenants in public housing. It asserted that a through investigation of prospective tenants was essential. Contact before tenants moved in was "the right psychological moment for real educative work" for prospective tenants who "may be dirty, irresponsible in their attitude to the payment of rent, destructive in their habits or likely to make trouble with neighbors." Collecting rents in the home, rather than in the housing office, allowed personal contact with tenants as well as supervision, without an "atmosphere of inspection." Rent collectors could detect and deal with tenants' personal difficulties before they became acute.[87]

Since apartments did not provide direct access to gardens, a serious disadvantage for families with small children, the report argued that every apartment should include an open-air porch or balcony. That way children could play outside and adults could escape a "physically or emotionally heated" atmosphere inside.[88]

The 1935 report also argued for mixed-income projects. It might be unwise to segregate too many of the lowest income families without opportunities for association with higher income people. Projects might be more satisfactory if they included people of "more ample means" who had enjoyed wider cultural opportunities and who could contribute more to communal life.[89]

Opponents

Talk of government funded housing prompted opposition. The United States Chamber of Commerce, the National Association of Real Estate Boards, and the U.S. Building and Loan League were the most prominent national organizations opposed to government-funded housing. Their principal spokespersons were Morton Bodfish of the Building and Loan League and Walter Schmidt and Herbert Nelson, both associated with the real estate boards. Since the debate about public housing often centered on New York City, joining the national organizations were landlord and real estate organizations from New York City, like the Bronx Borough Taxpayers League and the Real Estate Board of New York.

According to several opponents, housing was not properly an activity of the federal government. Government intervention into the housing market was unconstitutional and beyond what the founding fathers intended. Establishing a government as a landlord, especially on a large scale, was out of keeping with American practice. If citizens became government tenants, the nation's economic basis would be undermined. The government would be supporting citizens rather than the citizens supporting the government. The United States operated on the theory that people had to provide for themselves. It was not the government's place to provide housing, any more than it was the government's place to provide food and clothing.[90]

Owning one's own home was the American way. Widespread home ownership was the "bulwark of this nation," according to Walter Schmidt. Americans had proven that they wanted to own their own homes. Allie Freed, a real estate developer, argued that the property right of home ownership was "the greatest human right." Socialism and communism did not take root among American homeowners. If the government built affordable houses, it would destroy the ambition to own a home. Some Americans might occupy poor housing, but they need not remain there forever. "Advancement in the scale of life is the American ambition."[91]

Housing was properly the responsibility of the private sector, opponents often argued. Government intervention would inevitably undermine private efforts. Private builders would be unable to compete with government efforts; access to cheaper credit alone would give government efforts an in surmountable advantage. Frank Carnahan, testifying on behalf of the National Lumber Dealers Association in 1937, claimed that government efforts had already inhibited private builders. Any sensible builder would hesitate before competing with a government program. The Chamber of Commerce warned that federal interference in housing and slum clearance would demoralize community efforts to rebuild blighted areas and real estate industry efforts to construct better housing.[92]

Spokesmen for the New York City real estate interests were especially critical of potential competition from government-funded housing. They maintained that the city already had too many apartments; vacancy rates were in double digits in parts of the city. If there was to be any new public housing, they argued, one existing housing unit in the slums should be demolished for every new housing unit built. If New York families needed better housing, it was available. Decent housing was available all over Manhattan. New York City housing was much better than the housing reformers portrayed, the landlord organizations claimed. The city had one of the strictest housing codes in the nation. If private companies could not build affordable homes, the housing code was the culprit. If some properties had deteriorated, they could be renovated. If there was a housing problem, it was that many people could not afford the apartments that were available. Building more housing was unnecessary. It would impoverish landlords, many of whom "had worked and labored for twenty-five or thirty years in butcher shops and bakeries and delicatessen shops" in order to buy their properties to provide some income in old age. New York City's finances depended on property taxes; ruining landlords would undermine city finances.[93]

Walter Schmidt contended that once the government provided cheaper, better housing to some, the demand for more would be irresistible. No government could satisfy the demand. Others warned that building decent housing for everyone who lived in a slum would be huge task, perhaps two million new dwellings in New York City alone. The cost of such an effort would be "staggering."[94]

Schmidt and others saw a basic inequity in government-funded housing. The assumption was that the government-built housing would be superior to that occupied by most of the population. If that were the case, taxpayers would be paying more so that poorer families could have better houses than they themselves could afford. Why should families who worked and saved to buy a house provide housing to those who had not? The results would be a "social maladjustment" and political pressure to build better houses for more and more families.[95]

The United States did not have slums like those found in Europe, Schmidt told a Senate committee in 1935. Slum clearance was needed at most in "one or two congested centers." In any case, it was unfair to have the rest of the country pay to clear these slums. It was also expensive to build housing in big cities. Replacing slums with better housing would be astronomically expensive. The larger problem, he and others argued, was "blight." In many cities, blighted areas had appeared. Housing built originally for middle- or upper-class families had aged. The original owners had moved on and poorer families moved in. Single-family houses had been divided into apartments and allowed to deteriorate. These areas were now over-crowded and seemed to breed crime and disease. The solution was to rehabilitate blighted housing, not demolish it. This was something the private sector could do.[96]

Clearing what slums existed should not be paired with building low-cost housing, the argument went. Local governments could, and should, demolish unsafe buildings and buildings that lacked indoor plumbing. Once slum sites were cleared, private builders could construct new communities, not for the displaced families, but for families that could afford new private housing. Slum land cost too much to permit low rents. Any displaced families could find housing in buildings vacated as more affluent families sought better housing. Building new low-cost housing before clearing the slums was an especially bad idea. If families moved out of the slums, tenements would stand vacant, eyesores and menaces.[97]

If there were slums, the people who lived in them were at least partly to blame. Some slum dwellers would not spend even a little bit more to live in better houses. Some were content with where they were. They did not want to abandon familiar haunts and old associations. Moving them elsewhere would not eliminate crime and disease; slum dwellers would spread them to other neighborhoods. New public housing would become the warrens of the future. Representatives of the national real estate organizations made these arguments in polite terms. The New York groups were more direct and vivid.[98]

As the likelihood of government action increased, the groups that opposed government-funded housing warmed to other government measures. The federal government might expand the availability of mortgages by insuring them and creating a secondary market. The government could conduct housing research, especially into new methods and materials. Local governments could enact planning and zoning laws and enforce housing codes more aggressively. State and local governments could create city and regional plans.[99]

If there was to be a public housing program, it should not compete with the private sector. It should not increase the housing supply. Local governments, and not the federal government, should manage and operate it. Public housing should be as cheaply built as possible. It should serve only the poorest families. If rents in public housing could not be low enough to serve all families, the best solution was paying rent subsidies to families.

Local control was essential to a proper low-rent housing program, according to many critics. If local bodies were in charge, comprehensive city planning would be possible. Under local control, the housing program could proceed more slowly and might gain greater support and cooperation. Federal projects put the government in competition with the private sector and would provoke opposition. A few federal projects sprinkled around a city would do more harm than good.[100]

Herbert Nelson and others doubted that the government could build housing any more cheaply than the private sector. New housing in the United States was expensive for many reasons. The public or low-profit efforts so far had not achieved costs low enough to allow rents affordable by slum dwellers. The critics pointed out that the housing built by the federal government during the First World War involved many of the innovations advocated by housing reformers: comprehensive planning, large scale efforts, new construction methods and the like. Yet, the costs achieved were not significantly lower than the private sector could achieve.[101]

It was important that any new public housing be inexpensive. Bodfish told a House committee in 1937 that it must be "modest in its appointments and of as low a cost as possible." It should not cost more than the average housing unit built by the private sector. He was not, he added, advocating shoddy construction. He was advocating housing in which tenants would not want to linger. He claimed that public housing in Britain was decent and sanitary but lacked electrical equipment. Tenants moved out as soon as they could find better housing. Ernest Fisher argued that public housing design should start not with housing standards, but with a cost limit. If the government could not build decent housing at a price that families could afford without a subsidy, it should work to raise the general wage level rather than subsidize some housing. Housing subsidies merely created an unsustainable standard of living.[102]

In 1937, Bodfish said he could not sympathize with the reformers' view that the new housing might not serve the lowest income families. He said that starting with those at the very bottom, rather than those who could afford an economic rent, would provide the greatest public service. Allie Freed, speaking on behalf of the Committee for Economic Recovery, said that housing authorities should plan and operate the new housing, but local welfare departments should select tenants and determine the rents they should pay.[103]

To provide housing to the poorest, the critics proposed payments to families rather than subsidies to housing authorities. A rent subsidy intended to cover the difference between an economic rent and what a family could afford would address the problem best. It would allow housing authorities to operate the new housing on a business-like basis. As a family's circumstances or the nation's economic situation changed, the rent subsidy could be adjusted. Since everyone hoped that economic conditions would improve, the overall cost of subsidies might decline in the future.[104]

Just as in the Hoover Commission's work, the opponents of public housing included some who took a dim view of slum dwellers and the poor. In a 1936 book, *Slums and Housing* by James Ford, one of the editors of the Hoover conference's reports, recommended that anyone "constitutionally unable" to earn enough to afford the cheapest private housing be removed from the cities. Ford advocated that the authorities evaluate the families displaced by slum clearance. He anticipated that a large, but unknown, percentage were "misplaced in our competitive, industrial world," because of mental or physical handicaps, by "nature or mis-education." The authorities should remove such families to rural colonies where they would live and be trained to "contribute as much as possible."[105]

By the early 1930s, the deficiencies of America's housing were severe enough that even mainstream figures acknowledged them. Housing was too expensive for many. Too much of it was substandard. Slums and blighted areas afflicted many American cities.

The mainstream view was that expansion of existing patterns was the path to improvement. Singe family, detached homes owned by American families should remain the norm. The principal innovation should be large, integrated corporations capable of constructing large-scale developments and of achieving lower costs through more efficient methods.

A small group of Americans thought that such steps would be insufficient. They thought the private real estate industry was incapable of building decent, affordable housing for many Americans. They proposed a federally subsidized, locally controlled program to construct rental housing for what might be termed today the working poor, families that were poor but still capable of paying some rent. The new buildings ought to offer decent housing, housing that met basic standards. Without sacrificing quality, it also ought to be as inexpensive to build and maintain as possible. The new housing developments should include families of various income levels and buildings of various types. They should not include high-rise apartment buildings. The housing reformers were not necessarily committed to government built and managed housing; other mechanisms, like housing cooperatives or limited dividend corporations, were acceptable. While they imagined a large non-private housing sector able to operate wherever needed, most did not anticipate competition between private housing and a new non-private sector.

The most obvious disagreements within the public housing community involved the purpose and location of the new housing. For the "social workers," the new housing would replace the substandard housing found in slums. For the community planners and Catherine Bauer, the new housing would eventually lead to the elimination of slum housing, but the immediate purpose was to increase the supply of decent affordable housing. They would locate new developments on vacant land on the periphery of cities. They imagined large, planned communities constructed on inexpensive land.

Because the "social workers" saw public housing serving slum dwellers, they imagined that the new developments would offer more than housing. The housing reformers most focused on clearing slums assumed that the families living in slums needed other services, instruction in good housekeeping practices and the like. Most reformers assumed that the new housing would have a social aspect that single-family homes did not necessarily offer. Tenants would share some facilities and work together to build a community. Most reformers also assumed that potential tenants would be carefully chosen, but this was more important to the "social workers" than to others.

Some questions remained unresolved. The lack of meaningful operating or construction cost data inhibited discussion of the nature and extent of federal subsidies. Reformers were apt to be satisfied with wishful thinking about government's ability to build cost efficient housing. Likewise, the absence of family income data promoted vague discussions of the population to be served, its extent or its ability to pay rent.

CHAPTER TWO

The 1937 Housing Act

While housing reformers debated the merits of public housing, the executive and legislative branches combined to create a public housing program. First, under the aegis of the temporary Public Works Administration the executive branch built 58 projects containing about 25,000 housing units. The PWA program was, in effect, an experiment. It resolved some issues, raised others and set some precedents. Then, in 1937, the Congress drew upon the PWA experience and the reformers' ideas to craft what was intended to be a long-term public housing program. It proved a pale shadow of the reformers' ideas.

Public Works Administration

Roosevelt's New Deal saw a series of federal interventions into housing. In the National Housing Act of 1934 and other measures, the Roosevelt administration restored and reformed the private housing market. The National Industrial Recovery Act, passed in 1933, created the PWA, reporting to Secretary of the Interior Harold Ickes, and authorized it to support "low-cost housing and slum clearance projects." Mary Simkhovitch and Monsignor O'Grady used their contacts in the Roosevelt administration to have the provision inserted in the bill.

The PWA program quickly demonstrated that limited dividend corporations were not likely to build much low-cost housing in the United States. Despite offering relatively generous terms, the Reconstruction Finance Corporation created by the Hoover administration had funded only Knickerbocker Village on New York's Lower East Side and a small project in Kansas. PWA offered more generous terms: lower interest rates, four rather than 5 percent; longer repayment periods, 35 rather than ten years; and loans up to 85 percent. Nevertheless, while the PWA attracted 533 applications, it funded only seven, including two originally submitted to the Reconstruction Finance Corporation.[1]

The experience of Knickerbocker Village suggested that accepting low profits was not enough to produce rents low enough for most city dwellers. Financed by the Reconstruction Finance Corporation, the New York real estate developer, Frederick French, built Knickerbocker Village on the Lower East Side in 1933–34. After paying high land prices, the project charged rents of $12.50 per room per month, affordable only for middle-class New Yorkers. The project housed very few families from the buildings demolished for the project. The rest moved to housing little or no better than the demolished structures. Over 80 percent of displaced families moved to tenements built before 1901, so-called old law tenements. Half the displaced families lived in apartments without private toilets and a third in apartments without hot water.[2]

Knickerbocker Village also suggested that building on cleared slum sites might produce high population densities. The buildings demolished to make way for the project housed about 3,000 people. To reduce rents, the project included enough housing units to house as many as 5,000 people, or about four times the average residential density in Manhattan.[3]

Failing to attract enough viable limited dividend organizations, PWA turned to designing and constructing housing itself. In 1935, however, a landowner in Louisville contested the PWA's attempt to condemn his property under the right of eminent domain. A federal court sided with the landowner, ruling that the federal government could not condemn land in order to build housing. Fearing a judicial rebuff, the Department of Justice declined to appeal the ruling. The National Industrial Recovery Act authorized the PWA to grant public bodies 30 percent of housing construction costs and lend them the remaining 70 percent. In response, most states authorized and created local housing authorities. After the adverse ruling in the Louisville case, the PWA began working with the local authorities to carry out a public housing program.

Ickes and the PWA needed local allies. In Chicago, Ickes named an advisory committee to oversee the PWA housing program. It included Jane Addams and other prominent social workers, business leaders, clergymen, academics, real estate officials, union leaders and a representative of the Cook County Department of Public Welfare—a slice of the local establishment. Nevertheless, the relationship between the PWA and the local authorities was often not happy. Ickes was determined to prevent

(Left to right) New York mayor Fiorello LaGuardia, Nathan Straus, head of the United States Housing Administration and Langdon Post, chairman of the New York City Housing Authority, at Annual Conference of Mayors, November 17, 1937 (Library of Congress).

any fraud or waste and the Housing Division was equally determined to fund exemplary housing. Everything had to be reviewed in Washington and progress was often slow. Negotiations over land acquisition took time. Many participants were naïve about how long large-scale design and construction might take. The LaGuardia administration in New York City had plans for nearly 100,000 units of public housing. By 1937, many, especially in New York, thought federal control was a bad idea. Local housing authorities had to have a greater say in a low-cost housing program. Helen Alfred and Albert Mayer called for more local control. By 1937, Ickes agreed with them. He told a Senate committee that local control would bring greater local cooperation and perhaps financial assistance.[4]

PWA maintained high standards. Ickes was determined that public funds be spent carefully and wisely. He was especially opposed to paying high prices for land. Initially Ickes believed that the PWA projects could be self-supporting. Only after two years' experience did he accept that low rents were impossible without substantial subsidies. Even then he touted the PWA projects as simple and not pretentious. Unlike European projects, he asserted, they devoted more attention to interior livability than exterior ornament.[5]

The PWA's Housing Division considered itself a demonstration program. Initially under the guidance of Robert Kohn, a New York architect and member of the Regional Planning Association of America, the division thought it was creating a new means of planning, designing, and constructing housing for all Americans. At the same time, the division tried to adapt its vision to be consistent with the notion of low costs. It portrayed the result as European housing methods modified to fit local requirements and to create the most economical housing that assured health, safety and reasonable comfort.[6]

The Housing Division imagined that its housing would have to compete in the housing market. It had to offer economy, comfort and convenience. The PWA proposed to build multiple low-rise buildings (no higher than three stories) on large sites. The buildings would be surrounded by open space; the buildings themselves would cover no more than 25 percent of the site. The site would be separate from the usual urban street grid; no through traffic would be permitted. Buildings would be only one unit deep; every unit, therefore, would have direct light and cross ventilation. Access to apartments would be from stair halls and not internal corridors. Ceilings would be eight feet high; living rooms at least 150 square feet; bedrooms at least 100 square feet. One bedroom in every apartment would be big enough for two twin beds. Bathrooms would have a toilet, sink and tub. At a time when only 15 percent of American homes had both electric stove and refrigerator, every PWA kitchen was to have them. Every apartment was to have linen and coat closets and every bedroom a closet.[7]

Reconciling low-cost construction with perceived architectural merit proved difficult. Merely creating standards riled some architects. The Housing Division claimed that establishing standards did not imply standardization. It wanted to ensure that the new housing met basic requirements and opposed "regimentation." Alfred Mayer was not convinced. He saw PWA housing as "mechanically determined by sociological and cost data." It was not "inspired architecture." The PWA's methods did not allow for enough creative talent or aesthetic achievement. Oscar Stonorov, Bauer's colleague and designer of the Carl Mackley houses in Philadelphia, also worried about standardization. If the aim was to establish standards for American housing generally, it was critical that "trivial standardization" not lead to public housing that would be perceived as housing built for the poor.[8]

The two PWA projects in New York, Harlem River Houses and Williamsburg Houses, were hailed at the time as examples of good design and quality construction. Horace Ginsburg, responsible for several New York apartment houses intended for upper-middle-class tenants, helped design the Harlem River Houses and the project resembles New York garden apartments. It consists of three groups of four and five story, walk-up apartment buildings arranged around landscaped courtyards. The buildings occupy about a third of the site. Williamsburg Houses also drew on the New York garden tradition but with clear influences of European modernist ideas. The twenty 4-story apartment buildings, arranged around courtyards, featured horizontal bands on the exterior. Rather than paralleling the surrounding streets like the Harlem River buildings, the Williamsburg buildings are shifted 15 degrees away from the surrounding streets.

Lewis Mumford, from his perch as *The New Yorker*'s architecture critic, told readers that the Harlem River and Williamsburg Houses were projects worth seeing. They no longer had to travel to Europe to see the "new order of building." The new PWA projects reflected standards of housing superior to those of most buildings on Park Avenue, Mumford announced. By contrast, the rest of the city was "makeshift, congested, disorderly, and dismally inadequate." If commercial builders did not copy the PWA projects, "we are a race of Caspar Milquetoasts." Mumford was not sure about the Williamsburg buildings not paralleling the street, but there was little else he did not approve of. Both projects demonstrated, in his view, the importance of building large-scale projects, separating them from the street grid and including generous open space.[9]

Mumford was equally vehement about the faults of the New York authority's first project. In 1935, the New York City Housing Authority used its own funds to build First Houses, also on the Lower East Side. The authority demolished and replaced several tenements and the project occupied half of a city block. Mumford thought it too small. Its overall environment remained as before, "bleak, filthy, ugly." The rents were relatively low, but Mumford thought the standard of housing was unacceptable for a civilized country. The authority had, in his view, replaced one slum with another.[10]

Langdon Post, the head of the New York authority, was proud of First Houses. He claimed that, for the first time, housing with ample sunshine, space and air was available to every American regardless of income. This was the real test, not architectural innovation. The *New York Times* thought

Two. The 1937 Housing Act

Aerial view of Williamsburg Houses, Brooklyn, New York, 1939 (Library of Congress).

First Houses' homely appearance was to its credit. Unlike some slum clearance projects, it did not try to combine the best features of a "Harkness Quadrangle at Yale with the charm of an old Tudor mansion."[11]

If First Houses did not demonstrate good construction practices, it exemplified the ways low-cost housing could be managed. The authority screened potential tenants. They had to demonstrate that they had income at the proper level, no more than four or five times the rent; that they had been steadily employed for at least a year; and that they had no debts. They had to have savings of at least $100 but no more than $1,000 and insurance of at least $1,000 but not more than $3,000. Their current housing had to be substandard and lack heat or bath. The authority dispatched investigators to applicants' homes to interview them and evaluate their housekeeping practices. After investigators had rated the applicants, a committee, on which Mary Simkhovitch served, chose the tenants. The authority collected rents weekly. Rent collectors visited every apartment. In the process they were to inspect the apartments and establish a personal connection between the tenants and project management.[12]

The PWA projects followed similar practices. Ickes argued that unless the new housing was restricted to families that could not afford private housing, it would defeat its own purpose. Local authorities screened potential tenants in PWA projects. Only families were accepted, and they could not have lodgers. Families with children in the home received preference. Income, current housing conditions, and what could be summed up as "character" were evaluated. Total family income could be no more than five times the rent. Families on relief were not usually accepted. The family's current housing had to be substandard and the family had to demonstrate good housekeeping practices and reliable work habits. Many housing authorities subsequently inspected apartments on a regular basis. An advisory committee that included Mary Simkhovitch, Edith Wood, and Abraham Goldfield drew up management guidelines for PWA housing developments. The guidelines called for efforts to protect tenant health and morals. They imagined that a female housing assistant would be responsible for family casework and for arranging childcare and recreation within the project. The guidelines explicitly rejected any notion of tenant control through some cooperative arrangement.[13]

PWA told the Congress that it took pains to ensure that families whose houses was demolished to make way for the new housing found equivalent housing. In 1938, it reported that, on 33 sites, PWA projects had displaced nearly nine thousand families. Half had moved into better quarters at the same or lower rent. Twenty-five percent had moved into better housing at higher rents and the rest into housing that was no better than the demolished housing. Nonetheless families displaced by the new construction were not often rehoused in the new housing. Families displaced by the project did not usually get any preference. Often they could not afford it. Of the 533 families displaced by the construction of the Jane Addams Houses in Chicago, only 21 found places in the new housing.[14]

Some housing officials appreciated the quality of PWA projects but did not consider them a model for the future. Shortly after the Philadelphia Housing Authority was established, its members visited the PWA-funded

Jane Addams Houses, Chicago, Illinois, opened 1938 (Library of Congress).

Hill Creek project. The unanimous verdict was that the authority would not build another project like it. It was too good.[15]

Many observers were less impressed by the quality of the PWA projects than by their price, despite Ickes' concerns about economy. The Williamsburg site was a cleared slum site and cost $4.20 per square foot. The Harlem site had been vacant but still cost $3.40 per square foot. In contrast, the United States Housing Authority would later try to limit land costs to $1.50 per square foot. Even with 30 percent of construction costs paid by the federal government and, on the Williamsburg site, higher housing density that the neighborhood it replaced, the average rents in both projects were over $7 per room. Prevailing rents in the two neighborhoods were just above $4 per room. Very few families displaced by the Williamsburg project could, therefore, afford the new housing. The new tenants in PWA projects seem to have been the best off of all the families who could not afford decent private housing, skilled laborers and the lowest paid clerical and white collar workers. They were certainly not the poorest.

As one observer wrote, they were not "those families so touchingly described at Christmas time as the hundred neediest cases."[16]

Ickes told a House committee in 1937 that he thought the PWA had done everything possible to lower costs. Others were not convinced. Peter Grimm, a New York City real estate executive, told a Senate committee that all the PWA had proved was that you could build sumptuous dwellings as long as you did not worry about the costs. Loula Lasker, a supporter of public housing, argued that public housing needed to be adequate, not necessarily ideal. Including features beyond those necessary for health and safety was a mistake. The *New York Times* called the Harlem River Houses no more than a "fragment of a low rental utopia," because they could not be duplicated except at extraordinary expense.[17]

Ickes and the Housing Division recognized that cost management would remain a challenge for public housing. Operating costs would, in the long run, be greater than the initial capital costs. To minimize both, Ickes thought more research into construction materials and methods was needed. To fund future repairs and replacement, the Housing Division estimated the useful life of building components and had local authorities set aside reserves.[18]

Ickes' initial inclination was to confine PWA to slum clearance. Slums, he believed, were a national problem. He rejected some limited dividend applications because they proposed to build on vacant land in suburban areas. He saw no need for new housing in such areas and thought building it would put the government in competition with the private sector. Nonetheless, in order to speed construction, or to avoid high land prices or condemnation proceedings, the PWA and its local collaborators increasingly chose vacant land and not slum sites. In the end only about half the PWA projects were on slum sites; only one limited dividend project was on a slum site. Walter Schmidt deplored the practice; clearing the worst slums was, in his mind, the object of the exercise. For advocates like Henry Churchill, the initial focus on slum clearance was a mistake. It retarded progress and would have put the new housing in the wrong places.[19]

For Mumford and others, real estate interests were to blame. They wanted to rescue investments in slum properties and didn't mind slowing the housing program. From Mumford's perspective, opposition from the real estate industry had created a hostile atmosphere for government housing and had warped the government's efforts. Social workers and other concerned about the slums came in for their share of criticism as well. They had been "betrayed by imperfectly understood slogans." "The slums must go" was too appealing. The slum clearers had not thought their

Secretary of the Interior Harold Ickes testifying before the House Committee on Banking and Currency regarding the Housing Act of 1937, August 5, 1937 (Library of Congress).

ideas through; they did not understand that slum clearance and low-cost housing need not be part of the same program.[20]

The PWA program left many unhappy. The real estate industry opposed government intervention generally, and government funding and construction in particular. Intent on stimulating the economy, the Roosevelt administration thought the PWA was moving too slowly. At one point Roosevelt withdrew most of the PWA's funds. Ickes, who described himself as a "curmudgeon," was impatient with the Housing Division's efforts, eventually replacing Robert Kohn with Horatio Hackett who had a background in large-scale construction. Some housing advocates thought the program was too "ad hoc." They pointed out that no one had investigated at the outset whether the financial terms the PWA could offer were likely to yield low rents. Alfred Mayer wrote that "bringing housing in the back door" was a ghastly mistake.[21]

The community planners were the unhappiest. As Mayer put it, they wanted a "broadside attack" on the housing question. Housing was complicated and difficult. Hasty efforts targeted more on employment than housing endangered the entire program. Mumford thought that the PWA's early decision to limit itself to slum clearance and to housing rented at rates well below any available in the private sector was a serious setback. The bad old methods would still prevail in most of American housing. That the Congress had, in the meantime, passed the National Housing Act of 1934 which sought to bolster the private real estate industry and promote homeownership, made things that much worse.[22]

Federal Housing Administration

The Roosevelt administration was not of one mind regarding public housing. The Federal Housing Administration, established by the 1934 Act to support the private housing industry, endorsed public housing but only tepidly. FHA officials conceded that the private sector could not build housing for the lowest income groups and decent housing for low-income families would require subsidies. Nevertheless, they saw the future in terms of private construction on vacant suburban land. If enough families moved to new suburban homes, slum dwellers could move to the houses they vacated. Like many others, FHA leaders imagined public housing as the means to eliminate slums. They suggested that housing legislation require one slum unit to be demolished for every new public unit built and advocated that the legislation put more emphasis on rehabilitating slum housing.[23]

In congressional testimony, Stewart McDonald, Federal Housing Administrator, was less than approving of urban dwellers. He wondered aloud how many people really needed to live in cities. New York City was planning to build new housing for people in Harlem. Would not they be better off in Alabama or Arkansas? McDonald thought that they were attracted by the city lights and the "merry-go-round." For "humanity's sake," he presumed that the government had to take care of them. He observed that you could offer some foreign-born slum dwellers the "finest farm in Missouri" and they would not take it.[24]

Tenants

The debate about public housing before 1937 took place almost entirely without the people who lived in substandard housing or who might occupy any new housing. Architects, planners, writers, settlement workers, officials of trade and professional organizations and other middle- or upper-class thinkers dominated the discussion. Tenants rarely appeared at the congressional hearings, perhaps only twice. In 1935, representatives of the Lower East Side Housing Conference testified about conditions in their neighborhood and in 1937 the chairman of the New York City–wide Tenants Council spoke in support of the housing legislation.[25]

The Lower East Side Housing Conference owed something to the support of settlement workers. Simkhovitich and other settlement workers believed that they should train and prompt their clients to organize and act on their own. As early as 1912, the Association of Neighborhood Workers helped 26 Mothers' Clubs run by settlements to coalesce into a League of Mothers' Clubs that then lobbied city officials on various issues.

The city-wide Tenants Council was the latest expression of tenant organizing in the city. Typical of the "popular front" politics of the time and place, the council represented an array of tenant organizations from across the city as well as several political orientations. Groups from Knickerbocker Village and the Lavanburg Homes participated, as did groups with links to labor unions or the Communist Party.

Legislation

In March 1935, Senator Robert Wagner (D–New York) introduced housing legislation,[26] based on ideas provided by the National Public Housing Conference. It was a bare bones proposal. The bill replaced the PWA Housing Division, whose authorization was temporary, with a permanently authorized Division of Housing within the Department of the Interior. The new division's mission was to carry out slum clearance and low-rent housing programs. Its tools were loans and grants to local public housing bodies; the bill language did not define what qualified as a public housing body. Grants could be as much as 30 percent of the cost of labor and materials. The only stipulation for loans was that the interest rate not exceed the rate for ten-year federal bonds. Where housing conditions were poor and no local public housing body existed, the division would be authorized to carry out slum clearance and low-rent housing itself. Once a local public housing body came into existence, however, the division was to turn over its projects to the local body.

The same year, the Labor Housing Conference persuaded Congressman Henry Ellenbogen (D–Pennsylvania) to introduce a housing bill it had drafted.[27] The bill sought to implement many of Catherine Bauer's ideas. It contemplated an array of agencies providing "modern, large-scale" housing. An independent United States Housing Authority was to provide financial aid to state and local governments, public housing agencies, non-profit housing agencies, and limited dividend housing agencies. The authority could create regional or local federal housing corporations. The bill defined "large-scale" as projects designed and administered as a "neighborhood unit." To facilitate assembling large tracts, it allowed housing agencies to ignore local ordinances that mandated standard lot and block subdivisions. The new housing had to provide light, air, ventilation, safety and amenity at least equal to that mandated by local ordinances. Housing agencies were to prefer projects where land costs were no higher than the use value for "good modern housing."

Recognizing that the Ellenbogen bill was better than the conference's effort, Wagner persuaded Bauer and others to work with his staff, principally Leon Keyserling, to produce a composite version. Wagner introduced their product in 1936.[28] The heart of the bill was an independent United States Housing Authority. The authority could make grants up to 45 percent of a project's cost, payable in a lump sum or in annual contributions for up to 60 years. The authority could lend housing agencies the full development cost (85 percent in the case of limited profit housing agencies).

The bill took a stab at defining the intended beneficiaries of the new housing program. "Low rent" referred to decent housing for families of low income. "Families of low income" were those who could not pay enough for housing to induce private builders to build an adequate supply of decent housing.

The 1936 bill dropped many of the "modern" housing features; there were no references to neighborhood units, requirements regarding light and air, or permission to ignore local ordinances. The range of possible providers of low-rent housing was narrowed. States and localities could no longer receive assistance. Limited profit housing agencies and non-profit housing agencies, now called "public housing societies," were still included as possible aid recipients along with public housing agencies. The bill tried to avoid creating windfall profits for landowners by directing that land be purchased "at a reasonable price."

The federal role was somewhat smaller than in the 1935 versions. The United States Housing Authority could not create federal housing corporations. The authority could not build its own housing projects. It was empowered to carry out "demonstration projects" which it had to sell or lease to housing agencies as soon as practicable.

Wagner's 1936 bill circumscribed the federal role in still other ways. It stipulated that low-rent projects were to be limited to areas where there was a shortage of decent, privately built housing. The authority was to fund slum clearance projects only where the private sector was not adequately addressing the problem. PWA projects had displaced families that it failed to rehouse. The 1936 bill directed that slum clearance should not take place if it would make it more difficult for displaced families to find equivalent housing at no higher cost. The bill directed that displaced families were to be rehoused on the cleared site or elsewhere.

The 1936 bill addressed several issues that had arisen in the course of debates. In the face of fears that slum clearance and low-rent housing were only urban problems or even just New York problems, the authority was to distribute benefits as widely as possible throughout the country. Some local officials worried that housing projects exempt from property taxes would undermine their tax base. The bill therefore authorized housing agencies to make payments in lieu of taxes to local governments. The George-Healey Act, enacted in 1936, had permitted the PWA to make such payments.[29]

After the 1936 bill failed to gain passage, Wagner introduced a slightly revised version in 1937.[30] The requirement to rehouse displaced families was watered down to require only that "substantially all" the displaced families be accommodated in equivalent housing. The most important addition was language intended to specify the intended beneficiaries. The bill stated that the new housing was intended for families whose income was no more than five times the rent charged or six times in the case of families with three or more minor dependents. In the George-Healey Act, Congress had limited PWA projects to families whose incomes did not exceed five times the rent charged.

Senator Robert Wagner

Robert Wagner was a social and economic reformer. After a career in New York City politics often allied with Al Smith, Wagner was elected to the Senate in 1926. During the 1920s, he outlined a program intended to organize industrial society for the common good. He wrote about the need for economic growth, amicable labor relations, and shared prosperity. He thought that laissez faire economics were outmoded and that the nation needed national planning. Even before the Depression, he supported increased wages, decreased hours, and a program of social insurance.

Nonetheless, Wagner was a cautious reformer. He looked for cooperation, not conflict with business interests. As a result, business leaders were content with his playing a lead role in the labor relations machinery established by the National Industrial Recovery Act. Wagner avoided what he saw as utopian plans and radical changes. In Congress, he chose only proposals he thought could be enacted. He was comfortable defending limited measures as steps in the right direction or the half loaf that was better than none.[31]

Wagner accepted the main thrust of the housing reformers' argument. A great many Americans were too poor to afford the housing the private sector produced. Instead they lived in substandard, crowded homes. The private sector was incapable of solving the problem, at least not without financial support from governments. Wagner agreed that a program of low-cost housing subsidized by the federal government was the immediate answer.[32]

Wagner stressed that the proposed federal programs were to be limited. The housing efforts funded by the Reconstruction Finance Corporation and by the Federal Housing Administration had been, in Wagner's view, largely successful. In supporting low-cost housing, he was not proposing to displace or limit them. The private sector could produce housing for the middle and upper classes and might make a contribution to housing for low-income families. Wagner was not proposing to reduce the private sector's role or create a housing program that would compete with it. Making sure that public housing projects did not compete with private industry was "the most important consideration." Only the private sector could produce the volume of new housing that the country needed or that would stimulate the economy. Wagner saw government's role as only supplementing private efforts. Wagner argued that the private real industry had no reason to oppose a low-cost housing program. The beneficiaries of a new housing program were to be only low-income families living in substandard housing, not all low-income families.[33]

The new federal program might be temporary as well. Wagner claimed that government housing programs in Britain had stimulated private building. Perhaps the same would happen in the United States. If the U.S. economy revived and incomes rose, the demand for low-cost housing might decline. Subsidies might not be necessary. Wagner thought that, ultimately, responsibility for housing should return to the states and localities. Wagner argued that local control offered the private sector protection from government competition. Locally controlled programs would be "in close contact with the general business needs of the community." Local control might mean that states and localities eventually assumed responsibility for supporting low-cost housing financially.[34]

Wagner intended that public housing be simple and economical. He told the Senate in 1937 that the intent was not to build "palaces." Public housing was to be an ordinary type of construction, decent housing with running water and private toilets, but nothing more. Wagner thought that nearly all the PWA projects had been too expensive. Low-income families could not afford them, and, because they were well built and well designed, they threatened to compete with the private sector. Public housing was supposed to compete only with the "miserable conditions of slums and blighted areas." When Senator Harry Byrd (D–Virginia) offered an amendment to the 1937 proposal that limited the cost of public housing to $1,000 per room, Wagner offered little or no opposition.[35]

For Wagner, public housing was about eliminating slums. He was open to building new housing on vacant land outside the slums, but his focus was removing slums and blighted areas. In 1937, he was comfortable with language that described the proposed beneficiaries as the "lowest income" group, but explained it did not mean people who could not afford even subsidized rent. It meant the poorest families that could afford public housing rents. In Wagner's telling, slum dwellers were a menace to community health and wealth. Once the nation eliminated slums and provided better housing, juvenile delinquency, crime and disease would disappear. The cities' financial situation would improve.[36]

Senator David Walsh

The chairman of the Senate committee responsible for housing legislation (Education and Labor) in the mid–1930s was Senator David Walsh (D–Massachusetts). Like Wagner, Walsh was among the reform-minded Democratic senators whose tenure pre-dated the New Deal. Walsh participated in reform politics in Massachusetts and was first elected to the Senate in 1919. Unlike Wagner, he was at best a lukewarm supporter of the Roosevelt administration, opposing Roosevelt's foreign policies and his plans to remake the Supreme Court.

Walsh claimed that the PWA had no authority to enter the housing field. It had used, improperly in Walsh's view, a mandate to promote employment in the building trades as an excuse to build housing projects. PWA housing was too expensive. Walsh suspected that, if complete figures were available, they would show that the PWA projects cost more than any of

Senators Robert Wagner (left) and David Walsh (right) confer with William Green, President of the American Federation Labor, at the Senate Committee on Education and Labor hearing regarding the Housing Act of 1937, April 14, 1937 (Library of Congress).

the limited dividend projects. Walsh thought that, because the PWA could not use the power of eminent domain, it had been forced to buy expensive land. Because PWA projects were expensive, they served the wrong people, not the lowest income families. By building overly expensive housing, the PWA had allowed some low-income families to have better houses than "any moderately comfortable workingman" could afford. Walsh claimed that he would not deny any wage earner decent housing, but that he did not want to put the "owners of small homes" at a disadvantage. Subsidized public housing should not be better than the housing that self-sufficient families could afford.[37]

Walsh was adamant that public housing serve only the poorest. He said he wanted the "lowest income group" served, not merely the low-income group. The people to be re-housed were the families with the "lowest income, the largest family," "just struggling to make a living," and living in the slums. Walsh worried that political machines would take control of public housing. People with political "pull" or influence would get new housing and not the "poor widow, washwomen, orphans." Walsh was willing to contemplate income limits for public housing far lower than any of the reformers. Reformers, and Wagner, resisted any limit expressed in dollar terms, arguing that a national limit would be unworkable. Nevertheless while proposals to limit public housing to families earning less than $1,000 a year were floating around, Walsh suggested limits of $500 or $600 a year. Public housing advocates assumed that families that poor would not be able to afford even subsidized rents and would be on relief.[38]

For Walsh, public housing was supposed to rehouse slum dwellers, not to produce better housing generally. States and localities already had sufficient authority to tear down slum buildings; they did not need federal assistance for that, he argued. They did need help, Walsh accepted, building new housing for the families displaced by the demolition. Housing anyone else in the new housing was wrong and the federal government needed to guard against it. During the 1937 debate, Walsh noted that two different groups supported low-cost housing: those who wanted to clear the slums and those who wanted to build housing. Walsh claimed that he and Wagner sided with the proponents of slum clearance. Wagner agreed.[39]

New housing for slum dwellers, by itself, would not guarantee the end of slum conditions, in Walsh's view. Slum families did not all understand good sanitation and good housekeeping. Unless such families received health and housekeeping education, along with better houses, their new homes would soon be as dirty as their old.[40]

Walsh viewed a low-cost housing program that did more than re-house displaced slum families as an impending disaster. Walsh believed that building better housing for the 40 percent of American families who earned less than $1,000 a year was obviously impossible, beyond the financial means of the federal government. The government lacked the authority, Walsh argued, to provide subsidized housing to only some families, particularly if they did not come from the slums and were not very poor. If some families got subsidized housing, Walsh said he would expect all families to get subsidized housing. Doing that, however, would put the nation "on the road to socialism" and government ownership of all private housing.[41]

Congressional Opposition

The most common complaint from congressional opponents was that the proposed program was too expensive. Pointing to the PWA projects and the greenbelt communities developed by the Resettlement Administration, opponents like Senator Harry Byrd argued that government construction had been wasteful and extravagant. Even with construction costs limited to $1,000 per room, the new housing units would still cost more than the houses most Americans lived in. It was impractical to house families who earned very little in such houses, others argued; the subsidies would be too big. If the government attempted to build decent housing for every family that needed it, the cost would be astronomical.[42]

Like David Walsh, opponents thought that providing housing to some was unfair. Why should families that had worked and saved to buy a home pay for someone else's housing, especially housing that might cost more and be superior to their own homes? What would other slum dwellers think when they did not get any of the new housing?[43]

Wagner's bill was the "entering wedge," opponents claimed. At a minimum, taxpayers needed to know how big the program would ultimately be and how much it would cost. Senator Walter George (D–Georgia) argued that the bill would mark the end of private investment in housing. If the bill were enacted as proposed, the U.S. would end up with state socialism. Millard Tydings (D–Maryland) suggested that, once the government provided housing to some, everyone would want some, even people who did not live in slums.[44]

The new housing would serve only the big cities, critics complained. There was nothing in the bill, they pointed out, for rural areas or for small communities. Eight or ten cities would get all the benefits. Congressmen Hamilton Fish (R–New York) contended that even the proposed solution was too urban. Rather than concentrating people in "human beehives," the government ought to move people out of the cities and into little homes of their own. They could become "property owners, taxpayers and good American citizens." That would do more to offset "radicalism, socialism and communism" than anything else.[45]

Would public housing help the people who needed it? Some opponents doubted that better housing would transform slum dwellers in the ways Wagner described. Would someone unaccustomed to keeping a clean apartment keep his new public housing clean? Would the new housing go to the lowest income families? And what happened when public housing tenants lost their jobs? Wouldn't the public housing authority feel obligated to house them? Eventually, wouldn't public housing projects become "glorified alms houses" with only the most needy families in residence? Since public housing proponents did not plan to house undesirable elements, like prostitutes, what would happen to them when the slums were demolished? Would not they be scattered elsewhere in the community?[46]

If a public housing program was inevitable, congressional opponents had some suggestions. Some said they would support a slum clearance program. Restricting any new housing to displaced poor families might be acceptable. Otherwise, the key was to limit the program as much as possible. Public housing had to feature simple design and modest materials. There was no excuse for anything elaborate or pretentious. It should not be better than housing occupied by "the average homeowner and taxpaying citizen." Public housing should under local control. No city should be forced to accept public housing. The federal government need not build any projects on its own.[47]

The National Housing Act of 1937

The bill[48] passed by Congress authorized an independent United States Housing Authority (USHA), empowered to carry out slum clearance and low-cost housing programs. The USHA could provide annual grants to local housing authorities over 60 years that could cover up to 90 percent of a housing project's cost. Local authorities would be responsible for covering operating costs.

Wagner's latest proposal benefited from circumstances beyond his or the reformers' control. The Roosevelt administration and the Congress were still looking for programs that would boost employment and revive the economy. In 1937, the administration also needed a legislative victory. It was skeptical about Wagner's bill, but was willing to put its doubts aside. Furthermore, the administration still had enough clout with the Congress to push the bill through. Henry Steagall (D–Alabama), its sponsor in the House, had been opposed but pushed the bill through at Roosevelt's request. That Wagner focused on the art of the possible and was willing to modify the advocates' ideas to appease fellow Democrats like David Walsh helped.

The bill gave skeptics and critics much of what they wanted. Grants and loans could be made only to local housing authorities; references to limited dividend corporations were eliminated. The bill did not authorize federal demonstration projects. To ensure local commitment and to reduce the federal contributions, local authorities had to fund 20 percent of the cost. To promote slum clearance, localities had to demolish or rehabilitate one housing unit for every new public housing unit constructed. Projects should not be elaborate or expensive. Costs were limited to $1,000 a room or $4,000 per unit and, to meet the objections of New York representatives, to $1,250 a room or $5,000 a unit in cities larger than 500,000 inhabitants. To prevent New York getting too much money, no more than 10 percent of the funds could go to any one state.

The bill left key decisions to local housing authorities. Beyond the cost limits and admonition against extravagance, local authorities were free to build whatever kind of housing they chose. The requirement to demolish slum dwellings pushed local authorities towards locating the new housing on slum sites, but they were free to build on vacant land provided they demolished bad housing elsewhere. The bill set an upper limit on tenants' incomes (five times the rent), but local authorities were otherwise free to select tenants. The need to cover operating costs, of course, made it difficult to house tenants with little or no income. The bill made no mention of the facilities or services housing authorities should or could provide along with housing.

The size of the new housing program was dependent on congressional action. The bill did not attempt to identify the national need for low-cost housing or commit the federal government to meeting it. The funds made available in the bill were relatively small—$5 million in 1937—while discussions of the national need had been in the billions.

Catherine Bauer conceded that the requirement to demolish housing units in proportion to the housing units, the limitation on construction costs, the limit on funds to any one state, and the requirement for local funding were all "jokers." The *New Republic* published a similar assessment when the Senate passed the bill. Bauer thought the level of subsidy authorized by the bill, which she thought would reduce rents to about half of what they would otherwise have been, was positive. For Bauer, the most positive feature was that the legislation represented a victory for a coalition of labor unions, city officials and advocacy organizations. It was a popular measure, not an administration measure, a triumph of the Left over the Right, she wrote. Langdon Post wrote that the bill's importance rested on its acceptance that housing, for its own sake, was now a government responsibility. The federal government had set upon a course from which there was no retreat.[49]

The public housing program created by the Roosevelt administration and the Congress was an innovation for the United States, the first peacetime legislation authorizing government funded and managed housing. Nonetheless, it was a tightly constrained, even parsimonious, program, designed not to offend the real estate industry, compete with the private sector or intrude in local affairs. Rather than serving a third or half of American families, it could serve only some of the working poor. Its ultimate size was unknown; future construction was dependent on congressional action. At a time when even the Hoover housing conference was concerned about the quality of housing, the legislation's principal message was that public housing should be cheap. As Senator Walsh pointed out, it was intended to clear slums rather than build more houses. If it resembled any of the versions of public housing proposed by advocates in the preceding five or six years, it was the "social workers" slum clearance program. It repudiated nearly all aspects of the community planners' vision.

CHAPTER THREE

The 1949 Housing Act

In some ways the debate between 1937 and 1949 seemed like business as usual. The executive branch, in the form of the United States Housing Authority, and local housing authorities fleshed out the provisions of the 1937 Act to create their own version of public housing. Housing reformers, including important figures like Catherine Bauer, probed housing issues and offered solutions. Opponents, supported by the real estate industry, lobbied against public housing. The Congress then drew upon the stock of ideas and the accumulated experiences to produce a revised version of public housing in the Housing Act of 1949.

The post–1937 debate was, however, different in important ways. The debate was less ambitious or optimistic. The conventional assumption was that private sector would solve the nation's housing problems. Catherine Bauer and others offered alternative notions, but they had little impact. There was no broad agreement, in fact, that the country needed public housing. The best that advocates could hope for was a revival of the 1937 program, perhaps with a few refinements. Undoing the constraints imposed by Congress in the 1937 Act did not appear feasible.

United States Housing Authority

The program and organization established by the Housing Act of 1937 did not survive long. In Roosevelt's 1939 governmental reorganization, the USHA ceased to be an independent agency and was incorporated into the Federal Works Agency. In 1942, it was renamed the Federal Public Housing Authority and consolidated into a new National Housing Agency. In 1947, it became the Public Housing Administration (PHA), part of a new

Housing and Home Finance Agency (HHFA). More important, appropriations ceased or were diverted to defense housing. Through June 1941, USHA funded 585 projects including about 170,000 housing units. Almost no additional units were funded from then until 1949.[1]

The USHA foundered, first, on congressional opposition. In 1939, Congress failed to pass amendments to the 1937 Act intended to strengthen the program. Congressman Fritz Lanham (D–Texas), an opponent of public housing, drafted the 1940 bill authorizing government housing for defense workers so as to prevent USHA control of the program. He later secured an amendment that required congressional approval for conversion of any defense housing to low-income public housing. Although USHA, alone among federal agencies, had a program in place to construct housing, it received little of the funds appropriated for defense housing.[2]

Charles Palmer, Roosevelt's first choice as Defense Housing Coordinator, had been instrumental in Atlanta's first public housing project, Techwood Homes. Nonetheless, he favored private efforts for defense housing and, among federal agencies, did not favor USHA. In 1941, the United Auto Workers proposed construction of a 20,000 housing unit "defense city" for workers near the Willow Run aircraft plant outside Detroit. International Style architects were to design the homes and they were to be sold to workers on a cooperative basis. Palmer collaborated with Henry Ford and others to delay and, ultimately, derail the project. In 1942, National Housing Administrator John Blandford shifted efforts from permanent housing developments to temporary housing built to a low standard, unless a clear and long-term need for permanent housing in a community could be demonstrated. Real estate interests and their congressional friends had argued that permanent housing would depress real estate values. Blandford also ceded greater control over planning and development to local governments.[3]

USHA was also unlucky in its first administrator. Nathan Straus came from a prominent New York family, owners of Macy's department store. He had served in the New York State legislature and on the New York City Housing Authority and he funded Hillside Homes, a limited dividend project in the Bronx. Nonetheless, he did not impress senior figures in the Roosevelt administration. Ickes considered him a dilettante, "lacking in force, initiative and decision." Ickes lumped him together with his other critics from New York and claimed that, were Straus appointed administrator, he would have nothing more to do with public housing. Marriner Eccles, Federal Reserve Chairman, told Roosevelt that, if appointed, Straus "would probably find himself in hot water in about two

Building No. 16, Techwood Homes, Atlanta, Georgia, opened 1936 (Library of Congress).

weeks." Nevertheless, Roosevelt chose Straus. Of the five names offered by Eccles, Straus was the only one who wholeheartedly supported public housing and was acceptable to most housing advocates.[4]

Eccles was right. Straus irritated Congressmen on both sides of the aisle. Senator Albert Gore (D–Tennessee) took a particular dislike to Straus. In the crowded defense housing effort, Straus ended up in power struggles with other key officials, usually on the losing side, and was impolitic enough to air his grievances in public. None of this helped USHA get the resources needed to build housing. Straus resigned in 1942 after it was clear that USHA would not play a major role in defense housing.

As head of USHA, Straus set as his goal demonstrating that the government could build decent housing cheaply enough to accommodate the lowest income families. He wanted to show that the USHA could do better than the PWA in providing low-cost decent housing. The USHA's 1939 annual report acknowledged that public housing had multiple goals beyond building low-cost housing: promoting construction and employment, establishing fair labor standards and clearing slums. Yet, the report asserted that the program would not be a success until it could charge rents low enough to serve the lowest income group. The path to low rents was, it claimed, through low construction costs.[5]

How low would rents need to be to serve the families with the lowest incomes? No one really knew. Straus accepted that government subsidies equal to initial capital costs would be sufficient. Straus claimed that rents equal to operating costs were equivalent to rents paid by slum families. Construction costs are what he could try to control and he set out to do so.[6]

The 1939 USHA report claimed success. No matter how one defined construction costs, the USHA had done well, the report said. USHA projects had constructed housing units for an average cost of $2,821 per unit. Building permits issued to private builders suggested that private construction cost at least $3,448. The cost of construction plus facilities in USHA projects was well below the maxima set by the 1937 Act. The report claimed that total costs, that is, construction plus facilities and land, were lower than those of large-scale, privately-owned rental housing. And, the report claimed, the USHA would continue to push costs downward.[7]

To achieve cheaper construction, Straus set out to build minimal housing, "houses that are clean and decent and sunny, but homes built to standards set at the minimum compatible with decency and comfort." The goal was not to house a few families in ideal homes but to house as many slum dwellers as possible in decent homes. USHA mandated smaller rooms than the PWA had. Straus described with some pride the USHA method for determining the smallest possible rooms. Inside a garage USHA staff constructed a four-room residence with movable walls and, after adding furniture and equipment, moved the walls inward as far as seemed reasonable. The USHA standards eliminated what it considered frills—a door between the kitchen and other rooms, closet doors, floor moldings and the like. By 1940, USHA refused to approve projects unless construction costs were well below the limits set in the 1937 Act.[8]

The omission of closet doors caught peoples' attention and provoked much criticism. Eliminating closet doors came to be seen, and remembered, as evidence of public housing's indifference to human needs. After Straus left the USHA, he felt compelled to defend the decision. It was, he explained, an example of the right way to reduce costs, breaking construction down into component items and evaluating each. It was also an example, he wrote, of the difficulty of pleasing everyone.[9]

Housing advocates chafed at the 1937 Act's cost limits. A limit on unit costs, they pleaded, motivated housing authorities to build too many small apartments and too little housing for large families. If a cost limit was needed, it should apply to rooms and not entire units. Charles Abrams pointed out that a national cost limit, even if for just large cities, was unduly rigid and failed to recognize local conditions. He complained that most private construction was at a lower standard than public housing. Limiting public housing costs to private practices was therefore too restrictive. The National Public Housing Conference thought that cost limits were unnecessary. The stipulations that construction not be elaborate and not exceed private sector costs were sufficient. The National Association of Housing Officials thought the nation could do better. The USHA standards represented progress, but the rooms were too small and some projects lacked adequate outdoor space.[10]

The USHA's low construction costs failed to mollify critics of public housing. An employee of the U.S. Savings and Loan League, writing in 1940, accepted that USHA costs were lower than the PWA's, but added that PWA costs were so high that almost any project would appear cheaper. He pointed out that the figures quoted by USHA did not include the costs of acquiring and clearing the land. Housing that could last 60 years was a mistake and high-quality materials and high construction standards were wasteful, he went on. The government should not be building better houses for poor families than self-supporting families could afford. Private developers, with assistance from the FHA, were planning to build houses cheaper than the USHA units. They might be inferior in quality and conveniences than USHA construction, but it made more sense for poor families to live in them rather than houses that cost as much as middle-class housing. If the USHA had to build something, it should be the bare minimum, sufficiently Spartan so that families would not want to stay long.[11]

USHA-Funded Projects

The two biggest USHA projects in New York, Red Hook Houses (2,800 units) and Queensbridge Houses (3,000 units), started with plans drawn up under PWA guidance. Working under the USHA guidelines, the New York City Housing Authority reduced unit costs. Its architects added two stories and elevators to the four-story buildings already planned. The elevators were small and stopped at every other floor. The added stories increased the number of units and reduced average unit costs without increasing the amount of land covered. Coverage at Red Hook remained low, at 25 percent. Population densities were significantly higher than at the two New York PWA projects, Harlem River and Williamsburg. The density at Queensbridge was about a third bigger than at Harlem River. The costs per room were roughly half those achieved at the two PWA projects and rents could be about 30 percent lower.[12]

The six-story structures in New York were not representative of USHA projects nationwide. Row houses and two or three story apartment buildings were still the norm. USHA claimed that, while apartment houses might be cheaper to build than row houses, they were more expensive to maintain. Local authorities had to follow USHA guidelines but the final design decisions were theirs.[13]

Lewis Mumford did not like some aspects of USHA projects built by the New York authority. Their chief sin was trying to house too many people. Mumford preferred lower densities housed in row houses and three-story apartment buildings. The Red Hook buildings were unnecessarily barrack-like and monotonous. He called it "Leningrad formalism." The designers could have sited the school and community center so as to break the monotony but did not. Mumford thought that the use of colors and textures in the Queensbridge facades was better. The Red Hook apartments had insufficient air and ventilation. The rooms in the Red Hook and Queensbridge projects were too small and not well laid out. When New York built 10- and 11-story buildings at the East River Houses in East Harlem, Mumford liked them even less. They were the city of the past, he wrote, not the city of the future.[14]

At the same time, Mumford believed that, in some ways, developments like the Red Hook and Queensbridge Houses represented the way forward. They were large-scale projects. The fixtures and workmanship were good. They had internal gardens and playgrounds. They had community centers and stores. They were organic units for living, not "a clot of nondescript structures built anyhow." They were "miles above the product of any commercial apartment building." Even if architects learned nothing more, it would be worthwhile to rebuild New York on their pattern. Mumford thought architects could and should learn more. They did not have to repeat the mistakes of the past.[15]

Many supporters of public housing did not share Mumford's enthusiasm for projects like Red Hook and Queensbridge. Such projects were too big, too dense. Their exterior design was dull, monotonous and unimaginative. They were too different from existing housing in the same areas. Henry Churchill wrote that "stereotyped monotony was enforced from Washington in the name of economy." Mary Simkhovitch, who served on the New York City Housing Authority throughout the period, said she wanted smaller projects and more variety in design. The USHA projects were too clearly institutional, many argued. Several writers maintained that public housing's allegedly distinctive appearance labeled it as the home for the poor and separated it from the rest of the community. Public housing did not look like anyone's home, another critic claimed.[16]

Housing filled with poor people even if well designed and well built troubled outsiders, even those who supported public housing. No matter how good the housing was, public housing looked like "housing for poor people," observers concluded. It was "institutional." Worse, it "stigmatized" the people who lived these as poor. It set them apart from the wider community. Many observers conceded, however, that the USHA projects offered better housing than many Americans had.[17]

After the war and after Bauer had left USHA, she wrote articles that echoed these sentiments. She criticized "one class dormitory developments" and "bleak" projects that offered decent housing but were "not very warming to the spirit." She thought standardization of building types was matched by social segregation by class and "race." She criticized public housing tenant selection policies regarding "race." Nonetheless, Bauer was not so much discomfited by developments in public housing as hankering for a broader, more ambitious national housing policy. She was still interested in a comprehensive national housing program and better regional planning. She wrote about attracting more affluent families back to cities as well as finding places for poorer families in the suburbs. She imagined that housing authorities could construct and manage mixed income projects, where subsidized and non-subsidized housing existed side by side. She set the goal as providing all families with a choice of decent housing.[18]

Under Straus, the USHA appeared to embrace slum clearance as mandated in the 1937 Act. In 1939, Straus told the Congress that USHA efforts would lead to the elimination of 160,000 unsafe and unsanitary dwellings. He said that every USHA project involved a binding agreement with the local government to eliminate the appropriate number of slum housing units within a year of the project's completion. In 1945, the PHA Commissioner could report that USHA projects had caused the elimination of 114,000 deficient housing units, 83 percent of the number required by the law. Another 20,000 units remained to be eliminated, but action had been deferred because of the housing shortage.[19]

Insisting on low land costs was part of Straus' crusade to lower initial costs. USHA policy became that the cost of acquiring land, including the cost of demolishing existing buildings, could not exceed $1.50 a square foot. In the face of resistance from the New York City Housing Authority USHA modified the policy to allow higher costs if the local housing authority funded the difference. Nevertheless, USHA retained the right to review the land costs of every project. In the 1939 annual report, Straus claimed success regarding land costs. For the 346 projects approved before the end of the 1939, land costs averaged 29 cents per square foot.[20]

Average costs computed across the entire country are not especially revealing. The program extended beyond New York and beyond big cities, even if our knowledge of the rest of the country remains limited. Half the projects built before 1944 were in cities of less than 100,000 inhabitants and about one quarter in towns of less than 25,000 inhabitants. In many areas, land costs were much lower than in the New York and USHA's limit on land costs probably had less impact nationwide.[21]

In New York and other big cities, a limit on land costs was significant. It could push projects onto vacant land or prompt construction of taller buildings. The New York authority built the Queensbridge project on essentially vacant land. It built several other early projects in the outer boroughs on land that was not densely developed. As Alfred Mayer had argued in the 1930s, New York had within its boundaries vacant or cheap land suitable for large new housing projects. It was not until the East River Houses that New York built on what could be considered a slum site in Manhattan. In Cincinnati, limits on land costs prompted the housing authority to drop plans for a project near an earlier PWA development located near downtown and to consider two projects on vacant land further from the center. Opposition from real estate interests blocked those plans, nevertheless. Two of the three USHA funded projects in Philadelphia were on vacant land. As observers recognized and as the PHA Commissioner explained to Senator Robert Taft (R–Ohio) in 1945, building on slum sites was more expensive, but authorities thought they offset the additional costs by adding more units and taking advantage of infrastructure already in place. Thus, the East River Houses included 10- and 11-story buildings, rather than the six story structures at Red Hook and Queensbridge.[22]

Nathan Straus and the USHA deplored the move to taller buildings. At the dedication of the East River Houses, Straus warned against overcrowding people. On another occasion in New York, he warned that people were not intended to live in tall, crowded buildings. Children enjoyed a happy and healthy childhood, he said, when they lived in low-rise developments.[23]

Location

The debate over site selection continued, however. New York City Housing Authority leaders promoted the case for building on slum sites. Langdon Post and Alfred Rheinstein, his successor as head of the New York authority, argued that building on slum sites cleared slums, while construction on vacant land did not. Vacant land was usually at the city's periphery; building there would hollow out the city and undermine land values. Construction costs on vacant sites might seem lower, but they did not include the cost of new infrastructure, streets, schools, sewers and subways, that they city would be forced to provide.[24]

Alfred Mayer and Carol Aronovici argued for vacant sites. Land values in the slums were inflated. Acquiring land at existing values would make public housing too expensive and overly crowded. The only beneficiaries would be the owners of slum properties. Tearing down slum housing without first providing better housing elsewhere would push poor families into other slum housing, perhaps at higher rents. According to Mayer, the Metropolitan Life Insurance Company's Parkchester project in the Bronx was the model that New York City should follow, a very large project on vacant land in the outer boroughs. He claimed housing units there would cost 25 percent less than similar units built on the Lower East Side.[25]

Rent

Straus' USHA claimed success regarding rents in the new public housing. The 1939 annual report alleged that rents in the 17 newly opened projects were the lowest charged for decent housing in the 20th century. They were, the report added, lower than the average rents paid for slum housing in the same communities. In only four projects were the income limits for admission set at the highest level allowed under the law, that is, five times rent. The report offered this as proof that the lowest income families were being served. Straus claimed that public housing rents calculated to cover operating costs were about equal to the rent slum families could afford to pay.[26]

Local housing officials faced a more complicated situation. Federal and state subsidies paid the initial construction costs, but local authorities had to cover operating and maintenance costs. In the simplest terms, housing officials were looking for poor families, but not so poor that they could not pay enough rent to cover costs and not so well off that the rent was less than 20 percent of their income. Since the supply of public housing was small, much smaller than the demand, housing officials could not house all eligible families. They were, therefore, vulnerable to criticism that they were housing the wrong people, perhaps families who were not the poorest, perhaps families that were too poor.

In 1940, USHA recommended that local housing authorities adopt what it called "graded rents." Authorities would set two or more rent levels tied to units' size, location or other factors. If the rents were calculated properly, authorities could cover their costs and still accommodate families with different incomes. The National Association of Housing Officials included "graded rents" in its proposals for public housing after the war.[27]

In the midst of the Senate debate on the 1949 Housing Act, HHFA described how it thought local authorities set rents. Local authorities, the HHFA told the Senate, established a range of rents, the lowest of which the poorest slum families could afford. Income, however, did not necessarily define housing need. Among the families that could afford each rent level, authorities attempted to identify those whose housing needs were the greatest. Equating income with housing need and serving only the families with the lowest incomes would convert public housing into another form of relief, federal officials wrote, not what the Congress had intended in the 1937 Act.[28]

Housing Relief Families

Families whose income came from relief payments posed a particular problem to housing authorities. USHA's official position was that public housing should be available to families on relief provided their relief payments were sufficient to cover the rent. At the same time, USHA and its supporters argued that public housing could not, and should not, be expected to solve the nation's income problems. Public housing was for working families with too little income to afford decent housing. It was the task of relief agencies and social insurance programs to serve families with little or no income. Edith Wood likened public housing to public schools, not to relief agencies. In her view, public housing was not a form of relief; it was the same sort of subsidy that the government provided airlines that carried the mail.[29]

Local practices regarding families receiving relief varied. In 1939, housing officials assumed that relatively few relief families lived in public housing. Rents were too high and relief payments too low, they thought. In New York, rents were lower and relief payments higher than many other places. Nevertheless, Alfred Rheinstein, the head of the New York authority, resisted USHA's pressure to house poorer families. When USHA wanted to set the income limit at $1,399 per year, Rheinstein argued for $1,923. At the USHA's income limit, he complained, New York's projects would be filled with relief families. Rheinstein also clashed with USHA about limits on relief recipients. The New York authority has restricted relief families to 5 to 8 percent in the PWA projects. Only under pressure from USHA did it increase the percentage in the USHA funded projects to something over 20 percent. In Chicago, the housing authority refused to accept relief families until the USHA exerted pressure. In the District of Columbia, the housing authority limited relief families to 25 percent of any project. In 1949, the percentage of relief recipients housed at 14 housing authorities varied from 9 percent in the District of Columbia to 43 percent in Seattle, and averaged 17 percent. Twelve percent of New York's tenants received relief; 20 percent of Chicago's.[30]

Rheinstein and the New York authority offered several reasons for limiting the number of relief recipients. They assumed that relief payments would not cover the rent. Housing relief recipients would make covering operating costs more difficult and might require larger subsidies. Giving the poorest families preference might also discourage efforts to increase incomes. A project full of the poorest people, especially families on relief, would lack the good example set by self-supporting families.[31]

A 1939 conference of housing and welfare officials addressed the issues related to housing relief families. The conference accepted that housing relief recipients made considerable sense since they were among the most needy. If they lived in public housing, they would have better housing than otherwise and, provided the relief agency paid their rent, they would be no worse off in terms of buying food and other essentials.

Officials thought that housing relief families could have a profound impact on public housing, however. They thought that if housing authorities treated relief families like other families, a large proportion of housing units would go to relief families and the number would increase if economic conditions worsened. Officials worried about what that might mean. Public housing projects restricted to relief recipients were certainly a bad idea, they concluded. Such projects would be seen as modern day poorhouses and would stigmatize relief families. Conference attendees thought that relief families might benefit from living near self-supporting families. Officials were also concerned about how the general public would perceive housing relief families. Outsiders might think that the most needy should be served, but, if a preponderance of relief families created problems within public housing, it might lose public support. Housing officials worried that public housing's financial health could become dependent on relief agencies and their willingness to pay rent. Public housing had already encountered the criticism that it provided poor families with better housing than better-off families could afford. Housing relief families might provoke similar complaints.[32]

The 1939 conference's recommendations were consistent with the public housing community's views. Housing authorities, not welfare agencies, should be responsible for public housing. It recommended that community agencies, not housing authorities, should provide community facilities and services. Housing authorities should select tenants so as to dispel the notion that public housing was a form of relief. A majority of families in public housing should be self-supporting. The percentage of relief families in public housing should resemble the percentage of such families in substandard housing within the community. Otherwise relief and self-supporting families should receive equal treatment. The conference worried that any quota to limit the number of relief families would be arbitrary and would incite objections. Perhaps the only feasible policy was that relief families should neither be isolated in public housing project nor denied access to it.[33]

Selecting Tenants

Housing officials were uncomfortable with turning away poor families who were living in substandard housing. One rationalization was that Congress would not have approved public housing legislation with subsidies generous enough to serve the poorest families. Until greater subsidies became available, public housing would have to serve those it could, "the upper brackets of the low income." Catherine Bauer made the same argument. Congress had, if effect, set a bottom limit for public housing, she wrote. Until Congress enacted different legislation, the USHA would have to work within the established limits.[34]

Housing officials and housing advocates were, on the other hand, more comfortable with enforcing an upper limit on tenants' income. Housing authorities normally set the income limit for remaining in public housing higher than the income limit for being admitted. Families could increase their incomes somewhat without being forced to leave. In 1939, Straus considered it normal to have tenants with increased incomes, so-called "over-income" families move out and make room for other poor families. After the war, a representative of the National Public Housing Conference portrayed public housing as a means to improve families. He claimed that living in public housing improved motivation and led to higher incomes. The movement of families in and out of public housing was, therefore, understandable and a way to serve a large needy population with a limited supply of public housing. During the war, significant numbers of defense workers with incomes above the statutory limit moved into public housing. Officials told the Congress that they considered this an emergency arrangement and that, after the war, they wanted to move these families out as soon as possible. Bleeker Marquette, testifying for the National Association of Housing Associations, said that waiving income limits during the war worried him more than anything. He thought it made public housing that much harder to defend.[35]

Nevertheless, critics focused on USHA's failure to serve the poorest. If homes without private bathrooms and toilets, without light and air, and that required tenants to walk up six or seven floors were bad for people, if they bred crime and disease, how could public housing officials justify not housing the families who lived in the worst of these conditions? The public housing program was too small to accommodate every needy family, but why not start with the families at the bottom and work up the income scale, rather than starting somewhere in the middle and working down? Turning the housing as public service argument around, critics pointed out that the United States did not limit public schools to those that could afford them. The New York authority had selected 1,600 families from the 19,000 that applied to live in the Williamsburg Homes. It made little sense, one critic wrote, to house just a handful of slum dwellers, but why not at least house the most needy?[36]

Others, more sympathetic to public housing, worried about housing developments full of poor families. Edith Wood thought giving preference to the poorest families was too simple a solution. If public housing were just an emergency measure, it might make sense. If, as Wood imagined, public housing was a long-term public health program, it made more sense to prefer low-paid workers with children. It was better to ensure that children were raised in a healthy environment than to create asylums for problem cases. Alfred Rheinstein argued that housing the "independent, self-supporting individual" was the right choice.[37]

Consideration of applicants' and tenants' incomes raised administrative issues. Officials had to ask applicants for income information and they had to verify it. On a regular basis, they had to do the same for sitting tenants. Getting data might not be straightforward. Officials anticipated that tenants would be motivated to under report their income. Not all families were the same size. An adequate income for a family of four might not be sufficient for a family of six. Whose income should be included? Certainly the father's and mother's income, if any, should be part of the calculation. But what about any income children might earn? If children's income were included and pushed the total over the statutory limit, families would face the unenviable choice of leaving public housing themselves or having their child move out.[38]

Under the USHA regime, local housing authorities thought screening tenants was crucial. The head of the New York City Housing Authority claimed that "without scientific selection" even the best housing project would fail. Housing staff reviewed applications submitted by potential tenants and checked the information against other sources. They visited the current homes of families that had survived the initial screening. New York and Chicago, and perhaps other authorities, developed elaborate point systems to evaluate and rank applications.[39]

Given the paucity of public housing compared to the potential demand, authorities could afford to be selective. Tenants had, first, to meet the income criteria. They also had to live in substandard housing. Some authorities attempted to rate housing conditions and favor families living in the worst conditions. To reduce applications, the New York authority took a narrow view of substandard housing. It decided that substandard meant housing that violated the law, that is, health or building codes. Two-parent families with children received preference everywhere. Authorities might also prefer tenants who worked nearby or whose children attended the local school or who had special health or social problems. Authorities screened out most single parents, especially single mothers with children by multiple fathers. Anyone with a substance abuse problem or a criminal record or any other indication of anti-social behavior was unlikely to obtain public housing in this period.[40]

The preference for families with children was central to the USHA's approach. Bauer explained that favoring families with children was the most reasonable way to distribute a scarce resource. The current situation was inequitable. Eventually everyone who needed public housing might get it. In the meantime, serving families with children was a "reasonable interim course."[41]

Families whose homes had been demolished to make way for public housing sometimes received preferential treatment. Nevertheless it was apparent, from the start, that some, perhaps many, displaced people would not find places in the new public housing. In one Boston project, only 8 percent of the families displaced by the project found places in the new housing. Results in two Cincinnati projects were similar. Single people and childless families were not eligible for public housing. The poorest families and families on relief could not afford the new housing. As opponents of building on slum sites had predicted, such families had to look for their housing elsewhere, most likely in other substandard buildings. Welfare departments and housing authorities mounted efforts to help, but the general sense was that they were not successful. Without a massive increase in the housing supply, housing officials lacked the tools for the job.[42]

The failure to re-house displaced families was another vulnerability for public housing. Supporters pointed out that increasing the supply of decent homes was the basic answer. Others suggested that displaced families receive greater preference. At the same time, the picture of public housing projects pushing families from the their homes and into housing no better than what they had left was hard to combat.[43]

Public Housing's Impact

Mayor Fiorello LaGuardia of New York could wax poetic about public housing and its effect on poor families. He told a Senate committee in 1945 that when the city moved a family from slum housing into public housing, into an apartment with light and air, a "transformation of the human being" took place. Unkempt, harassed young mothers became nice and clean, no longer worried about their children or about where they will do the washing. LaGuardia claimed that there were no police troubles in the housing projects. Housing projects were easier to police than the neighborhoods that the tenants came from, he said. Tenants might organize and agitate, but that was okay with the mayor.[44]

A 1942 article suggested that such flowery talk posed risks for public housing's reputation. Emanuel Stein wrote that the housing problem amounted to an increased awareness that some people lived in bad housing and the parallel conviction that improvements were needed. Expectations about housing were likely to increase, however. Minimal housing built now might not seem acceptable in the future. Stein doubted that public housing would reduce municipal costs because the poor always consumed more public services. He wondered whether public housing would reduce crime and disease; he thought factors other than housing were at work. If public housing's real benefit was an improvement in "community morale," because the poor's living standards had improved, and not decreases in crime, disease or municipal costs, housing advocates needed to say so now. Otherwise, Stein warned, a failure to make demonstrable improvements in social conditions would give public housing's opponents a golden opportunity.[45]

In 1945, Monsignor John O'Grady confessed to a congressional committee that he believed that he, and others, had been too optimistic. Providing better housing did not always improve families' standard of life, he said. Many families had been living in bad conditions for years; it was not easy to change. Some seemed to prefer their old neighborhoods. Some apartments in the new housing were still dirty. Despite tenant screening, problem families found their way into public housing. Gathering hundreds of poor families together in one place created its own problems and perhaps the projects were too congested. The new housing did not create these problems, but unless housing authorities and social agencies provided more services, public housing projects would become slums. Monsignor O'Grady admitted that he had changed his mind, but, unless the government did something, public housing would not attain its objectives.[46]

Other housing advocates also claimed for public housing a role beyond just more and better housing. Beatrice Rosahn and Abraham Goldfield, in their 1937 book, *Housing Management*, wrote that public housing was more than mere operation of a building, more than introduction of a recreational program, and more than cultivation of public interest in a community undertaking. It was, they said, in varying degrees a combination of all three.[47]

Housing Management

Management practices in public housing remained as before. The New York authority imposed a wide array of rule: no pets, no boarders, no clotheslines and so on. The authority provided blinds for windows; tenants were forbidden to use any other. Initially, the authority used the Octavia Hill methods for collecting rents; social workers visited every apartment each week. In the face of tenant complaints, by 1944 the authority reverted to weekly or monthly payments made at the project office. The Cincinnati Metropolitan Housing Authority had staff inspect apartments on a regular basis and report any apparent problems to the management office. If there were a problem, the authority would dispatch a "homemaking adviser" from the private, voluntary Better Housing League to the home. The adviser would "read the riot act" to the tenants, warn them that they had to improve, and offer assistance. If the family did not follow the guidance offered, the authority would evict them.[48]

Observers questioned what they considered typical housing authority practices. Dorothy Canfield thought forcing "hard working American citizens" to reveal their income was wrong. Dorothy Rosenman, wife of one of Franklin Roosevelt's advisers and head of a post-war housing advocacy organization, the National Committee on Housing, complained about authorities that adopted a "you do as we tell you" attitude. Hugh Carter, writing in 1940, warned against making a fetish of a building's condition. Tenant relations were more important. He advocated definite long-term leases for tenants, with clear standards for terminations. Housing management needed to know what not to do. Making suggestions, about employment assistance or health care might be okay, but management had to realize that tenants were dependent on its approval. Charles Abrams suggested that "skillful indifference" was probably better than "benevolent interest." He thought housing authorities should welcome the formation of tenants' organizations.[49]

Renewed Debate

Between 1937 and 1949, housing issues remained alive and reformers remained active. According to critics, housing was still too expensive. Housing quality was too low. Slums remained and families in the middle and lowest thirds of incomes could not find decent affordable housing. Especially after the end of the Second World War, there was not enough housing. The halt in housing construction during the 1930s combined with increases in income and the number of households after the war to produce a housing shortage. Some thought that perhaps as many as 12 to 18 million new homes were needed over ten years. Calls for government action followed.[50]

The political climate did not favor public housing proposals, however. The Housing Act of 1937 was one of the last, if not the last, major "New Deal" measure. From 1938 on, control of the Congress passed to a coalition of Republicans and southern Democrats that resisted further innovations. The Roosevelt administration's attention shifted to foreign affairs and then

Robert Mills Manor, Charleston, South Carolina, opened 1938 (Library of Congress).

to war. Its domestic policy preferences inclined more to the private sector. After the war, the private sector and its adherents were in the ascendant. Nearly everyone imagined that, if enough housing were to be built, the private real estate industry would build it. For public housing, the question was one of survival, not of offering an alternative to private housing.

Observers saw the political odds stacked against public housing. The national real estate organizations had learned to coordinate their lobbying efforts in Washington. The National Association of Home Builders and the National Association of Real Estate Boards had members in almost every American community, prominent citizens with links to the local congressmen, the press, and civic groups. The real estate industry deployed their members to support their legislative agenda.[51]

After the war, homebuilders were more confident. They asserted that they could build more cheaply than any government agency. Joseph Merrion, from the National Association of Home Builders, claimed that, while the Chicago Housing Authority was building the Jane Addams Houses at over $6,000 a unit, he was building single-family homes in Chicago's suburbs for $5,500 a unit. When asked how his land costs compared to the Chicago authority's, he said he did not know. In 1949, another builder told a congressional committee that private builders could construct single-family houses for nearly every American family for less than the cost limits set for public housing. Public housing was unduly expensive because Washington wrote the specifications and did not take local conditions into account, he explained.[52]

Public housing had no such widespread network of support. The National Association of Housing Officials and the National Public Housing Conference remained but neither had the financial resources or the fervor of public housing's opponents. Both were cautious, perhaps complacent. Their ambitions did not go beyond reviving the 1937 program. For many other New Deal supporters, public housing was part of Roosevelt's legacy and therefore a program worth preserving. It might not serve one's own needs, but supporting it was the right thing to do.

Nevertheless some prominent, ostensibly liberal, proponents of ambitious redevelopment schemes raised doubts about public housing. Alvin Hansen was a Harvard economist and perhaps the most important American advocate for John Maynard Keynes' ideas. In 1941, he and the planner Guy Greer produced a pamphlet "Urban Redevelopment and Housing," that called for extensive urban redevelopment after the war. Like the builders, Hansen and Greer were troubled that the government was building better and more costly housing for low-income families than half or more of American families could afford. They wondered whether standards could be lowered so that the government did not appear to be favoring the poor. They accepted that a responsible government could lower standards only so far. Beyond that, they could suggest only that the federal government might assume responsibility to bring all housing, over time, somehow, up to the USHA standards. In the meantime, they thought basic elements of the USHA needed to be rethought. Did public housing need to last 60 years? Did poor families have to be housed in new homes? Did public housing need to give preference to the lowest income families?[53]

Labor unions continued to offer important support. During the Second World War, unions, especially those in the Congress of Industrial Organizations (CIO), took a deep interest in housing issues. As the end of the war approached, the CIO itself, the United Auto Workers, and the Textile Workers produced pamphlets laying out their visions for housing in the United States. They were ambitious, optimistic visions. Increased housing production, a reorganized building industry, an expanded government presence, urban redevelopment, and better planning all featured in the plans. They echoed themes raised by the community planners: neighborhood planning, satellite towns, and better links between work and homes. All the union plans had a place for public housing. The CIO recommended at least 500,000 units of public housing each year.[54]

The unions did not imagine that many of their members would live in public housing. Most union members earned too much to qualify for the housing authorized by the 1937 Act. The unions envisioned some form of cooperative housing for their own members, perhaps supported by limited government aid. One United Auto Workers pamphlet advocated that union members form housing committees that could plan and acquire sites where union members could purchase homes. R.J. Thomas, United Auto Workers president and chair of the CIO Housing Committee, explained that the CIO supported public housing, nor for its own members, but for poorer families. The CIO believed in good housing for every American family and supported subsidies for those families that could not afford decent housing.[55]

Catherine Bauer recognized the challenges advocates of public housing faced. Bauer worried that public housing had become too enmeshed in what she termed the principles and terminology of social casework to have any popular appeal. It might be something you supported, but not for yourself and your family. The real estate lobby, on the other hand, seemed to represent the average American family's desire to improve its housing and general living conditions.[56]

About the time the 1937 Act passed, Charles Abrams emerged as a housing expert. The son of Polish immigrants, Abrams grew up in Brooklyn, studied law at night, and, while practicing law during the 1920s, prospered by dealing in Greenwich Village real estate. In 1933, he helped write the legislation that established the New York City Housing Authority. After leaving the New York authority in 1937, he began writing on housing and planning topics.

Abrams was also not sanguine about public housing's prospects. Abrams doubted whether there ever was a housing movement. Unlike the pushes for labor union rights, social security, or veterans' benefits, public housing could not count on mass support. Public housing did not command popular support because it did not offer the prospect of immediate tangible benefits to many people. The public housing program was too small and construction of public housing too slow. Even the construction of a public housing project in a slum family's neighborhood increased its chances for better housing only slightly. The 1937 Act had passed, Abrams thought, only because its opposition had not coalesced. Advocates for an expansive public housing program were few and often not articulate. Even among supporters of public housing, they had to compete with what Abrams called the "paternalists," supporters of private enterprise who thought the government should offer a few benefits to those the private sector ignored. Abrams included Truman and Senator Robert Taft (R–Ohio) in this category. Abrams warned that public housing was also at risk of being taken over by the "aid to business" lobby, those who believed that funds intended for social reform should be funneled through private businesses. Public housing advocates had to be aware that slum clearance could become a financial rescue program for slum landlords.[57]

Some of the remedies proposed to cure the nation's housing ills followed familiar lines. Catherine Bauer talked about a "comprehensive housing policy," that would bring new homes within everyone's reach. Charles Abrams talked about an "integrated national policy." He thought government efforts so far had been random and undirected. To reduce housing construction costs, writers imagined bigger, better-organized home building companies, perhaps working in concert with government, using more efficient methods and materials. To reduce land costs, writers saw the government taking a larger role, acquiring large tracts of vacant, suburban land and assembling large parcels of urban land. Lewis Mumford and others continued to believe that better regional and urban planning had to be part of the solution.[58]

While many proposed solutions involved government action, the usual assumption was that the private sector would remain dominant in the housing market. Abrams argued that the government should build housing only when private builders could not meet housing demand or where government action would more effectively promote private ownership. Government-constructed housing should be sold to private owners and government-owned land turned over to private development wherever possible. When the government did construct housing, Abrams thought it should rely on private firms and financing to the greatest possible extent.[59]

Reformers usually assumed that private builders served the needs of the richest third. Subsidized housing seemed to be answer for the poorest third. Decent housing for the middle third remained problematic. The common assumption was that, although families in the middle third had sufficient income, the private sector was not providing adequate housing. Writers suggested several possible solutions. Nathan Straus proposed a variant of public housing, where rents covered operating and capital costs.

Government construction might lower costs and improve quality, but government assistance would be limited to lower interest rates or mortgage guarantees. Cooperative housing had its backers, especially a form referred to as mutual housing. During the war, the federal government built several mutual housing projects. Advocates imagined that they could be a pattern for the future. Limited dividend corporations still had their proponents. Some looked to large investors, particularly large insurance companies, as possible providers of middle-income housing.[60]

Abrams believed saw private homeownership as the goal, but he also thought that only the government could produce enough homes at affordable prices. Like Edith Wood, he thought that only governments were likely to achieve the economies of scale, the efficient organizations, and improved methods and materials needed to construct large scale, affordable housing developments. Other reformers remained skeptical of ownership as the answer for most Americans. Straus argued that for families of modest means owning a house could be a burden. It might swallow "earnings and hopes alike."[61]

Role of the Private Sector

The official view in Washington was not enthusiastic about public housing. Philip Klutznick, the head of the PHA in 1945, thought that the nation might need no more than 1.5 or two million public housing units, rather than the seven or eight million figures bandied about. Incomes were increasing and perhaps private builders would be able to lower their costs. For Klutznick, the principles undergirding the public housing program were that it not provide housing where existing housing could meet the need, that it not compete with private builders, and that there should be a gap of 15 to 20 percent between the lowest rent charged in the private sector and the highest rent charged in public housing. The government needed to leave room for the private sector to move into low-cost housing. Klutznick hoped that public housing would not expand to serve tenants better off than the current tenants. Instead, he hoped, expansion of the private sector into low-cost housing would push public housing to serve still poorer tenants.[62]

The 1937 Act relegated public housing to a subordinate position and barred competition between public and private housing. After 1937, spokespersons for federal housing agencies stuck to that script. Straus assured the Congress that the USHA did not compete with private housing. The

1937 Act prevented the USHA from building houses for middle-income families even though they could not afford private housing. The way was clear for private builders to move into this market. In any case, Straus added, public housing worked in concert with the private real estate industry. It employed private builders and architects and bought land from private landowners. Public housing might challenge private builders by producing better houses at lower costs, but federal housing officials said they welcomed an expansion of private building. In 1945 John Blandford, the Administrator of the National Housing Agency, told the Congress that it was his "sincere hope and expectation" that private housing would meet more of the need in the future.[63]

Future of Public Housing

The National Association of Housing Officials thought public housing could serve an important, but limited role. It maintained that some families would always be unable to afford private rental housing and public housing would have to serve them. Nonetheless, rising incomes and declining housing costs might mean that fewer families would require subsidized housing after the war. Private builders should expand as far down the income scale as possible and receive whatever government aid they needed to do so. The National Public Housing Conference held that there should be enough public housing for every family that needed it but that public housing should also be barred from any market that private firms could serve. At a 1945 hearing, a representative from the national conference described public housing as "the most effective piece of salesmanship for the private realtor." He said that public housing should seek to improve tenants and raise their aspirations. They would then move on to buy houses in the private market. A spokesperson for the National Association of Housing Associations hoped that the private sector would soon be able to provide housing for all American families.[64]

Charles Abrams saw the 1937 Act as a breakthrough and USHA public housing as a success. The 1937 Act marked, for Abrams, a break with the past. For the first time, the government had recognized that it could not leave low-income housing to private builders and that earlier housing reforms based on increased regulation had failed. The USHA had funded new housing units and caused substandard units to be demolished, all at a low cost per unit or per person rehoused. Public housing could be better designed and public housing management less paternalistic, but Abrams thought the basic formula was sound.[65]

At the same time, Abrams advocated important changes. Tenant management should be one of public housing's goals. A board of directors, with a tenant majority, should manage each housing development. Ultimately the government should turn the developments over to the tenants, through leases or even sales. Abrams thought that government involvement in housing need not involve government ownership. It was unhealthy for the government to be a major landlord, he argued. He also imagined a bigger role for housing authorities. Housing authorities should build units for sale as well as for rent. Housing authorities should build anywhere private builders failed to. Management of housing projects should be less "institutional"; privacy was important. The relationship between housing manager and tenant should be more like that of landlord and tenant than guardian and ward. Authorities should expand the range of rents so that housing projects did not become "economic ghettoes," filled with just poor families.[66]

Once Catherine Bauer left USHA, her views increasingly reflected that fact that what the 1937 Act authorized fell far short of the vision laid out in *Modern Housing*. USHA had funded decent, well-built housing at reasonable costs, she wrote. The public housing built by housing authorities demonstrated the value of neighborhood-scale planning, of building on large tracts and of including significant open space. Perhaps private builders would follow public housing's example. Public housing served the lowest income families, but many families with higher incomes still could not afford private housing. Sadly, the 1937 Act produced one-class neighborhoods, Bauer admitted.[67]

Bauer could still imagine something dramatically better. A "free and experimental attitude" was needed, fueled by imaginative architectural and managerial talent plus broad public interest and concern. Together they could sweep away the obstacles and create public housing that was not just for poor people and did not suffer from a "charity atmosphere."[68]

Advocates for public housing considered local control essential. Almost no one spoke up for a federal construction program like the PWA or the "demonstration" projects included in early versions of the 1937 Act. "Decentralization" was critical, according to Charles Abrams. It was one of the most salient of democratic principles and a necessary countercheck to the concentration of power at the center. Empowering housing authorities might increase the possibility of mismanagement, corruption and extravagance. Other municipal activities suffered from such problems, but the risk was worth it. Local bodies ought to set housing standards, several argued. Only then could public housing become acceptable to the whole community. Even Catherine Bauer came to view federal housing agencies as weak, unimaginative, and disorganized.[69]

Opposition

For some critics, public housing was "undiluted socialism" and a political and social menace. Embracing public housing would put the United States on the path to nationalization and dictatorship. On the other hand, home ownership was the bulwark of democracy. Public housing would undermine the private real estate industry. No investor would choose to compete with government efforts. Critics claimed that the USHA program was another in a long line of government housing failures, reaching back to the PWA and the Resettlement Administration. After the war, critics contended that the British experience demonstrated that public housing, once begun, would dominate the housing market. Providing public housing to some at the expense of the rest was unfair and would erode individual initiative. Eventually, everyone would want government-supplied housing. Once most people became tenants in government housing, they would no longer be free.[70]

Opponents did the math and concluded that the United States could not afford to build decent housing for everyone. Advocates for better housing claimed that about a third of the population, seven or eight million families, lived in relatively expensive but substandard housing. The available evidence in the late 1930s suggested that decent housing would cost $5,000 or $6,000 a housing unit. The price tag for solving the housing problem, if you accepted the reformers' numbers, was something greater than $35 billion, perhaps as much as $48 billion. Critics recoiled in horror at such numbers. If better housing cost $37 billion, the price would be four times total federal expenditures in 1938 and half national total income in 1936.[71]

Representatives of the real estate organizations repeated criticisms common among friends of public housing. The USHA program had not eliminated slums nor built many housing units, they maintained. Many USHA projects were not in slums at all. USHA projects did not serve the families most in need, they wrote. Local housing authorities had avoided housing families on relief or without employment. Herding poor families together was, in any case, a bad idea. Poor families needed contact with families that did not suffer from financial difficulties, critics argued.[72]

Opponents of public housing supported enforcement of existing building codes, demolition of substandard houses, and redevelopment of slum and blighted areas. To house the poorest third of the population, they promoted rehabilitation of existing housing and rent certificates. Enough structurally sound, but blighted, housing existed to meet the need, they maintained. The government should facilitate its rehabilitation. The government should subsidize families, not housing. If families could not afford decent housing, the government should issue them rent certificates with which they could obtain housing. Housing support should be no different from relief payments.[73]

Conservative Capital

"Conservative" capital was another alternative offered by opponents of public housing. Critics accepted that firms interested in quick turnover and speculative profits were unlikely to build housing that poor families could afford. Large organizations looking for safe, long-term investments and willing to accept modest profits might, however, produce low-cost housing. These would not be philanthropic, limited dividend corporations but profit seeking companies willing to trade lower profits for long-term security. Perhaps the government might guarantee them a certain yield on their investment in return for abiding by certain standards, regarding rents or population densities. The government might also set a limit on their profits.[74]

The Metropolitan Life Insurance Company was just the sort of company critics imagined. Under the leadership of Frederick Eckers, Metropolitan Life funded large housing projects in the 1940s, including one in the Washington, D.C., area and several in New York City. Metropolitan Life's Stuyvesant Town in New York provoked disputes that paralleled the debates about public housing.

Parkchester in the Bronx, Riverton in Harlem and Stuyvesant Town and Peter Cooper Village on the east side of Manhattan, all Metropolitan Life projects, represented significant departures from normal New York real estate practices. Together Stuyvesant Town and Peter Cooper Village comprise 110 buildings, most 13-story elevator buildings, and house more than 25,000 people in 11,250 apartments. By itself Stuyvesant Town covers 80 acres. Stuyvesant Town occupied a "super block" and approximated what later came to be called "towers in the park." The buildings' exteriors were plain, similar to those of buildings constructed by the New York

Stuyvesant Town, Manhattan, New York, funded by the Metropolitan Life Insurance Company, opened 1947 (Library of Congress).

housing authority. New York City allowed Metropolitan Life to close streets and ignore Manhattan's grid pattern in siting the buildings. Considerable open space surrounds the high-rise buildings. The city allowed Metropolitan Life to restrict access to the complex and to maintain its own security force.

Metropolitan Life's management of Stuyvesant Town resembled the methods used by housing authorities. Prospective tenants had to complete lengthy surveys and representatives of Metropolitan Life often interviewed them in their homes. Life in Stuyvesant Town was subject to a myriad of rules which management was quick to enforce. Dirty apartments, parking violations, misbehavior by children or pets, and a host of other failings prompted warnings, at a minimum, from the landlord. Metropolitan Life was, in part, reacting to tenants' own concerns. Tenants were apt to complain about noisy neighbors, inconsiderate children, garbage left in halls and the like.[75]

Housing activists, especially Lewis Mumford, detested Stuyvesant Town. Stuyvesant Town offended Mumford's humane values. He thought it was based on a faulty understanding of New York's situation, and presumably the situation of other large cites. For him, it represented a step backward in re-planning and redeveloping the city.

Stuyvesant Town's interior spaces, according to Mumford, were decent. The living rooms should have had more windows and the floor layouts created some wasted space, but the kitchens were better than in most prewar New York apartments. Nevertheless the site plan and the size of the project were poor. Mumford argued that the open space around the buildings was badly planned and insufficient for the population. What play spaces were offered were too similar and offered only "mechanical and organized" play. The arrangement of the buildings offered no vistas and gave a visitor the sense of being hemmed in. Mumford posited that the design confused open space with habitable open space, a mistake he attributed to the French architect Le Corbusier. The development also included no community facilities, no churches, schools, or libraries. Most damning, the buildings were designed for roughly four times as many people as Mumford thought appropriate. It was a development for 25,000 people on a site suitable for 6,000, he wrote.[76]

Mumford blamed Robert Moses for Stuyvesant Town. Moses, in one of his many roles within the New York City government, had negotiated the city's agreement with Metropolitan Life. Mumford viewed it as an unholy bargain in which the city condemned the land and granted long-term property tax exemptions so that Metropolitan Life could build inferior housing and make a profit. As Parks Commissioner, Moses had done good work, but, in housing, Mumford complained, getting things done quickly was not as important as doing the right things in the right way and in the right order.

Moses was wrong on several counts, according to Mumford. First, most housing in New York City, even upper-income housing, was deficient, in Mumford's view. It was too dense, included too little open space, and provided too little light and air. The goal was not to emulate Park Avenue; it was to follow the pattern set at Sunnyside Gardens. Moses contended that land values in Manhattan were too high to allow anything but high-density development. Mumford countered that reducing densities was essential for humane living even if it meant reducing land values. Government needed to limit densities, not let speculators and investors set the standards.

Despite government support, Stuyvesant Town did little for low-income families. Metropolitan Life's agreement with the city did not require it to relocate the families displaced by the project, but it did undertake efforts to do so. Critics doubted that these efforts were successful. They claimed that the displaced families moved into other slums. Rents at Stuyvesant Town were too high for nearly all families from the immediate area. Metropolitan Life was free, Mumford contended, to choose its tenants and they were "far from the economic edge."

Like Mumford, Bauer regretted the example set by Stuyvesant Town. Dense, relatively expensive housing developments were not part of her vision for cities. She criticized the homogenous character of Stuyvesant Town's population. Quoting Henry Churchill, she complained about "housing 12,000 families of one economic level in one spot in identical warrens."[77]

For Charles Abrams, Stuyvesant Town was another example of a pernicious trend that began in the New Deal: deploying profit-makers, subsidized by the government, to solve social problems. Public powers were put at the disposal of private companies that were allowed to evade public responsibilities. Government seized the land for Stuyvesant Town and allowed Metropolitan Life to police the site, but Metropolitan Life was not required to treat everyone equally. For Abrams, Metropolitan Life's refusal to accept African American tenants was especially galling.[78]

Developments like Stuyvesant Town were, however, central to Robert Moses' thinking about urban housing. Moses had not supported public housing at first, but came to recognize that it could play a role in his efforts to transform New York. By 1945, he accepted that much new housing in the city required government subsidies, large subsidies for poor families and smaller subsidies for middle-income families. Still his support for low-income housing was far from fervent. The city was reaching its limit for completely subsidized housing, he wrote. You could not rebuild all the slums for low-income families. If the city had to build low-income housing, it should be in the least attractive sites in Manhattan, not near parks or on the waterfront and not on vacant land in the outer boroughs. Building in outlying areas merely attracted slum dwellers to areas that had no slums and left old buildings empty and liable for default and foreclosure. Beyond subsidized housing for the poor, the way forward was government aid to private capital, what Moses called semi-public housing. The government would use eminent domain to assemble large tracts and turn them over to private companies. In return, developers would accept government standards for setting rents and selecting tenants.[79]

Moses had harsh words for the community planners, like Mumford and Mayer. Theirs were revolutionary plans, Moses claimed. They would tear up New York City and rebuild it on a different scale. They would abandon the older cities in favor of satellite towns. They could not succeed,

Moses argued, and should be eliminated from the picture. They ignored the vested interests and underestimated attachments to old neighborhoods. Sentiments for the old neighborhoods, and not the "pinks and reds," would create the need for gradual and conservative change.

Urban Redevelopment

After the 1937 Act passed, proposals emerged, from the National Association of Real Estate Boards and others, for "urban redevelopment." The idea was to enlist the government's right of eminent domain and government subsidies to redevelop slum and blighted areas. To overcome the problems posed by small lots and high land values in urban areas, government would take ownership of large urban tracts and make them available to private developers at below market prices. The developers would be free to build whatever they chose. Some proponents imagined urban redevelopment as an alternative to public housing. Slums and blighted areas would disappear but the government need not build anything itself and redevelopment need not involve housing for low-income families. Others acknowledged the need to rehouse families, almost certainly low-income families, displaced by urban redevelopment and saw urban redevelopment and public housing as complementary.

Most supporters of public housing, including the National Public Housing Conference, and the National Association of Housing Officials were comfortable with public housing and urban redevelopment proceeding side by side. If the government demolished housing, it was responsible for finding the residents someplace else to live. This was particularly true for poor families who lived in slums or blighted areas. Demolishing existing housing without providing an alternative would push families into other slum areas and increase the cost of bad housing. If redeveloped sites were to include housing, it would most likely be for middle- and upper-income families. Even with the government subsidizing land acquisition, developers were not likely to charge rents poor families could pay. Some public housing on redeveloped sites made sense for advocates of mixed income neighborhoods. Others doubted that there would be sufficient demand for middle- and upper-income housing on redeveloped sites. They wondered whether subsidized housing for poor families might not end up being the best use.[80]

Some housing advocates took a less charitable view of urban redevelopment. The United Auto Workers' 1944 memorandum on housing policy talked about the real estate industry "hoodwinking" the public into buying slum areas at a high price and turning them over to developers at a fraction of the cost. Catherine Bauer contended that urban redevelopment was a scheme to guarantee profits to slum landowners and a ploy to kill off public housing. She wrote that she did not object to paying inflated land prices if it meant better housing and workable cities. "Bailing the boys our" was okay as long as families were rehoused. She added that the focus on central areas was mistaken. The future of metropolitan areas depended on how suburban areas were developed. If the "oncoming tidal wave of suburban building" did not result in well-integrated satellite communities surrounded by open space and linked to workplaces, the result would be chaos and potential blight.[81]

The Housing Act of 1949

The Housing Act of 1949,[82] which revived the 1937 Act's public housing program, had a long and difficult gestation. In 1943, the Senate attempted to wrest control of post war planning from the Roosevelt administration by creating a Special Committee on Post War Policy Planning. In response to a call for a study of government housing policies from Senators Wagner, Taft, and Allen Ellender (D–Louisiana), the Senate had the Special Committee create a Subcommittee on Housing and Urban Redevelopment chaired by Taft. After hearing more than 50 witnesses and compiling more than two thousand pages of testimony, the subcommittee submitted its report in August 1945. Simultaneously, Taft, Wagner and Ellender submitted a comprehensive housing bill that called for, among many other things, revival of the 1937 program. Interest groups including the National Public Housing Conference, the AFL and the CIO had participated in drafting the measure. Opposition from House Republicans, especially Representative Jesse Wolcott (R–Michigan), and some southern Democrats blocked passage in successive congresses. In 1947, Wolcott secured creation of a joint congressional committee to study housing issues. After hearings in 33 cities involving more than 1,200 witnesses, the joint committee issued a report that repeated the 1945 proposals. Senator Joseph McCarthy (R–Wisconsin), who served on the joint committee, submitted a minority report. In the lead-up to the 1948 election, the Congress again failed to pass the measure, although it did pass a housing measure submitted by McCarthy. After Truman's re-election and election of Democratic majorities in the House and Senate, the measure finally passed with the public housing program intact. Its survival was a close call; the House considered three amendments that would have eliminated the public housing program; they failed to pass by one, three and five votes.[83]

S. 1592,[84] the bill submitted by Taft, Ellender and Wagner in 1945 re-enforced the limits imposed on public housing program by the 1937 Act. Nearly all the bill's key provisions survived in the 1949 Act. The 1937 Act sought to limit public housing to low-income families. The 1945 proposals, and the 1949 Act, mandated a 20 percent gap between the lowest rent in private housing and the highest rent in public housing. The notion of a 20 percent gap originated in USHA during Straus' tenure. It was intended as further demonstration that public housing would not compete with private housing. The 1945 proposals required that local housing authorities investigate every applicant's income and housing and review every tenant's income periodically. The 1949 Act stated that, to be eligible, families had to have appropriate incomes and to have lived in substandard housing, been displaced by a public housing project or been homeless.[85]

Amendments made during the legislative process strengthened these provisions. They required that the PHA approve income limits set by local authorities. They barred discrimination against families receiving relief payments and required that families receive preference based on the urgency of their housing needs.

The 1949 Act addressed some concerns about computing family incomes. It repeated the requirement that family incomes not exceed five times the rent, but, to benefit larger families, allowed housing authorities to deduct $100 for each minor child from the family's income when determining eligibility. When reviewing tenants' suitability to remain, the housing authority could deduct $100 per minor child or all or any part of a child's income.

Under the 1937 Act, Congress could control the amount of public housing constructed through the appropriation process. The same was true under the 1949 Act, but the Congress added a limit on the number of units constructed, 500,000 in the original proposal, and 810,000 in the final bill.

The 1949 Act retained the requirements for inexpensive construction. The 1945 proposal deleted the cost limit on housing units, as housing advocates had asked, but retained a limit on cost per room. It set the limit per room at $1,000 generally, at $1,250 in cities with more than 500,000 people and $1,750 in Alaska. The final bill set the per room limit nationwide at $1,750. The final bill added provisions barring elaborate or extravagant construction and requiring economy in construction and administration.

The 1949 Act allowed the PHA to increase the room limit by up to $750 per room. Some perceived the 60-year loans allowed under the 1937 Act as an incentive for overly expensive construction. The 1945 proposal limited loans to 45 years; the 1949 Act limited them to 40 years. The 1949 Act required the Public Housing Authority to approve all construction contracts "in light of prevailing costs."

The 1937 Act tried to ensure local control by giving local housing authorities the key role. The 1945 proposals, and the 1949 Act, went further to require the agreement of local government for any public housing construction. They required that a need for public housing be demonstrated. During the legislative process, the bill was amended to require that, before any public housing could proceed, the local government and the local housing authority had to sign an agreement.

Another new provision directed that any excess revenue collected by local authorities reduce the federal government's annual contribution. The 1937 Act assumed that the federal government would fund the initial costs and the local authorities would use rent revenue to pay operating and maintenance costs. It did not address the situations where rent revenues were more or less than operating and maintenance costs. The 1949 Act required that any surplus a local authority experienced would reduce the federal government's annual payment intended to pay off the initial costs.

The final measure attempted to assuage local concerns about public housing diminishing property tax revenue. The original proposal had been silent on the issue. Subsequent amendments authorized payments in lieu of taxes up to 5 or 10 percent of aggregate rents. The 1949 Act authorized payments in lieu of taxes, without specifying a limit, but it also required local governments to contribute 20 percent of initial costs if the public housing project were not exempt from local taxes.

The 1949 Act loosened the 1937 Act's requirement that housing authorities eliminate one slum housing unit for every new housing unit they built. The 1949 Act allowed localities to count the rehabilitation or removal of any unsafe or insanitary housing unit in the metropolitan area within five years of a public housing project's completion. Where there was a housing shortage, the federal government could defer the elimination requirement. The Act allowed authorities to count as units eliminated the number of families housed in substandard buildings removed or repaired. The Act removed the elimination requirement for public housing projects built on slum sites cleared after enactment of the new law.

The law was silent regarding the location of public housing. Like the

1937 Act, it connected public housing to slum clearance, but did not bar construction on non-slum sites. Nonetheless, letters between Senator Paul Douglas (D–Illinois) and Raymond Foley, head of the Housing and Home Finance Agency, demonstrated a preference for slum clearance over developments on vacant suburban land. Douglas entered the letters into the record. He wrote that he intended to create a plain record that urban redevelopment's primary obligation was to clear slums. Slum clearance might involve acquiring outlying tracts, but slum clearance was the primary justification for the program.[86]

Public housing was only one part of the 1949 Act. The principal innovation enacted by the Act was urban redevelopment, a program of federal payments to cities to facilitate the clearance and redevelopment of slum and blighted areas. The 1949 Act required local governments only to demonstrate that they were trying to rehouse families displaced by urban redevelopment. It did not mandate that they re-house them, on the redeveloped sites, in public housing or elsewhere.[87]

The 1949 Act was consistent with the reports submitted by the 1945 Subcommittee on Housing and Urban Redevelopment and the 1947 Joint Committee on Housing. Many American families could not afford decent housing, the reports stated. Housing was too expensive. The long-term solution lay with the private sector. The federal government should help the private sector produce more and better housing. While the federal government should continue to intervene in the housing sector, housing remained a local concern. Regardless of private efforts, it was highly likely that some families would not be able to afford decent housing without government subsidies. To eliminate slums and the worst housing, the reports recommended that the federal government should fund public housing for them. At the same time public housing should not compete with the private sector or serve families who could afford their own housing.[88]

The Act reflected the views of Senator Taft, who became the bill's chief spokesperson in the Congress. After the war Wagner was increasingly ill and absent from Washington. Taft told the Senate in 1949 that he knew of no method other than public housing for serving low-income families. The government needed to "start at the bottom" and replace slums with permanent buildings. It needed to subsidize the new housing so that it was properly maintained and did not become a slum. Some families failed to earn enough to provide for themselves. Perhaps it was their own fault, but some of these families had children, Taft argued. All American children deserved an equal opportunity. Americans, he claimed, were charitable and humane. They did not want to see hardship and poverty in the midst of plenty. Elsewhere Taft talked about providing a floor under essential services in order to eliminate extreme poverty and hardship. Housing, for Taft, was an essential service. Regional planning and urban redevelopment were not.[89]

Federal housing officials and most of the bill's supporters in Congress made arguments similar to Taft's. Supporters were, however, forced to explain limiting public housing to 810,000 units when the data indicated that as many as seven million families could not afford decent housing. Senator John Sparkman (D–Alabama) admitted that 810,000 units would not meet the need. His solution was to hope that the private sector would become more efficient and produce cheaper housing. Congressman Ray Madden (D–Indiana) argued that the bill demonstrated that the government was trying to be of service. If the United States could spend "billions across the water" to combat communism, he added, it could afford to offer housing assistance in order to curtail "communistic agitators" in America.[90]

Supporters

Most advocates outside Congress supported the final bill. They had accepted the program defined by the 1937 Act; reviving it made sense. The bill's final version satisfied complaints about the 1937 Act's cost limit per unit. It watered down the equivalent elimination requirement. Advocates argued, however, that the program authorized by the 1949 Act was too small. The mandatory 20 percent gap between public and private rents was also "morally and socially wrong," according to the National Public Housing Conference. Enacting a ban on housing assistance to a segment of the population was "unconscionable." Nonetheless, the measure was a start, a compromise, the only measure likely to pass; most advocates embraced it.[91]

Charles Abrams overcame misgivings to support the bill. For Abrams, the bill was another experiment, not a definitive answer to the nation's housing ills. Continuing the 1937 version of public housing was not enough for him. Government housing assistance needed to be extended to large families, middle-income families, the elderly, single persons and others. The number of public housing units authorized was no more than a quarter of what was needed. Abrams criticized the bill's lack of ambition in housing for veterans, clearing slums, and reorganizing the housing industry. The measure perpetuated a piecemeal approach to housing. Yet, the bill was the beginning of a sound program, a step in the right direction.[92]

For Catherine Bauer, the worst feature of the 1949 Act was the 20 percent gap between private and public rents. Barring a segment of the population from government housing assistance blocked what she called "a universally effective housing market." Without such a market, neighborhood planning, city rebuilding, and decent housing for everyone were impossible. Still, she thought that the bill ratified the notion of a national housing policy, one that included public and private efforts. She thought other provisions of the bill were the beginning of government support for middle-income housing other than homeownership. And she imagined that it would pave the way for regional planning. As she had for the 1937 Act, she hailed the bill's passage as a popular victory and a defeat for the real estate industry. She attributed the bill's success to a "consumer civil welfare coalition." For once, she wrote, the consumers had won.[93]

Opponents

According to Representative Edward Cox (D–Georgia), the bill made socialism the new national policy. He argued that any housing shortage that existed resulted from excessive regulation of private building. Representative Leo Allen (R–Illinois) thought it unfair to have some Americans pay for others' housing. Senator John Bricker (R–Ohio) said that the government should not be giving some Americans better housing than others could afford.[94]

Prominent among public housing's congressional opponents was Senator McCarthy. His minority report to the Joint Committee on Housing listed objections to the program. The argument he pushed hardest was that public housing was not serving the most needy families. He pointed to limits on welfare families and the presence of over-income families and contended that public housing had drifted away from its real purpose. According to McCarthy, very low-income families should get preference. That would require increased federal subsidies, but as long as the government was spending $15 billion adding another $400 million was not a big problem. Senator Harry Cain (R–Washington) joined in McCarthy's critique. Cain offered an unsuccessful amendment that would have required that welfare agencies choose public housing tenants. He claimed that he did not intend that public housing serve only welfare families. The aim, he said, was to make sure the most needy families got better housing.[95]

Public housing survived, but just barely. Even more than in 1937, Congress remained committed to the private sector and to private housing. Unwilling to discard a New Deal program, it imposed more constraints on public housing and tied it to urban redevelopment. Most public housing advocates accepted the result and were left with either administering public housing as housing authority officials or criticizing what public housing was built.

Chapter Four

After the 1949 Act

Public housing survived in 1949 but only as a straggler forced to wander through hostile territory. The real estate industry and most Republicans remained opposed. Democrats started out as lukewarm supporters but eventually lost whatever interest they had. After 1949, the political influence of the groups that advocated public housing declined further. Local housing authorities had different experiences; some more successful than others. Nevertheless, the flaws in the program's funding arrangements and the failure of either the Congress or successive administrations to fix them eventually ensnared many authorities. By the early 1970s, housing authorities lacked the money to operate the program as it was intended. Finally, public housing's luck ran out in 1973 when President Nixon halted all new construction and initiated a program of rent supplements.

A Small Program

The public housing program implemented in the wake of the 1949 Act proved too small to meet the need for decent, affordable housing. By 1949, earlier efforts had produced roughly 170,000 public housing units. The Truman administration created 200,000 more units. Under the 1949 Act, moving a public housing project from the drawing board to construction was a long process. If a locality did not have a housing authority, it had to create one. The housing authority had to draw up plans and secure the agreement of local government and the approval of the PHA. The local authority had to persuade federal officials that a need existed and that the proposed construction costs fell within acceptable limits. The time required to create this process and move proposals through it accounts, in part, for the Truman administrations meager public housing output. After the United States intervened in Korea, Truman also limited the amount of building materials that could be used for public housing.[1]

The eight years of the Eisenhower administration generated 100,000 or so units, leaving the 1949 program less than halfway to its original target of 810,000 units. The Kennedy and Johnson years produced something more than 300,000 units; the Nixon administration roughly the same number through the end of 1973. At that point, therefore, the 1949 program had produced a little more than the 810,000 units first envisioned and the total public housing stock stood at slightly more than a million units. At the same time, the nation's housing stock, as measured by the 1970 census, was about 68 million homes. Public housing, therefore, accounted for less than 2 percent of American homes.

A 1959 PHA background paper documented how far short of the need the public housing program was at the end of the Eisenhower administration. In June 1959, local authorities operated 455,000 housing units and another 132,000 were either under construction or planned. The report estimated that 86,000 families displaced by urban renewal would need newly constructed public housing by the end of 1960. The paper's avowedly conservative estimate was that the need for public housing could still be measured in the millions of housing units.[2]

By the early 1970s, the situation had not changed significantly. The public housing program served only a small fraction of the target population. In 1972, five million families were officially poor. About ten million American households earned less than $3,000 per year. Almost 18 million families earned less than $5,000 a year, about half the median family income. A little more than 5 percent of the families earning less than $3,000 a year lived in public housing. A little less than 5 percent of the families earning less than $5,000 a year did so.[3]

A Changed America

Public housing was at risk, in part, because housing in the United States underwent a transformation between the end of the Second World War and 1970. Increased incomes, new building methods, and federal loan guarantee programs combined to produce 30 million new housing units, most single-family homes in suburbs. At least a quarter of the new homes were purchased with a mortgage insured by the federal government. More than 60 percent of American families now owned their homes, compared to 44 percent in 1940. The quality of U.S. housing improved as well. The percentage of housing units that were overcrowded fell from 15.7 percent in 1950 to 8.2 percent in 1970. The percentage without indoor plumbing fell from 35.5 percent to 6.9 percent. The real estate industry could claim with more confidence that it could meet the nation's housing needs and the percentage of Americans who might see public housing as the solution to their housing problems decreased.[4]

The housing boom left some behind, nevertheless. The 1956 Housing Inventory counted about 13 million substandard housing units, most, but not all, in nonfarm areas. The 1956 data also reveal that 3.9 million households with incomes below $4,000 lived in substandard rented housing and 3.3 million in substandard owner-occupied housing. Over five million housing units were still overcrowded in 1970; over four million lacked indoor plumbing.[5]

After the war, incomes increased across the board, sometimes faster than the cost of living. Incomes of poorer families, however, increased more slowly than those of other families. Housing costs increased faster than costs in general. One study estimated that the median rent in Boston increased by 68 percent between 1960 and 1970, while family income increased only 33 percent and the overall cost of living only 27 percent. In 1970 rented housing was only about as affordable as it had been in 1945. Michael Stone contends in his book *Shelter Poverty* that, although the number of poor families declined in the 1950s and 1960s, the number of families who could not afford decent housing increased. He estimates that in 1970 over eight million families who rented could not afford decent housing.[6]

Edith Wood would have recognized the housing market portrayed in a 1971 book. Private developers built only for middle- and upper-income families in the suburbs, if only because the only vacant land was in the suburbs. Low-income families depended on the "filtering" process for their housing. Only when more affluent families vacated housing in search of newer, better housing could low-income families improve their situations. When builders cut back on production, the "filtering" process slowed and poorer families suffered. If housing production remained low even as incomes continued to increase, the housing situation for those at the bottom worsened still further. Fewer housing units were available, rents rose and landlords, realizing that they faced less competition, cut back on maintenance.[7]

Some observers did notice that, despite the housing boom, some things had not changed from the 1930s. A 1957 article in *The Nation* quoted a National Housing Conference study to the effect that in 11 metropolitan areas, the median-priced house was beyond the means of five out of six families. The same article complained that builders preferred to build expensive homes. Substandard homes persisted, even in relatively affluent suburbs like New York's Westchester County and Stamford, Connecticut. The article went on to argue that slum housing could still be profitable. A building in Columbus Ohio assessed at less than $2,000 yielded over $7,000 in rent each year from 11 tenants.[8]

Public housing was also at risk because between 1949 and 1973, the national political situation shifted still further away from federal governmental interventions like public housing. Republicans were never more than tepid supporters. When the Democrats regained control first of the Congress and then the White House, they proved more interested in stimulating the private sector than had been the Roosevelt or Truman regimes. Lyndon Johnson orchestrated a significantly increased role for the federal government, but his housing programs relied heavily on the private sector.

The platforms of the two major political parties document public housing's fall from grace. In 1952 and 1956, the Democrats supported the program embodied in the 1949 Act and criticized Republicans and special interests for opposing it. The 1960 Democratic platform promised to continue public housing but offered new housing programs for low-income families. The 1964 platform recounted the Kennedy and Johnson accomplishments in housing and promised to build more public housing, but largely for the elderly. The Democrats' principal claim in 1968 was that they had encouraged private enterprise to build more housing; they promised to continue. Providing every family the freedom to choose its housing also appeared as a goal. By 1972, public housing disappeared from the Democratic platform. The 1948 and 1956 Republican platforms supported federal aid for public housing albeit only where private builders or local governments could not meet the need. In 1964, the Republicans claimed that urban redevelopment under the Democrats had created new slums by forcing poor families from their homes to make way for luxury apartments. By 1968, the Republicans focused on home ownership; there was no reference to public housing. Their 1972 platform opposed housing programs that sought to impose "arbitrary housing patterns on unwilling communities." It opposed dispersing large numbers of people from their neighborhoods and favored helping communities create better housing for low-income families.[9]

Legislation

During the Truman and Eisenhower administrations, Congress remained hostile to public housing. In 1950, Senator John Sparkman (D–Alabama) introduced legislation that would have provided long-term, low-interest loans to housing cooperatives. For housing advocates like Catherine Bauer, this was a way to expand public housing beyond low-income families. Despite nominal support from the Truman administration, both House and Senate voted against the measure. Real estate groups opposed it, while unions, veterans' groups and women's organizations supported it. Between 1949 and 1952, members of Congress attempted three times to end appropriations for public housing; all three attempts failed, but two of the three came within five votes of passing. In 1951, the House Appropriations Committee inserted language into the Independent Offices Appropriation Act, which funded the PHA, limiting new public housing units in fiscal year 1952 to 50,000 units. Similar restrictive language appeared in annual appropriations measures or housing legislation throughout the Eisenhower administration. The 1951 appropriation bill also prohibited public housing projects in localities where the local government had rejected them.[10]

Eisenhower

Dwight Eisenhower was never more than a lukewarm supporter of government-subsidized housing. He saw it, at most, as a tool to promote employment and a means to cultivate a caring image. His appointee as head of the Housing and Home Finance Agency, Albert Cole, was a former congressman on record as opposed to public housing. Nonetheless, in 1954, Eisenhower and Cole promoted a smaller, perhaps temporary, version of public housing geared to re-housing people displaced by urban redevelopment.[11]

Eisenhower's chosen instrument was the Advisory Committee on Government Housing Policies and Programs. Cole convened the committee in 1953. James Rouse, a Baltimore developer, was the chair. Of the 23 members, 17 were from the real estate industry. The only member with experience in public housing was Ernest Bohn, head of the Cleveland housing authority and an adviser to Senator Robert Taft. At least seven members, including a former president of the National Association of Home Builders and a former head of legislation for the U.S. Savings and Loan League were longtime opponents of public housing.[12]

The Cole Committee made recommendations across the spectrum of federal housing and urban redevelopment programs with the centerpiece a renewed emphasis on slum clearance and prevention. For low-income families, it recommended a new program of home loans. The committee characterized it as an effort to stimulate private enterprise, not provide relief or subsidies to low-income families. Recognizing that the program would be an experiment and that some low-income families might never be able to afford to buy a home, the committee also recommended continuation of public housing as authorized by the 1949 Act. Tying public housing closer to slum clearance, it recommended that public housing be limited to communities that had in place a program to improve the existing housing supply through enforcement of building and health codes and that families displaced by any public program, not just urban redevelopment as stipulated in the 1949 Act, be given preference. It recommended that public housing make use of existing buildings where possible, rehabilitated if necessary. Whatever public housing was built, the committee said, should be at lower densities than local authorities were constructing and should more closely resemble local building practices. Building high-density projects on slum sites was a false economy, the committee wrote. The committee contemplated that public housing might not need subsidies in the long run. It recommended that local authorities continue to transfer any surpluses (of rent revenues over operating costs) to the federal and local governments until they had repaid their initial subsidies. The committee imagined that the need for public housing might disappear. One reason it gave for recommending building in local styles was to facilitate an eventual sale to private parties.[13]

Cole explained to the Congress that he was still opposed to what he called socialized public housing and to housing a large segment of the population in government subsidized developments. He opposed public housing that was provided regardless of a family's need, or any social need or impact. He had come to realize, however, that some low-income families displaced by federal actions could not find decent housing. The federal government had a responsibility to help them and that was what the program he was promoting was intended to do. It was not for everyone who lived in slums; at least half of them could afford their own housing, he thought. When pressed about the limited number of new units the administration was proposing, Cole explained that carrying out a bigger program was impossible. Even for the families who could not now afford decent housing, Cole saw public housing as a "conduit," a means for them to better themselves and eventually move out of public housing. He characterized his proposal for building 35,000 units a year for four years as a way to take public housing out of politics, a sound, careful approach that everyone could support.[14]

Congressional reaction to Eisenhower's public housing proposals was less than warm. Congressman Jesse Wolcott, chairman of the house committee responsible for housing legislation, remained opposed to public housing. In his mind, Congress had been sold a bill of goods by people claiming that public housing promoted slum clearance. Wolcott complained that, despite claims to the contrary, public housing did not house the poorest families. Congressman Charles Oakman (R–Michigan) explained at length that he was not opposed to public housing that facilitated slum clearance. What he was opposed to was building public housing on vacant land on the periphery of big cities, on land that could have been used by private builders. Wolcott's committee reported out a bill without any public housing but the version of the Housing Act of 1954 that eventually passed continued the program.[15]

The 1954 Act went further than the Eisenhower proposals in subordinating public housing to urban renewal. It enacted the Cole committee's recommendations for a mortgage program for low-income families and for laying the groundwork for public housing projects becoming self-liquidating. It also required local authorities to make payments in lieu of taxes to local government, another Cole committee recommendation. It limited public housing to no more than 35,000 units a year. A floor amendment limited public housing to communities that were carrying out a federally-subsidized urban redevelopment project and that could certify that the public housing was needed to relocate displaced families. The bill also limited the number of units to what the PHA determined was needed to relocate displaced families.[16]

Democrats

After 1956, when the Democrats retook control, Congress adopted a less hostile stance and tinkered with the 1949 Act program. In 1956, the Congress broadened the program to include the elderly. Legislation passed that year added single persons over 65 years of age to the list of eligibles, authorized local authorities to give the elderly preference for housing built specifically for them, and increased the construction cost limit for units built for the elderly. The Congress extended authorizations for new units from one to three years. To accommodate larger families, in 1957, the

Congress modified income limits for acceptance and continued occupancy. The limit remained five times rent but now less $100 for each minor and each adult, other than the principal wage earner and spouse, who lacked income and less $600 of the income of any wage earner other than the principal wage earner. In 1959, the Congress modified the declaration of policy to include serving larger families and the elderly among the program's goals. In reaction to complaints about the PHA and its dealings with local authorities, the Congress did away with national income limits and authorized local authorities to set them subject to federal approval.[17]

John Kennedy's key housing appointments seemed likely to support public housing. Robert Weaver, one of Kennedy's most senior African American appointments, became head of the Housing and Home Finance Agency. Weaver had served in the PWA and USHA and worked on housing issues in the New York state government and elsewhere. Maria McGuire, Weaver's choice to head the PHA, had been executive director of the San Antonio housing authority.

McGuire proved an energetic and innovative official. Improving the design of public housing was a key goal. To encourage better design, she made her agency's standards advisory rather than mandatory. She created an architectural advisory board and held regional seminars with local architects. She advocated, with limited success, scattering public housing throughout cities and using rehabilitated housing for low-income housing.[18]

Nevertheless, the Kennedy administration proved little more supportive of the 1949 program than the Eisenhower regime. Kennedy had only limited interest in housing and urban issues. To the extent that he did, he was more interested in urban renewal and suburban homebuilding than public housing. His transition team on housing and urban issues comprised city officials and bankers and their report reflected the their views and interests as well as those of city planners. Kennedy's principal proposal for government-subsidized, multi-family housing sought to serve low- and middle-income families who could not qualify for government guaranteed home mortgages. It provided 100 percent, below-market-interest-rate loans to non-profit cooperatives and limited dividend corporations. Kennedy proposed to build, over four years, the 100,000 public housing units authorized by the Housing Act of 1949 but still not built. Housing advocates like Monsignor John O'Grady and Leon Keyserling thought the proposal inadequate The Congress included it in the Housing Act of 1961. The resulting construction, between 20,000 and 30,000 units a year, was greater than in the last Eisenhower years but less than in the last Truman years.[19]

During the Johnson years, public housing experienced significant growth. In 1964, Lyndon Johnson called for construction of 50,000 units of public housing over each of the next four years. In 1965, he upped the amount to 60,000 units a year for four years. Beginning in 1967, the number of units completed per year increased from around 30,000 to a peak of 91,000 in 1971, remaining at about 58,000 a year in 1972 and 1973. The lag between signature of an agreement between the federal government and a housing authority and completed construction varied, but could be four years or more. It is probably safe to assume that some of the increased construction in the Nixon years originated in the Johnson administration.

Nonetheless, the thrust of Johnson's low-income housing initiatives was away from the 1949 model, that is, housing funded, built and managed by government entities, towards an increased role for non-public entities, including the private real estate industry. The Johnson administration proposed a program of rent supplements paid to low- and middle-income families not eligible for public housing. In the Housing Act of 1965, the Congress revised the program to include payments to non-profit landlords on behalf of families who were eligible for public housing. The 1965 Act allowed local housing authorities to buy or lease existing housing units. In 1966, the administration unveiled a "turnkey" construction program for public housing, whereby private developers designed and built public housing projects before turning them over to local authorities. The Housing and Urban Development Act of 1968, a large and ambitious piece of legislation, called for construction of 26 million new homes over ten years. It included a new subsidy program to promote home ownership among low-income families and another program intended to promote non-public rental housing for low-income families. It also authorized the sale of some public housing units to tenants. The bill was ambitious enough to incorporate an increased authorization for public housing, but it was clear that the Johnson administration, and the Congress, did not see the 1949 Act model as the way forward.[20]

Testifying before Congress in 1965, Weaver explained the administration's attitude. He questioned the feasibility of building large amounts of public housing. Pointing to arguments about site selection, he argued that communities could absorb only so much public housing at any one time. While he accepted that government-built public housing was more likely to produce a larger number of new units than the administration's proposed rent supplement plan, he doubted that sufficient sites could be agreed upon. He also suggested that public housing could be un–American. He said that, given the kind of economy and social system the United

States had, there were real questions about how much housing should be owned and built by public agencies.[21]

The proposals that led to the 1968 Act were based, in part, on the work of the President's Committee on Urban Housing, even though the committee's report appeared after the legislation passed. The committee, headed by Edgar Kaiser, an heir to the Kaiser shipbuilding empire, included prominent figures: Walter Reuther, George Meany and Whitney Young, Jr., among them. Johnson asked the committee to consider how private enterprise could build housing for the urban poor and how the nation could rebuild the slums. The committee conceived the nation's goals as increasing the production of housing for the poor and attracting the fullest private participation in all aspects of federally subsidized housing. The committee's report conceded that a direct federal program, that is, something like the PWA program, could produce the millions of new housing units needed by the poor. Such a program would, however, be too drastic since it would necessitate preemption of private as well as state and local efforts. It was unnecessary, the committee claimed. The existing approach, several subsidy programs plus an enlarged role for the private sector, would be sufficient. Nevertheless, in words reminiscent of the 1932 Hoover housing report, the committee warned that if the existing approach did fail, a massive federal intervention would be needed and the federal government would become the nation's "houser of last resort."[22]

In the wake of the urban riots in the late 1960s, Johnson set up two commissions to consider housing and urban issues. Both produced recommendations that did not fit his ideas and he ignored them. The National Advisory Commission on Civil Disorders, chaired by Governor Otto Kerner of Illinois, blamed federal programs for perpetuating neighborhoods populated solely by African Americans. The commission's remedies included expanded federal spending, including on housing. It recommended construction of six million subsidized housing units for low- and moderate-income families over the next five years. Public housing was only one of many issues discussed by the National Commission on Urban Problems, led by former Senator Paul Douglas. The commission detailed public housing's problems and offered explanations and remedies. Its basic recommendation was "emphatic" support for subsidized housing for the poor. It proposed at least 500,000 units a year exclusive of housing for the elderly. Its target clientele extended to families earning as much as $4,500 a year, that is, higher than the existing limits for public housing. The commission thought that resistance from local governments had restrained the growth of public housing. It recommended that, where state and local actions were not meeting the needs of low- and moderate-income families, the federal government step in and become the builder of last resort.²³

Nixon

Richard Nixon and his secretary of housing and urban development, George Romney, initially embraced Johnson's housing programs, especially the new subsidy programs. Approvals of new public housing units continued at relatively high levels. Romney added two new initiatives: Operation Breakthrough, intended to apply modern manufacturing methods to home construction, and the Open Communities Initiative, intended to open the suburbs to African American families. By the end of Nixon's first term, the administration's ardor had cooled. Suburban jurisdictions resisted Romney's fair housing efforts and Nixon undermined them. Problems emerged in the new subsidy programs. A disproportionate number of subsidized home purchases ended in default and foreclosure and federal housing officials were accused of mismanagement and corruption. Suburban officials also grumbled about the number of subsidized units in their jurisdictions. Romney eventually lost faith in the subsidy programs. In early 1973, he denounced the programs and, referring to them as a "Rube Goldberg structure," called for a different approach. On January 5, 1973, Nixon declared a moratorium on all federal housing programs, including public housing, pending completion of a thorough evaluation.²⁴

In a September 1973 message to Congress, Nixon recited a litany of complaints about public housing. The federal government, he said, had become the biggest slumlord in history. Public housing projects were too often monstrous, depressing places, rundown, over-crowded, crime ridden and falling apart. Tenants were strangers to each other and cut off from American life. Perhaps the worst project, St. Louis' Pruitt-Igoe, had not worked and was about to be torn down. Nixon claimed that public housing was inherently unfair. A few families got better housing at taxpayer expense, while many other taxpayers had to settle for inferior housing. Evicting families when their incomes increased promoted dependence and undercut self-reliance. Public housing was also wasteful. Nixon claimed that government-built housing cost 15 to 40 percent more than the same families would pay in the private sector. Public housing cost families their basic right to choose where they lived.²⁵

Nixon's answer was to focus on the income side of the problem, rather than the housing side. The absence of affordable housing was a symptom, not the problem itself, he argued. Giving families cash subsidies with which they could obtain housing was preferable on many counts, Nixon claimed. It was more efficient and preserved the right to choose one's own housing. It was what the real estate industry had been promoting since the 1930s. The Housing and Community Development Act of 1974 enacted Nixon's proposals in the form of the Section 8 program.

Opponents

Undeterred by passage of the 1949 Act, the bankers, builders and brokers opposed public housing at the federal and local levels. Eighteen national real estate organizations joined together to oppose public housing. They pressed for state laws requiring public housing projects to be approved by public referenda and campaigned against public housing in the referenda. Where there was no requirement for a referendum, they pressured city councils to reject public housing proposals. They mounted extensive and sophisticated efforts, distributing pamphlets and other materials to sympathetic groups across the country. They were not shy about associating public housing with communism or socialism. Opponents of public housing in California claimed that public housing was a "left-wing Communist scheme" intended to bring a "Hitler-Stalin housing program" to America. In Detroit, opponents of public housing warned that it was the work of "fringe disruptionists, the political crackpots and socialist double domes." In Oakland, real estate interests defeated proposals for public housing largely on the basis that they represented "socialized housing" and "CIO communism."[26]

Public housing's opponents tapped into homeowners' fears that public housing would promote "infiltration" on the grand scale. As the Home Owners' Loan Corporation housing maps document, the conventional wisdom was that a neighborhood's health and well-being depended in large part on keeping "lower grade" people out. People of lower status must not be allowed to infiltrate into sound neighborhoods. It was easy for real estate interests to portray public housing as the vehicle that would bring poorer people, often African Americans, into a neighborhood. In Detroit especially but elsewhere as well, politicians opposed to public housing played upon such fears, particularly among homeowners of modest means, to defeat proposals for public housing or to limit it to neighborhoods where the poor already lived. That African Americans represented a disproportionate share of the poor made these fears all the greater.[27]

By 1949, Chicago and Detroit had already witnessed street violence in response to African Americans moving into public housing located in white neighborhoods. Federally funded housing for war workers and, after the war, emergency housing for veterans were planned and built on an expedited basis. The careful negotiations between federal officials and local political leaders that preceded PWA projects did not happen or were foreshortened. Sites were chosen that would not have been considered in peacetime. In Chicago, war housing and postwar veterans housing were located in outlying areas, perhaps near-middle-class African American communities but not in the South and West side neighborhoods where African Americans predominated. City officials considered housing for veterans an emergency program and preferred land owned by a public agency regardless of the neighborhood. African Americans occupied relatively few units in Chicago's war or veterans housing. Nonetheless, in 1946 and 1947, riots broke out as whites protested the arrival of African Americans at two sites in white neighborhoods. In 1941, Detroit officials located 200 units of war housing in a northeast neighborhood that included an African American community. Fearful whites from surrounding areas rioted when African American families moved into the new housing.[28]

At a 1960 Senate hearing, Senator Joseph Clark (D–Pennsylvania) bemoaned opposition to public housing. "They don't care," he said. "They do not care whether the housing is built or not. They just want to be sure there are no undesirable people living near them." He and others were aware that the decision to concentrate public housing in the least sought after neighborhoods was a political decision. Those who lived in more sought after neighborhoods and the officials they elected did not want new residents, families with several children in particular, who might represent a tax burden. They did not want new residents of lower socio-economic status than the current residents. They did not want new residents with different racial or ethnic identities, especially African Americans.[29]

The real estate industry's efforts had considerable success. Despite the opposition of both Republican and Democratic parties, the industry secured passage in 1950 of a ballot initiative in California requiring all future public housing projects to be approved by a public referendum. Public housing programs were defeated in Los Angeles, Houston and Dallas. Between 1949 and 1952, opponents of public housing prevailed in 40 of the 60 public referenda held. Public housing lost most frequently in small and medium sized cities, along the West Coast, in Texas and the Midwest.[30]

Advocates

Public housing lacked any comparable lobbying organization. The National Association of Housing Officials, according to an observer in 1951, was "too stuffy and inhibited" to be effective. Its "stodgy and cautious leadership" reflected the conservative character of most housing authorities. The National Housing Conference, while still active, lacked the time or money to support or inspire local organizations. A 1966 assessment offered a similar judgment. The National Association of Housing Officials merely represented the interests of those employed by housing authorities, it claimed. The National Committee Against Discrimination in Housing and other "liberal" groups were loose confederations whose support for public housing was measured, at best.[31]

When housing legislation was before the Congress, several national organizations regularly testified in favor of public housing. The National Conference of Catholic Charities, the American Association of Social Workers, and Americans for Democratic Action spoke up for public housing. The most consistent and vigorous support for public housing came, however, from the national labor organizations, the AFL and the CIO. Boris Shishkin, the secretary first of the AFL's housing committee and then of the AFL-CIO housing committee, testified repeatedly on behalf of an expanded public housing program. Two hundred thousand units a year was the AFL-CIO's usual position. Shishkin maintained that low-rent public housing was the only proven means to house low-income families. The public housing program may have its flaws but no one had developed a better alternative, he argued. Eliminating construction cost limits, raising income limits, and providing more and better community facilities would improve the program, but the basic program created in 1937 and revived in 1949 remained the best option. As labor leaders had before, Shishkin said that the unions supported public housing not for their own members, but for the low-income families the private real estate industry did not serve.[32]

Urban Renewal and Relocation

In the 1950s and 1960s, urban redevelopment, or "urban renewal" as it was called after the Housing Act of 1954, focused less on housing and more on other kinds of structures. The original legislation imagined a slum clearance program whereby obsolete residential structures were demolished, perhaps to be replaced by better housing. Nevertheless, real estate interests secured amendments that exempted first 10 and then 20 percent of all projects from removing bad housing. The statutory language that the area cleared be "predominately" residential came to mean that housing had to occupy no more than half the designated site. The law did not require that land once acquired and cleared with federal urban redevelopment funds be made available for low-income housing. Local governments were free to treat housing authorities as another potential re-developer. Since most cities were eager to expand their tax base, they preferred private sector developers who would construct buildings subject to property taxes. If they built housing, it was likely to be for middle- and upper-income tenants. Local authorities could use federal public housing funds to acquire and clear sites for low-income housing. They saw little reason to use their urban renewal funds for the same purpose.[33]

For urban renewal's harshest critic, public housing was just another part of a flawed program. Martin Anderson, in his 1964 book, *The Federal Bulldozer*, spent several hundred pages attacking urban renewal. Maintaining that he accepted that goal of the 1949 Act, that every American should have a decent home, Anderson argued that urban renewal had worsened housing conditions. Anderson calculated that urban renewal had destroyed 126,000 low-rent homes and provided only 28,000 to replace them. Anderson accepted that the urban renewal program could be modified to proceed only as fast as replacement housing was built. Because he believed that the private sector could do everything that urban renewal and public housing purported to do, however, he dismissed the possibility. It would amount to modifying an inherently bad program whose costs outweighed its benefits. It was better to do away with both urban renewal and public housing.[34]

The failure to provide satisfactory housing for displaced families extended beyond urban renewal to all federally funded urban public works projects, including public housing itself. The most accessible data involve urban renewal, however. Anderson calculated that three-quarters of the families displaced by urban renewal found new housing on their own, usually substandard and more expensive than their original housing. Chester Hartman, who would have a long career as a planning and housing expert, claimed in a 1963 article, based largely on research in Boston's West End, that only 17 percent of families displaced by urban renewal found homes in public housing. About half of the displaced households were eligible for public housing. The others earned too much or too little. Some were single men or adult couples without children; neither qualified for public housing. Still others did not meet the local housing authorities' criteria. Perhaps they were credit risks or had police records. Hartman contended that, of the half that was eligible for public housing, only about a third moved into public housing. Data for housing projects in Chicago and Atlanta suggest that the experience of families displaced by public housing projects was much the same. Most families whose homes were torn down to make way for public housing did not find places in the new housing.[35]

The failure to relocate displaced families led to criticisms of the public housing program. Some observers concluded that there was not enough public housing. They thought that federally funded public works projects, including urban renewal, highways and public housing, should be required to create as much housing as they destroyed. Others pointed to public housing's income limits and selection procedures.[36]

Chester Hartman saw the failure to rehouse displaced families as a fundamental indictment of public housing. Based on a study of white families displaced from Boston's West End, he concluded that most displaced families did not want to move to public housing. He reported that they thought public housing projects were too big or too crowded. They thought the tenants and the environment were undesirable. They thought that public housing had too many rules. He perceived significant differences between the families willing to move to public housing and those that were not. The families that moved to public housing, Hartman claimed, were the "deprived and incapacitated—those families with some social or personal impairment or disadvantage." They were the poor, the old, single parents, and the parents of large families. Among them, he could find few he considered "upwardly mobile," who were looking to buy a home or otherwise improve their housing. The families who rejected public housing, Hartman reported, were the "respectable working class," those with a "normal family structure, residential stability, steady employment and a commitment to the place where they live." Because respectable working people did not want to live in public housing, Hartman argued, it would inevitably become an island of "poverty, segregation, deprivation and despair." Perhaps grouping deprived families together might offer an opportunity to provide "intensive, comprehensive social and personal services" to families needing help. For the respectable working class, however, the government needed something other than public housing: rental subsidies, support for rehabilitating housing, small and scattered projects and the like.[37]

Local Housing Authorities

The PHA supervised local housing authorities, issued rules and guidelines and reviewed proposals. Although local housing authorities and others complained about the extent and nature of federal supervision, the law allowed local authorities considerable discretion. Under the 1949 Act, local authorities designed, built, and managed projects. Local authorities selected tenants and enforced rules. In some cities, decisions about sites fell to local government, but authorities usually played a role as well. In 1983, the Congressional Budget Office counted nearly 2,800 local authorities across the country. Most authorities were relatively small. Twenty-two authorities, each with more than 6,500 units, managed a third of all public housing units. The other 2,775 authorities managed the remaining two-thirds; on average, these authorities managed a few hundred units.

The membership of the local housing authorities followed the pattern set by Harold Ickes' first advisory committees. A survey from the late 1960s revealed that they were generally middle-aged or elderly white males, in the middle- or upper-middle-income ranges, well educated and employed in business or the professions. Only 11 percent had incomes close to those of public housing tenants and, in most cases, their incomes were low because they were retired. Only 3 percent had ever lived in public housing. The original notion had been that the local authorities would be independent and professional, free of ties to local politics. Since mayors and city councils appointed most members, authorities were generally in step with whoever presided in city hall. In some cases, as in Philadelphia before 1949, the housing authority was an extension of the political organization then in power. Elsewhere, as in New York before the late 1950s, the local authority maintained some space between itself and city hall. Membership could readily follow a "balanced ticket" pattern common in some cities. In Chicago, the understanding was that the housing authority should include one housing reformer, one labor leader, one African American, one Jewish member and one business executive.[38]

The managers employed by housing authorities, while were more diverse and similar to public housing tenants than authority members. About a third were female. Twenty percent were not white. Most of the non-white managers worked in large projects with many non-white tenants. Almost half of public housing managers had not completed college. Seventeen percent had lived in public housing at some point.[39]

The typical housing authority member in the late 1960s was comfortable with the existing program. When asked if they favored new methods then being proposed, three quarters said they did not know enough about them to decide. Of the quarter that professed to be knowledgeable, most preferred the methods established by the 1949 Act. Two-thirds said that their communities needed more traditional public housing. Most thought that their authorities needed strict rules to promote good behavior. Most members were not interested in negotiating with tenant groups or allowing a tenant to serve on the housing authority.[40]

New York

In 1955, Martin Meyerson and Edward Banfield wrote that in no American city was public housing "developed as part of a long range plan for all types of housing or as part of a reasonably detailed comprehensive plan for the growth and development of the community." They were right, but New York City came closer than any American city. By the late 1960s, the New York City Housing Authority managed 157 housing developments for 500,000 people, or 6 percent of the city's population. Nearly 20 percent of U.S. public housing was in New York City. Sixty-nine of the New York projects contained at least 1,000 apartments, usually in high-rise buildings. In the late 1950s, the New York authority also began to build so-called "vest pocket" projects, projects of only a few hundred units scattered throughout the city. To the projects funded by the federal government, New York added city and state funded projects, most frequently low-rise buildings built on vacant land in the outer boroughs. The subsidies provided to them were limited to low-cost financing and exemption from property taxes. Rents were higher than in federally funded projects and the population better off than the residents of federally funded projects.[41]

New York built more public housing units because housing conditions in the city were different than in the rest of the country. From the Second World War onwards, the city experienced a severe housing shortage. In 1946, the City Planning Commission estimated that the city needed a million new units by 1970. Twenty years later, the city had 850,000 new units and still had a housing shortage. A 1960 report conducted for the city claimed that another 356,000 housing units were needed. In 1968, the housing vacancy rate in the city was 1.23 percent. In addition, much of the city's housing was old. In 1963, 43,000 old law tenements remained, that is tenements built some time between 1879 and 1901. The same 1960 report claimed that 20 percent of the city's housing was substandard, more than in 1950, with another 15 percent on their way to being substandard.

Typically New Yorkers rented apartments in multi-family housing. In the 1960s, households rented 80 percent of the city's housing units.[42]

Eighty percent of New York City's voters were renters in the 1960s. Housing remained a contentious issue and support for government interventions was strong. New York was one place where a broad array of politically active people campaigned for public housing for themselves and their families. That state and local politicians launched programs for families who were not considered poor, who were thought of as of moderate or middle income, was both a response to such campaigns and a reason why they continued. Although the image of public housing in New York declined as it did elsewhere, support persisted. As late as 1960, Mayor Robert Wagner moved to expand the city's middle-income housing program.[43]

Through the late 1950s, public housing in New York City fell within the Robert Moses' municipal empire and was shaped by his views. Moses' main purpose was to make the city, especially Manhattan, more attractive for the middle class. For Moses, low-income housing was a source of funds from the state and the federal government and a means to make urban redevelopment projects more attractive to federal and state officials or to local communities. Moses offered the prospect of public housing to deflect charges that his proposals would displace families. He was given to optimistic estimates of the number of displaced families who would be, or could be, re-housed in public housing. While the data suggested that no more a third of displaced families had found places in public housing, Moses claimed that at least 40 percent would be re-housed. He characterized displaced families whose fate was unknown as having "self-relocated" and counted them as successes. Moses was willing to construct low-income housing in neighborhoods that he thought would never attract private builders, the Lower East Side, Harlem, the south Bronx, and central and eastern Brooklyn. Elsewhere his preferences were private development and middle-income tenants.[44]

Construction of public housing in New York City came to a virtual halt when, in the middle 1960s, New York voters rejected state bond issues for public housing and constitutional amendments intended to facilitate public housing. Voters in Queens and Staten Island joined much of the rest of the state in rejecting the measures. Opponents of the measures offered familiar arguments: that public housing served only a select few and was somehow un–American. The city would also have received most of the new money. At least one commentator attributed the defeats to fears about the apparently mounting cost of public housing and about the possibility of public housing spreading to new neighborhoods.[45]

Moses' willingness to demolish existing neighborhoods provoked opposition. On the Lower East Side and in the area on the West Side that became Lincoln Center, neighborhood groups launched campaigns to stave off demolition. The failure to relocate displaced families in adequate housing or even to accommodate the displaced families who were eligible for public housing were key parts of opposition groups' indictment of Moses' version of urban redevelopment. One umbrella group, the New York State Committee on Discrimination in Housing, issued a report in the late 1950s that claimed that Moses' proposals threatened to dislocate nearly 10,000 families, nearly half of whom were African Americans. The committee estimated that just over a third of the displaced families would be eligible for public housing and only 15 percent would be able to afford the other apartments that would be constructed on the cleared sites.[46]

In the late 1940s and early 1950s, Lewis Mumford continued his critique of New York's public housing. He conceded that it was superior to the slum buildings it replaced or the earliest efforts at model tenements. The New York authority's latest efforts, he argued, were decently designed and constructed. Yet he persisted in his belief that high-rise construction was a mistake. It detracted from good interior design. It crowded too many apartments around the elevators and made rearing children more difficult. Most important, it crowded too many people together. Mumford thought that the increased densities made the latest New York projects inferior to the first PWA projects or the best privately built developments. Mumford wrote approvingly of the Fresh Meadows apartment complex in Queens, funded by the New York Life Insurance Company. The exterior design was ordinary, but the use, for the most part, of two- and three-story buildings combined with an excellent site design created what Mumford considered a "beautiful community."[47]

Mumford's criticism went beyond architecture to include the city's, really Robert Moses', approach to urban development. Replacing crowded slums with high-density public housing was, in Mumford's terms, replacing a pathological condition with a pathological remedy. The housing authority and the City Planning Commission had frozen the design of public housing in "an obsolete, congested mold that ignored the needs of tenants and the city." By concentrating on low initial costs, ignoring long-term costs, and preferring quantity to quality, the city had created a pernicious model that it was spreading even to less crowded parts of the outer boroughs and that private investors were copying. Re-developing the city at high densities would increase traffic congestion. Building more highways, Moses' remedy, would draw more people into Manhattan and divert funds from other public facilities. In Mumford's view, the New York public housing projects were big enough to be communities, but, because they were not diverse, either in terms of family incomes or building uses (no shops, churches or movie theatres), they fell short. According to Mumford, there was "no architectural substitute for the variety and stir of a real neighborhood."[48]

Jane Jacobs was, at one time, a friend of Mumford's. The two were part of a group that resisted Moses' attempt to push a highway through Washington Square in lower Manhattan. Jacobs had come to New York from Pennsylvania in the late 1930s. She eventually settled in Greenwich Village and worked as a writer for *Architectural Forum*. In the late 1950s, her criticism of Moses attracted attention and, then, financial support from the Rockefeller Foundation. Despite sharing a dislike for what Moses was doing to New York, Jacobs' analyses of urban development and public housing were dramatically different from Mumford's.

In the late 1950s, concern about street crime in New York was on the rise. Starting with that concern, Jacobs' 1961 book, *The Death and Life of Great American Cities*, attempted to describe how cities can be safer and therefore better. According to Jacobs, the "bedrock of a successful city district is that a person must feel personally safe and secure on the street." For a neighborhood to be safe, Jacobs thought, it had to have lots of streets, lined with shops and filled with pedestrians. In effect, Jacobs was arguing that her own neighborhood, the West Village in lower Manhattan, defined the essence of a great city.[49]

From Jacob's prescription for the ideal neighborhood flowed other judgments. Jacobs was no fan of the suburbs, believing that they were diverting resources from the cities. "Superblocks" were anathema. Jacobs poured particular scorn on large planned developments that eliminated through streets, that sought to create an entire community, and that controlled the number and kind of non-residential uses. Jacobs disliked "towers in a park," high-rise buildings surrounded by considerable open space. She welcomed high population densities, but thought that diverse building types, another facet of a great city in her view, and low ground coverage were incompatible. High densities and low ground coverage could yield only large apartment houses, not the variety of buildings found in the West Village.[50]

Blame for these and the other ills Jacobs saw in urban development she attributed to "planners." Among those she named were Ebenezer Howard, the British originator of the garden suburb; Patrick Geddes; Clarence Stein; Raymond Unwin, another British urban thinker; Le Corbusier, the

French architect; Lewis Mumford; and Catherine Bauer. Jacobs conceded that most of their proposals had never been implemented in the United States, but claimed that their ideas had nevertheless shaped city planning. Changes in the city and the region were the work of "a new aristocracy of altruistic planning experts," "paternalists" and "utopians" whose objectives were "semi-feudal." According to Jacobs, low-density urban development, regional planning and satellite communities, the ideas of those she called "de-centrists," was really an effort to "jettison" the cities.[51]

Jacobs detested public housing. The projects in East Harlem were "almost pathological displays of slum troubles." According to Jacobs, low-income projects were "worse centers of delinquency, vandalism and general social hopelessness than the slums they were supposed to replace." In Jacobs' view, public housing was irrelevant to urban problems, to the needs of ordinary Americans, to the American economic system and to the concept of "home" in the American tradition.[52]

Never one to duck an argument, Mumford responded. Jacobs' analysis and remedies were trivial, he wrote. To imagine that a "few tricks of planning" could restore order to city life was as foolish as imagining that too much open space and superblocks had caused the city's problems. Rather than considering how the city could be renovated, Jacobs had settled for measures that allowed slums and blighted areas to preserve their congenial human features without radical change. As Mumford saw it, Jacobs' social and aesthetic goals were attainable by housing people in sufficiently congested quarters, but not in superblocks, and providing for a "sufficient mish-mash of functions and activities." The city's problems, Mumford wrote, stemmed from "overgrowth, purposeless materialism, congestion and insensate disorder," the dynamic forces that Jacobs seemed to favor. Mumford's solution lay in encouraging not these forces, but the "formative, stabilizing, coherent, order making" forces. Only then could there be a truly human urban civilization, one that was self-limited and self-directed.[53]

The sociologist Herbert Gans thought that Jacobs' book was a path breaking achievement. He thought it was often right, but, disappointingly, often wrong. Gans was open to paying rent supplements to poor people and scattering public housing throughout the city, notions that Jacobs had offered. He agreed that public housing did not promote the sort of street life the tenants wanted. Nevertheless, he thought Jacobs, like the planners she criticized, over estimated the possible effect of physical design and under estimated the impact of social, cultural and economic factors. The latter were much more likely to shape a neighborhood than the former.

Gans thought that Jacobs did not understand the political and economic forces that had shaped the cities and public housing. Public housing and the cities were the way they were because private enterprise and the middle class had shaped them. In preferring private enterprise to planners, Jacobs was returning to the 18th or 19th century, asking private enterprise to do something it had failed to do, and ignoring the role of the "well-heeled builder and the realtor lobby in Washington" in creating the more obnoxious elements of urban renewal and hamstringing public housing.[54]

Chicago and St. Louis

Two other local authorities attracted considerable attention, Chicago and St. Louis. In neither Chicago nor St. Louis did public housing have the broad political support it did in New York. Public housing in Chicago and St. Louis was a program for low-income families. There was no push to expand it beyond poor families and it received little local financial support. The city of Chicago spent almost nothing on public housing. The Chicago housing authority subsisted on state and federal monies plus whatever revenue rents produced. Because public housing lacked wide popularity or interest, in both cities it remained the preserve of local politicians and housing officials, with local politicians eventually gaining the upper hand. Likewise, public housing readily became an adjunct to urban renewal.[55]

The Chicago housing authority is usually seen as a well-intentioned organization that ran afoul of local politics. By 1950, the authority had built 6,300 units in nine projects, most row houses or low-rise apartment buildings. The executive director, Elizabeth Wood, was winning a reputation as an effective administrator. Wood had degrees from Illinois Wesleyan and Michigan, taught English, and worked as a social worker before being named the authority's first executive director. By 1949, the authority had plans for 40,000 additional units, an ambitious amount in the context of the 810,000 national total enshrined in the 1949 Act, but small compared to the authority's estimate of Chicago's need, 270,000 units. The authority's plans called for public housing throughout the city, with 15,000 units on vacant land. Projects would be large enough, at least 1,000 units, to create a neighborhood but densities would be moderate, no more than 30 units per acre. Half the units would be for African Americans. As Martin Meyerson, a former authority planner, and Edward Banfield described in their 1955 book, *Politics, Planning and the Public Interest*, the city council seized control of the planning process after a long struggle and restricted public housing to slum neighborhoods south and west of the Loop populated largely by African Americans. By 1954, Elizabeth Wood was out of a job, replaced by someone more in tune with city hall.[56]

By the early 1960s, the Chicago authority had moved to constructing very large projects consisting entirely of high-rise buildings in African American neighborhoods. African Americans predominated in the oldest, least attractive Chicago neighborhoods. The Federal Street slum on Chicago's South Side included five census tracts where, in 1950, 46 to 80 percent of the houses lacked private baths. Most houses dated from before 1900 and were overcrowded. Starting a slum clearance program in such areas made sense and, to the city council's relief, left the rest of the city undisturbed. The authority began with plans for low-rise buildings, but, after a long, difficult interaction with the PHA, settled for high-rise elevator buildings. Chicago's costs were high, for construction and land acquisition. Outsiders assumed that the city administration was content to pay owners of slum properties high prices and to accept high bids from favored contractors. The PHA balked, however, at designs that seemed still more expensive. The authority and the PHA finally agreed on very large projects like the Robert Taylor Homes, 28 sixteen-story buildings containing more than 4,400 housing units, built to replace the Federal Street slum. Economies in shared facilities, like a central heating plants and those allegedly inherent in high-rise construction made Chicago's higher cost somehow more palatable.[57]

In the late 1940s and early 1950s, the city of St. Louis contemplated large-scale urban renewal. As the Second World War ended, the city faced serious problems. It was one of only four U.S. cities whose population declined between 1930 and 1940. Its population accounted for only 51 percent of the metropolitan region's population. Thirty-five percent of its housing units were substandard. Decent, affordable housing was in short supply. In response the city administration developed plans for large-scale redevelopment. The aims were to eliminate slums and make the city more attractive for middle-class families. New neighborhoods would be built, complete with public facilities, churches, stores and recreation spaces. The worst slums around the city center would be replaced by high-density public housing. One of the most notorious slums, populated predominately by African Americans, would be replaced by two public housing projects: one, Igoe Apartments, for whites; the other, Pruitt Homes, for African Americans.[58]

The St. Louis authority, like its counterpart in Chicago, was far less

Pruitt-Igoe Homes, St. Louis, Missouri. Demolition began in 1972 (Wikimedia Commons, credited to U.S. Department of Housing and Urban Development, Office of Policy Research and Development).

adept than the New York authority, especially at managing costs. Site acquisition and construction costs for Pruitt-Igoe were significantly higher than in New York or earlier St. Louis projects. Cost cutting measures produced smaller rooms, bedrooms of fewer than 100 square feet, for example. Finishing details, such as paint on hallway walls, screens on gallery windows, and insulation on steam pipes, were omitted or of low quality. Public toilets on the ground floor were dropped from the plans. Landscaping of the open spaces was rudimentary. Based on faulty market research, Pruitt-Igoe included too many small apartments and not enough big ones. The authority's occupancy guidelines, which allowed two persons per bedroom, produced significant over-crowding. The Pruitt-Igoe buildings proved difficult and expensive to maintain.[59]

The high construction and operating costs in St. Louis suggested to Eugene Meehan, author of several analyses of public housing in the late 1970s, that public housing there had, perversely, met its goals. Pointing to public housing's origins in the New Deal, Meehan argued that providing work for contractors and construction workers, creating jobs for unionized janitors and maintenance staff, and rescuing owners of slum properties were among public housing's goals, perhaps more important goals than creating better housing for low-income families. Pruitt-Igoe, Meehan observed, may have been the most successful project since its construction generated public works spending; it did not last long (and therefore did not disturb the rest of St. Louis); and its demolition produced still more public works spending.[60]

Finances

The 1937 and 1949 Acts had the federal government paying for construction of public housing and local housing authorities paying for their operation and maintenance. Some authorities included utility costs in the rent. After the early 1950s, all authorities made payments in lieu of taxes to their local government. Local authorities borrowed the construction funds and the federal government contracted to pay the debt service over a fixed period. Edith Wood had originally proposed that the federal government make guaranteed fixed payments to local authorities over a period of time, as had been the case in Britain, but the Congress altered the plan so that only the number of years was fixed and only debt service guaranteed. The revised scheme made local housing authority bonds attractive to investors, but left local authorities with a considerable challenge. They were charged with providing housing to low-income families, presumably charging below market rate rents, while collecting enough rent to cover operations and maintenance. Even when housing authority finances seemed healthy, observers recognized that housing authorities intent on balancing their books risked driving away the lowest income families when they raised rents.[61]

Through the late 1950s, local authorities met the challenge. Operating and maintenance costs were manageable, in large part because overall price inflation was low. During the 1950s, only in 1950 and 1951 did the consumer price index increase by more than 3.6 percent. Most public housing buildings were relatively new and required only routine maintenance. Rent income was healthy. For a time the presence of over-income families may have bolstered revenues. During the war, public housing served many war workers who earned more than the statutory income limit and were supposed to pay market rents. One estimate was that over-income families represented 25 percent of public housing families in 1948, but only 1 percent in 1957. Nevertheless, local housing authorities continued to show a considerable surplus of rent revenue over operating and maintenance costs for the remainder of the 1950s.[62]

Federal officials and members of Congress saw the surplus as a way to reduce or even eliminate the federal subsidy. The PHA instituted a policy whereby local housing authorities could retain a surplus no greater than 50 percent of a year's revenue. It would transfer any further surplus to the federal government to reduce its annual contribution. In 1952, Truman's PHA Commissioner, John Egan, imagined a long-term scenario in which the incomes of public housing tenants and the rent they paid continued to increase and the federal subsidy decreased. The 1954 Cole committee recommended continued payment of surpluses to the federal and local governments until their subsidies had been repaid. Albert Cole did not dismiss the idea that public housing could, in this way, become self-liquidating. As late as 1958, Cole worried that, if local authorities were allowed to retain more surplus funds, they would use them for something other than low-income housing. Through 1957, authorities transferred nearly $250 million in surplus funds to the federal government, reducing the federal subsidy by nearly 39 percent. At the same time, local authorities found themselves with limited reserves.[63]

By the end of the 1960s, the picture looked different. Statistics compiled by HUD showed that 16 housing authorities were nearly bankrupt and another 19 headed in the same direction. Fifty-one of the 82 largest authorities, accounting for two-thirds of all public housing units, were in critical financial shape. In Chicago, operating and maintenance expenses equaled rent revenue in 1967. Thereafter the authority experienced a budgetary deficit and had to draw upon its reserves. By 1970, it had exhausted the reserves. New York started drawing on its reserves in 1962. It had paid the federal government nearly $20 million in surplus revenues, but, as it entered 1970, faced an estimated deficit of over $9 million with reserves of only $5 million.[64]

Operating and maintenance costs had outrun rent revenue. Between 1952 and 1967, the average tenant income in New York public housing increased by $1,600 a year or 65 percent. The average rent increased nearly 72 percent, but operating and maintenance costs increased over 125 percent. A national study of 23 large housing authorities pointed the finger at increased price and wage inflation between 1965 and 1968. Over that period, the consumer price index increased steadily from 1.6 percent per year to 5.4 percent per year. The large authorities increased rents, but the increases trailed increased costs by about 25 percent. For every dollar increase in costs, the authorities collected only 75 cents. The same study concluded that only price inflation explained the overall increase in costs. It looked at the age of the public housing buildings, local wage patterns, the size of the housing authority, the number of children per housing unit, and the percentage of housing units with no wage earner present. It concluded that none of these factors had had a significant impact on costs. A 1970 Rand study reported that, between 1951 and 1967, operating and maintenance costs in public housing had increased by over 5 percent per year, while the Consumer Price Index had risen less than 2 percent a year. In the same period, public housing rents had increased only 3 percent a year. The Rand report stated that the faster growth in maintenance and operating costs was largely a product of price inflation although deterioration due to age and changes in maintenance services also played a role.[65]

Generating enough revenue to cover costs while still serving appropriately low-income families was a challenge built into the basic public housing legislation. How housing authorities dealt with the challenge is unclear. Many commentators believed that housing authorities normally charged tenants 20 percent of their income. The statute set five times income as the admission standard for public housing, but said nothing about the rent to be charged. In the early 1960s, the Boston authority discarded rents based on income in favor of rents tied to the size of an apartment. It believed, as many did, that income based rents pushed out higher income families. Fixed rents, the authority hoped, could allow it to charge higher rents and still retain higher income families. The Chicago authority took similar steps about the same time. Fixed rents generated more income only if the authority could offer various sized apartments and especially if it could offer larger apartments, with three or four bedrooms. Part of the Chicago authority's thinking was that larger families, who needed larger apartments, often included more employed members and that could, therefore, afford higher rents.[66]

When the Congress re-considered income limits and rents in the late 1950s, witness' testimony demonstrated the contradictory pressures housing authorities faced. Most witnesses wanted lower rents, but for different reasons. The Eisenhower administration wanted lower income limits and lower rents because it feared that, otherwise, housing authorities would seek to serve mainly families who could pay higher rents. Public housing might end up competing with private housing in violation of congressional intent. Housing groups wanted lower rents because they thought existing rents were too high for many low-income families. The National Housing Conference advocated setting rents in relation to a family's need and imagined that housing authorities could do this and still cover their costs.[67]

A housing authority could take steps to secure the right mix of tenants, poor enough to qualify but still able to pay enough to cover costs. It had less control over other factors. It could not always control how many welfare recipients it housed or how much it could charge them for rent. The Boston authority charged welfare families lower rents. Like any other landlord, housing authorities had to compete for tenants. As low as public housing rents seemed to some, rents in other housing could be lower still, especially in substandard buildings. Data from 1950 suggested that 60 percent of families and individuals renting substandard housing in metropolitan areas paid less than 20 percent of their income for rent. Such figures varied by place and time, but it was possible that moving to public housing meant increased rent for some low-income families. Housing authorities also had to compete in terms of type and quality of housing. Larger apartments were always easier to rent than smaller apartments. Public housing had a distinctive image and reputation. Not everyone wanted to live there.[68]

The St. Louis authority got it all wrong. St. Louis city officials viewed Pruitt-Igoe as part of program that would attract middle-income families back to the city. By the time Pruitt-Igoe opened, more middle-income families had moved to the suburbs. As a result, more housing became available within the city. In 1950, the overall housing vacancy rate in St. Louis was 2 percent. It increased to 5 percent in 1960 and 10 percent in 1970. The vacancy rate at Pruitt-Igoe started at 9 percent in the early 1950s; increased to 16 percent in 1960 and 65 percent in 1970. Pruitt-Igoe contained too many small apartments and too few large ones. The vacancy rate for smaller apartments was always higher. Despite high construction costs, the Pruitt-Igoe buildings were expensive to maintain and operate. To meet rising costs, the authority raised rents, so that, by 1969, 15 percent of tenants were spending more than 50 percent of their income on rent. Less than half were paying 25 percent or less. Nonetheless, with the average tenant income less than $3,000 a year, rents could go only so high. Extensive publicity about crime in Pruitt-Igoe and a nine month rent strike by tenants in 1969 almost certainly discouraged families from moving in and pushed still more families out. Through the early 1970s, the St. Louis authority rarely covered it costs at Pruitt-Igoe.[69]

In the early 1960s, advocacy groups began lobbying for more generous treatment of the housing authorities. The National Association of Housing and Redevelopment Officials called for the federal government to make its full annual contribution regardless of the state of the housing authority's finances. The National Housing Conference pushed for additional financial assistance to housing authorities to pay for non-housing services such as employment and family counseling. As housing authorities raised rents, tenants pushed back. In the most vivid example, limiting rents to 25 percent of income was one of the chief demands of the rent strikers in St. Louis in 1969.[70]

The Housing Act of 1969 was Congress' attempt to correct the situation. In 1968, it had made things worse by authorizing housing authorities to provide a variety of services to tenants, especially employment and family counseling. In 1969, at the behest of Senator Edward Brooke (R–Massachusetts), it limited rent in public housing to 25 percent of income. It authorized the payment of operating subsidies to housing authorities as well as modernization grants, intended to correct some of the worst maintenance problems. The Nixon administration was slow to implement the operating subsidies. In the first year of operation, it spent only $33 million of the $75 million appropriated for operating subsidies. The administration worried that the housing authorities had caused their own financial problems and that operating subsidies would undermine any incentives to manage funds properly. The administration attempted to direct them only to what it considered efficient authorities. Neither the operating subsidies nor the modernization grants cured the housing authorities' financial woes during Nixon's time.[71]

Even the Congress' meager effort seemed too generous to some. Anthony Downs characterized the operating subsidies as covering the difference between costs and 25 percent of tenants' income. He claimed that many tenants paid no rent and might, in fact, receive money from the authority to pay their utility bills He argued that such measures removed any incentive, on the part of authorities or tenants, to manage properly. He thought limiting rent to 25 percent of income treated tenants in identical apartments differently. This, he argued, undermined tenant morale.[72]

In 1971, the Congress enacted another amendment proposed by Senator Brooke. It limited rent payments by welfare recipients to 25 percent of their adjusted income and prohibited welfare agencies from reducing the housing portion of welfare payments. The amendment was another episode in a long-term struggle between housing authorities and welfare agencies about paying for welfare recipients' housing. Both sides looked to the other to foot the bill. The immediate impact of the 1971 Brooke amendment was to shift more of the cost to housing authorities, further undermining their financial health. One estimate of the annual cost was $77 million.[73]

It took a while but the real estate industry and its congressional supporters got their way. Having imposed significant constraints on the program in the 1949 Act, they eventually halted construction of new public housing units and converted federal housing aid to low-income families into cash subsidies. In the meantime, the public housing legislation starved housing authorities of the resources needed to maintain their buildings. By the early 1970s, many of them faced bankruptcy and were at the mercy of federal willingness to increase subsidies. The nation's housing ills remained, but it turned away from the solutions promoted by the 1930s housing reformers.

Proponents and opponents of public housing thought that the 1937 Act was an important milestone. By having the federal government intervene directly in the housing sector, they thought it marked the beginning of a continuing and growing federal involvement in low-income housing beyond the assistance offered to the private housing industry in the 1934 housing legislation. They were wrong. The 1937 Act was a false dawn. The United States proved more resistant to change after 1937 than before. Public housing's origins in the New Deal caused elected Democrats to support it for a while, but eventually even they preferred reliance on the private sector.

CHAPTER FIVE

Buildings

In a 1958 book, *The Shook-Up Generation*, Harrison Salisbury, a one-time Moscow correspondent and longtime *New York Times* writer and editor, described his visit to the Fort Greene Houses in northern Brooklyn. Salisbury wrote that he had never expected to find the equivalent of Moscow's newly built slums in the United States. Even in Moscow, he had not seen elevators that children used as toilets. At Fort Greene he saw "broken windows ... cold drafty corridors ... playgrounds that are seas of muddy clay ... the planned absence of art, beauty or taste, the gigantic masses of brick, of concrete of asphalt, the inhuman genius with which our know-how had been perverted to create human cesspools worse than those of yesterday." Some might describe Fort Greene as the world's largest housing project, Salisbury wrote, but it was really a $20 million slum.[1]

Salisbury's account was especially vivid, but still symptomatic of attitudes towards public housing's buildings after 1949. Nearly every aspect of typical public housing construction, or what commentators thought was typical, was the subject of criticism; location, size, site design, maintenance, exterior design and interior design.

Location

After the 1949 Act, the sites chosen for public housing, or at least the public housing that attracted outside attention, were almost always in cities, not the growing suburbs, and, within cities, on cleared slum sites, not vacant land. The Congress, the federal agencies responsible for public housing and local housing authorities combined to resolve the argument about location in favor of the slum clearers. The 1949 Act, like the 1937

Act, was silent on the question of location, but its legislative history signaled Congress' preference for building on slum sites. The 1949 Act also left public housing to the discretion of local governments. Local governments were not required to build any public housing. If a suburban community did not want public housing, it could decline to create a housing authority or request federal funding. Some advocates, like Catherine Bauer, read the 1949 Act to allow the use of urban renewal funds for planned communities outside cities, but HHFA interpreted the legislation narrowly, allowing urban renewal projects only near or in slum areas. The PHA's initial guidance limited site acquisition costs for public housing to 20 percent of total project costs. Strict enforcement might have eliminated the most expensive slum sites. Yet, the administration, under pressure from the New York housing authority, first raised the limit to 25 percent as long as an authority was pursing a balanced program of slum and vacant sites and then interpreted the limit as applying to the total site acquisition costs for all the projects an authority was planning, not to individual projects, and regardless of the mix of slum and vacant sites. Housing authorities, as Meyerson and Banfield recounted in the case of Chicago, usually located federally funded public housing where it would disturb neighborhoods that were not considered slums or blighted areas as little as possible. In most, but not all, cases, this meant building in slum neighborhoods, although in the early 1950s, the Boston authority found vacant land for most of its projects.[2]

Traces of the old argument about location remained. The National Federation of Settlements and Neighborhood Centers echoed the views of earlier social workers. The Federation argued that public housing needed to be centrally located, near poor peoples' jobs, institutions and social networks. It was not so much a preference for locating public housing in the slums, but for locating public housing where tenants could access stores and public transportation. Catherine Bauer and Albert Mayer continued to make the community planners' case. They pressed for public housing outside slums, on vacant land within cities and in new communities outside cities. In the early 1960s, Mayer saw the prospect of new communities modeled after the British new towns as an opportunity to increase the supply of decent, affordable housing for low-income families. Critics who worried about public housing's costs complained that building on cleared slum sites was expensive. One analysis claimed that land acquisition and construction costs were significantly higher on cleared slum land than elsewhere. It claimed that six housing units could be built for the cost of five constructed in the slums.[3]

Locating public housing in what were or had been slum neighborhoods came to be considered a bad thing. Writers did not always feel required to explain why being located in a slum neighborhood was problematic. Others were more specific. A 1971 article saw slums as having adverse influences that better housing could not overcome. If prostitution and addiction were rife in the surrounding streets, if jobs were scarce, if residents did not feel safe, if the schools were inadequate, a public housing project would suffer the same problems, they thought.[4]

In the sociologist Nathan Glazer's assessment, locating projects in slum neighborhoods facilitated ties to outsiders, which could reinforce "low income life styles." Support from fellow slum dwellers could mean less motivation to change. Glazer maintained that husbands were less responsible when they realized their wives could call upon formal and informal networks rooted in the neighborhood.[5]

A 1979 study commissioned by the Department of Housing and Urban Development could be interpreted to support the notion that public housing projects could not escape the influences of the surrounding area. The study identified 7 percent of housing projects that HUD staff considered "troubled," a total of 700 projects with 180,000 units. The troubled projects were disproportionately large, older, urban projects in what could be equally considered "troubled" neighborhoods. Only 5 percent of projects were in "high crime" neighborhoods, but 42 percent of the troubled projects were. Only about a third of projects were in neighborhoods with fair or poor police protection, but more than half the troubled projects were.

The HUD study also suggests that judgments about projects and neighborhoods need to be treated carefully. Designation as "troubled" depended on the judgment of HUD staff, distant observers at best, and was impressionistic. The allegedly troubled projects were more likely to be in African American neighborhoods. Thirty percent of all projects were in neighborhoods where African Americans constituted more than half the population. Nearly 60 percent of the troubled projects were in such neighborhoods.[6]

Size

Nationwide, the average project became smaller from the first PWA projects in the middle 1930s through 1957. Even in New York, the authority built some smaller projects starting in the late 1950s. By the 1970s, more than half of public housing projects included fewer than 200 units. Nevertheless, housing officials, in places like Chicago and New York, built large projects, visually separated from the surrounding neighborhoods. It was these big projects that attracted comment. Authorities acquired large plots of land, and separated them from the surrounding neighborhood and street grid by closing off existing streets. Within the resulting "superblocks," authorities sited buildings in a fashion that made sense within the project but without regard to older, existing buildings. For authorities focused on clearing slums, large projects offered an opportunity to make a significant dent in the inventory of substandard housing. For those interested in building new communities, a large project approximated Clarence Perry's neighborhood unit. With the right design and community facilities, it was thought, a large project could become a functioning, healthy neighborhood. A large well-designed project, it was hoped, could withstand the deterioration underway around it. It might even promote improvements in neighboring blocks.[7]

When critics saw large projects apparently separated from the neighborhoods around them, they saw problems. Charles Abrams though public housing ought to fit into existing neighborhoods. For him, New York's initial project, First Houses, was superior to later projects because it was small and resembled the buildings around it. Jane Jacobs was sure that large projects isolated their tenants. She claimed that public housing tenants might cross over to other neighborhoods, but outsiders rarely entered public housing projects. Public housing tenants might visit their friends elsewhere, but their friends did not visit them in their public housing apartments. When Anthony Wallace studied a Philadelphia project in the early 1950s, he reported that tenants were more likely to visit their friends outside the project than have their friends visit them. Wallace thought that some tenants were embarrassed to have their friends come to the project. Wallace was, however, far more positive about public housing than Jacobs. He thought a public housing project could become a real community. The key for Wallace was including the right community facilities and locating them so that they served both public housing tenants and people from elsewhere. That way, a project could fit within the surrounding area and offer the basis for what he called "an independent social structure." Observers complained that public housing projects did not promote improvements around them. By tearing down parts of existing neighborhoods, they might even harm their environment, disrupting existing neighborhood ties and irritating existing residents.[8]

In part, the criticisms of large projects flowed from changing views of poor neighborhoods. Commentators had come to question the negative portrayals of poor, urban neighborhoods current before World War II. If the old neighborhoods were not so awful, there was less reason to obliterate them and build large public housing projects. Salisbury saw in East Harlem before the advent of public housing "institutions that have the neighborhood stability," street fiestas and "the interwoven relationship of stores and neighbors." Jacobs, given her fascination with busy streets, perceived in the old neighborhoods' crowded sidewalks "exuberance" and "gaiety" that she did not find in public housing projects. Monsignor O'Grady lauded the old immigrant neighborhoods that "gathered around the church." These neighborhoods had a "certain bond of union" that was lost when people moved into large apartment buildings.[9]

Michael Harrington, in his book *The Other America*, elaborated the theme. Slum neighborhoods were narrow, centers of poverty and physical misery, he conceded. The old slums had, he claimed, a vital community life organized around a national culture or religion. Their inhabitants had real aspirations; their shabby surroundings goaded them to better themselves. The old slums were melting pots and way stations to something better. The new slums, on the other hand, had collected society's failures, rootless people, people born at the wrong time or in the wrong industry. Although the new slums often had large minority populations, they were integrated in that they contained the poorest and most miserable of every race, creed or color. Their inhabitants suffered from a sense of hopelessness and a culture of poverty, according to Harrington.[10]

The changed views of poor neighborhoods reflected, in part, the work of scholars like Herbert Gans. In *The Urban Villagers*, Gans argued that Boston's West End, a neighborhood that had been "renewed," had been a low-rent district, not a slum. Gans argued that buildings and neighborhoods were slums only when they were physically, socially, or emotionally harmful to their inhabitants. While accepting that many West End structures were deficient in some way, he claimed that the standards normally applied to buildings reflected middle-class values. Failing such standards represented an inconvenience and did not pose a threat of harm. Gans argued that areas like the West End gained bad reputations because their inhabitants often indulged in "overt and visible behavior considered undesirable by the majority of the community." Instead of bad behavior, Gans saw in the West End poor people who sought out housing they could afford.[11]

Unlike Harrington and Jacobs, Gans was not arguing that urban villages were superior to high-rise housing projects or any other kind of community. In a note added to a second edition, he reiterated his opposition to urban renewal as practiced in the West End, the unfairness of destroying poor people's homes and replacing them with luxury housing, all at public expense. He added that, while he liked the West End, he was not arguing for or against urban villages or ethnic enclaves. As far as he was concerned, debating whether they were superior to other types of communities was irrelevant.[12]

Gans did not see public housing as it then existed as a way to rehouse poor people. Nevertheless, he thought public housing had been subjected to inaccurate and unfair criticisms. Many people did not recognize that public housing was the creation of federal and local governments. Nevertheless, Gans preferred the notion of new communities built on vacant land as a solution to housing problems.[13]

High-Rise Buildings

Besides the size of some public housing projects, critics objected to the presence of high-rise buildings. The tallest building at Fort Greene was 15 stories high. Once again, the discussion of public housing diverged from public housing as it existed. High-rise public housing, like Fort Greene or the Robert Taylor Homes and Pruitt-Igoe, was almost unknown before 1950 outside New York and common before 1960 only in New York, Chicago, St. Louis and Philadelphia. Outside New York, public housing before 1950 almost always featured low-rise (no more than three stories) construction. Boston built seven federally funded projects between 1949 and 1954, none of them high-rise. Five combined low-rise and mid-rise buildings; the others had only three-story buildings. The 1950s did see a surge in high-rise construction. Whereas only two high-rise projects were built outside New York before 1949, the PHA approved 70 between 1949 and 1959. Still, not all consisted of only high-rise buildings. In Philadelphia only one project built before 1955 included only high-rise buildings. Overall, three-quarters of public housing projects that served families, not the elderly, were four stories or lower.[14]

In choosing to build tall apartment buildings, local authorities sought to achieve at least three aims: lower per-unit construction costs, lower land acquisition costs and the maximum number of new housing units. Not everyone agreed, but studies dating back to the 1930s suggested that taller buildings yielded lower per-unit costs. Once the additional cost of an elevator had to be spread over all units, going beyond four or six floors made sense. Virtually everyone acknowledged that slum sites were more expensive to acquire than vacant land on a city's periphery. Achieving acceptable per-unit land acquisition costs required higher densities. Accommodating open space, recreational space, community facilities and parking on limited slum sites similarly pushed local authorities to build taller.

Building as many units as possible was consistent with the local authorities' mandate. Everywhere, the need for affordable, decent housing exceeded the authorities' capacities. As urban renewal projects destroyed old, substandard housing, the number of displaced families alone exceeded the authorities' resources. Federal dollars were limited and suitable sites were hard to acquire. If federal money and a site were available, a local authority was likely to make the most of them.[15]

Beginning with East River Houses in 1941, the New York authority built increasingly tall buildings. Convinced that constructing taller buildings was the way to make the most of limited resources, the authority moved from six stories, to ten or 11, to 13 or 14. The authority believed that a 14-story building was at least 10 percent cheaper than a low building. By the middle 1960s, the authority's rationale was that building at the highest density zoning regulations permitted was essential to controlling the cost per unit and that high densities demanded high-rise construction. Securing enough open space for parking and for recreational spaces was still another reason to build tall. The first high-rises in New York were Y-, X- or T-shaped. When the authority perceived that the "slab" buildings (long, narrow buildings with a single corridor on each floor) constructed in Chicago and St. Louis were still cheaper, it adopted the same design.[16]

The Chicago authority's trajectory was similar. Its first projects were low-rise buildings. Cabrini Homes featured two-story row houses with private backyards. In the early 1950s, while Elizabeth Wood was executive director, the authority moved to mid-rise buildings, on the grounds that they allowed more open space than three-story walkups. The authority's 1957 report stated that, although two-story row houses were still the best housing for families with children, cost limits had made their construction impossible. In the following years, the authority moved to high-rise construction. Of the 7,800 units the authority built between 1959 and 1963, 7,500 were in high-rise buildings.[17]

The Philadelphia authority's decision to build high-rise projects was intended to solve several problems. In 1951, the authority wanted to build 20,000 units but it assumed that obtaining approval for its preferred option, low-density projects on vacant land, would be difficult and time consuming.

Constructing tall buildings on slum sites already approved for public housing would be fast and less contentious. The prospect of adding many units quickly would offset any additional costs for acquiring the sites.[18]

The original scheme for the Pruitt and Igoe projects in St. Louis called for garden apartments similar to PWA projects in Atlanta and Philadelphia. The city administration elected in 1949, however, was intent on building as many units as possible, partly to accommodate the families displaced by highway and urban renewal projects. The new mayor, Joseph Darst, had also been impressed by high-rise developments in New York. The St. Louis housing authority contracted with a young enthusiastic proponent of high-rise buildings, Minoru Yamasaki, to design the new buildings. In articles and speeches, Yamasaki hailed high-rise buildings as the most practical means to rid cities of slums, which he termed "cancers" on the city. High-rise buildings took into account, he contended, the high cost of inner city land and the need to provide recreational spaces on limited sites. Yamasaki's initial plan called for a mix of mid-rise and high-rise buildings. He copied two distinctive features from other high-rise buildings, elevators that stopped only at every third floor and long, wide galleries intended to provide play space and access to laundry and storage rooms. In 1951, *Architectural Forum* praised the design as an innovative approach to replacing ramshackle single-family houses with "vertical" living. Nonetheless, as the St. Louis authority, the PHA and the architects sparred over the plans, they discarded some of Yamasaki's ideas. The projects had to accommodate more people and the buildings had to be taller. The final results, opened in 1954, were two projects encompassing 2,870 housing units, in 33 11-story buildings on 57 acres, taken together the biggest U.S. public housing project at the time.[19]

Outside New York, high-rise buildings were a highly visible departure from traditional housing patterns. Anyone driving on the Dan Ryan expressway in Chicago, for example, could hardly miss the Robert Taylor Homes. Some people objected to high-rise buildings for public housing simply because they were different. The possibility that public housing in Los Angeles might include high-rise buildings intensified opposition there. Congressmen, residents of existing neighborhoods and public housing tenants themselves, were on record wishing for public housing that looked like everyone else's housing. Usually high-rise buildings were the focus, but residents of a public housing development, Easter Hill Village, in Richmond, California, told a researcher that their row houses were an innovation for California and they would prefer detached, single-family homes like the neighborhoods around them.[20]

Easter Hill Village, Richmond, California, opened 1954 (Library of Congress).

Some people objected to all high-rise buildings. Mumford, Bauer and others had expressed such views in the 1930s. When the anthropologist, Anthony Wallace, evaluated the Jacob Riis Houses in New York in the early 1950s on behalf of the Philadelphia housing authority, he found many things he did not like. He thought high-rise buildings inappropriate for raising children. He concluded, nevertheless, that the deficiencies he saw were not confined to public housing. Middle class developments, like Stuyvesant Town, were as bad or worse.[21]

Much of the criticism of high-rise buildings in public housing came from those who supported the program. Housing advocacy groups, settlement house organizations, and committees of architects came out against high-rise construction. Charles Abrams preferred smaller, less costly buildings because he imagined that public housing was a temporary phenomenon and someday housing authorities would want to tear down and replace the first generation of buildings. Elizabeth Wood liked the row houses the Chicago authority had first built. She argued that row houses with backyards allowed children to play near their mothers. To care for children properly and meet other human needs, high-rise buildings required community resources, childcare in particular. Wood doubted that American cities would ever include sufficient community facilities in public housing.

Catherine Bauer wrote that row houses were preferable. Americans knew how to live in such houses and preferred to do so. Americans, according to Bauer, lacked the desire or gift to follow the "highly organized, impersonal and relatively inflexible mode of living" required in an apartment house. In the 1930s, one might have thought that Americans were moving towards more collective ways of living, subsequent experience had proved otherwise. Bauer warned that designers of public housing needed to take heed.[22]

In the late 1960s, the Douglas Commission set out a more nuanced approach. First, it pointed out that tall buildings were the exception rather than the rule. In any case, it did not want to rule out any approach to public housing. In the commission's opinion, walk-up garden apartments offered better housing and could accommodate somewhat higher densities than the slum buildings they replaced. Where large projects containing high-rise buildings stood out from the rest of the housing stock, they risked labeling the tenants as poor and isolating them from the rest of the community. Elsewhere, well-designed tall buildings that included sufficient community resources could house low-income families effectively, the commission argued.[23]

In the end, critics of high-rise buildings won the day. The Housing Act of 1968 contained language prohibiting high-rise buildings with elevators for low-income families with children unless the secretary of housing and urban development determined there was no alternative.[24]

Density

The high population densities that high-rise buildings brought also attracted criticism. As New York moved to increasingly tall buildings, population densities grew. The earliest New York projects produced densities around 235 persons per acre, higher than the residential New York average of 190. Taller buildings pushed the densities to above 300 persons per acre and then to over 400 persons per acre. Mumford had long contended such densities were unhealthy. Martin Meyerson argued that, for high densities to be tolerable in Chicago, a host of other changes to the city would be required, to the transportation system and to the distribution of schools, stores and other community assets. For Anthony Wallace, even low-rise buildings built to relatively high densities were unacceptable. Once a project involved more than 20 low-rise units to an acre (or about 80 people), providing enough open space became difficult.[25]

Open Space

In the earliest public housing, open space took the form of backyards connected to row houses or open courts surrounded by garden apartments. The latter approach was consistent with New York apartment buildings of the 1920s and with innovative designs like Clarence Stein's Sunnyside Gardens. Where housing authorities moved to high-rise buildings, site design changed to a "towers in a park" approach, tall buildings surrounded by park-like expanses of open space.[26]

Critics, notably Jane Jacobs, disliked the new open spaces. Given Jacobs' conviction that personal safely was the goal of urban design and that safety outside the home depended on the presence of many other people, space filled with grass and shrubs was unacceptable. She had a particular aversion to grass lawns. She considered the open spaces in public housing inherently unsafe. For her, they lacked the hustle and bustle that she associated with healthy urban neighborhoods. Since Jacobs sought relatively high population densities without high-rise buildings, open space had no place in her ideal city neighborhood. The only way to accommodate large numbers of people was to crowd many low-rise buildings together.[27]

Writers more favorably inclined to public housing had their doubts about the changed approach to open space as well. Anthony Wallace argued that backyards promoted family solidarity and community organization. Backyards were places where fathers could be something more than "the star boarder" and opportunities for fathers to establish working relationships with their male neighbors. Elizabeth Wood remained convinced that families with children needed private backyards. Failing that, housing authorities needed to design open spaces in ways to encourage people to linger and mingle. Anything that got people to interact and recognize their common interests was a good thing. Alfred Mayer worried that too many open spaces were inert and lifeless. Like Wood, he thought better design could overcome the problem, even at Pruitt-Igoe where the open spaces were particularly bare. Mayer thought the open spaces could re-connect public housing with the surrounding neighborhoods. Well-designed open spaces could attract people from outside the project. Rather than a separate enclave, public housing could become part of the wider neighborhood. Mumford thought that the most recent designs amounted to "mere openness." Architects needed to created "public enclosures" where people could recapture a sense of "intimacy and innerness." Designers needed to rediscover the cul de sac, the court and the cloister.[28]

Interior Spaces

Interior spaces in public housing, living spaces and public spaces, contained evidence of penny pinching. Critics were on firmer ground when they blamed Washington for them. Missing toilet seat covers and closet doors were standard in outsiders' complaints about federally-funded public housing, along with asphalt tiles and concrete floors and ceilings. The impact of federal rules became particularly apparent when Chicago and New York built state- and locally-funded public housing within more generous cost limits. According to one account, Elizabeth Wood felt free to instruct the architects responsible for a state-funded project to "give us the best you have." Eugene Meehan, writing about Pruitt-Igoe, noted that the federal government imposed cost limits but did nothing to ensure the quality of the housing produced. By the 1960s, the PHA loosened some of its strictures and the New York authority adopted more generous standards. Closet doors and toilet seat covers appeared along with larger windows, showers, brighter colors and tile floors. Nevertheless, for many, the image of public housing as minimum housing remained.[29]

The Truman administration retained Nathan Straus' emphasis on cost control. John Taylor Egan, an architect who had risen through the federal public housing organizations to become commissioner of the PHA, insisted that low costs were essential to the program's ultimate success. Egan worried aloud that public housing was becoming more expensive than private construction. To his mind, the program's goal was to provide low-income families with decent housing at "low rents geared to their income." If costs could not be kept close to a "fair and achievable national average," the program risked congressional wrath. The PHA argued that lowering operating costs was not always sufficient justification for higher construction costs. It accused local authorities of using more expensive materials than private builders used and forbade them from exceeding the standards established in local building codes. It warned against building on sites with inherent disadvantages that private builders had avoided because of the additional costs involved. It set maximum room sizes, smaller than those recommended by the American Public Health Association or by PHA's own 1945 study. As in Nathan Straus' day, the PHA under Egan urged local authorities to overlook no detail in their search for lower costs.[30]

The Eisenhower administration was no less focused on controlling costs than its predecessors. The statutory limit applied to a room's initial construction costs and did not include the cost of acquiring a site, providing public utilities or streets, and building non-dwelling elements, like community centers or meeting rooms. As local authorities built apartments with more rooms to accommodate larger families, added community facilities, and chose expensive inner city locations, overall costs increased. For at least one 1950s New York project, the construction costs subject to the statutory limitation represented only about half the total cost. The PHA worried that public housing was becoming more expensive than private housing or, at least, could be portrayed as more expensive. In 1957, the PHA imposed a limit of $17,000 on the total cost per unit, even though it had no legal authority to do so. Charles Slusser, the head of the PHA, explained that the limit was consistent with the statutory requirement to promote economy and promoted the production of the maximum number of units with the funds available.[31]

Worries about public housing's costs persisted through the 1970s, among both supporters and opponents. The notion persisted that public housing's standards had been set without regard to cost. Instead, the argument went, the government should decide what it could, or would, pay and then design housing to fit within a budget. At a 1952 appropriation hearing, Senator Albert Gore (D–Tennessee) fussed about housing authorities moving tenants' belongings from one apartment to another. He complained that ordinary American families paid their own moving expenses. Charles Abrams thought that public housing was built to an overly high, and expensive, standard. He anticipated that the current generation of public housing would be demolished as urban renewal progressed. Cheaper, smaller buildings made more sense. Skeptics pointed to the overall cost of public housing. The billion dollars expended through the middle 1960s sounded like a lot of money. Total construction costs of $13,000 to $20,000 per unit in the late 1950s prompted complaints that housing authorities could purchase modest suburban homes for less.[32]

In the eyes of many outside observers, the interior public spaces of high-rise public housing contained at least three objectionable features: long hallways, elevators and an absence of public restrooms on the ground floor. In many walk-up buildings, tenants entered their apartments from stairways that served only a few apartments on each floor. Tenants in row houses entered their homes from the street level. When housing authorities started constructing taller apartment buildings, lobbies, elevators and hallways leading from the elevator to apartments became the norm. So-called "slab" buildings incorporated a single long hallway on each floor. The earlier Y, X or T buildings had had several shorter hallways leading from the elevator to apartments. At Pruitt-Igoe and a few other buildings, the long hallway became a gallery along one of the long, outer walls, with apartments on one side and windows on the other. Also at Pruitt-Igoe and a few other buildings, so-called "skip-stop" elevators stopped at every other second or every third floor. In such buildings, tenants had to negotiate stairways and hallways to get to and from their apartments.

Long hallways, galleries and skip-stop elevators were not unique to public housing. Hallways and elevators were standard features of apartment houses. A few privately built developments included skip-stop elevators. When the St. Louis authority announced that galleries and skip-stop elevators would be part of Pruitt-Igoe, commentators saw than as useful innovations borrowed from other designers. In the original concept, the galleries were meant to be play spaces as well as spaces where tenants could interact on their way to the elevators, shared laundries and storage spaces.[33]

Elevators in particular posed design challenges. The New York authority started with slow, relatively small elevators, some of them skip-stop. Over the 1950s, it discovered that such elevators could cause problems. At lunchtime and after school, lobbies could be crowded with children waiting for the elevator. The authority adopted larger, faster elevators and discarded the skip-stop design in new buildings. There are indications that when St. Louis and Chicago started to build high-rise apartments, their initial elevators were similarly inadequate.[34]

To critically-inclined visitors to public housing, the problem in the interior public spaces was not that tenants had to wait for elevators or did not have access to a freight elevator when they moved in or out. What several of them perceived first was that the elevators smelled like toilets. The conventional explanation was that public housing buildings did not normally have public restrooms on the ground floor and the many children living there used the elevators rather than travel all the way up to their apartments. The smelly elevator was central to Harrison Salisbury's portrayal of public housing. Michael Harrington also wrote that smells were a characteristic of a tenement, of cooking, of human beings and of bad plumbing. When he encountered smelly elevators and hallways in public housing, he concluded that the "old culture of poverty" had survived in a new environment.[35]

Crime

To Jane Jacobs and Oscar Newman, the interior public spaces were at least as unsafe as the exterior public spaces. Jacobs saw the stairways, hallways and elevators as the equivalent of streets. Since they were closed to public view, they could not be safe. Tenants could readily become prey for anyone loitering in the building. Newman was of similar mind. He pointed out that tenants had to use the elevators even if they were screened from public view.[36]

The core of Newman's 1972 book, *Defensible Space*, was the contention that good design could lead to greater safety. Based on research in New York public housing, Newman claimed that high population densities produced crime. He detected a marked increase in crime once densities exceeded 50 units per acre. Newman's larger argument was that private spaces, or spaces that were perceived as private, were safer than public space. People, Newman argued, acted to protect space they perceived as their own, but not space that seemed to belong to everyone. By Newman's logic, single-family homes were the safest, because their ownership was clear. As housing became denser, as it moved from row houses to high-rise apartments, the amount of space that did not obviously belong to anyone increased and safety declined. Public housing, with few through streets, entrances that did not face the street, numerous open spaces, hallways, stairways and elevators were, in Newman's view, particularly unsafe. There were too many places that tenants could perceive as someone else's responsibility. Newman thought architects could design even high-density housing so that the inhabitants would be inclined to claim ownership of more spaces. Having apartments open onto a landing shared with only a few other apartments was safer than having them open onto a hallway.[37]

The connection between hallways and safety was, to an extent, in the eye of the beholder. The sociologist Lee Rainwater, who studied Pruitt-Igoe in the late 1960s, reported that tenants there preferred apartments opening onto hallways, because they were public spaces, rather than onto a space, a landing in the stairwell, shared with only two or three apartments. Hallways, Rainwater wrote, were thought to be safer because there was a greater likelihood of help.[38]

Although design was at the heart of Newman's work, he hedged his bets. Location in high crime areas, a lack of exterior embellishment, and overwhelming size and scale contributed to crime in public housing, Newman claimed. It was hard to build safe homes for low-income people, he wrote. They lacked the "refined sense of property and ownership" and self-confidence that the middle class exhibited. Unlike the middle-class, low-income people had experienced little success in improving their lives. They were that much less likely to act to create a safer living environment. Newman believed that sharply defined class lines promoted safety. Southern cities before the Second World War were safer because a "strongly defined social structure" existed. Contemporary American cities contained little physical structure that marked social stratification. Different ethnic and income groups were forced to live close together, a situation neither rich nor poor liked, according to Newman.[39]

Newman claimed that the police operated better and had better relations with tenants in low-rise buildings than in high-rise buildings. Nonetheless, Newman did not look to the police to solve crime problems. Additional police manpower and equipment were "palliatives." The current atmosphere was, he wrote, one of "pervasive crime and ineffectual authority." It was up to the tenants to ensure a policeman's safety within a building. It was up to the tenants collectively to assert community control. Rather than "surrender their shared social responsibilities to any formal authority," tenants must come together "if only for the limited purpose of ensuring survival of their collective milieu."[40]

Harrison Salisbury's *The Shook-Up Generation* recounted the problems afflicting American youth. Youth gangs were one of Salisbury's principal concerns. He quoted Ralph Whelan, a senior New York City official, to the effect that the opening of a new housing project led to an increase in gang violence during the first six to 18 months. The housing project brought young men and their gangs into the neighborhood; they struggled with the existing gangs in the surrounding neighborhood. According to Salisbury, the newcomers often had a different racial or ethnic identity from the existing gangs intensifying the conflicts.[41]

The material in Salisbury's book first appeared as a series of articles in the *New York Times*. Similar newspaper stories highlighting crime in public housing were common. The *Christian Science Monitor* ran a series in 1955 about crime in Boston's public housing. Similar articles appeared in Chicago and New York papers over the next two decades. A 1970 *Barron's* article, entitled "Worse Than Slums," cataloged notorious crimes committed in public housing.[42]

Although the description of new housing projects provoking gang conflict in the short term was virtually Salisbury's only bit of evidence, he denounced public housing as a source of crime. Public housing projects, he claimed, spawned teen-aged gangs. They incubated crime. They "debased family and community life to the lowest common mean." They were worse than anything George Orwell conceived.[43]

Michael Harrington considered Salisbury's book a "brilliant study." He combined it with the report of a 1959 St. Louis grand jury to argue that public housing projects promoted violence and juvenile crime. The grand jury claimed that crime in housing projects was more prevalent than in the city generally. Gangs from outside the projects had made themselves at home and the city's law enforcement apparatus had had no impact. For Harrington, the culprits were the culture of poverty and public housing's "bureaucratic aspects." Despite improved housing, tenants' "long schooling in the slums" made them resist better times, Harrington wrote. Public housing itself promoted "alienation and rootlessness."[44]

Salisbury's account was also grist for Jane Jacobs' mill. She used the quote from Ralph Whelan as the basis for the claim that the Lower East Side's public housing was the area "highest delinquency belt." According to Jacobs, the two most formidable gangs in Brooklyn had their home bases in public housing projects. She cited a Pittsburgh study that reported that crime in public housing was higher than in the city's slums. For Jacobs, this proved that some things were more important than good housing. Those who believed that good housing could promote good behavior were deceiving themselves. She quoted Reinhold Niebuhr to the effect that this self-deception amounted to be belief in "salvation by bricks."[45]

Crime and the fear of crime were serious concerns for public housing tenants. Pruitt-Igoe tenants quoted in Lee Rainwater's work complained about the lack of order in the project. Surveys of public housing tenants in Chicago in 1970 showed a high level of concern about vandalism and gang activity. Rabushka and Weissert's study of Wilmington's public housing revealed that nearly two-thirds of the tenants were worried about being robbed. Nearly half were concerned about being assaulted. A 1973 study of welfare recipients in New York told the tale of a young mother living in public housing who took a knife with her when she left her apartment for fear of being robbed.[46]

More than anything else, tenants wanted better police protection. Testimony from tenants about their fear of crime nearly always included complaints that the police could not or would not do their job. Pruitt-Igoe tenants blamed the absence of police for the breakdown of law and order in the project. They claimed that the obvious lack of police attracted criminals to Pruitt-Igoe and that non-residents committed most of the crimes within the project.[47]

Concerns about crime were prevalent enough that tenants were willing to take action on their own. In the late 1960s, tenants in a Brooklyn project started their own safety patrol. By the early 1970s a hundred such patrols were active in New York City developments. In projects where tenants participated in management or formed tenant unions, rigorous enforcement of housing authority rules, better policing, and eviction of troublemakers were high priorities. Between 1963 and 1980, New York public housing tenants held nearly 40 demonstrations, rent strikes and other actions demanding more police in public housing.[48]

Police could be hard to find in public housing. A report compiled by Pruitt-Igoe tenants claimed that only two watchmen were at work in the 30-block project over a 24-hour period. In New York, St. Louis and Chicago, the police's initial position was that they would patrol only the perimeter of large projects. In the 1950s and 1960s, police forces were moving away from foot patrols to using patrol cars. They resisted requests that they leave their cars and patrol public housing projects. By the late 1940s, New York employed watchmen in most projects. Despite mounting concerns about maintaining order, the New York authority did not create its own police force until 1952 and then only for the projects it considered trouble spots. By the 1960s, the New York housing authority police had expanded its patrols to all public housing. The Chicago authority did not create its own police force until the middle 1960s. San Francisco and Boston did likewise, but their forces remained small through 1980.[49]

Adding police to public housing faced several hurdles. Some were jurisdictional. City police did not see public housing as a high priority, but were not necessarily eager for another police force to take shape. Coordination between the housing authority and city agencies seems to have a particular problem in Chicago. Additional police cost money. By the early 1970s, the New York housing authority police cost $10 million a year and was the fourth largest police force in the country. Neither cities nor housing authorities were eager to pick up the tab. The federal government helped Chicago pay for its police force in the middle 1960s, but was reluctant to have security included among housing authorities' normal expenses. Many housing projects were located in neighborhoods where police protection generally was weak. The police treated public housing the same way they treated the surrounding neighborhoods.[50]

The notion that public housing was especially crime-ridden was not universally accepted. A 1964 article by Albert Mayer contended that studies in Chicago and St. Louis showed lower crime rates for public housing than for the surrounding areas. William Moore's *Vertical Ghetto* reported that the project he studied in a mid-western city did not have an unusually high crime rate. A literature review sponsored by the Department of Housing and Urban Development in the late 1970s provided limited support, at best, for the picture of public housing bedeviled by crime. The review identified only a handful of studies, three sponsored by HUD, plus Oscar Newman's research in New York. The review noted that the sponsored studies focused on only a few projects and that relevant data were unavailable from other projects. The review concluded that insufficient data were available to create a national picture of crime in public housing. The review was more comfortable with the assertions that public housing tenants were afraid of crime and that this fear significantly affected their lives. One study, of public housing tenants in Boston, reported that more than half were afraid to carry out normal activities at night: waiting for a bus, shopping, riding the elevator or walking in the hallway.[51]

Subsequent studies support the HUD review's conclusion about crime in public housing. A 1982 study repeated the concerns that the studies cited in the review were not typical of public housing nationwide since they were chosen because they seemed to have crime problems. The same study analyzed St. Louis police data from the 1970s and concluded that crime in St. Louis public housing was no greater than the city average and comparable to crime in similar areas.[52]

Common Facilities

Churches and places of entertainment like saloons were not found in public housing projects. Playgrounds and other outdoor recreation spaces were common, however. By the mid–1950s, developments in New York also hosted 53 nursery and school age centers, 25 health centers, 12 libraries, and six mental health centers. Many projects in New York and elsewhere included a community center that included meeting rooms and spaces for childcare or other services. A survey of large housing authorities in the middle 1970s indicated that more than 90 percent provided day care centers and roughly 80 percent offered recreational programs for children and teenagers.[53]

Nevertheless, housing authorities struggled to fund activities in their common facilities. Typically, the housing authority provided space for outside groups, such as settlement houses or city agencies, to provide clinics, childcare or other services, but did not provide funding itself. The PHA advised housing authorities to consider the availability of other community resources before constructing their own and the PHA expected outside groups to pay for community services. Enticing charity organizations to participate was not easy and relationships with other city agencies not always cooperative. In New York, in the mid–1950s, only half the 50 community centers within public housing had private sponsors. Even they served only a small fraction of the tenant population. Later the New York authority paid for youth programs in public housing projects.[54]

The first New York projects included spaces set aside for retail shops. New York could not, however, rent all the spaces it set aside for shops. Alfred Rheinstein subsequently opposed stores that might compete with privately-owned businesses. By 1944, the authority had decided that it was in only the housing business. Later, state and federal rules forbade stores in public housing. Existing shops in New York hung on, however. In the late 1950s, nine of 82 New York developments still contained shops.[55]

Tenants wanted community facilities. When Beatrice Friedman asked New York public housing tenants about community facilities, they overwhelmingly expressed a desire for childcare and other facilities. Nearly 80 percent said that public housing should include childcare centers. Similar percentages expressed support for recreational facilities for teenagers, meeting rooms for adults and social rooms for the elderly.[56]

Most commentators agreed. Some focused on community centers and the social services they might bring. More objected to the absence of stores. In part, the concern was that tenants were forced to travel too far to shop and, perhaps, to pay too much because they had little choice. In part, the concern was that stores helped make a collection of homes a neighborhood and, perhaps, a community. Mumford suggested that a profitable, successful shopping center might help create a neighborhood and subsidize housing for the low-income families. Elizabeth Wood pointed out that, while planners might refer to the neighborhood unit idea, Clarence Perry's template included stores and other community assets that were usually not included in public housing. The Douglas Commission, echoing these views, said that every project should include a childcare center and playgrounds.[57]

The absence of stores in the several public housing projects in East Harlem troubled the settlement workers at the Union Settlement Association. Like many settlement houses and the settlement movement generally, the Union Settlement Association supported public housing but felt obliged to raise what it believed legitimate concerns. In the 1950s, the Union Settlement Association, spearheaded by Ellen Lurie, was at work in East Harlem. Responding to complaints from local business owners, it determined that public housing had destroyed over 1,500 storefronts in the area. Most of them housed retail ships, but clubs, churches and cafes also disappeared. When the stores were demolished, they took many small businesses and an estimated 4,500 jobs with them. The settlement workers, like other commentators, thought that the stores' demise deprived the neighborhood of important social resources, the glue that held the community together. For the settlement workers, this meant that public housing needed some changes, not that it was fatally flawed.[58]

Jane Jacobs got to know the workers at Union Settlement, served on its board of directors and adopted their critique of stores in East Harlem. Small shops along crowded streets were at the heart of her idealized neighborhood. The fact that there were rare in New York public housing in the 1950s was just another black mark against the program for her. Jacobs saw the demolition of East Harlem's small shops as another example of planners and architects interfering with private businesses. For Jacobs, redevelopment, like public housing, used public funds to destroy the livelihoods of shopkeepers without offering any real public benefits. Even when public housing included community centers and shops, Jacobs was sure that they did not function properly. She claimed that people in one East Harlem project never used their community center. When Jacobs visited one of the stores in a New York public housing project, she came away complaining that it was too noisy and crowded. It would fail, she wrote, if it had any competition. In any case, she added, most customers did not like the manager. He was not the friendly shopkeeper found on one of Jacobs' idealized streets.[59]

Oscar Newman parted company with Jacobs and other critics regarding stores in public housing. The notion that adding stores would increase activity and improve safety was too simple in his view. Before an authority allowed stores, it needed to evaluate several factors: the nature of the business, the probable customers, and their relationship to the neighborhood. The PHA and housing authorities had banned stores to prevent competition with other businesses, Newman wrote, but their policies might have another rationale rooted in safety.[60]

Maintenance

Salisbury thought Fort Greene badly maintained. Lisa Peattie, writing about a Boston project, described apartments not painted for years, missing doors and locks, leaky faucets, dysfunctional boilers and broken windows. The *Wall Street Journal* printed a description of a Chicago project. Among its flaws, it listed rags stuffed in windows, missing light bulbs, cockroaches everywhere and missing fire hydrant caps.[61]

By 1970, Pruitt-Igoe was a shambles. The St. Louis housing authority's management record was not strong and the 1969 rent strike had left it virtually without funds. At the end of the strike, 23 of the 33 buildings were closed; nearly two-thirds of the original units were unavailable. Estimates for the repairs needed throughout St. Louis public housing started at $30 million. The repair estimates for some units exceeded their original construction cost.[62]

Salisbury blamed the New York authority for the problems he saw at Fort Greene. He thought other cities managed public housing properly. He thought that all New York needed was a little money, foresight, common sense and a regard for human beings. Public housing need not, he wrote, be a combination of almshouse and ghetto. Others agreed that management was at fault. It did not budget enough for maintenance and did not take tenant complaints seriously. It was too ready to overlook featherbedding and overly restrictive work rules imposed by unions.[63]

Tenants came in for their share of blame as well. Newman worried that placing welfare families in high-rise buildings would lead to the destruction of the buildings in five years' time. He contended that poor families, single-parent families, immigrant families, and families from rural areas could not adapt to living in high-rise buildings. Housing authority managers complained about tenants' destructive behavior. Others thought the large number of children in public housing increased wear and tear to a significant degree.[64]

Once again, tenants viewed the situation differently. A survey of public housing tenants in the early 1970s revealed that 57 percent viewed building maintenance favorably. About a third thought that housing authority management was very concerned about maintenance; another third thought it was somewhat concerned. Roughly half of the tenants surveyed thought that their building had stayed the same in recent years; nearly 20 percent thought it had improved. Rabushka and Weissert reported that 62 percent of the Wilmington tenants they interviewed had no problems with management. A 1974 Urban Institute report concluded that, housing authorities were providing housing services that residents viewed favorably.[65]

What data are available do not support the picture of poorly maintained public housing. When the New York authority surveyed its buildings in 1957, it judged that 20 percent suffered from serious vandalism. Ten years later, the authority thought that the vast majority of its projects were satisfactorily maintained. Of the 123 projects, four had unsatisfactory open spaces; seven had mechanical maintenance problems; and ten had structural problems. In the late 1970s, HUD considered no more than 7 percent of projects troubled. A 1980 national evaluation judged the vast majority of public housing buildings to be in good condition. Rehabilitation was needed to counteract aging, wear and tear, minor vandalism and changes in building codes but the overall condition was good.[66]

The New York authority was cognizant of the challenges maintenance posed. As early as 1943, senior officials were aware that wear and tear in large, high-rise buildings might necessitate different approaches. Highly glazed surfaces on hallway walls and grills over windows might be needed. By the middle 1950s, the authority concluded that construction materials and methods used during the Second World War represented false economies. The buildings constructed during the war, including Fort Greene, did not withstand heavy usage well. In 1957, the authority renovated the Fort Greene buildings, installing new plumbing and replacing wooden doors with metal ones. The New York authority prided itself on having adequate maintenance staff in place, in the early 1950s one employee for every 20 families and a caretaker in every building.[67]

Impact

Parkchester, Stuyvesant Town and other privately built developments in New York were at least as big, had as many high-rise buildings, and were almost as densely populated as any public housing project. Critics struggled to explain why a collection of tall buildings could work in some instances but not in public housing. The problem was especially acute for those that claimed that the buildings found in the allegedly typical public housing development were not just unattractive but had deleterious effects on the tenants. A mid–1960s article offered three reasons that high-density housing was okay for middle- and upper-income families but not for poor families. It claimed that more affluent families could afford to spend time away from their apartments, on vacation or otherwise, while poor families could not. Rents were higher in middle- or upper-income developments and, therefore, the buildings were more attractive inside and outside. The article maintained that there was no stigma attached to living in the middle- or upper-income apartment complex.[68]

The supposedly noxious effects of public housing's architecture were central to Oscar Newman's analysis. He expended considerable effort explaining why the same designs did not have the same effects in other housing. He argued that more affluent families did not spend as much time in their apartments and that high-rise buildings elsewhere were more attractively decorated. He added that some apartments intended for higher income families included balconies, which were rare in public housing.

Newman ignored developments like Parkchester and argued that public housing developments were generally larger than other housing developments. Consistent with Newman's focus on crime, he claimed that public housing lacked the doormen, guards and resident superintendents commonly found in apartment complexes built for better-off families. Finally, he shifted his focus away from the buildings to the tenants. He argued that families with children rarely predominated in middle- or upper-income apartment buildings and that middle-income children were supervised more carefully and taught better behavior than poor children.[69]

Nathan Glazer argued that the tenants' "social circumstances," not its architecture, created the ills detected in public housing. The "jungle" was not created by the 20-story apartment building. To the extent that architecture adversely affected tenants, its "deviant" nature was at fault. The distinctive character of public housing had come to symbolize lives set apart, of lives in a "ghetto."[70]

Blame

For those who disliked high-rise construction and other aspects of public housing's structures, the PHA made a convenient target. The PHA already had its critics. Local authorities complained about interference from Washington throughout the 1950s. Critics talked about miles of red tape and "over-caution" and "manualization" in Washington. The PHA remained fixated on reducing costs, even beyond the limits established in legislation. Before the end of the Truman regime, it added guidance about minimum densities for construction types. One-story row houses had to be at least 15 to the acre; two-story apartment houses, 36 to the acre; and multi-story apartments, 50 to the acre. Such limits offered a ready explanation for the increase in tall apartment buildings.[71]

Nonetheless, a 1975 analysis absolved the cost and density guidance, but not the PHA, of responsibility. The study contended that local authorities could have remained within the PHA's cost limits and met its density targets without building high-rise buildings. To do so, however, they would have had to reduce the number of units. It pointed to pre–1949 low-rise projects that had managed densities of 45 units per acre or higher. It made the point that, since federal funds covered all construction costs, local authorities had no incentive to reduce total construction costs, only to remain within the per-unit or per-room limits. In 1950, the PHA told local authorities that apartment buildings higher than three stories were the least livable arrangement, especially poor families raising children. Such buildings would be appropriate only if they were the only solution that met local conditions. The PHA's guidance remained silent on high-rise construction until the 1960s. The 1975 study argued that it was this silence was the problem. The PHA could have banned high-rise construction, but did not.[72]

To what extent were architects and architectural styles responsible for public housing allegedly inferior buildings? Some critics, often architects, placed the blame on the PHA's guidelines and local housing authorities' decision. Obsessed with lowering costs, federal and local agencies had created a situation where architects could not do good work. Officials insisted on low construction costs and were content with plain, repetitious designs. Architects might draw up interesting schemes, as Yamasaki had done for Pruitt-Igoe, only to be told that they were incompatible with decisions the local authority had already made or that cost limits dictated modifications. In other instances, local authorities, it was alleged, hired inferior architects and relied on stock plans.[73]

The architects' critique could be largely an aesthetic one, with only limited connection to how the housing suited the inhabitants. Uniqueness was more important to architects than to others. As in earlier periods, the fact that public housing often included many similar buildings represented, for at least some architects, a failure. Repetitive, standardized designs were not architecture, but merely shelter engineering in Percival Goodman's view.[74]

Others, less frequently architects, blamed the then current taste for Modernist architecture. Planners and designers were allegedly enamored of the ideas of Le Corbusier and other European architects and had imposed them, inappropriately, on American cities and on poor families. Commentators noted the similarity between the "towers in a park" design and Le Corbusier's ideas and assigned him the blame for public housing's supposed ills. Galleries and skip-stop elevators were also considered unhelpful imports.[75]

By the middle 1960s, Catherine Bauer had reconsidered her views on public housing architecture. It was not that the Modernist style was flawed or harmful or even inappropriate for housing. Instead she thought that the architects and planners had prematurely and inappropriately settled on a set pattern. Notions that had been new and cathartic had become rigid. The designers of public housing in the United States had allowed their work to become overly institutional. They failed to translate Modernist ideas into useful social architecture.[76]

Bauer came to believe that she and other housing advocates had misread historical trends. The European architects who influenced Bauer focused on providing essential housing, the minimum standards for housing. Housing legislation in the United States did the same. Bauer saw this as a reaction to the economic conditions of 1930s, when growth did not seem possible and the best use of existing resources seemed to be the right goal. The post-war period proved very different. Technology, rising incomes, and a growing population created new possibilities. "Decent, safe and sanitary" housing no longer seemed sufficient and yet it remained the goal of public housing. In the 1930s, standardization and collectivism seemed the way forward. Events in the United States had proved otherwise. Variety and individualism became more important. The version of public housing implemented in the United States was, from Bauer's perspective in the middle 1960s, a relic of the 1930s and unsuited to American conditions.[77]

Tenants' Views

Public housing tenants generally thought their housing was better than where they have lived before, but they too could be critical of the buildings and their surroundings. A 1946 survey of tenants in Chicago public housing indicated that they did not like the ways the housing authority had economized. Small bedrooms, insufficient closets, the absence of closet and kitchen doors, concrete floors and ceilings, all elicited complaints. A New York survey about the same time revealed the same opinions. A PHA survey in 1945 reported that tenants preferred one and two story buildings to high-rise apartments. Outside space of one's own, where children could play, was cited as an important reason for preferring low-rise buildings. When Lee Rainwater studied Pruitt-Igoe in the middle 1960s, tenants said that they preferred apartments that opened onto the much-criticized galleries because they were that much closer to the outside. Oscar Newman attributed a preference for low-rise buildings in large part to concerns about status. Tenants, like other Americans, considered the single-family house the ideal. A row house, Newman claimed, was seen as closer to that ideal than an apartment.[78]

Tenants were far more critical of the area outside their public housing apartments. Whereas Rainwater reported that 80 percent of Pruitt-Igoe tenants were satisfied with their housing, only 49 percent were satisfied with living in the project. Most wanted to move to a nicer, safer neighborhood.

A mid–1970s survey indicated that more than half of public housing tenants did not like their neighborhood. Tenants complained about a lack of recreation facilities, dirty streets and sidewalks, drug addiction, crime, and noisy neighbors.[79]

It would be unwise to dismiss all the criticisms of public housing construction. Nonetheless, they were usually long on opinion and short of facts or data. None of the critics lived in public housing or spent much time there. With the exception of Oscar Newman, the best critics could normally offer were anecdotes and subsequent analyses have cast doubts on even Newman's conclusions. Few critics attempted to consider a broad range of projects. Most were content to focus on a few, often atypical, examples. What contemporaneous data we have often casts doubts on commonly held beliefs.[80]

The criticisms of public housing construction demonstrate how far public housing, especially the public housing that attracted the most attention, had strayed from the ideas of the early reformers, especially the community planners. Most reformers had never, for example, favored high-rise construction. Many had favored large developments separated from existing neighborhoods, but they had also imagined public housing as a humane place where community might flourish. The projects actually built seemed to fall short. The community planners had warned against building new housing in the slums and predicted that doing so would drive housing authorities towards constructing large, tall apartment houses.

The criticisms of public housing also suggest that Americans, even some in New York and even many reformers, resisted innovations in housing. Housing developments that were obviously different garnered little support. The single-family, detached house remained the norm. If anything, the post-war building boom seems to have reinforced its status as the proper housing for American families.

The HOLC maps incorporated the idea that a neighborhood's reputation depended on both the nature of its buildings and the character of its inhabitants. A slum was a slum because both its housing and its inhabitants were somehow unacceptable. Attitudes towards public housing construction appear to bear to support this notion. Public housing design was different from what Americans were accustomed to, but it was reasonably well designed and constructed. It offered low-income families better housing than they were accustomed to. Nevertheless, observers could not get past the idea that these were buildings full of poor people. Stuyvesant Town, built according to the same template but populated by middle-class Americans, was acceptable in ways that public housing was not.

Chapter Six

Tenants

After 1949, the United States underwent important changes. The economy grew steadily, more than doubling by 1970. Poverty declined. The population grew by more than 40 percent, from 149 million to 211 million. Thirty million new housing units were built, most in the suburbs. The composition of the country's urban population changed and American family structures were beginning to change. Against this background, writers and experts debated the character of public housing tenants. Were they ordinary people who happened to be poor or were they dysfunctional in some way? Were they good for public housing? Was public housing good for them?

A Changed Population

By 1980, women headed more U.S. households than in 1940. In 1940, women headed 12.3 percent of U.S. households; by 1980 the percentage had grown to 16.6 percent. For non-white, non–Hispanic households, the percentage grew from 20 percent to 34.5 percent. The number of children living in single-parent families increased. Nine percent of U.S. children in 1960 lived in single-parent families; in 1980 19 percent did. The number of births to unmarried women also increased. In 1940, 3.8 percent of all births (a total of 89,500) were to unmarried women. In 1973, 13 percent (or 407,300 births) were to unmarried women.[1]

Poverty declined after the war, but not equally for all groups. Estimates of poverty that take into account a household's total money income show poverty declining from over 40 percent in 1949 to 13.1 percent in 1979. The poverty rate in 1979 was lowest for white households where husband and wife worked (2.4 percent) and highest for non-white, non–Hispanic households headed by a woman who did not work (69.5 percent) and Hispanic households headed by a woman who did not work (72.1 percent). For households headed by a white, employed woman, the poverty rate in 1979 was 19.6 percent. For households headed by an African American, employed woman, the poverty rate was 32.1 percent.[2]

The number of Americans on welfare increased significantly. Changes in southern agriculture and northern manufacturing, the increase in female-headed households, changes in federal and state laws, the emergence of welfare advocacy organizations, and a series of court rulings combined to expand the number of families and people receiving welfare payments. In 1950, the most significant federally mandated program, Aid to Dependent Children (after 1956 Aid to Families with Dependent Children [AFDC]), served 651,000 families that included 2.2 million people, children and their parent or caretaker. In 1975, AFDC payments went to 3.5 million families that included 10.4 million people. Whereas only about a third of eligible families received payments in the early 1960s, 90 percent did in 1971.[3]

The Public Housing Population

Between 1949 and 1973, the tenant population in public housing changed. Households became poorer compared to the rest of the population. Households were more likely to be headed by a single mother and were likely to include more children. Tenants were more likely to be unemployed and to be welfare recipients. They were more likely to be African Americans. Data about the tenant population are far from complete and conditions varied from city to city, but the trends are clear.

In real terms, the incomes of public housing households remained little changed in the period. Between 1944 and 1957, the median annual income for both households entering public housing and being reexamined for continued occupancy in public housing increased in nominal terms. In 1944, the figures are roughly $1,200 and $1,500; in 1957 they were $2,100 and $2,200. In real terms, the median annual incomes remained constant or even increased slightly in this period. The Douglas Commission concluded that the incomes of public housing households between 1956 and 1966 remained more or less constant in real terms. Data from 1970 indicate that that the trend continued through the end of the sixties.[4]

Compared to other families public housing tenants did less well. In 1950, the average annual median income for public housing families was about 45 percent of the national family median income and about 80 percent of the African American families' median income. Through 1961, the relationship between public housing incomes and the national averages appears to have remained about the same. Between 1960 and 1972, however, the national median family income increased by 90 percent, while the median income for public housing tenants increased by only 21 percent. By 1970, public housing incomes had declined to about 37 percent of national family median income and 55 percent of African American families' median income. By the middle of the decade, families in public housing were earning only about a quarter of what families nationwide earned and 37 percent of what African American families were earning. Public housing tenants as a group went from being merely poor to being dramatically poor.[5]

The make-up of public housing families underwent parallel changes. Public housing initially gave preference to two-parent families with children. The elderly became eligible in 1956. One observer claimed that in the early 1940s females headed fewer than 10 percent of public housing families. Reports suggest that, through the mid–60s, two-parent families still represented more than half of all public housing families, perhaps as much as two-thirds. By the time of the National Housing Policy Review in the middle 1970s, the percentage of public housing families headed by females had grown to nearly 60 percent. In families with incomes less than $3,000, a female was the head of household in 68 percent. By the middle 1970s, 40 percent of tenants were elderly. Despite the increase in elderly tenants, children comprised a large and growing proportion of the tenant population. In 1956, children under 21 made up more than half the tenant population. In 1968, children comprised two-thirds of the tenants in Chicago public housing. In Boston in the late 1960s, school-aged children were 26 percent of the public housing population, whereas in the city as a whole they were only 12 percent. The average number of minors per housing unit ranged from 1.4 in Cleveland and Minneapolis, where more than half the public housing units were occupied by the elderly, to more than three per unit in Chicago, Los Angeles, St. Louis and Washington.[6]

Social workers from the Union Settlement in East Harlem, concerned as they were about the demise of urban communities, catalogued the differences between the population of the George Washington Carver Houses and the housing it had replaced in 1958. Seven percent of the old neighborhood earned more than $4,000 a year, the upper limit for admission to the new project. As a result, the new project housed more poor people, laborers and clerical workers, and fewer of the slightly better off, schoolteachers, small business proprietors, and professionals, than the old neighborhood. The old neighborhood had housed 3,255 families and 1,420 "unrelated individuals." The new housing was limited to families of two or more; almost none of the single adults resident in the old neighborhood found places there. Construction of the new project nearly doubled the number of children under five in the neighborhood and cut the number of people over 45 in half.[7]

In the early 1950s, about 30 percent of public housing tenants received some form of public assistance, including Social Security; about a quarter of families moving into public housing did so. By 1957, these percentages had increased to nearly 40 percent and 32 percent. Over the same period, the percentage of public housing families with no employed adult increased from 25 to 32 percent. These trends continued until, in 1970, 48 percent of white families and 53 percent of non-white families in public housing received public assistance, including Social Security, and nearly 40 percent of all public housing families had no employed adult. In Chicago in 1950, 27 percent of public housing families received public assistance. In the Robert Taylor Homes, the percentage of AFDC families increased from 36 percent to more than 80 percent between 1967 and 1974. The percentage of working families declined from 50 percent to 10 percent. In New York, where the housing authority resisted admitting welfare recipients, the percentage of welfare families increased from 12 percent in 1960 to 34 percent in 1973. In Wilmington's public housing, welfare families increased from 35 to 71 percent in the same period.[8]

The number of non-white tenants increased. In 1952, about 40 percent of tenant families re-examined for continued occupancy were classified as non-white. The percentage had changed little from 1944. By the middle 1970s, the percentage had grown to 60 percent. In some cities and projects, it was much higher. In the late 1960s, more than 90 percent of public housing tenants in St. Louis and Washington were non-white, almost all African Americans. Almost everyone in the Chicago's Robert Taylor Homes was an African American. On the other hand, in the Twin Cities and Pittsburgh, the percentage of non-white residents was less than 25 percent.[9]

All these trends came together in the Pruitt-Igoe project. Nearly all the tenants were African Americans. In the 1965, half of Pruitt-Igoe families depended on public assistance of some kind and women headed half of Pruitt-Igoe families. Only 30 percent included husband, wife and children. Two-thirds of the nearly 10,000 inhabitants were children; 25 percent of all children were less than six years old. Fewer than 900 of the inhabitants were adult men. The median family income was $2,454, relatively high for St. Louis public housing, but because of the large number of children, the per capita income was less than $500 per year.[10]

Pruitt-Igoe was not typical of public housing in the middle 1960s. Nevertheless, for the debate about public housing, the key point is that the poor, welfare-dependent, African American family headed by a woman and including several young children came to be identified with public housing. The population that Rainwater portrayed in St. Louis came to stand for all public housing tenants.[11]

Perceived changes in the tenant population became central to discussions of public housing. Lawrence Friedman, writing in the middle 1960s, produced an oft-quoted description. According to Friedman, the original public housing tenants were perceived as part of the middle class, "submerged" by the Great Depression. They were articulate citizens, "angry and dispirited by their unjust descent into poverty." They were not the "dregs of society," but people of high demands and high expectations who insisted on decent housing.[12]

Several writers elaborated on the nature of the new tenants. They were from "special deprived groups with chronically low incomes." They were African Americans faced with discrimination, the aged unable to work or on small pensions, the broken family and the family with no wage earner. They were "severely disorganized" families. They were depressed, untutored and dependent, "alcohol and dope ridden, criminally disposed, mentally and physically unfit." Instead of housing normal people and families, public housing had come to house "inadequate personalities and problem type persons." They allegedly brought with them a host of personal and social ills, from feeble-mindedness to sexual deviation, and from juvenile delinquency to extreme poverty and inadequate housekeeping.[13]

In the simplest version of the changed tenant story, normal, white, working but temporarily poor families gave way to abnormal, African American, unemployed and permanently poor families. Sometime after the war, as the economy boomed, the capable families increased their incomes, found better housing, perhaps purchased a single-family house and moved out. Public housing functioned as a "way station," a stepping-stone to a better life, not as a permanent alternative to private housing. In some accounts, providing a boost to the middle class became public housing's real purpose and the fact that it no longer seemed to be doing so counted against it. Worse yet, the persistent image was that once poor families moved in, they never moved out. No longer a stepping-stone, public housing had become a sinkhole where the poor remained trapped.[14]

In most accounts, the key changes took place in the early 1950s, not in the late 1960s, when, in fact, the tenant population did change significantly. Observers pointed to the 1949 Act and its provisions giving preference to the most needy and to those displaced by urban renewal. Income limits came in for their share of blame as well. To a lesser extent, critics pointed to the subsequent admission of the elderly to public housing. Faced with the need to house displaced families, housing authorities, it was argued, relaxed their selection criteria and admitted less capable, less worthy families. Once such families were in place, they changed the project's atmosphere, making it less attractive to normal families. From there, public housing began a downward spiral, at each turn losing capable families and having to settle for more problem families.[15]

In the mid–1950s, Elizabeth Wood, one-time head of the Chicago Housing Authority, was the most prominent proponent of the downward spiral notion. Wood objected to income limits. She believed that tenants resented the annual income reviews and the increased rent and possibility of eviction that they brought. Administering a means test pushed working families out of public housing, she believed. The bigger problem was the character of the families who filled the resultant vacancies. Wood argued that, while the earliest public housing projects included some "bad families," they were inconspicuous. Tenants had created their own communities without management's intervention. Before 1949, housing officials could be comfortable in the view that people did not cause slums. With the arrival of families displaced by urban renewal, however, Wood thought conditions were different. The displaced families brought with them disorderly behavior and low standards. With their arrival, juvenile delinquency, prostitution, and crime increased. Most important, their presence gave public housing a bad reputation. Wood was convinced that the tenant population was changing for the worse because more capable, intact, working families refused to live in public housing. She argued that, by the late 1950s, the only families willing to be considered low-income were "the apathetic, the damaged, the problem families and those restricted to the fulfillment of their aspirations by their race or color."[16]

Although the tenant population changed and became relatively poorer from the end of the war until the mid–1970s, what we know about the movement of individual families does not support the notion of public housing as a trap. Families moved in and out of public housing regularly. Throughout the 1950s, families left public housing at about the same rate that families in general moved. From 1950 to 1957, the annual move-out rate for public housing families was never lower than 22 percent and was as high, during 1956, as 27 percent. As of 1970, 70 percent of white families and 60 percent of non-white families had been in public housing for three or fewer years.[17]

Some commentators saw problems in such statistics. Anthony Wallace thought a turnover rate of nearly 29 percent in a Philadelphia project signaled an unstable community. Chester Hartman conceded that turnover in public housing was no greater than in the general population. He argued, nevertheless, that it should have been lower because public housing provided superior housing at lower rents. Hartman thought that public housing tenants were less likely than members of the middle class to move for job-related reasons. Hartman concluded that if public housing did not suffer from other problems, tenants would be staying longer.[18]

Income Rules

Until 1959, the maximum income allowed for a family entering public housing was set by federal law, basically five times the rent. Subject to approval by the PHA, housing authorities were responsible for setting rents, keeping in mind the requirement that the rent remain 20 percent below the lowest rent charged in private housing, and for setting income limits, both for admittance and continued occupancy. Usually, the income limit for remaining in public housing was about 25 percent above the limit for initial admittance. Income limits varied according to family size. In 1959, the Congress yielded to complaints from housing authorities and gave them greater flexibility in establishing income limits.

Since rents and therefore income limits were tied to the local rental real estate market, they varied across the country. At the high end, the maximum income for a family of four in New York public housing in 1967 was $5,760; in Chicago, $4,600. At the low end, the limit in Fort Worth was $2,700 and in New Orleans $3,000. In New York, the limits ranged from $3,888 for a single person to $7,896 for a family of 12.[19]

Throughout, housing authorities faced contradictory pressures. Their mandate to provide decent housing to low-income families pushed them towards lower rents and lower income limits. Their need to cover operating and maintenance costs pushed them towards higher rents and income limits. A particular issue was the treatment of families whose incomes increased above the limits.

The first and largest group of over-income families posed a highly visible problem. During the Second World War, the families of war workers in several areas found places in public housing despite having incomes above the statutory limits. Forty percent of Baltimore's public housing tenants in 1946 and about a third of Boston's in 1947 were families of war workers. The initial push from Congress after the war was to evict such families, but in the face of a housing shortage and pushback from tenants and others, the rules were relaxed. Nonetheless, the families of war workers eventually moved out of public housing. The PHA reported that whereas 25 percent (nearly 42,000 families) of public housing tenants in June 1948 had excessive incomes, housing authorities had reduced the figure to 13 percent by December 1949. By 1953, over-income families were only about 8 percent of the tenant population. By this time, they would have included families other than those of war workers.[20]

Over-income families comprised a much smaller proportion of the tenant population in later years. The Douglas Commission reported that they were only 3.3 percent of the total in 1966. Nevertheless, they remained a concern for housing authorities and the Congress. In 1967, the New York authority's policies allowed them to stay regardless of any excess income. The 1961 Housing Act authorized housing authorities to allow them to stay if they could not find standard housing at an affordable price.[21]

The income rules remained a controversial topic. Critics and supporters of public housing criticized them. Some thought them too high; some too low. Usually, the concern was not their tie to the housing authorities' financial situation but to their impact on the nature of the tenant population.

In the early 1950s, public housing's opponents in Congress complained that it did not serve the lowest income groups. They were worried that income limits were high enough that public housing might compete with private housing. Similar concerns persisted through the late 1950s. Critics charged that housing authorities used inflated estimates of private rents to set their own rents, did not check incomes properly and did not evict over-income families. Those more favorably disposed towards public housing complained that income limits were too high. Many needy families could not afford public housing. Surveys in the middle 1960s revealed that 7 percent of families in the District of Columbia were so poor that they could not afford public housing and that 30 percent of families who rented housing in New York City were in the same situation. Several critics bemoaned that fact that the nation's principal housing program for low-income families did not serve those with the lowest incomes.[22]

The more common complaint was that the income limits were too low. Elizabeth Wood thought that New York's limits in the late 1950s were arbitrary. Family incomes were likely to fall above or below them from year to year without the family's circumstances changing significantly. Charles Abrams was only one of several who thought that the income limits represented a disincentive for economic improvement. Why should a government housing program penalize families because someone had gotten a raise? Ira Robbins warned that evicting over-income families would send them back to substandard housing. Families might earn too much to qualify for public housing, but they did not necessarily earn enough to pay for decent housing in the private housing market. If housing authorities enforced the statutory 20 percent gap between their rents and the lowest rents in the private sector, the chances of an over-income family finding decent housing would be especially slim. The notion that over-income families should be able to stay in public housing until they could find other decent housing gained considerable support by the early 1960s.[23]

Critics thought that income limits deprived public housing of its most capable residents and its leaders. According to Elizabeth Wood, "middle status" people were the neighborhood leaders. They had organized the recreation committees and other collective efforts in public housing before the war. According to Wood, lower status people viewed groups like the PTA as foreign to their lives. If public housing was to succeed, it needed to retain the "urbanized, higher standard" families. For other writers, families who increased their incomes were the more "disciplined families," the "more energetic, ambitious and responsible tenants," and the "more intelligent, skillful, and emotionally better adjusted" families. Albert Mayer thought that permitting over-income families to remain was the single most important measure for public housing to succeed.[24]

Discussions of income limits proceeded, in nearly all cases, without benefit of any real data. Data from St. Louis public housing suggest that having too little income to live in public housing was a far more common problem than having too much. Between 1954 and 1969, nearly 17,000 tenants left St. Louis public housing. Only 393 (or 2.3 percent) left because their income was too high. On the other hand, 642 left because the rents were too high and another 2,081 left without notice, but presumably because they were delinquent in their rent. Together, these two groups comprise nearly 15 percent of the tenants who moved out.[25]

Another study, of tenants leaving Buffalo, New York, public housing over a two-year period in the early 1960s, provides a glimpse of how public housing and public housing tenants fit within the larger housing market.

The study was based on a 10 percent sample, a total of 223 families, chosen to create two groups separated by income. About 60 percent of the families earned less than $4,000 a year; the other 40 percent earned more than $4,000 a year. Ten percent of those earning more than $4,000 were African American; half the poorer families were African American. Only 3 percent of the better-off families received welfare; at least 25 percent of the poorer families did. Three quarters of the better-off families moved into standard housing. None moved into a blighted or slum neighborhood. The families from the better-off group that moved into substandard housing were more likely to be African American and to be relatively large, with four or more persons. Eighty-five percent of the poorer category moved into substandard housing. Twenty-seven percent moved into a neighborhood considered blighted. Of the seven poorer families who purchased homes, five were in blighted neighborhoods and were substandard. None of the poorer families who moved into standard housing were African American or received welfare.[26]

Screening Applicants

Housing authorities continued to screen applicants and enforce rules. Policies varied but it appears that authorities rejected applications from those that abused alcohol or drugs, had criminal records, had borne out-of-wedlock children, whose homes were untidy, or who had irregular work histories. In 1953, the New York housing authority adopted a list of 21 "moral factors" on which to judge applications for public housing. The Boston authority applied 15 similar criteria. New York also sought to limit the number of welfare recipients accepted for public housing. In 1957 it adopted a policy that no family receiving welfare would be accepted into a project where welfare recipients were already 20 percent or more of the tenant population.[27]

By the middle 1960s, housing authorities' rules and their procedures for screening, fining, and evicting tenants had provoked opposition among tenants, welfare advocates, and lawyers concerned about civil rights. In New York, lawyers associated with the youth services and advocacy organization Mobilization for Youth saw the New York housing authority's rules and procedures as arbitrary, based on inappropriate middle-class values, and violations of tenants' individual rights. In response to lawsuits filed by such lawyers, the courts ordered changes. Housing authorities could not deny access or evict a family because of the presence of out-of-wedlock children. Housing authorities had to use a reasonable and consistent system for screening applicants and had to give preference to those with the greatest need. In a series of decisions, the courts applied logic used in earlier rulings about welfare and ruled that public housing tenants were entitled to due process regarding acceptance, evictions and alleged rule violations.[28]

As the number of welfare recipients increased across the country, pressure to house them in public housing increased. A 1968 study funded by the Department of Health, Education and Welfare reported that at least half of all welfare recipients, both the elderly and families, lived in substandard or overcrowded housing. A 1973 work argued that being a welfare recipient in New York was a greater barrier to obtaining good housing than being African American or Hispanic. Much of the pressure was at the grass roots, with public aid caseworkers trying to find better housing for their clients. Some was more public. Mitchell Ginsburg, New York's welfare commissioner, told a congressional committee that welfare recipients in his city were not getting their fair share of public housing. New York's 21 moral factors included behaviors that were endemic in the welfare population, Ginsburg contended.[29]

Housing authority practices changed. Authorities established new procedures for screening applications. New York dropped its 21 criteria. The general sense was now that authorities, including New York, were more willing to accept welfare families. Authorities established new procedures for enforcing rules and evicting tenants. The Department of Housing and Urban Development, after negotiations with the National Tenants Organization and the National Housing Law Project, developed a model lease and a model grievance procedure for public housing. The Department agreed that eight clauses formerly considered standard in public housing leases were unfair and unreasonable.[30]

Some critics agreed with the public interest lawyers. Selection criteria were based, they claimed, on unexamined assumptions and preconceptions. Why should single mothers be excluded? Or people who did not meet middle-class standards in speech and demeanor? Others argued that the selection process was often flawed and based on incorrect or incomplete information. Often a single official could impose his or her prejudices on the entire tenant population. Alvin Schorr reported that a review of the New York authority's rejection of 82 families showed that 33 should have been accepted. Others objected that the selection process ignored the fate of those it rejected. The assumption was that any family rejected for public housing would struggle to find decent housing.[31]

Still others saw housing authorities creating a hostile, institutionalized environment. They argued that the rules made no sense to children and they were apt to resist them. Housing officials worried about public housing's image had reverted to an authoritarian approach, introducing rules far more complex than private landlords, one critic argued. Another worried that the procedures and rules were doomed to failure because imposing middle-class values on poor people was impossible. Ellen Lurie thought the government as landlord was the problem. Public housing was impersonal, bureaucratic and afflicted with red tape in ways, she claimed, that private housing was not.[32]

On the other hand, housing experts who embraced the notion that public housing was intended to transform or rehabilitate tenants considered careful screening and vigorous rules enforcement vital. Anthony Wallace thought that rules were far more effective in inculcating middle-class values than improved housing. For another writer, public housing offered the possibility of creating a "total environment" in which social services could be successfully offered to poor families. Public housing could be a stable environment in which a community could be rebuilt. For Agnes Meyer, wife of the *Washington Post*'s publisher, evicting mothers of illegitimate children was part of the battle against illegitimacy. She thought that women who had several out-of-wedlock children were often mentally deficient. Preventing them from having more children was necessary to defend civilization.[33]

Less optimistic observers saw screening and rules simply as the means of preserving public housing. If problem tenants were not barred, no one would want to live there, they wrote. Alcoholics, drug addicts, unwed mothers, and families inclined to cause trouble had to be kept out. Otherwise conditions in the projects would deteriorate and conscientious families would have no opportunity to improve themselves. Outsiders would withdraw their support. You could not manage public housing as if it were a middle-class apartment house. Housing officials were no longer dealing with the working poor or the "submerged middle class." Screening was essential to preserve the program. Problems had to be dealt with before families were admitted to public housing.[34]

For such writers, the courts' intervention on behalf of public housing tenants was a disaster. Recognizing tenants' due process rights made it more difficult for public housing projects to function. It had made enforcing rules and evicting tenants difficult and costly. Housing officials were now less likely to act. According to J.S. Fuerst, who had worked for the Chicago authority, judges and lawyers had used the high ideals of the 14th

Amendment to bludgeon housing authorities to death and the tenants were the real victims.[35]

Communities of the Poor

Parallel to concerns about the departure of over-income families were concerns that communities comprised only of poor people were bad for the residents and bad for public housing. The steady increase in the number of welfare recipients in public housing provided a ready index for the increasing poverty of tenants. In New York, where the housing authority had resisted housing welfare families, the percentage of tenants receiving welfare grew from 13 percent in 1956 to 16 percent in 1961 and to 26 percent in 1970. According to Harrison Salisbury, public housing in New York had become a "catch basin for the dregs of society." It lacked the capability to help itself. It breed "endless social ills" and constituted "an ever replenishing vessel for trouble." It was a "built-in consumer of limitless social assistance." Some public housing projects had become monsters, "devouring their residents." They polluted the area around them and spewed "a social excrescence" which infected the whole of society.[36]

Discussions about neighborhoods inhabited solely by the poor led to discussions about the poor themselves and their behavior and how it affected their surroundings. Mirroring a larger debate, writers concerned with public housing disagreed. Some thought that poor people were ordinary Americans who happened to be poor. If their behavior seemed different, it was because they were coping with difficult circumstances. Others thought that some or all of the poor were dysfunctional. And dysfunctional poor families came to be seen as a threat to public housing.

While Lee Rainwater's research at Pruitt-Igoe, especially *Behind Ghetto Walls*, was located in public housing, it was less about the housing itself than about the behavior of poor people. Rainwater's basic conclusion was that what seemed to outsiders as unreasonable behavior on the part of poor people represented their efforts to cope with the predicaments and opportunities they encountered in the world. The world inhabited by the poor presented them with two basic problems, according to Rainwater. They did not have enough money to live the way average Americans did and they found themselves living among people in the same situation. They learned over time that other poor people could pose a threat to them and that their communities could not expect good public or private services. In the end, Rainwater's solution had little to do with housing. He argued that the United States had to deal with the underlying income inequality if it wanted to deal with poverty and its consequences.[37]

Alvin Schoor's *Slums and Insecurity*, a report prepared for the Department of Health, Education and Welfare, took a similar stance. Schorr argued that poor people perceived the city differently from middle class. They were more closely tied to their neighborhood. They preferred the familiar and intimate to the open and challenging. Changes like urban renewal had a greater impact on the poor than on others. The fundamental reason was the poor's lesser capacity to bend events to their will. They lacked the money, contacts and attitudes needed to influence events. They were at the mercy of events.[38]

Nevertheless, as early as the middle 1950s, negative ideas about the poor and public housing coalesced into a consistent narrative. It appeared even in a 1957 Public Housing Administration circular. The narrative held that many, if not most, poor people and families were dysfunctional in some way. Those most likely to be dysfunctional were unmarried women and their children. If allowed into public housing, the deviant behaviors of such people created problems for housing managers. They damaged the buildings. Their presence and the damage they caused undermined the quality of life in projects and damaged public housing's image. Normal families moved out and other normal families did not want to move in. Support for public housing declined.[39]

One thread held that people created slums and damaged public housing. Miles Colean, a longtime housing expert, argued in the late 1950s that the perceived deterioration in public housing was the work of tenants. Slums were the product of the people who lived in them. Daniel Seligman, in an oft-cited contribution to William Whyte's *The Exploding Metropolis*, quoted an un-named housing official to the effect that better housing did not improve people. Housing officials may have anticipated that moving problem families into better housing would improve their behavior, but they proved to be "the same bunch of bastards they always were." Seligman argued that slums did not create crime and disease. Instead they attracted problem families. An anonymous respondent to the HHFA's survey about public housing commented, "The occupants of a palace could turn it into a slum."[40]

In another variant, poor families, especially families who had recently migrated to the cities, could not cope with urban life. According to Seligman, migrants tended to be semi-literate, low income, of rural origins and members of racial minorities. Their impoverished rural backgrounds were key. They did not know how to live in cities. Their standards of sanitation were low; they didn't understand building maintenance. Agnes Meyer told the National Association of Housing and Redevelopment Officials that expecting recent migrants from the South or Puerto Rico to develop middle-class standards over night was absurd. They could not overcome a long background of deprivation quickly. The National Federation of Settlements and Neighborhood Centers told the Senate that many alleged problem families came from parts of the county "where facilities were meager and educational standards low."[41]

Michael Harrington framed the problem in terms of a culture of poverty. Borrowing a concept usually attributed to the anthropologist Oscar Lewis, Harrington saw poor people, including public housing tenants, caught in a vicious circle. Defeated in attempts at improvement, the residents of what Harrington saw as a new kind of slum became listless and passive. The slum dweller's lack of aspiration and ideals decreased his chances of advancement still further. Observers saw such people, the poor families trapped in "imprisoning and self-perpetuating" circumstances, occupying a disproportionate and unhealthy share of public housing.[42]

Harrington and others thought that family structure and composition were at the heart of the problem. The Douglas Commission noted that over 40 percent of families in public housing in 1966 included only a single parent, usually a woman, 9 percentage points higher than ten years earlier. Harrington thought the old, ethnic slum had been centered on stable family life. In his view, the new slum was characterized by serial monogamy, women living with one man for a period, bearing his children, and then moving on to another man. Ray Vicker, writing in the *Wall Street Journal*, saw public housing filled with "broken families, families with big broods of children by nameless fathers." Another writer described a social world "dominated by women, women hostile to men, needing men and trying to keep from being overwhelmed by the problems of a woman managing alone, bringing up children poor." The number of children in public housing drew particular attention. According to one account, the presence of large families was the single largest factor behind crime, vandalism and social dysfunction in public housing.[43]

Still another variant focused on substance abuse, mental illness, sexual behavior and emotional problems as key factors in poverty and in allegedly poor conditions in public housing. At a minimum the presence of people who exhibited "extreme behavior deviations" gave public housing a bad name. Coleman Woodbury and Agnes Meyer thought such "deviant" people did not belong in public housing at all or, if they did, only in limited numbers. Concerns about such behaviors account in part for the concept of the "multi-problem family," families "weighted by various adversities associated with chronically low income." Such families suffered from various ills and needed extensive social and other services, but often showed little interest in changing. Roughly 45 percent of housing authorities queried thought such families did not belong in public housing.[44]

Much of the discussion of problem families or multi-problem families owed something to Elizabeth Wood's 1957 study, *The Small Hard Core*, an analysis of families living in a New York housing project. At Wood's request, housing managers identified 109 families (from a total of 1,526 apartments) that they considered problem families. Wood reported that for only 12 families rent delinquency and poor housekeeping were the only problems reported. All the other families suffered more than one other condition Wood considered problematic. Her list of problems was extensive. Some families were single-parent families or included illegitimate children. Adults had been arrested for narcotics or other major crimes. They abused alcohol or drugs. Children chronically misbehaved and the behavior of adults put children at risk. For Wood, these problems were significant because they impacted the quality of life within public housing. They disturbed neighbors and brought police into the building. Wood was concerned that such problems needed to be addressed. She accepted that some behaviors should bar families from public housing but her principal concern was that public housing officials and social service agencies work together to address what she saw as problems.[45]

In some accounts, the culture of poverty accounted for only some poverty. Some poor people were in a chronic state of failure and dependency. At the same time, there remained the working poor, people who shared middle-class values and aspired to middle-class status and incomes. Some writers argued that many, if not most, poor families and public housing tenants lead decent, hardworking lives. They were poor because they had fallen on hard times or had large families to support. Given the role Elizabeth Wood played in the discussion of problem families, it is only fair to note that she did not accept the culture of poverty argument, at least not for the vast majority of poor people. In her telling, almost all slum families had a healthy spirit; they were not defeated or hopeless. For Wood, the key test for aspiration was that, according to her, most families resented receiving welfare payments or, even, living in public housing.[46]

The discussion of the dysfunctional poor and public housing reached a climax of sorts in the Roger Starr's 1971 article, "Which of the Poor Shall Live in Public Housing?" Starr came from a well-to-do New York family, managed his family's business and then turned himself into a housing expert and writer. Starr divided the poor into the working poor and the dependent poor. The working poor included the elderly and families headed by employed males. The dependent poor, in Starr's analysis, were predominately families headed by females who were unemployed and received welfare assistance. Starr qualified his critique by saying that not every welfare family suffered from the kinds of psychological problems that made it a menace to its neighbors. Nevertheless, he argued that crime, vandalism and substandard housing conditions proliferated where welfare families lived. New York public housing "worked," he claimed, because it had served the working poor. Allowing members of the dependent poor to fill projects would lead to their deterioration. Once projects visibly deteriorated, the federal government, Starr warned, would be unwilling to fund them.[47]

Some housing officials and experts rejected the problem family theory. They pointed out that a range of behaviors could be, and were, considered problems. Problem tenants could be sloppy housekeepers or psychopaths; noisy neighbors or drug dealers. Some behaviors made a difference to housing managers and other tenants; others did not. Some behaviors were not found only or even primarily in public housing. They might be found in families across society. Perhaps the only consistent feature was that a housing manager or some other outsider considered them a problem.

Commenting on an analysis of alleged problem families, Lee Rainwater asserted that it was not clear to whom such families were a problem—to the housing manager, themselves or the taxpayer. Nor was it clear what their problems were. Rainwater argued that rather than participating in a culture of poverty or being psychologically ill, the families that came to the attention of housing managers were struggling to adapt to their straitened circumstances. As poor Americans, they found certain behaviors, stable family structures, for example, difficult and other behaviors, desertion and impermanent sexual liaisons, much easier.[48]

When managers' assessments of tenants were analyzed, they could prove unreliable. Reacting to Starr's article, Richard Scobie looked at the families housing managers in the Boston housing authority considered problems. Managers identified relatively few problem families, no more than 4.1 percent in any project. The families identified showed no clear profile. Identity, size of family, source of income, age of children, and other characteristics showed to relationship to problem status. Scobie found no correlation between the presence of alleged problem families and the areas within projects that managers considered problem areas. He found little connection between the families managers identified and any complaints recorded by the authority. Scobie concluded that families appeared to managers as problems largely because of their interaction with their immediate neighbors, not because they harmed the buildings or did other damage. When Rabushka and Weissert tried to find tenants who generated excessive costs for the Wilmington housing authority, either rent in arrears or extra maintenance, they found none. A 1980 study of managers' perceptions and actual complaints or maintenance issues in a small southern city yielded similar results. Complaints were far fewer than managers' perceived and there was no obvious connection between alleged problem families and maintenance expenses. A HUD study in 1970 found no correlation between the presence of welfare families and high costs for maintenance and operations.[49]

Starr's response to Scobie's analysis was that even 3 or 4 percent of the tenant population could disrupt an apartment building. Starr was not alone in this argument, nor was he the first to make it. In the early 1950s, Anthony Wallace had written about the damage a "small number of dirty, disorderly, quarrelsome, emotionally disturbed and sometime criminal persons" could cause. Elizabeth Wood argued that the 7 percent of the tenant population she identified as having problems could have a greater impact than their numbers might suggest.[50]

Several writers thought that uniformly poor neighborhoods were bad for their residents. The most common complaint was that, as Elizabeth Wood argued, they lacked the "capable, honest and ambitious" that could provide leadership. You could not have a good neighborhood with just the "damaged, non-normal, and deceitful." Other writers thought that lack of exposure to people with middle-class aspirations confirmed poor people in their current standards of behavior. Rather than assuming citizen responsibilities, they remained lethargic.[51]

Other commentators objected to uniformly poor neighborhoods in principle. Lewis Mumford thought that social ghettos were as bad as racial ghettos. Catherine Bauer thought that residential segregation, whether according to income or identity, was harmful. She wrote that only "feudalistic fascism" or "pure, old-fashioned Marxist communism" could countenance consciously segregating people. Others agreed that there was something repulsive about segregating poor people from the rest of the population, particularly when a government program was the principal tool. It seemed inappropriate in a society that claimed to value social fluidity.[52]

Not everyone agreed that economically and socially diverse neighborhoods were better, especially for low-income families. Chester Hartman thought the arguments for diverse neighborhoods were based on assumption and ideology rather than any concrete evidence. He pointed out that several kinds of observers doubted their wisdom. Economic conservatives worried about incentives if families of different incomes lived in similar housing. Sociologists worried that life style differences between low-income and middle-income families could provoke tensions. Others saw the movement of middle-income families into low-income areas as cultural imperialism that destroyed unity and vitality among low-income families. Alvin Schorr opined that heterogeneous neighborhoods played a role in preventing poverty. The presence of whites and African Americans and of families of varying financial statuses demonstrated that self-improvement was possible. Nonetheless, such neighborhoods did not come about easily and differences could promote conflict and difficulties. Wide gaps among families in the same neighborhood might inspire low-income families to improve their lot, but they could also emphasize the hopelessness of a family's situation.[53]

If uniformly poor neighborhoods were bad for their residents, public housing projects filled with poor people were at least as bad. In Elizabeth Wood's view, income limits motivated tenants to hide any additional income but put them at the mercy of neighbors who might inform management. She thought this produced a noxious atmosphere within public housing. Writers like Michael Harrington and Daniel Seligman thought public housing was cold, impersonal, and cheerless. There was nothing that communicated warmth, compassion or love of one's fellow man. Projects readily became institutions, rather than homes. Tenants were subject to too many rules.[54]

Partly because of the uninviting atmosphere, public housing did not promote communities, the argument continued. Elizabeth Wood, in particular, thought that the size of public housing projects and the design of open spaces militated against a sense of community. Jacobs and Harrington were certain that even the community facilities, like meeting rooms or nurseries, within public housing did not function as they were intended. Tenants kept to themselves and did not know their neighbors. Harrison Salisbury found no political organizing in public housing, no ward bosses as in the old neighborhoods and no tenant organizations. According to Jacobs, attempts at tenant organizing invariably failed.[55]

Because public housing was limited to the poor and increasingly to what observers saw as the dysfunctional poor, critics argued that public housing imposed a stigma on its tenants. In a society that valued social status and economic advancement, they were labeled as low status and poor. Tenants were seen as having low self-esteem. They were humiliated and separated from the rest of society. The Douglas Commission held that living in large public housing projects produced a sense of inferiority, especially in children. Lewis Mumford believed that limiting public housing to the lowest income group would lead to the same slum conditions that had motivated housing activists to promote public housing in the first place.[56]

Critics claimed that public housing bred resentment among the tenants and resentment pushed them to neglect or even damage the buildings. Jacobs argued that few people entered public housing willingly. Most moved in because urban renewal had destroyed their old neighborhoods or because they could not find better housing. According to Jacobs, tenants were unhappy, often angry with housing management and uncomprehending of their new environment. Jacobs wrote about a rectangular lawn in an East Harlem project and how much the tenants hated it. She claimed that it symbolized for the tenants their forced move out of their neighborhoods and into housing designed by others. Oscar Newman saw the impersonal surroundings motivating tenants to treat public housing like a prison. At a minimum they would do nothing to make it nicer.[57]

If public housing did nothing for tenants and, indeed, harmed them, it had failed its principal goal, critics contended. After the 1949 Act, the notion that public housing was intended to transform tenants became a commonplace. The conventional view became that public housing was supposed to eliminate crime and juvenile delinquency, reduce disease and cure whatever social ills slum dwellers suffered. In the best case, it would prepare them to become members of the middle class and owners of their own single-family homes. Public housing was to be a "sociological conveyor belt," taking people from the slums, rehabilitating them and sending them on to their own homes. Lee Rainwater, hardly a critic of public housing, thought the original logic of public housing was that by removing people from the slums and into better housing, their other difficulties would disappear and they would be able to take advantage of opportunities to improve themselves. Writers acknowledged, but minimized, evidence that safe, sanitary housing lowered the incidence of certain diseases or that it reduced overcrowding. Instead an increasingly poor tenant population, afflicted with what were considered social ills and living in deteriorating conditions, demonstrated that public housing had failed and that the original reformers had been wrong.[58]

According to Chester Hartman, the public debate had changed. In his view, housing reformers in the 1930s had focused on housing that was healthier and safer. By the late 1960s, the focus had shifted to a broader set of social issues, ranging from social status to residential choice. A housing program now had to be more than bricks and mortar. Robert Weaver saw better housing as only a part, perhaps a small part, of a social reform program. He told a Senate committee in 1965 that many poor people had needs beyond better housing. Kenneth Clark observed that moving people into better housing without providing better jobs and increased incomes would not break the cycle of poverty. For Albert Mayer, public housing attracted criticisms that were really aimed at social ills that better housing alone could not fix. Public housing was highly visible and made a convenient target.[59]

Evidence that public housing conferred benefits beyond better, cheaper housing was available. The 1962 study *The Housing Environment and Family Life* cited 40 studies that generally showed a positive connection between public housing and better health. The body of the study compared the family experiences of tenants in a Baltimore housing project and similar families housed in poor housing. The authors found that public housing appeared to improve the health of several population segments, especially women between 20 and 36 years of age. The study identified other positive effects: positive reactions to public housing on the part of tenants, more positive attitudes to the immediate neighborhood and a greater willingness to maintain the neighborhood.[60]

In *Slums and Insecurity*, Alvin Schorr catalogued the physical and emotional ills that poor housing, particularly overcrowded housing, generated or exacerbated. Housing reformers like Edith Wood and Mary Simkhovitch would have been familiar with the list. Schorr argued that acute respiratory infections, digestive ailments and infectious diseases of childhood were all more common in poor housing. Lead poisoning in children was found more frequently in substandard housing. Schorr connected bad housing conditions, especially overcrowding, with higher levels of stress which, he believed, were related to other harmful behaviors. Schorr reported that families in deteriorated neighborhoods reported higher levels of pessimism and passivity. Inadequate indoor space prompted adults and children to spend a great deal of time outdoors. Schorr thought that, for children, this could put them beyond parental control.[61]

Other writers were dubious about making connections between housing and physical or psychological conditions. Anthony Wallace thought that almost no useable data connecting social structure and housing existed.

He thought that nearly everything written about public housing amounted, instead, to "warmly-held opinions." Irving Rosow found little research that related housing design to human psychology. He observed that notions of privacy and adequate space could readily have different meanings for people of different classes. Overall, he was more impressed with how much people remained the same after they moved into new housing than how much they changed. John Dean argued that the tenant population in public housing was probably different from the general slum population. Single people and some large families could not find places in public housing. Housing authorities chose what they thought were the most suitable families. Some eligible families were not interested in public housing. Dean thought that comparisons between the two populations were probably not valid.[62]

Social Services

Elizabeth Wood argued that the division of labor between housing authorities and social welfare agencies, public and private, needed revision. The original understanding had been that housing authorities provided housing while other agencies provided social services. Housing authorities might provide space to settlement houses and public agencies from which to operate a range of social and recreational services, but, in the main, housing managers referred families to outside agencies for social services. While Wood thought that some problem families should be kept out of public housing, she conceded that housing authorities had to house some of them and that their number was increasing. She argued that public housing could not continue as a just a housing program. It needed to provide enough welfare services for a housing authority to be able to absorb problem families. She recommended programs of tenant education for the more or less normal families and more intensive services for the "more damaged" families. Tenant education would help families that struggled with the "complexities of urban living" or with good housekeeping.[63]

A great many agreed with Wood. In the 1950s and 1960s, housing authorities across the country, including New York and Chicago, took steps to increase the social services they provided or to coordinate better with social service agencies. In the late 1950s and in the middle 1960s, Congress considered legislation mandating wider social services. In 1962, the National Association of Housing and Redevelopment Officials produced a report calling for more social services in public housing. In 1963, the Department of Health, Education and Welfare and the Housing and Home Finance Agency created a joint task force to promote coordination between housing authorities and local social agencies.[64]

Lee Rainwater raised fundamental objections. He wrote that relying on special services for the poor assumed either that the poor would remain that way indefinitely or that services could somehow change the poor. He contended that whatever difficulties the poor experienced in improving their lot stemmed from being poor. By his standards, social services seemed a weak intervention, unlikely to make a real difference. "Better than nothing," but "not much better than nothing."[65]

Money remained the principal stumbling block to wider social services. Housing authorities were less than enthusiastic. Even in the late 1960s, only 8 percent of housing authorities members surveyed thought that their organizations should be responsible for social services. Housing authorities did not want housing funds diverted to other purposes. At the federal level, there was consistent resistance to making housing authorities responsible for social services. The Eisenhower and Johnson administrations sought better coordination between housing authorities and social service agencies. They welcomed housing authorities educating tenants in good housekeeping and the like, but they drew the line at using housing monies for other social services. Even Senator Joseph Clark (D–Pennsylvania), a public housing supporter, wondered why, if cities regularly provided police and social services to their inhabitants, anyone expected the federal government to pay for them for public housing tenants.[66]

Tenants' Views

Public housing tenants were concerned about what their neighbors did. Rainwater's work at Pruitt-Igoe found evidence that tenants were most concerned about the behavior of other tenants. Pruitt-Igoe tenants said that they felt more in common with people from their old neighborhoods than with fellow tenants. Mothers receiving welfare in New York in the early 1970s told researchers that a lack of adult supervision for children in public housing created severe problems. Longtime residents of the Chicago's Cabrini-Green project worried about an influx of welfare families beginning in the late 1950s. Tenant organizations in New York complained about similar changes there.[67]

Otherwise, what little we know about tenants' attitudes is at odds with what passed for conventional wisdom. Tenants in an Oakland project reported that other tenants could present problems but they also said that living in public housing did not confer any stigma. Only a quarter of Wilmington public housing tenants said that they felt trapped in public housing. Only 12 percent said that they were ashamed to live in public housing. Fewer than 30 percent found their project unattractive and only 14 percent thought it was overcrowded and therefore not a good place to live.[68]

Throughout the discussion of public housing, the almost universal assumption was that tenants were at best passive, at worst hostile and troublesome. Observers recognized that some tenants were capable of improving their situation by increasing their incomes, but otherwise the tenant population was portrayed as incapable of either individual or joint action on their own behalves.

Tenants in cities like New York, Baltimore and St. Louis as early as the 1950s tried to maintain order in their projects, forming patrols and agitating for better police protection. In the middle 1960s, tenants in Chicago's Robert Taylor Homes organized a law and order committee. Women from the project picketed the Chicago authority's offices, demanding more police, elevator attendants, and quicker elevator repairs. Across the country, tenants organized day care centers for themselves and created scout troops, sports teams and other activities for young people. Mothers took responsibility for supervising elevators, especially when children were going to and coming from school. Tenants participated in the tenants councils that some housing authorities created.[69]

In New York in the 1940s and early 1950s, public housing tenants formed local and citywide organizations to protect their interests. Tenant organizations had a long and colorful history in the city. Bolstered by connections to other tenant groups, CIO trade unions, the American Labor party and the Communist party, tenants in several New York projects organized themselves at the project level and then into the Inter-Project Council which aspired to represent public housing tenants across the city. The council took positions on housing authority policies and plans. The authority's efforts to evict over-income tenants were high on the council's list of grievances. The council supported Henry Wallace's presidential campaign in 1948. Over the next decade, project and citywide organizations withered. As economic conditions improved, many members moved out of public housing. The involvement of Communists made the organizations a target for outside attacks. In 1953 Congress passed legislation barring members of any organization on the attorney general's list of subversive organizations from living in public housing. Tenants had to sign affidavits stating that they were not Communists. In 1955, one of the most active tenant groups, the Queensbridge Tenants League, was added to the attorney general's list.[70]

In the late 1960s, tenants in New York public housing, concerned about crime and vandalism, organized tenant patrols. Within two years, the New York housing authority forged a partnership with the tenant-organized patrols and expanded the program. By the middle 1970s, 11,000 tenants were participating. Tenants involved in patrols also organized recreational and other community programs. In the wake of the tenant patrols' success, the New York authority created a 49-member Residents Advisory Council whose members were elected by tenants. The council went on to organize voter registration drives, lobby in Albany and Washington for public housing, and lead other community programs.[71]

In the late 1960s, public housing tenants, now largely African American, also created local and national organizations for themselves. Inspired by rent strikes in Harlem in 1964–65, public housing tenants in several cities formed their own organizations. In January 1969, the Chicago Tenants Union hosted a meeting where a new national group, the National Tenants Organization, took form. With help from the American Friends Service Committee and other groups, the National Tenants Organization held its first convention later in the year. Within two years, it had affiliates in most large and medium sized cities.[72]

In at least two cities, public housing tenants took forceful and dramatic action to protect their interests. In 1967 public housing tenants in St. Louis began campaigning for better maintenance and police protection, tenant representation on the housing authority and rents limited to 25 percent of income. When the housing authority failed to respond, tenants began to withhold their rent in February 1969 and did so for nine months. By fall 1969, 2,400 families had withheld of total of $600,000. Supported by the Teamsters and local political leaders, the strikers won their key demands, limits on rent and representation on the housing authority. A rent strike in Newark followed a similar path. There, roughly 11,000 families from three large projects withheld their rent, seeking limits on rents, better maintenance, and a tenant role in management. Eventually, with assistance from the courts, the strikers achieved most of their demands.[73]

The discussion of public housing's tenants parallels the criticisms of public housing construction in key ways. The commentary was generally negative. The usual question was "What was wrong with tenants?" The answer was often that they were inherently flawed. Much of the criticism was unsupported by real data or analysis. The experts were almost always outsiders who may have visited public housing, but not lived there; the voices of tenants were rarely in evidence.

Prejudice against poor people was explicit and widespread. Poor families were a tribe apart, not like normal Americans at all. Commentators readily concluded that, even among poor people, those slightly better off would, and should, set an example for others and would be the natural community leaders.

Some writers put public housing into a wider context and recognized that the changes in the tenant population were consistent with national trends. At least as frequently public housing was blamed for developments beyond the housing authority's control. It seemingly never occurred to some that the number of poor African American women with small children was increasing in inner cities generally and not just in public housing.

The tenant population did not coincide with most of the early reformers' expectations. As was the case with public housing construction, reformers of the community planner persuasion remained unhappy with public housing projects that housed a narrow range of incomes. Reformers more in the "social worker" tradition became unhappy as they perceived that public housing did not transform families and that, despite screening techniques, the tenant population became poorer and less like the middle class.

Finally, the tenant population presents a certain irony. Many opponents of public housing argued that, if there had to be any public housing, it should house the very poorest. And, yet, when public housing started to do just that, they did not like the result.

CHAPTER SEVEN

African Americans

Poor and barred from many neighborhoods by formal or informal restrictions, African Americans found housing in the least attractive neighborhoods, at the bottom of the nation's hierarchy of neighborhoods. In Philadelphia in 1939, more than half the housing African Americans rented was substandard while only 14 percent of the housing rented by whites was. Anyone seeking to build better housing or to change slum neighborhoods could not avoid dealing with African Americans' housing situation. Even in the late 1920s, when Lewis Mumford and others were planning Radburn, a new community distant from any African American neighborhood, they realized that, at some point, they would have to decide whether to sell or rent to African Americans. They skirted the issue and the relatively high cost of Radburn's housing eventually made the issue moot. Public housing planners and officials could not so easily avoid the issue.[1]

Migration to the Cities

Between 1940 and 1980, the number of African Americans in large cities increased dramatically. In 1940, the ten largest U.S. cities (New York, Chicago, Philadelphia, Detroit, Los Angeles, Cleveland, Baltimore, St. Louis, Boston and Pittsburgh) included almost 20 million people, of whom 1.6 million or 8.3 percent were African Americans. In 1980, the same ten cities included 18.7 million people, of whom six million or 32 percent were African Americans. In 1940, in only three of the biggest cities (Philadelphia, Baltimore and St. Louis) did the African American population represent more than 10 percent. In 1980, none of these same cities had an

African American population less than 17 percent. African Americans were the majority in Detroit and Cleveland. Even if one adds the population of the rapidly growing four cities (Houston, Dallas San Diego, and Phoenix) that were among the largest ten in 1980 but not in 1940, including two (San Diego and Phoenix) that had small African American populations in 1980, African Americans still represented nearly 30 percent of the total.

The increased number of African Americans combined with other population shifts to change many neighborhoods in the three decades after World War II. After the war, housing construction resumed after a nearly 15-year hiatus. Middle class and lower middle-class families, usually white, moved to new houses in the suburbs. In their wake, other families moved to what were for them better houses in the outlying areas of cities. African American families moved into the neighborhoods surrounding those where they had predominated before the war. To a certain extent, the availability for African Americans of housing in urban areas reduced the demand for public housing. More immediately, the population changes meant that, in many cases, public housing projects built in what had been mixed or white areas were, by 1970, in African American neighborhoods.

Neighborhood succession had a mixed impact on African Americans. Those with higher incomes obtained better, less expensive housing in northern cities. Poorer families, the majority, were still likely to find themselves in substandard, but expensive housing. In the mid–1960s, one estimate was that only 5 percent of African American households in Philadelphia could afford a house costing more than $12,000. Even while the number of nonwhite households in substandard housing declined 17 percent nationwide between 1950 and 1960, it increased in the northeast. In 1960, nonwhite households were twice as likely as white households to live in substandard housing. Despite changing neighborhoods, the neighborhood pattern as it applied to African Americans remained essentially unchanged. In the 1960s, scholars developed indices to measure urban residential segregation. By these measures, segregation in both northern and southern cities declined between 1950 and 1970, but only slightly. In Chicago, as neighborhoods opened up south of the existing African Americans neighborhoods on the South Side, it was middle-class African Americans who moved there. The overall African American community on the south side continued to occupy a contiguous area, only now divided by class.[2]

Early Debates

The first discussions of the United States' housing problems acknowledged the special situation of African Americans, but proceeded as if a sound housing program would benefit African Americans along with other Americans. Once the federal government and local housing authorities built and operated public housing, it became clear that the presence of African Americans in urban neighborhoods raised issues for public housing that could not be avoided. For some housing experts and officials, the challenge was to determine ways to serve African Americans without endangering the entire public housing program. Their fear was that public housing would be perceived as a threat to existing neighborhood patterns and would provoke even greater opposition. The goal was locating public housing and selecting tenants in ways that did not disturb existing neighborhoods. Other writers added a more positive approach. They saw public housing as a vehicle for improving the lot of African Americans, an opportunity to break with existing patterns and provide African Americans with decent, affordable housing.

The Hoover conference's report on "Negro" housing described the considerable difficulties African Americans had obtaining decent, affordable housing, but offered much the same solutions as for the overall housing problems. Secretary of Commerce Lamont argued that the answer was not to build housing for African Americans alone. Rather the range of measures proposed by the Hoover conference, large-scale enterprises, housing standards and the like, would be sufficient to create decent housing for every American. The conference's report did advocate national, state and local commissions to advocate for better housing for African Americans. It urged construction of housing for low-income urban and rural families and, like the report on slums, offered government-built housing as the alternative should the private sector fail.[3]

The 1937 Housing Act

In the period leading up to the 1937 Act, the housing problems of African Americans hardly figured in the debate. Reformers acknowledged that African Americans represented a special case. Regardless of income, they struggled to find decent, affordable housing. Nevertheless, mentions of African Americans were rare and the general sense was that a properly designed and implemented public housing program would serve their needs along with everyone else's.

The housing problems facing African Americans received only a few mentions during the congressional hearings before 1937. Organizations concerned about African American issues supported public housing. On behalf of the NAACP, Walter White advocated a ban on discrimination in the new housing. White also argued that rents in the new projects should be affordable for the people displaced and that displaced families should get first preference. The National Urban League's Reginald Johnson pointed out that bad housing promoted family instability, juvenile delinquency, and disease. Citing the Hoover conference's report, Johnson reminded a Senate committee that the housing choices facing African American urban families were bleak: paying inflated rents, settling for substandard housing, or both. Johnson cited statistics from Chicago and New York. In Chicago, rents increased 20 to 50 percent when properties were first rented to African Americans. In New York between 1919 and 1927, rents for African Americans rose 100 percent while average rents across the city increased only 10 percent.[4]

PWA Housing

Under Harold Ickes' direction, the PWA tried to address African Americans' issues. Ickes was a longtime supporter of civil rights for African Americans and had been president of the Chicago branch of the NAACP. He desegregated cafeterias and rest rooms throughout the Department of the Interior, including in the national parks. An African American, Robert Weaver, served as his adviser on "race" relations. All PWA contracts contained a clause forbidding discrimination on the basis of color or religious affiliation and specified the minimum percentage of labor costs that had to be devoted to African American workers.[5]

Ickes directed that public housing be provided to African Americans "in accord with their numbers and needs." Of the 49 projects the PWA built between 1934 and 1937, 14 were for African Americans alone and 17 included both white and African American tenants. Of the projects that included white and African American tenants, about half were completely integrated. The other half separated whites and African Americans in different buildings or wings of buildings. By 1940, when African American families constituted only 8 percent of urban families, African Americans occupied about a third of the housing units (7,507 out of 21,640 units) constructed by the PWA.[6]

Ickes was proud of the PWA's record. Addressing a largely African

American audience at the opening of an Atlanta project in 1934, he told them that the Roosevelt administration had learned that the whole country benefited when everyone was prosperous. Discriminating against a race, a religion or an occupation harmed everyone and interfered with building a balanced economy.[7]

Despite Ickes' personal views, he had no mandate to combat segregation or promote African American interests. Although the PWA paid for and built public housing, it and Ickes needed the cooperation of local housing authorities and, behind them, the local establishments. Ickes' principal tool for easing the way for African Americans to occupy public housing was the so-called neighborhood composition rule. The tenant population of any public housing project was to reflect the population of the neighborhood in which it was built. Projects built in white neighborhoods were to be for white tenants. Projects built in African American neighborhoods were for African American tenants. The neighborhood composition rule signaled that the PWA was implementing a housing program for whites and African Americans but not attempting to overturn either legally mandated segregation in the South or the neighborhood pattern elsewhere.

The rule was fuzzy on at least two counts. "Neighborhood" has no fixed meaning; what constitutes a "neighborhood" remains very much in the eye of the beholder. In the case of public housing in the 1930s, it could mean the few blocks around the proposed site for public housing or a much larger area. Similarly, what qualified an area as an African American neighborhood was left undefined. Some projects intended for African Americans were built in areas that were integrated, but with a large number of African American inhabitants.

The neighborhood composition concept took several forms over time. In the simplest version, a housing authority built equal number of units for whites and for African Americans, usually in separate projects. Other versions distributed units, whether in the same or separate projects, in proportion to the characteristics of either the entire population or of the eligible population in the immediate neighborhood or in the entire community.[8]

The two PWA projects in Atlanta, Techwood Homes for whites, and University Homes for African Americans, were slum clearance efforts. Both projects eliminated decrepit housing adjacent to institutions of higher learning, Georgia Tech and Atlanta University, and displaced the existing populations in the process. At best, they created as many housing units as they destroyed. The Atlanta authority claimed that the Techwood site had housed whites and African Americans, but most of the displaced families were African American. The original inhabitants of the University Homes site were especially poor African Americans. More than a third of the adults were out of work and few of those who were employed could afford the rents charged in the new housing. More than 80 percent of the original inhabitants told researchers that they did not know where they would go after their homes were demolished. Some of the African American families displaced by the Atlanta projects moved into hitherto white neighborhoods, sparking cross burnings and protest marches.[9]

The first two PWA projects in New York, Harlem River Houses and Williamsburg Houses, were examples of what could be thought of as managed integration. Both were built on largely vacant land and did not raise the displacement issues the Atlanta projects did. Harlem River was in an African American neighborhood; Williamsburg in a largely white neighborhood. Both housed a few tenants different from the population of the surrounding neighborhood and the housing authority could claim that both were integrated. Nonetheless, the authority maintained separate offices for processing applications. An office at the Harlem River development processed applications for it, presumably from African Americans; an office on 14th Street also processed applications, presumably from all other potential tenants.[10]

Elsewhere, housing authorities found their own ways to fit PWA projects into the existing neighborhood pattern. In Chicago, the housing authority decided to accommodate African Americans in the Jane Addams Houses in proportion to their presence in the surrounding neighborhood. The Cincinnati authority planned to build two segregated projects, but, in the face of complaints, built a single project with separate buildings for whites and African Americans. In Dallas, the original plan was to build two segregated projects, largely to avoid charges of favoritism. The Dallas authority saw better housing in African American neighborhoods as a way to avoid African American migration into other neighborhoods. When the authority could not find an economically feasible site in an African American neighborhood, it built only a project for whites. The Baltimore authority set out to build two projects for whites to block the migration of African Americans into white neighborhoods. In Cleveland, like New York, most projects were technically integrated but with only a few families from outside the neighborhood. As is Atlanta, the Cleveland projects in African American neighborhoods ended up serving better-off African Americans and pushing poorer African Americans into other neighborhoods. The overcrowding that resulted was obvious enough to attract criticism in African American newspapers.[11]

USHA Housing

By 1949, out of the roughly 140,000 units funded by USHA, 46,000 (or about a third) were occupied by African American families. Since African Americans were more likely to be poor than white Americans, these numbers flatter public housing. Nonetheless, statistics maintained by the federal housing agency suggest that a little more than half of the applicants for public housing subsequently deemed eligible in 1941 were African American as were a little less than half the successful applicants. Numbers for war housing are sketchy but African Americans appeared to have lived in around 15 percent (roughly 80,000 units) of the war housing built by the federal government. The parallel program of war housing built by private firms and backed by FHA loans allocated only about 5 percent of its units (or 15,000–20,000) to African Americans.[12]

Most USHA housing units were in projects that housed only whites or only African Americans. Thirty-five percent of units were in projects that included only African Americans; 21 percent in projects that included only whites. The remaining 44 percent were in projects that housed both whites and African Americans, although not necessarily in the same building.

In some cities between 1937 and 1949, especially in the South and West, public housing, including housing for war workers, reflected local laws and customs and was explicitly segregated. In the District of Columbia, the housing authority's stated policy was that projects would include only one "race" and that projects would house the same sort of people who lived in the surrounding neighborhood. In Dallas and Houston, the first projects were intended for a single group, in most cases African Americans but, in some, Americans of Mexican descent. The intent was to eliminate the city's worst housing, which such populations normally occupied; satisfy in part their demands for better housing; and reduce the chance that they would seek to move into white neighborhoods. Projects usually respected the existing neighborhood pattern. Opposition quickly emerged when they did not. After a white riot greeted a war housing project for African Americans in Detroit, the housing commission determined that future projects should not change a neighborhood's composition.[13]

In Chicago, Philadelphia and New York, USHA projects were integrated but most tenants resembled the population of the surrounding neighborhood. Two Philadelphia projects were in or near African American neighborhoods and 95 percent of the tenants were African American. The third project was near a white neighborhood and 95 percent of its tenants were white. By 1949, the authorities in both Chicago and New York had official non-discrimination policies, but their tenant populations resembled Philadelphia's.[14]

The Chicago and New York authorities went to considerable lengths to manage integration. They worked to preserve what they considered the correct mix of tenants in individual projects. The New York authority would leave apartments vacant rather than admit more African American tenants than it thought appropriate. Mary Simkhovitch, vice-chairman of the New York authority from 1934 until 1948, responded to calls for a tenant selection policy that ignored identity with the statement that the authority was committed to housing, not social experimentation. Accepting African Americans in equal numbers in all projects might satisfy social justice, but it would doom public housing, she said. New York's white residents were not ready for it. As it was, African Americans occupied nearly 15 percent of public housing units, twice their share of New York's population.[15]

The executive secretary of the Chicago authority, Elizabeth Wood, worked to shape tenant populations that might be integrated but did not offend the white majority. Most Chicago projects housed only whites or only African Americans. A few were integrated but subject to unofficial quotas. In the Jane Addams Homes and Cabrini Homes, both located in mixed neighborhoods, Wood attempted to have the tenant populations reflect the neighborhoods' proportions. The challenge was to find enough white tenants. The authority would leave apartments vacant until white applicants appeared and accept white applicants whose housing needs were not as pressing as some African American applicants.[16]

The tools available to housing authorities were no match for changing housing patterns, however. As sacrosanct as neighborhoods might be to some, people felt free to move from one to another. When the Frances Cabrini Homes opened in the early 1940s, the surrounding neighborhood, dubbed "Little Italy," was 80 percent white. The Chicago authority set the proportion of white to African American tenants at 4:1. White residents were not happy with the decision, if only because many white families displaced by the project's construction were not eligible for public housing. For a period, neighborhood opposition forced the authority to keep apartments intended for African American families vacant and in 1943 street violence broke out in response to an African American family occupying an apartment. At the same time, white families continued to leave the neighborhood, to be replaced by African American families. By 1949, more than half the neighborhood's inhabitants were African American. The authority could not maintain the original 20 percent quota for African American families. Leaving apartments vacant and favoring white applicants over needier African American applicants became embarrassing. By 1949, the quota had become 40 percent, twice the original figure, but still below the African American share of the neighborhood.[17]

African Americans' Views

Beginning in 1937, national organizations that advocated for African Americans took a greater interest in public housing. The 1937 NAACP convention came out in support of low-cost housing for the poor. It urged construction of public housing in the blighted areas where African American workers had to live. The NAACP criticized the 1937 Act's local control provisions. Local control over site and tenant selection would put African Americans at a disadvantage and perpetuate segregation, they claimed. Walter White, NAACP president, praised USHA efforts and Nathan Straus and Robert Weaver in particular. White said that they had resisted the extension of segregation despite the political dangers. In the early 1940s, the NAACP lobbied for African Americans to be included on housing authorities. In the debates preceding passage of the 1949 Act, most national African American organizations advocated an anti-discrimination provision in the bill.[18]

In 1940 Weaver, still working for USHA, penned a defense of its efforts. Weaver argued that USHA had broken new ground by neither ignoring African Americans nor treating them as a special case. Instead it had sought to address their needs within its basic programs. There was no African American housing problem, Weaver wrote, only national housing problems. The situation of African Americans was but one factor in a complex situation. USHA efforts reflected this reality. USHA had included African Americans in planning public housing projects because effective programs demanded the involvement of those to be served. USHA had made sure African Americans got their share of public housing construction jobs and of public housing units because all Americans deserved jobs and housing. USHA policy, Weaver contended, was that African Americans should not be displaced from stable and integrated neighborhoods and that no more housing units occupied by African Americans should be demolished than the number of new units made available to them.[19]

Turning to the future, Weaver struck a more cautious and ambiguous note. He declared that public housing should not establish "racial" patterns "less democratic" than those that already existed in a community. He warned that public housing could be used to expand segregation. African Americans might be excluded from public housing or public housing might be used to push them out of desirable neighborhoods. He wrote that the initial composition of public housing should include all groups who might conceivably live in the project during its lifetime. Neighborhoods changed and, if "separate facilities" were built now, they would be hard to change even if the neighborhood changed.[20]

In 1948, after Weaver had left federal service, he again addressed the housing problems African Americans faced. His judgment of federal programs to that point remained positive. The PWA, USHA and war housing programs had provided African Americans a fair share of housing units and of construction and management jobs. In most cases public housing had not pushed African Americans out of desirable neighborhoods. Public housing had provided poorer African Americans an opportunity to demonstrate that they could pay rent on time and maintain their homes properly. Unlike other federal housing programs, PWA and USHA projects had avoided making residential segregation worse. Weaver thought that the sites selected were "no less progressive" that the existing neighborhood pattern. On several occasions, USHA had urged local authorities to establish integrated housing. Because the war program built more units outside African American neighborhoods, its projects were less often in African American neighborhoods and more frequently integrated. Weaver acknowledged that war housing had created controversies as a result.[21]

Weaver thought the New York housing authority was outstanding, especially regarding housing for African Americans. He pointed to the authority's explicit non-segregation policy and to the fact that all of its projects were integrated. Authorities in Seattle and Los Angeles also seemed successful to Weaver.[22]

Federal efforts through the end of the war were far from perfect, in Weaver's view. As positive as efforts to serve African Americans were, the overall program remained muddled. Federal policy tried to sidestep residential segregation by building on slum sites and selecting tenants who resembled the neighborhood population. Housing officials thought that addressing the needs of African Americans directly would endanger the public housing program. African Americans were so in need of better housing that they welcomed decent housing in their current neighborhood and were willing to ignore the long-term issue of gaining access to other neighborhoods. Weaver argued that both housing officials and African American tenants were guilty of postponing the fundamental problems.[23]

Weaver worried that, if and when Congress re-authorized public housing, the most likely outcomes were more projects in slum neighborhoods filled with African American tenants and a few small, all-white projects elsewhere. Weaver thought the country could do better. Public housing was still the answer in Weaver's view. Most African Americans could not afford to purchase private housing or even federally subsidized private housing. Public housing could rehabilitate the slums and open new neighborhoods to African Americans. The federal government should not stand aside and watch African American neighborhoods expand in the face of opposition from surrounding areas.[24]

New, large, integrated communities on vacant land were the key, according to Weaver. Sites needed to be some distance from existing large African American communities but still accessible to them. Weaver thought sites in integrated neighborhoods or African American neighborhoods that could attract some whites would suffice. The new communities needed to be large enough to constitute their own neighborhoods. It would easier to create new attitudes in a new community than combat community wide opposition in old neighborhoods. Weaver thought the Queensbridge and Red Hook projects in New York had succeeded in creating new neighborhoods. The Cabrini Homes in Chicago was too small to offset the existing community's attitudes. Tenant selection policies needed to be flexible, according to Weaver. African Americans were accustomed to living in their own neighborhoods; they might be slow to move to a new integrated neighborhood. Weaver thought that, if the new public housing program were large enough, it might drain enough population from slum neighborhoods so that they could easily be redeveloped. Perhaps then African Americans could move back to the redeveloped areas. Weaver wanted to avoid allowing integrated public housing become entirely African American. His solution was a public housing program big enough to meet the needs of the entire low-income population.[25]

George Nesbit, who worked for the Public Housing Administration as a racial relations officer, raised similar fears. He pointed to past failures to relocate families, especially African American families, displaced by federal projects and predicted that relocation would be even more difficult in the future. Little vacant land remained within African American neighborhoods; almost any new construction would require demolition of existing homes. African American neighborhoods were even more over-crowded than before the war. Many African Americans would not eligible for public housing; many were either single or, if married, childless. Without careful planning and vigorous relocation efforts, urban renewal was likely to become "Negro removal."[26]

Nesbit anticipated that most public or non-profit housing in Chicago would be in the south side neighborhoods already dominated by African Americans. Even with an official open occupancy policy, tenants in any new projects were likely to be African Americans. Nesbit thought this unfortunate because it would buttress the notion that the South Side was for African Americans only and private developers would refuse to build there.[27]

As early as 1936, an observer had pointed out the risk that construction in slum areas would displace poor African American families. Karen Dash, writing in *The Nation*, reported that Detroit's first slum clearance project had demolished homes, but not provided any relocation housing. The Detroit housing commission, Dash wrote, claimed that a hundred families had been successfully relocated, but could not provide a list of the families. A commission official told Dash that the relocated families had had to pay only a few dollars more in rent to secure new housing. The official said that the public housing planned for the site was not necessarily for families like those displaced. It was for "industrious, low income" families who could pay $26 to $25 a month in rent. Rents in the demolished houses had been $3 to $10 a month.[28]

In Chicago, at least, African American attitudes towards public housing before 1949 were mixed. Most welcomed the new housing and saw it benefitting African Americans in ways that most federal housing programs did not. A few worried about the long-term impact of public housing built largely in existing African American neighborhoods. Others saw public housing disrupting existing communities or bringing the wrong kind of people into their neighborhood.

The African American press and politicians supported public housing as it was built in Chicago through 1949. From an elected African American's perspective, public housing benefited his constituents and left intact the communities from which he drew his support. In 1941 an African American member of the Chicago City Council sponsored a study of African American housing. The final report cataloged the crowded, substandard housing that many African Americans occupied in Chicago and praised the public housing recently made available to several thousand African American families. In describing the impact of poor housing, the report echoed themes from the wider housing reform literature. It claimed, for example, that poor housing prevented children from becoming fully formed adults.[29]

Some prominent African Americans did not value preserving the existing African American neighborhoods so highly. Robert Taylor, chairman of the Chicago Housing Authority, and Earl Dickerson, a onetime City Council member, opposed temporary war housing in African American neighborhoods on the grounds that it would "preserve the ghetto."[30]

Still other African Americans in Chicago opposed public housing because it would disrupt or diminish their neighborhood. An African American minister opposed a post-war public housing project because it would demolish the homes of his congregants. Affluent African Americans in a far South Side neighborhood fought a war housing project planned for their neighborhood because it might attract poorer African Americans. A similar project in Detroit met similar resistance from African American homeowners.[31]

Pre–1949 Act Debate

The debate about public housing preceding the 1949 Act acknowledged the plight of African Americans in a way that was not true before 1937. Even the 1948 Joint Committee on Housing accepted that African Americans faced serious problems obtaining decent housing. It argued that segregation was a local or regional problem but added that, until the national consciousness was ready for "radical adjustments," special provisions needed to be made for African Americans. The CIO and UAW included steps to improve housing for African Americans in their housing proposals. In 1945, the CIO told a congressional committee that federal aid should be withheld from any housing subject to restrictive covenants. In 1949, the National Federation of Settlements passed a resolution condemning discrimination in public housing. Other writers and congressional witnesses at least mentioned housing for African Americans.[32]

Catherine Bauer opposed residential segregation, whether it was based on "race" or class. She saw zoning and large-scale housing operations narrowing the income range within neighborhoods. She argued that restrictive covenants and public housing tenant selection policies were pushing the United States further toward "the most complete and absolute segregation by race." Some housing authorities had taken a stand against "racial" segregation, but most had followed the path of least resistance. Bauer thought that they needed to do better so that the country could make rapid progress toward "full integration of ethnic minority groups" into American democracy.[33]

In the 1940s, Bauer remained optimistic about public efforts to create integrated communities. She saw the "day of enforced residential segregation" drawing to a close in northern cities. How swift and smooth the transition would be would depend on the quality of civic leadership. Bauer still considered it possible that popularly based housing organizations could push cities towards "bona fide neighborhood planning" and away from harmful standardization. She imagined that, once the United States had a "broad-based and efficient home building mechanism," it would be possible to build diverse neighborhoods that included both private and public housing. If urban renewal meant attracting more affluent families back to cities, the country needed to find places for lower income families in the suburbs.[34]

Charles Abrams

Charles Abrams was among the leaders of a protracted effort to open the Metropolitan Life's Stuyvesant Town to African Americans and to have New York City adopt an anti-discrimination ordinance. Abrams was skeptical about Metropolitan Life's decision to build, and New York City's decision to subsidize, the Riverton development for African Americans in Harlem. Abrams saw the move as an effort to deflect criticism from Stuyvesant Town. Abrams criticized Metropolitan Life's efforts to relocate families displaced by the Stuyvesant Town and Riverton projects, many of who were African American.[35]

Robert Moses was Abrams' principal antagonist in city government. He countered pleas for non-discrimination in Stuyvesant Town or the city by arguing that reformers had to choose. In Moses' view, you could not have both non-discrimination and a vigorous public housing program. You could not have successful slum clearance and oppose a development like Stuyvesant Town. If the city made "social objectives" its first priority, private developers would refuse to submit redevelopment proposals.[36]

Abrams thought that public housing proved that "inter-racial" housing worked. According to Abrams, public housing had, in some cases, been large enough to create a self-contained community. It created its own environment and fixed the "long-term patterns of living." When such developments were managed in a way that demonstrated that neither whites nor African Americans were likely to "overwhelm" the neighborhood, whites and African Americans lived together with no problems. When

African Americans had the same privileges and responsibilities as other tenants, any initial tensions subsided and cooperation developed.[37]

Abrams believed that the federal government should oppose discrimination, especially in housing. Federally-funded public housing should not allow discrimination based on "race," color or religion. Federal agencies should not promote either discrimination or segregation. The civil rights statutes needed to be strengthened and restrictive covenants needed to be banned. The law needed to define the public role broadly and ban discrimination wherever federal funds were involved.[38]

Abrams thought that the country needed enough decent, affordable housing for everyone. If everyone had a place to live, no one need think that one's neighborhood or one's home was threatened by an influx of outsiders. Fears about outsiders "infiltrating" neighborhoods generated prejudice and undermined values in many neighborhoods, according to Abrams. New neighborhoods, integrated from the start and managed to preserve integration, would avoid these problems.[39]

Abrams was not clear about how one managed a project or a neighborhood to achieve and maintain integration. He contended that quotas were not required; there need be "no fixed rule" for selecting tenants by "racial" percentages. Administrators did need the authority to arrange the greatest heterogeneity with no predominance of any one group. Abrams wrote that tenant selection had to weigh the character and responsibility of potential tenants as well as the ability to meld into a community.[40]

If African Americans were to solve their housing problems, they needed to see the larger picture, Abrams argued. Local control meant segregation in many places, but a federally directed effort was likely to produce only declarations of equality that would not be honored at the local level. Local housing efforts that benefited African Americans represented real gains. Public housing built in African American neighborhoods was a real benefit. Nonetheless African Americans would be better off resisting "isolation" in these developments and fighting for a fair share of all new housing.[41]

The 1949 Act

Congressional consideration of the 1949 Act included a discussion of discrimination. In an effort to entice southern Democrats to vote against the bill, Republicans Senators submitted an amendment banning discrimination in public housing. As Senator John Sparkman (D–Alabama), a supporter of the bill, acknowledged, the conventional assumption was that no southern locality would propose additional public housing if discrimination were banned. No southern Senator was, therefore, likely to vote for an amended bill. National African American organizations disagreed about the amendment. The NAACP and the National Negro Council supported it; the National Council of Negro Women opposed it.[42]

It fell to Senator Paul Douglas (D–Illinois) to argue against the amendment on behalf of the Democratic majority. Douglas began by admitting that the amendment created a conflict for him and the 25 to 30 Democratic senators he characterized as liberals. They wanted to clear the slums and provide better housing for slum dwellers, but they also believed that no American should be treated like a second-class citizen. They were opposed to segregation in the North and in the South. Nevertheless, Douglas argued, the amendment would doom the bill and "non-segregated housing without a housing bill" would amount to nothing. Building better homes for what Douglas estimated would be 10 percent of African Americans was better than an empty gesture. Trying to get everything at once could defeat the possibility of getting something substantial now. The Congress could not legislate on everything at once and some problems had to be left to the future.[43]

Robert Taft opposed the amendment by arguing for the status quo. He maintained that anti-discrimination was unnecessary since site selection provided equal opportunity. Projects in African American neighborhoods served African Americans; projects in white neighborhoods served whites. "Forced integration" was to be avoided. Taft was willing to include an anti-discrimination statement, but thought that circumstances might require a certain amount of segregation and preferences for one group or another.[44]

The Senate agreed with Douglas and Taft. The vote on the amendment had 31 senators for and 49 against.

On the Senate floor, Douglas was arguing, in essence, that public housing in African American neighborhoods was better than no public housing at all. Advocates like Bauer and Weaver could imagine public housing outside slum neighborhoods, on outlying or suburban land. They could imagine new developments as integrated communities. Douglas and the 1949 Act's authors had foregone those possibilities. On the same day as the discussion about discrimination, Douglas read into the record his correspondence with Raymond Foley, the head of the HHFA. Douglas' letter to Foley clarified that the 1949 Act was intended to clear slums and build public housing on slum sites. It might be possible to build on open sites, but that was not the bill's main purpose.[45]

Public Policy After the 1949 Act

The 1949 Act did not prompt any change in federal policy regarding public housing's treatment of African Americans. According to PHA guidance in 1952, to be eligible for federal funds, public housing projects needed to make "equitable provision" for all "races" based on the "approximate volume and urgency" of their needs. Urban redevelopment and public housing were not to decrease the housing units available to minorities. Areas occupied by minorities were to be redeveloped only when relocation of displaced families was feasible. At the same time, PHA policy reaffirmed that tenant selection and assignment of housing units were local matters. When pressed by civil rights groups, PHA's position through the beginning of the Kennedy administration was that it lacked the authority to mandate non-discrimination in public housing.[46]

The Eisenhower administration professed concern about the housing needs of African Americans but did little or nothing to address them. The Cole Committee's report acknowledged that the lack of adequate housing for minorities was an important and difficult part of the nation's housing problem. Public housing represented an improvement, but, the report argued, was not the entire solution. The private sector had to step up as well. The 1954 Act tied public housing to urban renewal; public housing was to provide housing for families displaced by federally-funded urban renewal efforts. Since a majority of the displaced families were African American, the Eisenhower administration increasingly saw public housing as a program for minorities. It was content to see what few public housing units it was willing to fund go to African Americans pushed out of their homes by urban renewal. The administration was unwilling, however, to use public housing as a tool to promote integration or fair housing.[47]

In the late 1940s and 1950s, advocacy groups gravitated towards fair housing as the solution to African Americans' housing needs. In 1950, prominent national organizations, including the American Civil Liberties Union, the National Urban League and the American Friends Service Committee, joined with the NAACP to form the National Committee Against Discrimination in Housing. Robert Weaver and Charles Abrams were among its first leaders. Initially public housing remained part of the proposed solution, but over time ending housing discrimination took on greater prominence.[48]

Framing housing needs as a civil rights issue had important successes. In 1948, the Supreme Court (*Shelley v Kramer*) ruled that restrictive covenants on residential real estate were unenforceable. By 1954, 21 cities, including New York, had passed fair housing legislation. Eight states, including New York, had passed laws banning discrimination in public housing. In 1954, the U.S. Supreme Court left in place a state court ruling (*Banks v Housing Authority of San Francisco*) outlawing denial of public housing on "racial" grounds. The San Francisco authority maintained both a non-discrimination policy and a policy to distribute public housing proportionate to need. The authority argued that rejecting an African American family's application for an apartment in all-white project was consistent with the proportionate need policy. The California courts disagreed, citing the equal protection provision of the 14th Amendment.[49]

Pressure from civil rights groups eventually prompted President Kennedy to issue an executive order in November 1962 banning discrimination in all housing programs funded by the federal government, not merely public housing. The order's impact on public housing was limited since PHA interpreted the order as applying only to new projects, not to existing projects. In any case, PHA focused on tenant selection procedures, not site selection, and was content if housing authorities included non-discrimination language in their annual contracts.[50]

Title IV of the Civil Rights Act of 1964 banned discrimination in PHA-funded projects. At least one contemporary observer thought that PHA's initial enforcement of the non-discrimination provision was ineffective. PHA's first preference was a "free choice" program. Applicants could choose the project where they wanted to live and could not be forced to accept one that they did not want. Insisting on "color blind" tenant selection did not change the location of public housing projects and "free choice" seemed to do little to promote integration. The same observer held out hope that a "first come, first served" policy administered centrally could have more impact, but it is not obvious that it could, or did.[51]

The Fair Housing Act of 1968 directed the federal government to "affirmatively" promote fair housing. Initial implementation fell to the Nixon administration. George Romney, Nixon's HUD secretary, made opening the suburbs to African Americans a high priority. His principal housing tool was subsidized private housing, not traditional public housing. Nixon halted Romney's efforts once they attracted attention and before they could have any impact.

Public Housing After the 1949 Act

Between the end of World War II and the mid–1970s, the share of public housing units occupied by African Americans increased. In 1944, roughly 40 percent of the families re-examined for continued occupancy, that is families already living in public housing whose incomes were verified, were "non-white." In 1949, the percentage was 36.0. By 1957, it had risen to 47.8 percent. In 1966, HUD reported that 50 percent of families living in low-rent housing were "Negro." As of June 1974, this figure was 46.7 percent. As of June 1978, it was 47.1 percent.[52]

The national figures understate African Americans' share of the public housing that attracted the most debate, family units operated by local housing authorities. According to data collected by HUD in 1977, African Americans occupied 47.2 percent of all low-rent housing units subsidized by the federal government, including both public housing and private housing, and both projects intended for families and for the elderly. For housing units owned by local housing authorities, the percentage was 53.7 percent and for such units in projects intended for families, that is, public housing as understood by most writers, the percentage was 63 percent.[53]

Scholars have used the 1977 HUD data to calculate the likelihood that African Americans living in public housing lived in a project with only other African Americans, in other words, the degree to which African Americans were isolated in public housing. Among the 15 urban regions (standard metropolitan statistical areas) considered, Chicago was the region where African Americans were most likely to be isolated in projects designed for families and operated by the local housing authority. In Chicago, it was nearly a certainty that an African American living in public housing lived in a project with only African Americans. Baltimore, Dallas–Fort Worth, Detroit, St. Louis and Washington, D.C., were not far behind. At the other end of the spectrum, African Americans in the New York region were considerably less likely to be isolated in this sense.[54]

Impressions probably mattered more than actual figures. The changed population in the nation's largest public housing system, New York's public housing, would have been hard to miss. The white population of New York public housing declined from 58 percent in 1954 to 14 percent in 1974. The African American population increased from 33 percent to 57 percent and Americans of Puerto Rican descent accounted for 8 percent in 1954 and 28 percent 20 years later.[55]

If Pruitt-Igoe in St. Louis and the Robert Taylor Homes in Chicago defined public housing, as they did for many observers, public housing was occupied almost entirely by African Americans. When the journalist Elizabeth Drew discussed the prospects for Lyndon Johnson's housing proposals in 1965, she thought it relevant to mention that 95 percent of Chicago's public housing tenants were African Americans.[56]

Public housing remained tied to the slums after 1949. New public housing was intended to clear slums or to house families made homeless by urban renewal projects. Since African Americans lived in many neighborhoods considered slums, new public housing after 1949 was most often built in African American neighborhoods. Building new public housing on outlying vacant sites was no longer an option. At the same time, "color-conscious" or discriminatory practices persisted at least until the middle 1960s. In many cases, projects originally built for whites continued to have white majorities even as African Americans filled newly built projects. Housing authorities treated applicants differently depending on their identity. In some cases, housing authorities continued segregation policies. In others, they tried to manage integration. In 1969, 48 percent of housing authority officials (and 62 percent of officials in larger authorities) surveyed thought authorities should use tenant assignment policies to keep projects integrated.[57]

In cities like St. Louis, Baltimore, Detroit, Kansas City, Dallas and Philadelphia, housing authorities located post–1949 projects in slum or blighted areas, usually in African American neighborhoods. In places like St. Louis and Dallas, the choice of location was part of larger redevelopment scheme drawn up by city government and supported by important real estate and business interests. In places like Baltimore or Philadelphia, resistance from residents in the neighborhoods selected for public housing was apparent. In 1950, the Baltimore authority proposed two projects to be built on vacant land and to be occupied by whites. White neighborhood residents pushed back. They did not want low-income housing or housing that might someday be filled with African Americans. In the middle 1950s, the Philadelphia housing authority promoted a program of 21 small public housing projects scattered around the city, half of them in white neighborhoods. The plan collapsed in the face of widespread neighborhood opposition.[58]

Public housing projects in the South remained segregated through the 1970s as did some in northern cities. In Marietta Georgia, one project served whites; another African Americans. In Detroit and Baltimore, projects were officially for whites or for African Americans until pressure from civil rights groups or new laws forced changes. The Detroit authority opened all projects to African Americans in 1956; Baltimore made the change in 1954. It was not until the early 1960s that Boston adopted an official non-discrimination policy.[59]

Adopting a non-discrimination policy did not immediately change the composition of housing projects, especially if they were in white or mixed neighborhoods. Boston's public housing was distributed around the city and were 85 percent white when the authority changed its official tenant selection policy. It was still two-thirds white towards the end of the decade. The Cleveland authority had managed some limited integration from the start, although two of the earliest projects were clearly intended for whites. Three-quarters of the tenants in one project were still white into the middle 1960s. Despite Baltimore's official policy of non-discrimination, three projects remained all white in the middle 1960s. Four Detroit projects were virtually all white at the same time.[60]

The tenant selection process offered housing authorities tools with which to shape the tenant population beyond overt or covert discrimination based on identity. A housing authority intent on keeping a group out of a project or on managing the numbers of groups within a project could look to income limits or to the criteria used to gauge suitability. In the early 1950s, the Baltimore authority saw higher income limits as a way to maintain the number of white tenants while raising rent revenue and excluding welfare families. When the Baltimore authority decided to introduce some African American families into what had been white projects, it chose two-parent families without "social problems" and no more education that their likely white neighbors. The Boston authority's first instinct when pushed to discard discrimination was to substitute a renewed emphasis on avoiding "serious multiple social problem" households.[61]

Promoting integrated housing was not necessarily a housing authority's highest priority. In 1960 the Buffalo housing authority converted a low-income project into a middle-income project, thereby replacing an integrated project, the only project in the city outside an African American neighborhood with a sizeable African American population, with one that was almost entirely white. The project was adjacent to the waterfront and to downtown and appeared to city leaders a prime candidate for redevelopment. Converting the project also served to deflect criticism of the authority's management practices. Almost none of the low-income African American families in the original project could afford the increased rents and were, therefore, relocated to other projects in largely African American neighborhoods.[62]

Chicago

Chicago featured business and real interests eager to clear and rebuild slums, a city administration eager to accept federal funds for public housing and urban development, and a neighborhood pattern that sharply divided white and African American communities. By the middle 1950s, the mayor and city council wrested control of site selection from the housing authority. Responding to pressure from both business interests and white neighborhoods, it discarded whatever plans the authority had to disperse public housing throughout the city. Fending off civil rights and good government groups as well as half-hearted interventions from Washington, the city located virtually all public housing (other than housing for the elderly) in slum neighborhoods, nearly all with overwhelmingly African American populations. Neighborhoods that were mixed, but changing, when the initial plans were announced were heavily African American by the time the projects were completed. This pattern persisted until Chicago stopped building public housing in the late 1960s despite a long series of lawsuits, protests and demonstrations, some led by Martin Luther King, and a 1966 agreement between King and Mayor Richard Daley.[63]

When the city government gained the upper hand, it removed Elizabeth Wood as the housing authority's executive secretary. Her departure ended efforts to manage integration in certain projects. At least four Chicago projects were in white neighborhoods. Their tenants were all or almost all white, with the proportion of African Americans governed by informal quotas. Wood's successor, William Kean, continued Wood's practices and these projects remained as they had been through the middle 1960s. In other projects with more mixed tenant populations, Wood had worked to maintain the same proportions. Kean stopped this practice and African American families eventually filled the projects. In 1969, near the end of the period under consideration, Chicago changed its tenant selection policies in response to a lawsuit filed by the federal government. It returned to imposing quotas on African Americans in largely white projects.[64]

New York

New York resembled Chicago in at least three respects. Important business and real estate interests pushed for slum clearance and urban renewal. The key figure in New York's redevelopment efforts, Robert Moses, was uninterested in changing neighborhood patterns. He doubted that public projects, including public housing, could be, or should be, used to open new neighborhoods to minorities, African Americans or Puerto Ricans. Moses believed that public housing should be located in neighborhoods that private builders found unattractive, usually slum neighborhoods populated by minorities. Second, New Yorkers living outside slum neighborhoods were often opposed to public housing in their neighborhoods. Neighborhood groups in the outlying areas, Staten Island, the northern Bronx, eastern Queens, and southern Brooklyn, resisted new projects. When the city, under Mayor John Lindsay, proposed 13 "scattered site" projects in 1967, local opposition forced the abandonment of at least eight. The project slated first for Corona and then Forest Hills, in Queens, generated a highly publicized controversy that eventually undermined support for public housing. Finally, New York had a large and growing minority population. In 1940, African Americans numbered 458,000 and comprised a little over 6 percent of the city's population. In 1980, African Americans in New York numbered 1.7 million, a quarter of the city's population. In the same years, Americans of Spanish-speaking origins accounted for another 1.4 million or 16 percent of the population. New York's minorities often lived in the worst housing and were most likely to be displaced by slum clearance and urban renewal.[65]

For some authors, the population changes in New York, not the state of the city's housing, were the problem. Harrison Salisbury noted the arrival between 1950 and 1958 of 600,000 African Americans and Puerto Ricans, mostly poor. He thought many remained jobless and received welfare. Roger Starr contended that New York had built enough standard housing between 1948 and 1968 to have eliminated its substandard stock and accommodated a decrease in average family size were it not for the arrival of many poor families. Migration to the city had caused the overall housing stock to decline in quality, he claimed. Buildings that were considered standard in 1945 had deteriorated under the weight of over-crowding.[66]

New York was, nevertheless, different from Chicago and most other American cities. Residential patterns were more complex. There were several neighborhoods around the city where African Americans predominated, not just one or two at the city center. The indices that attempted to measure segregation suggest that New York was slightly less segregated than Chicago in 1950 and that segregation in New York declined further by 1970 than in Chicago. There were more mixed neighborhoods as well as slum or blighted neighborhoods where minorities did not predominate. The first public housing projects were on the Lower East Side, where recent immigrants, many of them Jewish, lived. East Harlem, where several projects were built after 1949, was an Italian neighborhood. New York's public housing program was bigger and more varied than those elsewhere. The housing authority was able to locate projects, frequently middle-income projects, in the outlying boroughs, in white or mixed neighborhoods. It served a broader population and had real popular support. It was not just a slum clearance tool wielded on behalf of real estate interests.

The New York housing authority continued efforts to manage integration until the middle 1960s. In the early 1950s, the authority prided itself on its ability to create and maintain integrated projects. It offered itself as proof that people of different identities could live together. Nonetheless, the number of minority tenants continued to increase. By 1959, African Americans and Puerto Ricans occupied 56 percent of public housing units in New York, although their share of the population was only 20 percent. Minority tenants were in the majority in 19 of 87 projects. That year, the authority changed its selection procedures in an attempt to preserve integrated projects. Depending on the composition of a project's tenant population, it gave preference to white or non-white applicants. About a third of all projects were thereby closed to new African American tenants and some projects closed to new Puerto Rican tenants. The projects where African Americans received preference were often middle-income projects in outlying areas, where applications from African Americans were uncommon. Advocacy groups initially supported the changes, but their success was limited. New applicants generally resembled the tenant population and the population of the immediate neighborhood. Apartments in heavily African American projects and neighborhoods remained vacant in the absence of white applicants. African American organizations eventually objected. At a time when 85,000 families applied each year for 6,000 public housing vacancies, it was hard to defend vacant apartments. In 1964, the authority moved to a first come, first served policy, while still "encouraging" applicants to choose a project where their presence might promote integration.[67]

In a 1960 article, Bernard Roshco, a former housing authority employee, denounced the housing authority's new selection procedures. Roshco accused the authority of "operating behind a fog of obscurantism." Even while maintaining to the federal Civil Rights Commission that it did not impose quotas, authority had implemented the new policy without public notice. Ends and means were both important, Roshco argued, and the authority had avoided analysis and debate of both. A large-scale expansion of public housing would be needed if New York were to absorb its rapidly growing minority population. Yet the authority had decided to act as a "benevolent autocracy" and exclude from public housing for an indeterminate time many who needed it most. Dispelling the idea that public housing was "minority" housing had become the goal. Confronted with resistance from white neighborhoods as well as complaints from African American leaders concerned about the number of projects in Harlem, the authority had set out to appease both. It promised neighborhood associations that it could maintain "racial" balances and worked hard to attract white tenants. To minority groups, it had offered the advice that they could promote integration by steering non-white applicants to largely white projects.[68]

When Ellen Lurie and the Union Settlement workers came to East Harlem in the 1950s, they encountered a neighborhood undergoing significant change. What had been an Italian neighborhood was becoming a Puerto Rican and African American neighborhood. Despite the departure of many Italian families during the 1940s, East Harlem's population was still more than half white in 1950. In 1959, it was only 21.4 percent white. The change in areas impacted by public housing was greater. Although as many as 40 percent of the families displaced by construction of the Washington Houses were white, only 12.5 percent of the tenants were white in 1956 and only 7.5 percent in 1959. The same pattern re-occurred in projects across East Harlem, even in areas with larger white populations or in projects built before 1949. East River Houses, built in 1941, saw its white population decline from an initial 89 percent to 36 percent in 1956. By 1959, none of the nine projects in East Harlem had a white population over 30 percent. By 1965, the average white population was 19 percent.[69]

Some New Yorkers saw such changes in a negative light. The Union Settlement team reported that Italian families in East Harlem felt threatened. They saw their neighborhood dissolving around them. Often with incomes too high to qualify for public housing, the original inhabitants saw newcomers better housed than themselves. White public housing tenants were, according to the settlement workers, an "unhappy lot to interview." Some were trying to make the best of their situation. Others were embarrassed by living in a project, amidst a "poor class of people." The settlement workers shared some of these feelings. They perceived a vibrant neighborhood being undermined, in part by the public housing they otherwise supported.[70]

African American Tenants

African Americans who lived in public housing generally approved of it. An opinion poll conducted in the middle 1970s on behalf of HUD suggested that African Americans served by public housing and the new, subsidized private housing programs were happier with their housing situation than African Americans generally. Nationwide African Americans were more disenchanted with their living conditions than any other segment of the population; only 56 percent gave their housing a positive rating. Nevertheless, African American participants in federal housing programs registered a 57 percent positive rating. African American public housing tenants were more concerned about the problems their communities faced than white tenants, but much less than African Americans generally. African Americans living in public housing thought poor schools, drug addiction, poor street lighting and poor housing conditions were less serious issues in their communities than did their counterparts in private housing across the country.[71]

Outsiders' Attitudes

When outsiders saw the African American population within public housing increasing after 1949, it became, for some, another reason to oppose public housing. A public housing project populated by African Americans was, in itself, something negative and not something you would want in your own neighborhood. Still others, both African Americans and whites opposed to housing discrimination, saw public housing filled with African Americans as segregation reinforced. For them, public housing had become a problem for African Americans, not a solution.

Some of those who supported public housing remained optimistic. While they were concerned about the increase in African American numbers, they saw public housing as a vehicle for integration and better housing. Others remained committed to managed integration. Like the increase in poor families or welfare recipients, the increasing African American tenant population was a problem to be managed. Finally an increasing group had their doubts about the prospects for residential integration and thought it unwise to sacrifice public housing in a vain search for integrated suburban housing.

An Extension of the "Ghetto"

Image counted as much as numbers. The fact that African Americans lived in public housing readily became one more thing that counted against the program. A series of articles that appeared in the *Chicago Daily News* in 1965 criticized the Robert Taylor Homes as the "world's biggest and most jam-packed housing development," a "$70 million ghetto," and a "civic monument to misery, bungling and a hellish way of life." The articles went on to say that the Taylor Homes were an "all–Negro city within a city," referred to by its tenants as the "Congo Hilton."[72]

Such characterizations fit into wider concerns about the increasing numbers of African Americans in the cities. In the 1940s, advocates for African Americans had borrowed the term, "ghetto," to dramatize the enforced isolation of African Americans in certain neighborhoods. Over time and in others' usage, it threatened to replace "slum" as the designation for the neighborhoods with the worst housing and poorest inhabitants. It came to be applied to any neighborhood with a predominance of African American inhabitants, regardless of their incomes or the quality of their housing. When working-class African Americans bought houses into formerly white neighborhoods in cities like Chicago, some saw the "ghetto" expanding. A critic of public housing policy in the middle 1960s could equate the increase in the urban African American population with an "explosive" growth of the "ghettos." He saw a "problem-ridden" population compressed in the neighborhoods "most deficient in housing and other facilities and services."[73]

In some accounts, ghetto inhabitants took on all the negative qualities formerly attributed to slum dwellers. Writing about the poverty and bad housing in the Williamsburg section of Brooklyn, Michael Harrington noted the arrival of African Americans and Puerto Ricans starting in 1955. All this produced in the neighborhood, Harrington claimed, was "an environment of social disintegration" and violent gangs. The most spectacular effect of the neighborhood transition, Harrington argued, was a marked increase in juvenile delinquency.[74]

When Lawrence Friedman attempted to explain public housing's declining reputation in the middle 1960s, he turned to the increased numbers of poor African American tenants as part of the explanation. The decline in public housing's fortunes, he wrote, had "gone hand in hand" with the increased numbers of African American tenants. When public housing meant "Negro ghettoes," whites abandoned it. They moved away or withdrew their political support. Whereas public housing once served "marginal whites," it now housed "the most despised and dispossessed group," "the urban problem-family Negro." Friedman thought that once whites perceived that public housing was home to "degraded, hopeless people, the victims of weakness, fate and prejudice," they became hostile.[75]

Congressional supporters of public housing voiced similar thoughts. In 1960, Senator Joseph Clark recounted that, when he had served as mayor of Philadelphia, public housing had lost popular support, largely because of fears of integration. Planners and social workers supported public housing, but the city council resisted. Clark conceded that the council probably reflected popular sentiment. He thought a "very real public education job" was needed before public housing would be acceptable at the local level.[76]

A Vehicle for Integration

In the 1950s and 1960s, Charles Abrams remained the most prominent advocate for public housing as the solution to African Americans' housing problems. In articles and his 1955 book *Forbidden Neighbors*, he described how public housing had benefited African Americans. According to Abrams, public housing was the first government program to provide African Americans decent, affordable housing and seemed to be the only program capable of doing so. Public housing had demonstrated that integrated housing could work. He claimed that it had created decent, integrated neighborhoods and stabilized property values in many places.[77]

Although cognizant that African Americans were occupying an increasing share of public housing units, Abrams was still convinced in the 1950s that the kind of managed integration practiced in New York could produce integrated public housing across the country. Abrams thought that keeping African American occupancy below 30 percent was critical. Otherwise, whites would feel like an oppressed minority and seek to leave. Abrams was comfortable with projects where African Americans predominated, as in Harlem. He thought fears about "ghettos" overblown. If people freely chose to live among people like themselves, that was okay. The keys for public housing were that African Americans have access to all projects and that housing authorities actively pursue integration.[78]

Success was not assured. Abrams thought that public housing could be the wedge that destroyed enforced segregation or it could destroy hope for "inter-racial" understanding and harmony. Abrams worried that Congress and the Eisenhower administration failed to see that housing problems and minority problems were much the same thing. Without a more ambitious housing program, African Americans would monopolize public housing and it would no longer be integrated.[79]

A decade later, Abrams was less optimistic about public housing. He still believed that federal government housing programs could satisfy African Americans' housing needs. Abrams was now open to supplementing government-built housing with subsidies paid to private developers. An ambitious housing program was still needed as was direct federal intervention to secure integration. The federal government should build where segregated housing persisted and housing authorities would not, or could not, act.[80]

Like Abrams, Robert Weaver remained optimistic during the 1950s about public housing's possible contribution to solving African Americans' housing needs. He praised housing authorities that had moved towards non-segregation policies. He was particularly positive about the New York authority's practices. New York's public housing had done more than anything else to introduce African Americans to all parts of the city, he claimed.[81]

Weaver worried that urban renewal was making residential integration more difficult. Most families displaced by urban renewal and other public works projects were African Americans. Giving displaced families preference in public housing brought more African American families into public housing and pushed whites out. Weaver believed that any project where African Americans comprised more than 40 to 60 percent of the tenants was likely to become all African American. Families dislocated by urban renewal but not rehoused in public housing looked for new housing in existing African American neighborhoods or in transitional neighborhoods. In the former case, the arrival of dislocated families led to overcrowding. In the latter, it led to more rapid neighborhood succession. Neighborhoods that were integrated, even if only temporarily, became all African American that much sooner.[82]

Weaver acknowledged that only a significant increase in low-cost housing could facilitate residential integration. Without more affordable housing, tearing down slum properties merely pushed poor African American families into other neighborhoods. Yet, Weaver's vision had become markedly less ambitious. He saw the greatest hope for integrated housing in middle-income projects located away from African American neighborhoods. Only then were whites likely to remain and the demand from African Americans likely to remain manageable.[83]

As the number of African American tenants increased, some writers expressed support for housing authorities' attempts to manage integration. Quotas, separate application procedures or any other tools housing authorities tried to wield were unattractive and had negative consequences, but the alternative was worse, they argued. If public housing were to remain viable, if it were to retain any public support, if public housing were to remain at least as integrated as it was, housing authorities had to be free to take "race" into consideration when choosing tenants.[84]

James Fuerst was the most vocal proponent for such measures. Fuerst worked for the Chicago housing authority under Elizabeth Wood and, after leaving the authority, had a lengthy career as an academic. Fuerst thought that firing Wood had put the Chicago authority on the wrong path, on the path to projects full of poor African Americans. Fuerst argued that public housing could be integrated housing, in terms of class and identity, but doing so required careful tenant selection, including quotas on African American tenants. "First come, first served" policies were a mistake. Filling vacant apartments quickly, rather than waiting for suitable tenants, was a mistake. Heeding pleas from African American leaders for more public housing in African American neighborhoods was equally a mistake. With careful tenant selection, housing authorities could demonstrate that public housing posed no threat to other neighborhoods. Once it was clear that public housing need not house just poor African Americans, housing authorities would be able to build more projects throughout the city.[85]

As support for civil rights increased, quotas were increasingly hard to defend. Before the 1964 Civil Rights Acts and the 1968 Fair Housing Act, commentators could speculate whether quotas were legal or constitutional. The three court cases that involved quotas before 1968, including *Banks v. Housing Authority of San Francisco*, suggested that the courts were unlikely to look favorably on them. A lengthy article in the 1960 *Howard Law Journal* reviewed the relevant legal precedents as well as the pros and cons. In the end, it concluded that, while quotas might be acceptable under the law, better alternatives existed—a much larger housing supply combined with measures like fair housing ordinances.[86]

Those that argued for non-discrimination and against measures like quotas had to confront the fact that non-discrimination in public housing did not necessarily produce integration. After the Civil Rights Act, HUD recognized two non-discriminatory tenant selection processes. Housing authorities could give prospective tenants a free choice of the unit they would occupy or an authority could adopt a "first come, first served" policy, in which applications were filled in order of receipt and applicants could turn down one or two units before being assigned to the end of the list. The first indications were neither produced integrated housing projects. Beginning in 1956, Louisville tried first a "first come, first served" policy and then one that limited applicants to a choice of three units. Both seemed to accelerate the departure of whites and the arrival of African Americans. An observer could see this as an "anomaly" created by site selection and housing discrimination elsewhere, but the immediate remedy for public housing was not obvious. Once the Civil Rights Act of 1964 passed, housing authorities, like the one in Chicago, that advocates thought did not serve African Americans' best interests, could defend their lack of concern about increasing African American numbers as consistent with the law.[87]

A Barrier to Integration

After passage of the 1949 Act, African American leaders remained of two minds about public housing. The desire for better housing was universal. Some leaders, often politicians and businessmen, welcomed public housing, and even urban renewal, in existing African American neighborhoods and were less enthusiastic about dispersing public housing elsewhere. Public housing was better housing and a boost to their communities. Others, often middle-class activists associated with NAACP, worried that public housing was replicating the pattern of segregation. Their attention turned to pushing public housing into white neighborhoods or even to the suburbs. Still a higher priority was ending discrimination in private housing and in Federal Housing Administration mortgage policies. As early as 1951, the NAACP leader Clarence Mitchell attacked federal housing policies as promoting segregation more successfully than the Ku Klux Klan. In 1955, the NAACP opposed a FHA-funded project in an African American neighborhood in Dayton on the grounds that it would "add" to the ghetto and expand segregation in the schools.[88]

For many advocates, housing came to be seen as an individual issue, not a social issue. Edith Wood and Catherine Bauer may have thought in terms of society building housing for those that needed it but could not find in the private market. Now writers saw an individual's freedom of choice as the goal. Once everyone, including African Americans, was free to buy or rent the housing they wanted, all would be well, they argued. Frank Horne, an African American employed at the HHFA, complained that, when "race" was involved, the laws of supply and demand no longer applied. In his view, the objective was that African Americans gain the right to bargain in an open market for shelter, just like everyone else.[89]

The NAACP and others turned to the courts to shift public housing policies and practices, especially site selection. In at least two cases, litigation overturned local efforts to block public housing. Another lawsuit produced a 1973 federal court order that suburbs around Cleveland sign cooperation agreements with the Cleveland housing authority. Their refusal to do so had, according the federal district court judge, prevented poor African Americans from finding decent housing outside the slums. Neither this suit nor a similar one in the Detroit area produced any public housing in the suburbs. In another case (*Shannon v U.S. HUD*), a federal judge directed HUD to establish an official site selection policy that took "racial" concentrations into account. The court ruled that the absence of a policy had adversely affected African Americans and violated the Civil Rights Acts of 1964 and 1968.[90]

The most noteworthy housing litigation was the Gautreaux case in Chicago. In 1966, lawyers from the American Civil Liberties Union filed suits against the Chicago Housing Authority and HUD on behalf of Dorothy Gautreaux and other public housing residents. The suits alleged that the housing authority's site selection practices, condoned by HUD, were discriminatory and violated the plaintiffs' civil rights. The lawsuits followed a long, complicated, and controversial path until their conclusion in 1976. The end results included an order that, in effect, the housing authority could build only small, scattered projects and that it could not build in African American neighborhoods until it had built in white neighborhoods, either within the city or the adjacent suburbs. Since the courts declined to force the housing authority or the suburbs to build any housing, the immediate result was a halt to public housing construction in Chicago.

The way the Gautreaux litigation unfolded forced the plaintiffs and their supporters into the same choice discussed during the final debate regarding the 1949 Act: public housing in African American neighborhoods or a declaration in favor of integrated housing. The plaintiffs' lawyer and the NAACP chose a statement favoring integrated housing. Alexander Polikoff, the longtime lead attorney, told a reporter in 1970: "if public housing must die because of business as usual practices, let it die." A NAACP official negotiating with the housing authority was asked whether she preferred decent housing or worrying about its location. Her reply was that she would prefer that no more public housing be built and people stay in the slums rather than more public housing in African American neighborhoods.[91]

Not everyone agreed. Once it became clear that the Gautreaux litigation put additional public housing at risk, some African American leaders in Chicago dissented. Outsiders had their doubts. A 1970 *Yale Law Journal* article pointed out that the decision ignored the fact that many people preferred to live in homogenous neighborhoods, even Chicago's

South Side, and put forward an alternative solution. On the theory that integration was meaningful only if between equals in fact as well as in law, it advocated building up African American neighborhoods and African Americans as a prelude to integrated housing across the region. Somewhat later, a piece in *The Public Interest* faulted the litigants as overly ambitious. By trying to integrate the metropolitan area and provide low-income housing at the same time, they had created a dilemma they had not escaped.[92]

In a 1966 article, Herbert Hill, a longtime NAACP official, forcefully elaborated the integrationist argument against public housing. African Americans had never received an adequate share of public housing, according to Hill. The presence of a few whites did not mean integration. Reserving a few apartments for whites in an otherwise African American project was a feeble attempt to avoid the real problem of integrated housing. Public housing in its current form was perpetuating housing segregation. Municipal governments were using public housing, along with welfare programs and urban renewal, to maintain and expand the "Negro ghetto." Segregation, poverty and exploitation were creating a "ghetto underclass." Public housing located in African American neighborhoods was not just an opportunity foregone; it harmed the African Americans it housed, Hill charged. Public housing was unhealthy, unattractive, and built to minimum standards. It isolated its residents from their surrounding neighborhood and the larger community. It alienated them from society and undermined their dignity and self-esteem. It penned people in and bred slum living.[93]

That public housing was a deliberate government effort to reinforce residential segregation gained wide currency. The National Committee Against Discrimination in Housing published a pamphlet in 1967, entitled "How the Federal Government Builds Ghettos." A national study published in 1960 considered a public housing project occupied solely by African Americans as "an extreme of racial segregation seldom equaled even in Negro neighborhoods." The study concluded that public housing had established or strengthened segregation in communities where "racial separation" had not previously existed. A 1967 article contended that "racial ghettos" were "chiefly creations of public policy," especially public policy since World War II. A critic of Chicago housing, writing in the 1970s, wrote that, because of the housing authority's site selection policies, public housing now perpetuated the "urban diseases" it was once designed to cure.[94]

At least two studies cast doubt on the notion that public housing reinforced residential segregation. One study, of 44 U.S. cities between 1940 and 1960, found no connection between public housing and residential segregation. The presence of public housing neither increased nor decreased residential segregation. Another study, of Philadelphia housing between 1930 and 1980, discerned no connection between public housing and a neighborhood's transition from majority white to majority African American. Instead it found that factors like low real estate values, location near the center city, and propinquity to industrial jobs explained how neighborhoods changed. In general African Americans moved into neighborhoods more affluent families or industrial corporations no longer wanted.[95]

Public housing also suffered guilt by association with urban renewal. By the early 1960s, it was obvious that urban renewal projects failed to rehouse most of the families it displaced. As many as 70 percent of families whose homes were demolished found new housing in equally poor housing conditions. It was also obvious that most displaced families were African American. Urban renewal came to be seen as "Negro removal." Although public housing gave preference to displaced families and remained the principal means to provide better housing for them, its location in African American neighborhoods reinforced the perception that public housing was just another part of a federal policy designed to reinforce segregation.[96]

Better Housing for African Americans

Despite the passion and persistence with which the NAACP and others pursued residential integration in the suburbs, other voices counseled caution. Wide scale integration might not be feasible in the short term, they warned. It might be possible only for middle-class African Americans. Some, perhaps many, African Americans preferred living in their own homogenous neighborhoods. Poor urban neighborhoods still needed better housing and other government assistance. Their needs should not be sacrificed while African American struggled to open up white suburban neighborhoods.

Herbert Gans saw new towns built on vacant land as solutions to the nation's housing problems, including residential segregation. Nevertheless, he cautioned that a new towns program would necessarily start slowly and relocate only a few African Americans at first. The most likely candidates were young, upwardly mobile families with decent incomes. Gans wondered whether "an unwed Negro mother" would want to move to a middle-income project filled with married couples and distant from her mother and other female relatives she was likely to have relied on. Gans was open to government programs that would help African Americans move into existing city neighborhoods even if it meant that cities became largely or wholly African American. He wondered whether fears of cities dominated by African Americans were not overblown. If the government provided decent services and housing to African Americans within their own neighborhoods, Gans speculated that the next generation of African Americans would be more accepting of residential integration.[97]

Frances Piven and Richard Cloward thought a rights-based attack on residential segregation was a mistake. The numbers involved alone made rapid, widespread residential integration highly unlikely. They claimed that if New York City applied all its housing and planning resources to integration, the best it could do was halt the expansion of predominately African American neighborhoods, not create more diverse neighborhoods. Piven and Cloward argued that non-discrimination statutes and other legal measures had proven ineffective. Typically anti-discrimination laws were weak and lacked enforcement provisions. Such statutes left control of the housing market in the hands of the private real estate industry and the industry was adept at maintaining the class and "racial" character of neighborhoods regardless of any legal requirements. Suburban housing was too expensive for most African Americans. Middle-class families might benefit from banning discrimination in suburban communities, but poor families would not.[98]

More government spending on housing in African American neighborhoods was a big part of the solution, according to Piven and Cloward. Despite public housing's poor reputation, more was needed. Piven and Cloward imagined a broad range of government interventions—rent supplements, low-cost mortgages, revised building codes, private buildings bought or rented by housing authorities, rehabilitation programs. Only the worse housing should be torn down. Housing authorities should build in marginal or underused areas, where African American neighborhoods could be extended without provoking opposition from whites.[99]

Public housing's relationship to African Americans' housing needs was complicated. From the start, African Americans occupied more public housing units than their share of the population might suggest. Most of these units fit within a "separate but equal" model. Yet some early public housing projects were vehicles for integrated housing and important proponents of public housing were opposed to residential segregation of any kind. After the war, African Americans' share of public housing increased steadily, until they dominated the public housing managed by local housing authorities and intended for families. Even so, the public housing program was too small to meet the needs of all low-income African American families. Critically, public housing, after the 1949 Act, was no longer a plausible tool for housing integration. After the war, African American advocacy organizations reshaped their goals so that an African American family's right to choose its housing became the principal aim. "Fair housing" replaced decent, affordable housing as the goal. Within this framework of individual rights, public housing, usually in African American neighborhoods, was no longer relevant, largely because it did not promote housing integration.

The identification of public housing with African Americans created critics for public housing. For some, the presence of so many African Americans was just another reason to oppose public housing. It was bad enough if public housing brought poor families into the neighborhood. It was worse if the new families were African Americans. For others, it was another sign that public housing had "failed." It had not promoted integration or improved neighborhoods. Still others saw living in an integrated, middle-class suburb as the ultimate goal for African Americans, or at least some of them. Public housing, from this perspective, was irrelevant or, worse, a barrier to be overcome.

CHAPTER EIGHT

Final Judgments

"We have, in short, a paradox: nobody likes public housing except the people who live there and those who want to get in." So Alvin Rabushka and William Weissert wrote in their 1977 work *Caseworkers or Police*.[1] The variant of public housing implemented after 1949 had very few enthusiastic supporters, other than tenants. The debate after 1949 featured commentators who disliked aspects of public housing for different reasons, those who wanted to do away with the public housing altogether and those who preferred some other government intervention into low-income housing. Judgments about public housing became so negative that, by the late 1950s, it was conceivable to ask whether public housing had "failed."

Tenants

Rabushka and Weissert interviewed public housing tenants in Wilmington, Delaware. Five out of six tenants reported that their housing was satisfactory and most had a positive opinion of the housing authority's management of the buildings. A Harris survey conducted as part of the Department of Housing and Urban Development's National Housing Policy Review in the early 1970s revealed that public housing tenants approved of their housing. Fifty-eight percent viewed their housing positively; two-thirds thought it better than their previous housing and nearly 80 percent gave the public housing program positive ratings. Ten percent of public housing tenants reported that their previous housing lacked a complete kitchen; similar percentages reported the lack of hot water, bathtubs or flush toilets in the housing they left. Even in the ill-famed Pruitt-

Igoe project in St. Louis the great majority of tenants believed that their apartments met their needs and were superior to their previous housing.[2]

Data collected by the 1968 National Commission on Urban Problems also provided evidence that public housing was popular with low-income Americans. According to the commission, the vacancy rate for public housing in the 50 largest American cities during 1967 was 2.2 percent. If one eliminated the four cities that had unusually high vacancy rates (St. Louis, Dallas, Kansas City and Fort Worth), the vacancy rate for the remaining 46 cities was 1.5 percent. The turnover rate (that is, the percentage of tenants leaving during a year) in public housing was 16.3 percent, compared with 20 percent in all American housing. During 1967, there were 28 applicants for every public housing vacancy. In New York City, there were 762 applicants for every vacancy; in Chicago, 126.[3]

Tenants evidenced significant concerns about other aspects of their housing situation, especially the neighborhood in which it was located, management's ability to maintain the building, and management and the police's capacity to enforce law and order. Public housing tenants were not as positive about their housing as Americans in general. According to the Harris survey, eight out of ten Americans viewed their current housing positively, while only six out of ten public housing tenants did. Individual projects experienced high turnover and vacancy rates from time to time. Nonetheless, through the 1970s, if you asked the Americans for whom public housing was built, they said that it did what it was intended to do, provide better housing for low-income families.

Public Image

Immediately after World War II, media portrayals of public housing projects were usually favorable; they appeared as at least a partial solution to urban problems. By the late 1950s, however, the media were most likely to portray public housing as segregated, rundown and crime ridden. Newspapers in cities like New York and Chicago printed articles depicting in vivid terms the alleged problems of public housing. Only 7 percent of public housing units were in high-rise projects that included more than 200 units. Yet, the popular image of public housing came to be large urban projects featuring multiple high-rise buildings. The Robert Taylor Homes in Chicago and the Pruitt-Igoe projects in St. Louis came to represent public housing. Even after the Pruitt-Igoe project was demolished in the early 1970s, the media equated it with public housing. The only form of public housing that could count on favorable press coverage was housing for the elderly.[4]

By the early 1960s, the conventional wisdom was that public housing had acquired a poor image. Both opponents and friendlier critics concluded that public housing's reputation was, perhaps irredeemably, bad. In a 1963 report for the Boston housing authority, Elizabeth Wood painted the grim picture: "According to its image, public housing has inferior architecture; looks institutional; is inhabited by people who are inferior by virtue of their residence or because they are all on public assistance, or because the projects are rife with crime and muggings or because they are spied on by management which makes them turn out their lights by ten o'clock but allows crimes to rampage." By the early 1970s, public housing had become, in the popular imagination, the housing of last resort, "a place nobody would live unless they had no choice."[5]

Some attributed public housing's bad reputation to the work of its opponents. The program's enemies had managed to crystalize a negative portrait. Others saw it merely as the inevitable product of public housing's many alleged problems. Chester Hartman wrote about the "litany of social, aesthetic and administrative defects" that were "widely known and acknowledged." Others perceived class prejudice at work. Both middle- and working-class Americans allegedly looked down upon anyone who needed help to pay the rent. The urban unrest of the 1960s, which the Kerner and Douglas Commissions had attributed, in part, to the failures of federal housing policies, seemed to have undermined public housing's support. Even the rent strikes launched by public housing tenants in St. Louis and Newark contributed to the negative image.[6]

Association with African Americans worked against public housing. It was easy to think that public housing projects were now just another African American neighborhood, an extension of the "ghetto." For those hostile to African Americans, this was more than enough reason to resist construction of more public housing. For those supportive of African Americans, it could lead to negative conclusions. What was the point of a government program that, at best, expanded the "ghetto"?

Reinforcing public housing's poor reputation was the oft-reproduced pictures of the high-rise buildings of the Chicago's Robert Taylor Homes and of St. Louis' Pruitt-Igoe Homes. As Lawrence Friedman put it, when people saw the projects, "drab, ugly blocks of cement standing like soldiers," they lost faith in public housing. A St. Louis newspaper described Pruitt-Igoe as a "terrified city within a worried city, a matriarchal society of too many unwed or deserted mothers and uncontrollable children, a community on the dole." By the 1970s, photos of Pruitt-Igoe "crumbling to earth" seemed to offer proof that public housing had outlived its usefulness.[7]

As of the mid–1970s, ordinary Americans were of two minds about public housing. Only a third gave the federal government's efforts in low-income housing a positive rating, but two-thirds said they favored housing for low-income families. Nearly 90 percent said they favored government housing for the elderly. More people favored building low-income housing outside inner city areas than opposed it. Fifty-two percent favored building low-income housing in the suburbs.[8]

"Expert" Opinion

Only a few months before the 1949 Act passed, an article debunking the traditional arguments in support of public housing appeared. In "The Myths of Housing Reform," John Dean cast doubts on the social impact of housing, on the relationship between slums and social disorder, and on the financial impact of slums on municipal finances. He thought it difficult to distinguish standard from substandard housing and to link poor housing conclusively with social welfare. Dean argued that reformers overemphasized the physical environment of poor neighborhoods and underemphasized the social environment. At a time when public housing tenants still had a positive reputation, Dean pointed out that they were the product of rigorous selection. Not only had they chosen to apply, but housing authorities had eliminated most kinds of "social misfits" found in the typical slum or blighted area. Even so, Dean thought public housing had not visibly improved the social welfare of its tenants. Housing authorities were geared to collecting rent and maintaining buildings and not to improving tenants. They did not promote social relationships among tenants. They did not encourage them to participate in community life or take advantage of whatever social services were available.[9]

By 1957, Catherine Bauer had lost faith in the public housing being built by housing authorities. The program, she wrote, dragged along in "a kind of limbo," "continuously controversial, not dead but never more than half alive." The approach adopted in 1937 was natural, valid and necessary at the time, but it had jelled too soon and become inflexible. The housing that was built was better than what it been available before. Nevertheless, the program had not adapted itself to American values and traditions. A healthy experiment with "functionalist and collectivist architectural theories" had gone on too long and been reduced to a rigid formula. Housing authorities interpreted their missions too narrowly. They were concerned only with slums and not with housing and not with entire metropolitan regions.[10]

The biggest mistake, according to Bauer, was establishing a separate program for rehousing slum dwellers. Legislation and administrative machinery that dealt only with poor families from the slums had detached public housing from other federal housing policies. Sole reliance on public initiative and public ownership plus narrow eligibility rules had isolated low-income families and led to their treatment as "a special charity case." In Bauer's view, public housing shared with the real estate industry responsibility for creating "lily white suburbs."[11]

Federal housing programs had produced a "few expensive, high density, over-controlled municipal projects mostly on central sites" and a "vast chaotic flood" of middle-class, single-family homes in the suburbs. The apartments built by housing authorities were, Bauer claimed, more expensive that modest suburban homes. Large housing projects were deliberately cut off from their surroundings. Their bleak architecture and minimum standards were incompatible with the "values associated with American home life." The projects built to date left no room for individual deviation, or for personal initiative and responsibility. The small-scale business enterprises that played important roles in poor neighborhood were forbidden. The rules and regulations went far beyond anything in private, multi-family housing. Welfare services had their place, but paternalistic landlords did not attract normal families. Public housing could not accommodate even the families uprooted by slum clearance, much less the many other families in need of decent affordable housing.[12]

Bauer thought that the country still needed a sizeable federal housing program. Despite more than 15 years of prosperity and feverish housing construction, the country had nearly as many "insanitary, congested, and dilapidated" houses as it did in the middle 1930s. Millions of slum dwellings should be demolished. Millions of new, better, affordable homes should be built for the families who were still not served by the private housing market.[13]

Bauer had little to suggest as a way forward. The object, she wrote, was to give low- and middle-income families choices regarding location, dwelling type and neighborhood character. There should be some real selection at all economic and social levels. Bauer was willing to forego public ownership in favor of subsidies paid to private developers if it meant a wider range of housing options and, even, support for public efforts from the real estate industry. Her most specific suggestion was a pilot program in which communities experimented, free of federal policies and procedures but with federal financial assistance.[14]

The dozen experts asked to comment on Bauer's article were even less supportive of a public housing program. The majority view was that home ownership should be the goal. If the government was to build any housing, it should be sold, not rented. To the extent possible, existing public housing should be sold, to the current tenants or to tenant cooperatives. Any new public housing should pay for itself, with rents covering costs. Income limits on public housing should be raised or eliminated. Whenever possible, tenants should be charged an "economic" rent.[15]

The experts did not agree about public housing's goals. One city planner argued that public housing was only about improving housing conditions. "Fix the buildings, not the people," was his advice. On the other hand, William Wheaton, another city planner, thought "rehabilitation and encouragement of people" was the goal, not maintenance of "safe and sanitary dwellings." Elizabeth Wood worried that public housing could not serve normal families and those "who could not accommodate themselves to urban standards of living." The latter group included both families from rural backgrounds unfamiliar with cities and families in need of social services.[16]

In 1959, at the end of the Eisenhower administration, the Housing and Home Finance Agency solicited the views of a similar cross-section of housing experts. With one notable exception, they echoed the reactions to Bauer's article. On the other hand, Lewis Mumford had not changed his views. Mumford argued that, unlike the program authorized by the 1937 and 1949 Acts, a successful public housing program would do more than provide bare minimum housing to the poorest families. For Mumford, a successful public housing program would be allowed to compete with private housing where their target populations overlapped. Mumford remained adamant that linking public housing to slum clearance and building high-density, high-rise housing were fundamental mistakes. They increased long-term costs and produced inferior housing.[17]

Charles Abrams, as a writer and as a lobbyist for the Americans for Democratic Action, continued to point to public housing's accomplishments. Public housing might be unpopular, even with its own tenants but it had demonstrated the feasibility of improved housing in slum areas. It had shown that slum dwellers could be responsible tenants. It had made clear that housing authorities could operate in a businesslike, honest fashion.[18]

Nevertheless, Abrams joined the chorus calling for a larger private role in what had been the preserve of public housing. Subsidies to private developers, sales of public housing projects and apartments, and a focus on home ownership were all parts of Abrams' preferred program by the 1960s. Abrams offered two distinctive arguments for an enlarged private presence. He maintained that allowing the government to be the landlord for a large number of U.S. families was inconsistent with American values. "Monolithic landlordism" had no place in an America that prized a diversity of choices, he argued. Abrams also saw subsidies paid to private developers as a way to bring low-cost, low-income housing, and minority families, to the suburbs. Suburbs could refuse to create housing authorities, but they could not bar private developments, Abrams argued.[19]

A larger private role still had its critics. Alvin Schoor, in his 1963 report prepared for the Department of Health, Education and Welfare, doubted that the private housing sector could, or would, serve the poorest American families. Historically, private builders had hesitated to build houses for families earning $5,000 a year (a little more than the median family income in the early 1960s). The possible profits were too slim and the risks too great. Schorr wondered why they would look for buyers among families earning much less than that. Families earning half the median income struggled to pay for food and clothing, much less rent or a mortgage. Schorr doubted whether the usual expectations about housing costs could apply to low-income families. It was probably not sound public policy to expect poor families to spend 25 or 30 percent of their income on housing.[20]

Alternatives

If there was anything like a consensus view of what public housing should become, aside from a larger private sector presence, it was the opposite of public housing's image. Public housing projects should be small, not large; low-rise, not high-rise. Public housing should fit into neighborhoods. It should be "scattered" throughout cities and metropolitan regions, not concentrated in former slum neighborhoods. Architecture and design should be indistinguishable from other housing. Public housing should be managed just as private, multi-family housing was. Tenants should come from various income and social groups, not just poor African Americans. Housing authorities ought to be re-integrated into city governments.[21]

Jane Jacobs subscribed to most of these notions. Consistent with her belief in the benefits of busy sidewalks, she added some distinctive ideas to what she referred to as "un-slumming" public housing. She would push new streets through housing projects and connect them to existing streets. She would add new, non-residential uses to the ground floors of apartment buildings. She might even add vendors with their carts. Such steps would promote her key to healthy cities, "lively, well-watched, continuously used public spaces."[22]

If the government needed to do something about urban housing, Jacobs thought rent supplements paid to families were preferable to government funded and managed housing. At the heart of Jacob's thinking was a return to pre–New Deal thinking. Under the right circumstances, slums could regenerate themselves. If "paternalistic" planners would get out of the way, an urban economy could transform poor people into middle class people; illiterates into skilled workers; and "greenhorns" into competent citizens.[23]

A Failure?

As early as 1957, it was possible to ask if public housing had "failed." By the early 1970s, it was conceivable to answer in the affirmative. It was not just that public housing had defects or problems. Somehow the entire program had failed. Henry Aaron could report in his 1972 survey of federal housing programs that tenants liked public housing; that vacancy rates were low; and waiting lists for public housing were long. The private sector produced nothing of comparable quality that public housing tenants could afford. Nonetheless, a considerable body of opinion held that the program had failed and ought not to be continued.[24]

Catherine Bauer was virtually alone in discussing how the situation might be changed. Nearly everyone else saw themselves as observers and critics, not potential participants in an effort to expand, improve, or even replace public housing. Bauer, on the other hand, continued to envision a broad popular movement that would bring about a better version of public housing. Over time, she became less optimistic but even in her "Dreary Deadlock" article, she wrote that "sooner or later" grass roots demands for improved public housing would defeat the special interest lobbies.[25]

Nathan Glazer, for one, raised fundamental doubts about the public housing program. Writing in 1967, Glazer judged public housing largely a failure, in the sense that it was unpopular with just about everyone. There might be long waiting lists, but poor families had no alternatives and public housing represented a bargain, he pointed out. Glazer was sure that tenants did not like public housing and would prefer to be elsewhere.[26]

Public housing was a "graveyard of good intentions," Glazer claimed. Limits on welfare families had forced welfare agencies to find more expensive private housing. Barring those with criminal records or drug habits denied decent housing to those who needed it the most. "Ethnic" quotas created perverse outcomes.[27]

Glazer set the capacity to improve family life as the test for public housing. It was not enough that public housing create safe, sanitary, un-crowded housing for poor families. To be judged a success, public housing needed to cure the perceived ills of poor families, especially African American families: "family breakdown, illegitimacy, dependency." Glazer could see no connection between housing quality and healthy families, specifically between public housing and African American family life. He concluded that, if the United States were to do something for the minority of American families who did not have "minimally desirable" housing, rent supplements or an income maintenance program was preferable to public housing.[28]

Over-crowding was at the heart of Glazer's argument. According to Glazer, the United States had virtually eliminated dilapidated housing and un-sanitary housing (housing without running water and toilets) in urban areas. The problem that seemed to remain, and that might afflict poor, African American families, was over-crowding, including population density and the number of persons living in a housing unit. Citing Oscar Lewis' work *Children of Sanchez*, Glazer conceded that over-crowding adversely effected families. He questioned whether, outside a few exceptional cases in New York and Boston, American cities were so densely populated that they harmed their inhabitants. He doubted that the usual American measure for an over-crowded housing unit, more than one person per room, identified harmful housing. Some higher income families lived in crowded apartments without obvious negative consequences.[29]

Glazer wondered whether agreement on the nature of family life was possible at all or possible enough to create the basis for a national housing policy. Whatever the standard, Glazer did not see connections between over-crowded housing and family life. Over-crowding had declined for African American families over the 1950s, but their "family disorganization" had increased. Low income, African American neighborhoods seemed to have the same problems regardless of housing quality. Moving into decent housing in a public project did not appear to transform poor, African American families. Perhaps if poor families moved into the superior housing typical of the middle class, family life might improve. Otherwise, Glazer was skeptical about the wisdom of public housing.[30]

Nevertheless, there was no consensus about how public housing had failed. Diagnoses fell into at least two categories: those that saw public housing as simply a housing program and those that imagined that public housing was geared to social transformation. Those who maintained that public housing was intended only to provide better housing bemoaned "grim, dull, drab" apartment towers and the like. Advocates for African Americans pointed to public housing's failure to create integrated housing. Others complained that public housing had not made slums go away. New York had nearly as many substandard housing units in 1960 as it had in 1935. Among those that looked for social impacts, Glazer argued that public housing had not improved its tenants; their "family lives" were no different than those of families living in poorer housing. Some claimed that living in public housing undermined healthy family life. It promoted "social disorganization" and despair. Others argued that public housing had not promoted social mobility. Tenants, rather than increasing their incomes and moving to better housing, remained poor and stayed in the projects. Elizabeth Wood thought that public housing had not "regenerated" neighborhoods.[31]

The confusion about public housing's objectives was, itself, seen as a problem. Henry Aaron observed in 1972 that public housing faced an uncertain future until and unless its goals became clearer. Whom was it to serve: the poorest or the working poor; the elderly poor, usually white or single-parent families, usually African American? Should public housing be tied to slum clearance? Should it provide housing only or housing plus social services? Should it be seen as a tool for creating integrated housing? In the middle 1960s, Alvin Schorr had laid a similar array of choices: a housing program for the working poor; a rehabilitative program for the poorest, less functional families; or a much larger program intended to expand housing opportunities for a substantial fraction of the population.[32]

One explanation for public housing's apparent failure was that it was being blamed for problems it could not solve. The solutions lay, instead, in different, broader public programs. Writers like Lee Rainwater and Leon Keyserling offered increased incomes as the fundamental solution to poverty and poor housing. For Keyserling, creating enough jobs was the key step. Some writers concerned about urban problems warned that a few housing projects could never remake American cities. Authorities needed first to address the problems of poverty and discrimination. To fix urban housing, they needed to deploy an array of remedies: better building code enforcement, rehabilitation of older buildings, more and better private housing, and new public facilities.[33]

Some explained that the public housing program was too small and too poorly funded to succeed, even if its only goal was to provide better housing for slum dwellers. According to a 1970 article, public housing's major problem was that it was "under-subsidized and over-controlled" at the federal level. In the late 1970s, Eugene Meehan wrote that, for public housing to succeed, the federal government needed to create enough housing to meet society's needs, especially the needs of the poor. It needed to properly subsidize the difference between public housing's costs and what housing authorities could reasonably collect in rents.[34]

Several experts, most supportive of public housing, saw "failure" in political terms. They thought the public housing program suffered from the continued opposition of the real estate industry and others. Public housing had little or no organized support, especially beyond national organizations headquartered in Washington. The public housing produced by housing authorities was not popular with ordinary Americans. Catherine Bauer thought the influence of builders, lenders and property owners had increased by the middle 1950s. Albert Mayer thought that real estate industry had been instrumental in creating a form of public housing that was unlikely to succeed. Public housing had, in his view, become "straitjacketed, unadventurous and non-evolving." It remained isolated and evidenced "a penury of spiritual outlook." Mayer explained that public housing remained "a prisoner of its original opponents and detractors" and they had determined its character, "to an unbelievable extent."[35]

The groups that had pushed for public housing in the 1930s and 1940s had drifted away. Bauer acknowledged support from labor unions, but still felt they were more interested in creating jobs than speaking for those without decent housing. In one view, "liberals" and Democrats had shifted from the ideological to the pragmatic during the 1950s. By the middle 1970s, Rabushka and Weissert could write that public housing had no support in universities or "policy making corridors" in Washington.[36]

When others looked at public housing, they saw the workings of a deadlocked, perhaps even stagnant, political situation. Observers wrote about "muddling through" and about "mindless incrementalism." In postwar America, public programs could not threaten the status quo. They needed to offer liberals and conservatives something. The government could build a token number of public housing units, too few to solve any problem, but not so many that conservatives felt threatened. Neither camp was satisfied, but could not conceive any alternatives. A public housing program big enough to meet the apparent need was politically inconceivable. Charles Abrams thought that public housing had failed to change as the housing market had changed, but public officials were unwilling to admit policy failures. One writer commented that the most remarkable aspect of public housing was not that it had been limited, but that it existed at all.[37]

A parallel argument was that public housing suffered because it had become the preserve of local housing authorities. Bauer talked about public housing as a "separate little pocket of city government," divorced from the community's needs and hamstrung by federal regulations. She saw housing officials under constant attack from real estate interests. Frightened and insecure, housing officials suffered from excessive caution, administrative rigidity and a lack of creativity. Chester Hartman was especially critical of housing authorities. He thought that because they were distant from the tenants they were supposed to serve, they were insensitive to their needs. They did not advocate effectively for public housing or represent tenants' interests. He charged that they were often the most effective brake on public housing construction. Harrison Salisbury attributed public housing's problems to poor concepts, administration, and "often deliberate sabotage by cruel, stupid, heartless men."[38]

Bauer thought that ordinary Americans did not want to live in the kind of housing local authorities built. The size, design, and exterior spaces found in a typical housing project did not fit post-war American values. Public housing's opponents had an important advantage because they appeared to support what Bauer characterized as "that vast inchoate American force," the average family's desire to improve its housing and living conditions. Bauer believed that the "charity stigma" attached to public housing repelled ordinary Americans. The "social work" notions that were part of the build up to the 1937 Act had proven serious handicaps to public housing's public acceptance.[39]

That public housing tenants were among the "undeserving poor" explained public housing's lack of popularity for some writers. Like welfare, but unlike Medicare, public housing seemed to serve society's failures and under-achievers. Homeownership signified civic virtue and individual worth. Subsidized rental housing signified the opposite. Lawrence Freidman connected the argument to social and economic changes. Friedman characterized the first public housing tenants as members of the "submerged middle class." Impoverished by the Depression, they nonetheless retained middle-class values and were perceived as such. After 1949, their poverty proved temporary and they moved on. In their place were the permanent poor and problem families. Once public housing became the home of the poor and powerless, it lost whatever public acceptance it had enjoyed.[40]

The Douglas Commission emphasized one further explanation for ordinary Americans' rejection of public housing, "racial" prejudice. The commission's report maintained that fears that low-income families, especially African American families, would lower property values were virtually universal. Such concerns and the "deep racial prejudice" held by some whites had slowed public housing to a "faltering walk."[41]

Richard Nixon's decision to end public housing construction rested, in part, on a review of housing policy conducted during 1973 by the Department of Housing and Urban Development. The review conceded that public housing offered real benefits. On average the families served were in the lowest income groups and were poorer than those who were not served. The benefits provided by public housing tended to be larger for the poorest families. The average public housing unit was almost as good as the average private rental dwelling. The vast majority of public housing tenants occupied better housing and could purchase more non-housing goods than they would have without the program.[42]

At the same time, public housing did not, the report contended, provide the same benefits a welfare program would have. A welfare program of cash payments to families gave the poor more options while public housing provided only housing. Because tenants were not free to choose among all the combinations of goods with the same market value as provided by public housing, public housing was less efficient. Using estimates of the market value of private housing units, of the market rents public housing tenants would have paid had they lived in private rented accommodations, and of what tenants would spend if they did not occupy public housing, the report produced numerical indices purporting to demonstrate the inefficiencies of government-constructed housing.[43]

HUD's 1973 review made popularity the fundamental criterion for judging public housing's success. The report conceded that a majority of Americans surveyed supported government help for housing for low-income families, but the report also used public opinion to counter some of the traditional arguments for public housing. It was difficult, the report argued, to determine whether public housing was having any desirable effects. The few social science studies completed had yielded limited information. Instead, one had to rely on the collective judgment of the community. Did the wider community think public housing was good for families? The report also reduced the question of housing quality to a matter of opinion. Everyone lived somewhere, the report claimed, so the issue was not about housing quantity, but about housing quality. And there the test was not some concrete measure, of the existence of toilets or indoor plumbing perhaps, but of public opinion. Did the majority of the public believe that poor families were living in minimally adequate housing or not?[44]

Weighing heavily against public housing, in the report's view, were negative reactions from communities and individuals. Many communities, particularly in the suburbs, did not want public housing. They thought it lowered property values and imported social problems from the cities. Public housing meant federal interference in local affairs and threatened to overburden schools and other community facilities. People living near public housing, according to the report, resented the fact that it allowed people with lower incomes to afford better housing than they themselves occupied.[45]

The report used public housing's popularity among low-income families and its limited size as arguments against it. Public housing was unfair because it served so few of the eligible families. The long waiting lists for public housing demonstrated only that it was a lottery benefitting a handful of families at everyone else's expense.[46]

Building more public housing units was not the answer. The report argued that it would increase overall government spending. Since the poorer the family the greater the chance the project would fail, more spending would only increase the risks of failure. More building would provoke more opposition. Locating more poor people in projects would lead to higher operating costs, reinforce public housing's negative image and increase opposition.[47]

In the end, it didn't matter what tenants thought or wanted. Hardly anyone else thought that public housing, as the Congress and local housing authorities had constructed it, was worth continuing. Opponents had persisted and, in documents like HUD's 1973 review, found new language with which to attack public housing. Proponents had run out of ideas. If public housing as implemented after 1949 was the only version that had any political viability, they could offer only complaints. What passed for alternatives amounted to abandoning government-funded and -managed housing.

As Catherine Bauer herself observed, the early reformers misread American politics. From the vantage point of the late 1930s, they thought that the United States was headed away from the private sector and towards more collective ways, just as they thought that the American public was moving away from single-family houses to row or apartment houses. Just as public housing's apartment houses seemed out of place in mid-century America, a program that involved a social solution rather than an individualist solution did not fit. Converting housing, or some large portion of the housing market, into a public utility resonated in the 1930s in ways that it did not in the 1950s or 1960s.

Writers concerned about public housing became more detached from politics over time. Perhaps out of necessity, the early writers discussed how public housing might be enacted and implemented. Catherine Bauer was especially concerned about the political actions needed to bring about housing reform and remained so throughout her career. Mary Simkhovitch and others practiced a kind of elite politics, dependent on links to influential Americans. Later Charles Abrams, for one, had comparable ties to political figures. Nevertheless, the majority of commentators functioned as distant observers and critics. They spent far more time enumerating public housing's flaws than they did imagining plausible alternatives. They spent little or no time considering how an alternative might be put in place.

Conclusions

America's conversation about public housing began with a burst of creativity and optimism. The apparent collapse of the economic order and the election of a president seemingly open to experiment prompted writers to propose new solutions to old problems. Public housing, that is, government-funded, -built and -managed housing, was itself an innovation for the United States. Some reformers would have gone further to create a large non-private housing sector, free to compete with the private housing industry. Before enactment of the 1937 Housing Act, reformers proposed new types of housing: large planned developments, perhaps separate from existing neighborhoods; buildings other than single-family, detached homes; and architectural styles that owed something to European models.

Reformers offered public housing as the solution to one or more problems. Some thought public housing could create decent affordable housing for the least affluent third of the population, if not the bottom half. Others saw public housing as a way to eliminate slums and provide better housing to slum dwellers. Among those interested in slum clearance were reformers who thought that public housing could improve slum dwellers and propel them out of poverty and dysfunction.

The legislative history of public housing suggests, however, that, despite the Depression and the Roosevelt administration, the United States remained resistant to significant changes in housing in the late 1930s. In the 1937 Housing Act, the Congress designed a public housing program that was not to compete with the private housing industry. It was to build only inexpensive housing and serve only low-income families. The 1937 Act did not specify the size of the public housing program, but the initial appropriation was small.

Despite the limited nature of the program enacted, proponents and opponents of public housing thought that the 1937 Act was an important milestone. By having the federal government intervene directly in the housing sector, they thought it marked the beginning of a continuing and growing federal involvement beyond the assistance offered to the private housing industry in the 1934 housing legislation. They were wrong. The 1937 Act was a false dawn. The United States was more resistant to change after 1937 than before. Opponents of public housing failed to block the program's revival in 1949. They did not stop new construction until 1973, but in the meantime they imposed more constraints in the 1949 act and elsewhere. They limited the number of units constructed. They reduced the federal subsidy and blocked housing authorities from amassing adequate financial reserves. They imposed tight cost limits. Finally, in 1973, the opponents prevailed when President Nixon ended new public housing construction.

Most politicians who supported public housing and most officials responsible for its implementation were not visionaries like Catherine Bauer or even Edith Wood. They were not interested in a public housing program that would unsettle the status quo. Housing authorities and housing officials were content to work within the program parameters established in the 1937 Act. They were content to limit the number of public housing units and to build only on slum sites. They were usually committed to reducing construction costs as much as possible and avoiding expenditures for anything other than basic housing. Community facilities and police protection should remain someone else's responsibility. Sometimes housing officials built large, plain apartment houses in effort to produce the most housing units possible, even if outsiders found the result unattractive.

Public housing fits within the broader framework of American history. During the Depression, expansion of the state seemed a solution. Before the Second World War, a reaction against state intervention set in and persisted. Important parts of the Roosevelt administration and of the Democratic party retreated from some forms of state intervention while retaining parts of the New Deal's legislative legacy. Continued Democratic support for public housing seemed to owe as much to nostalgia as to concern about the housing needs of low-income families. Key labor unions, public housing' most influential supporters, supported the New Deal and public housing, but their influence waned after the Second World War.

The political strength of the real estate industry, the builders, bankers, and brokers, was an important reason for public housing's fate. The real estate interests may have been discredited by the Depression, but, even in the 1930s, they remained influential. After 1938 and especially after the Second World War, their influence rebounded. They were well organized and well funded, with members in every community. Most housing officials did not intend that their program threaten the private sector's hold on the housing industry, but industry leaders were unconvinced. No matter how limited the program became or how discredited it might seem, the real estate industry saw government-funded, -built and -managed housing as a threat. If the United States was to offer poor families any housing assistance, it should be via direct subsidy payments, not government managed rental housing.

The post-war housing boom strengthened the real estate industry's hand. After 1945, it seemed that the builders, bankers and brokers had the answers. They built, financed and sold millions of homes to ordinary Americans. It was easy to ignore that federal reforms and subsidies created the basis for the boom or that the boom left many American families behind. The private real estate industry was prospering and building new homes for America's middle third. The middle third did not need government-built housing and could be convinced that further government intervention was unnecessary.

The real estate industry and America's homeowners agreed that a good neighborhood was a homogenous neighborhood. A good neighborhood belonged to a specific group, defined by a bundle of identity and class. White, "Anglo-Saxon," Protestant professionals lived in the neighborhoods with the best housing. Manual workers of more recent immigrant backgrounds lived in neighborhoods with less attractive housing. The poorest families, often but not exclusively African American or of Spanish-speaking descent, lived in the neighborhoods with the worst housing. Protecting the value of one's home and neighborhood required protecting this hierarchy of neighborhoods by keeping lesser families from infiltrating into better neighborhoods.

Public housing could threaten the hierarchy of neighborhoods. A large apartment project populated by poorer families, perhaps African American families, was infiltration on the grand scale. Light, airy, spacious apartments with modern conveniences rented to families who could not afford comparable private housing disturbed the proper order. Why should hard working families pay taxes so that poor families could have better housing than they did? Homeowners who lived near sites proposed for public housing needed little or no encouragement from real estate interests to oppose a project. Only obviously inexpensive housing built in the slums was compatible with the established housing order.

The limited, cramped nature of the public housing constructed in the United States, particularly that built after 1949, provoked criticism from writers who supported government intervention in principle. After 1949, praise for public housing was rare, much less support for expanding the program. Early advocates, like Catherine Bauer, as well as commentators who emerged in the 1950s and 1960s, worried and complained about almost every aspect of public housing: buildings, tenants, sites and management. After 1937, almost no one beyond Catherine Bauer and Lewis Mumford contemplated a public housing program that competed with the private sector. Very few commentators advocated a much bigger program. To the extent that commentators offered alternatives, they were the opposite of whatever public housing was or did. Projects should be small and not large and so on. They did not constitute a cohesive solution to the housing needs of low-income families. Public housing's opponents did not confront equally committed advocates. Instead public housing's ostensible friends generated complaints that opponents could convert to their own purposes.

Class prejudice was a persistent feature of debates about public housing. At every stage from the early 1930s onward, some writers expressed disdain for the poor. They were disorganized or dysfunctional. They created the slums; the slums did not create them. They were a menace to society. As the United States appeared to prosper after World War II, class prejudice became more apparent. Writers were more ready to see public housing tenants as dysfunctional, as problem families. Some thought that they posed a threat to public housing and would have barred them. Others thought that they were responsible for public housing's problems. Still others thought that public housing was responsible for helping problem families through the provision of social services of some kind.

The fact that the United States was experiencing unparalleled prosperity contributed to the negative views of the less affluent after World War II. If the United States had solved its economic problems and if most people were doing well, there must be something wrong with those who were not. During the Depression, looking for economic or political explanations for poverty was acceptable. During the post-war boom, it was much less so. In addition, the appearance of large developments full of poor families was an affront to middle-class American sensibilities. The "$20 million slum" did not belong in post-war America.

"Racial" prejudice compounded the impact of class prejudice on public housing and public housing tenants. Some early housing officials tried to use public housing as a vehicle for integration but discrimination against African Americans in public housing projects was widespread. Most housing authorities were committed to maintaining segregation in the South and the hierarchy of neighborhoods in the North. Even the measures adopted to promote integrated housing projects could work against the interests of some African American families. In northern cities at least, as the number of African Americans increased and as more affluent families moved to the suburbs, discrimination became less of an issue. African Americans came to occupy a large and increasing share of public housing units.

The large African American presence in public housing influenced the debate in several ways. For some, African American families were essentially problem families, especially when many African American families consisted of a single mother with several children. As such, they represented a threat to public housing, either because they might damage the project or because they might undermine the project's reputation. Others saw the increasing number of African American tenants as a challenge, either to the goal of integrated housing or to preserving the housing projects. Still others saw the location of public housing in African American neighborhoods as part of a wider, government-supported effort to limit African Americans to certain neighborhoods.

Public housing was blamed in some cases for economic, social and demographic changes beyond any housing authority's control. Changes in family incomes in the post-war years as well as increases in the welfare population and in the urban African American population profoundly affected public housing and attitudes towards it. Inflation undermined public housing finances. Some observers ignored the wider context.

After 1949, the debates about public housing demonstrated that most Americans, even housing experts, were uncomfortable with housing other than the single-family, detached house. Row houses or low-rise apartment houses might be acceptable for public housing. Except in Manhattan, however, apartment houses, especially large collections of tall apartment houses, seemed out of place. Observers were quick to see them as grim and unwelcoming. If the apartment house's architecture owed something to foreign models, it was even less acceptable. Observers were quick to blame European architects like Le Corbusier for public housing's problems.

The debates about public housing, if not actually fact-free, relied on impressions and anecdotes. Even when data were available, writers often ignored them. Many of the criticisms of public housing were at variance with what data were available. Writers made easy assumptions about complex social phenomena, the impact of living in a poor community or the role of the slightly better off within a poor community, for example. None of the principal contributors ever lived in public housing even for short periods. Few spent much time in public housing or interviewed many tenants. Yet they wrote with great certainty about tenants, their behaviors and their attitudes.

The largest, most notorious projects came to stand for all public housing. The many projects in smaller cities and towns became invisible. Even the many New York projects that many observers thought "successful" were obscured by Pruitt-Igoe and the largest Chicago projects.

Tenants and the poor featured very little in the debates. Participants were almost all middle class or upper middle class. Many were self-educated "experts," but over time more had advanced training and connections to universities.

Despite being known collectively as "housers," the early proponents of public housing were not a single, cohesive group. Most of the earliest proponents cooperated with each other and produced at least one statement of common ideas and aims. Nevertheless, they differed about the kind of public housing to be built and the purpose for which it was to be built. Catherine Bauer's version of public housing was different from Mary Simkhovitch's. Bauer, for example, would have built community-sized developments on the periphery. Simkhovitch was content with smaller projects in the slums.

Some of the early reformers, mainly but not exclusively the community planners, anticipated the 1937 Act's negative consequences. They foresaw that building in the slums might not produce enough housing for the families it displaced and that it might push them into other neighborhoods, with just as bad housing as they had left. Mumford and others warned against high-density development and tall apartment buildings. Albert Mayer counseled against drab, unimaginative architecture.

Compared with the spectrum of political views current in the 1930s, the original generation of housing reformers was not especially radical. Despite accusations of socialism or communism leveled by opponents, nearly all the proponents fit within the political mainstream. In the middle 1930s, some voiced concerns about capitalism, but none was a socialist. Catherine Bauer, perhaps the most outspokenly radical reformer, supported Harry Truman in 1948, not Henry Wallace. Subsequent writers about public housing were even less interested in anything like left-wing politics.

Conclusions

As Catherine Bauer herself observed, the early reformers misread American politics. From the vantage point of the late 1930s, they thought that the United States was headed away from the private sector and towards more collective ways, just as they thought that the American public was moving away from single-family houses to row or apartment houses. Just as public housing's apartment houses seemed out of place in mid-century America, a program that involved a social solution rather than an individualist solution did not fit. Converting housing, or some large portion of the housing market, into a public utility resonated in the 1930s in ways that it did not in the 1950s or 1960s.

Writers concerned about public housing became more detached from politics over time. Perhaps out of necessity, the early writers discussed how public housing might be enacted and implemented. Catherine Bauer was especially concerned about the political actions needed to bring about housing reform and remained so throughout her career. Perhaps naively, she continued to foresee a broad grass roots movement that would push the country toward different housing policies. Mary Simkhovitch and others practiced a kind of elite politics, dependent on links to influential Americans. Later Charles Abrams, for one, had comparable ties to political figures. Nevertheless, the majority of commentators functioned as distant observers and critics. They spent far more time enumerating public housing's flaws than they did imagining plausible alternatives. They spent little or no time considering how an alternative might be put in place.

Chapter Notes

Preface

1. Richard Nixon, "Special Message to the Congress Proposing Legislation and Outlining Administration Actions to Deal with Federal Housing Policy," September 19, 1973. Online by Gerhard Peters and John T. Woolley, *The American Presidency Project.* http://www.presidency.ucsb.edu/ws/?pid=3968.

Chapter One

1. John M. Gries and James Ford, eds., *Slums, Large Scale Housing and Decentralization* (Washington, 1932) xi.
2. John M. Gries and James Ford, eds., *Housing Objectives and Programs* (Washington, 1932), 151.
3. Gries and Ford, *Objectives*, 174.
4. Gries and Ford, *Objectives*, 177–180.
5. Gries and Ford, *Objectives*, 182, 183.
6. Clarence Perry, "The Neighborhood Unit," *Regional Plan of New York and Its Environs* 7 (1) (1929): 21–140.
7. Gries and Ford, *Objectives*, 150.
8. Gries and Ford, *Objectives*, 162, 194–195.
9. Gries and Ford, *Slums*, xiv, xv, 87.
10. Gries and Ford, *Slums*, xiv, 1–2.
11. Gries and Ford, *Slums*, 2–3, 41ff.
12. Gries and Ford, *Objectives*, 198; Gries and Ford, *Slums*, 4, 6, 166–167.
13. Gries and Ford, *Slums*, xi–xii, 7, 76.
14. Gries and Ford, *Slums*, 88.
15. Gries and Ford, *Slums*, xiii, 85, 155, 156.
16. Gries and Ford, *Slums*, 10, 166, 167.
17. Gries and Ford, *Slums*, 32–33.
18. Gries and Ford, *Slums*, 31–32.
19. For this and the following paragraphs. Peyton Stapp, *Urban Housing: A Summary of Real Property Inventories Conducted as Work Projects, 1934–36* (Washington, 1938), 3–8.
20. For this and following paragraphs, Home Owners Loan Corporation, *Residential Security Map and Area Descriptions* (Hartford, CT, 1937).
21. James Greer, "The Home Owners Loan Corporation and the Development of the Residential Security Maps," *Journal of Urban History* 39 (2) (March 2013): 286, 287.
22. Senate Committee on Education and Labor, *Slum and Low-Rent Public Housing, Hearings on S. 2392,* 74th Cong., 1st sess. (1935), 53, 54, 56; Edith Elmer Wood, *Recent Trends in American Housing* (New York, 1931), 9, 43–44.
23. Senate Committee, *Slum and Low-Rent Housing*, 53; Wood, *Recent Trends*, 60ff.
24. Wood, *Recent Trends*, 1–2, 3, 60ff; Edith Elmer Wood, " A Century of the Housing Problem," *Law and Contemporary Problems* 1(2) (March 1934): 137.
25. Edith Elmer Wood, "The Statistics of Room Congestion: Purpose and Technique," *Journal of the American Statistical Association* 23 (163) (September 1928): 263–264, 266.
26. Edith Elmer Wood, "The Costs of

Bad Housing," *Annals of the American Academy of Political and Social Science* 190 (March 1937): 147.

27. Wood, *Recent Trends*, 4–7.

28. Wood, *Recent Trends*, 41–42.

29. Wood, *Recent Trends*, 35–36, 38, 188, 192.

30. Wood, *Recent Trends*, 14–15, 46; Senate Committee, *Slum and Low-Rent Housing*, 53–54, 56; Senate Committee on Education and Labor, *To Create a United States Housing Authority*, 75th Cong., 1st sess. (1937), 165; Senate Committee on Education and Labor, *United States Housing Act of 1936*, 74th Cong., 2nd sess. (1936), 212.

31. Wood, *Recent Trends*, 7, 13, 280; Wood, "Century," 137, 138, 146.

32. Wood, *Recent Trends*, 77, 83, 94, 102, 278, 281–282; Senate Committee, *United States Housing Authority*, 165ff.

33. For a fuller discussion of the Regional Planning Association, see Edward K. Spann, *Designing Modern America: The Regional Planning Association of America and its Members* (Columbus, 1996).

34. Lewis Mumford, "The Skyline: The New Housing," *The New Yorker* (7 December 1935): 134.

35. Henry Wright, *Rehousing Urban America*, with a foreword by Lewis Mumford (New York, 1935), ix, 9; Albert Mayer, "New Homes for a New Deal I: Slum Clearance, but How?" *New Republic* 78 (1002) (14 February 1934): 9; Lewis Mumford, "New Homes for a New Deal III: The Shortage of Dwellings and Direction," *New Republic* 78 (1004) (28 February 1934): 70; Lewis Mumford (unsigned), "Housing versus Ownership," *New Republic* 69 (889) (16 December 1931): 123; Albert Mayer, "Why Not Housing," *New Republic* 78 (1002) (4 September 1935): 97.

36. Lewis Mumford, *The Culture of Cities* (New York, 1938), 459.

37. Wright, *Rehousing Urban America*, 4, 9; Lewis Mumford, "The Chance for Civilized Housing," *New Republic* 64 (824) (17 September 1930): 116; Lewis Mumford, "The Plan of New York II," *New Republic* (22 June 1932): 149; Albert Mayer, "Can We Have a Housing Program? I," *The Nation* 141 (3666) (9 October 1935): 401; Henry Wright, "New Homes for a New Deal II: Abolishing Slums Forever," *New Republic* 78 (1003) (21 February 1934): 41.

38. Mayer "Slum Clearance," 9; Mumford, "Civilized Housing," 115, 116.

39. Albert Mayer, "Housing: A Call to Action," *The Nation* 138 (3589) (18 April 1934): 435; Wright, *Rehousing Urban America*, xi, xii; Albert Mayer, Henry Wright, and Lewis Mumford, "New Homes for a New Deal IV: A Concrete Program," *New Republic* 78 (1005) (7 March 1934): 91; Mumford, "Plan of New York II," 152; Wright, "Abolishing Slums Forever," 43.

40. Lewis Mumford, "What Prevents Good Housing?" *New Republic* 67 (866) (8 July 1931): 209; Mumford, "Plan of New York II," 149; Wright, "Abolishing Slums Forever," 41; Mayer, "Call to Action," 436; Mayer et al., "Concrete Program," 91, 93–94; Albert Mayer, "A Practical Housing Program," *The Nation* 141 (3667) (16 October 1935): 434.

41. Mayer, "Practical Program," 433; Mayer, "Housing Program," 400.

42. Mayer, "Housing Program," 403–405.

43. Mayer, "Practical Program," 433; Mayer, "Call to Action," 436.

44. Albert Mayer, "Why the Housing Program Has Failed," *The Nation* 138 (3588) (11 April 1934): 409; Mumford, "Shortage of Dwelling and Direction," 69, 71.

45. Spann, *Modern America*, 135–136, 137; Mayer, "Slum Clearance," 7, 8.

46. Mayer, "Slum Clearance," 9; Wight, *Rehousing Urban America*, 5, 6.

47. Mayer, "Slum Clearance," 9; Wright, *Rehousing Urban America*, 9; Wright, "Abolishing Slums Forever," 43; Mumford, "Shortage of Dwelling and Direction," 71.

48. Mayer et al., "Concrete Program," 92; Mayer, "Slum Clearance," 9.

49. Mayer, "Slum Clearance," 7, 8; Wright, "Abolishing Slums Forever," 44.

50. Catherine Bauer, *Modern Housing* (New York, 1934).

51. Bauer, *Modern Housing*, xv, 115; Catherine Bauer, "Slums Aren't Necessary," *American Mercury* 31 (123) (31 March 1934): 299–301.

52. Bauer, "Slums Aren't Necessary," 299–301; H. Peter Oberlander and Eva Newbrun, *Houser: The Life and Work of Catherine Houser* (Vancouver, 1999), 70.

53. Bauer, *Modern Housing*, 44, 238, 242; Bauer, "Slums Aren't Necessary," 298; Senate Committee, *Slum and Low-Rent Housing*, 84.

54. Senate Committee, *Slum and Low-Rent Housing*, 85–86.

55. Bauer, *Modern Housing*, 237; Catherine Bauer, "Individualism and Housing," *The Nation* (10 February 1932): 173.

56. Bauer, *Modern Housing*, 241; Senate Committee, *Slum and Low-Rent Housing*, 84, 90; Bauer, "Slum Clearance or Housing," 731.

57. Senate Committee, *Slum and Low-Rent Housing*, 86; Senate Committee, *United States Housing Act of 1936*, 191; Senate Committee, *United States Housing Authority*, 80ff.

58. Bauer, *Modern Housing*, 84, 98, 136.

59. Bauer, *Modern Housing*, 121–122, 253, 254.

60. Senate Committee, *United States Housing Authority*, 3f.

61. Senate Committee, *Slum and Low-Rent Housing*, 27; Senate Committee, *United States Housing Authority*, 3f.

62. Senate Committee, *Slum and Low-Rent Housing*, 10, 46, 83, 126; Senate Committee, *United States Housing Act of 1936*, 41.

63. Alexander von Hoffman, "The End of the Dream: The Political Struggle of America's Public Housers," *Journal of Planning History* 4 (3) (August 2003): 226.

64. Senate Committee, *United States Housing Act of 1936*, 136ff; Maurice Leven, Harold Moulton, and Clark Warburton, *America's Capacity to Consume* (Washington, 1934).

65. Senate Committee, *United States Housing Act of 1936*, 136ff; Senate Committee, *United States Housing Authority*, 157ff; Helen Alfred, *Municipal Housing* (New York, 1935), 12.

66. Senate Committee, *United States Housing Act of 1936*, 123, 137; Senate Committee on Education and Labor, *Slums and Low-Rent Housing Public Housing: Hearings on S.2392*, 74th Cong., 1st sess., 13, 14.

67. Senate Committee, *United States Housing Act of 1936*, 67f.

68. Senate Committee, *Slum and Low-Rent Housing*, 104, 105; Senate Committee, *United States Housing Act of 1936*, 133; Alfred, *Municipal Housing*, 27.

69. Senate Committee, *Slum and Low-Rent Housing*, 13, 15, 96; Senate Committee, *United States Housing Act of 1936*, 89ff, 137, 239, 242; Senate Committee, *United States Housing Authority*, 157ff.

70. Alfred, *Municipal Housing*, 19; Senate Committee, *Slum and Low-Rent Housing*, 95, 104; Senate Committee, *United States Housing Act of 1936*, 136ff.

71. Warren Jay Vinton, "A Survey of Approaches to the Housing Problem," *Annals of the American Academy of Political and Social Science* 190 (March 1937): 13; Coleman Woodbury, "Integrating Private and Public Enterprise in Housing," *Annals of the American Academy of Political and Social Science* 190 (March 1937): 173; Charles Ascher, "The Housing Authority and the Housed," *Law and Contemporary Problems* 1 (2) (March 1934): 250; Langdon Post, "How Not to Plan Public Housing," *The Nation* 144 (13) (27 May 1937): 346; Senate Committee, *United States Housing Authority*, 170ff.

72. Frank Watson, *Housing Problems and Possibilities in the United States* (New York, 1935), 17–18.

73. Ascher, "Housing Authority," 255; Senate Committee, *United States Housing Authority*, 249.

74. Woodbury, "Integrating," 171, 173, 174; Senate Committee, *United States Housing Authority*, 249.

75. Ascher, "Housing Authority," 252; Ira Robbins, "Methods of Holding Residential Property," *Annals of the American Academy of Political and Social Science* 190 (March 1937): 115; Senate Committee, *United States Housing Authority*, 193ff.

76. Abraham Goldfield, *The Diary of a Housing Manager* (New York, 1938), 1.

77. Goldfield, *Diary*, 3, 6–7, 7–8, 9, 14, 41.

78. Goldfield, *Diary*, 44, 107–108.

79. Goldfield, *Diary*, 13, 19, 23–24, 43.

80. Elizabeth Milnarik, "The Federally Funded American Dream: Public Housing as an Engine for Social Improvement, 1933–1937" (Ph.D. diss. University of Virginia, 2009), 91, 93.

81. National Association of Housing

Officials, *A Housing Program for the United States* (Chicago, 1934), 6, 8.

82. NAHO, *Housing Program*, 6–7, 10–12.

83. NAHO, *Housing Program*, 17.

84. NAHO, *Housing Program*, 5, 7, 13, 14.

85. NAHO, *Housing Program*, 14, 15.

86. NAHO, *Housing Program*, 5, 16, 17–18.

87. Public Administration Service, *A Housing Program for the United States: A Report Prepared for the National Association of Housing Officials* (Chicago, 1935), 22, 23.

88. Public Administration Service, *Housing Program*, 20.

89. Public Administration Service, *Housing Program*, 6.

90. Senate Committee, *United States Housing Act of 1936*, 330f; House Committee on Education and Labor, *To Create a United States Housing Authority*, 75th Cong., 1st sess. (1937), 223ff; Walter Schmidt, "Private versus Public Enterprise in Housing," *Journal of Land and Public Utility Economics* 11 (4) (November 1935): 346; Edmond Hoben, "Realism versus Real Estate in Housing," *Journal of Land and Public Utility Economics* 12(1) (February 1935): 85.

91. Schmidt, "Public versus Private," 344, 346–347; Senate Committee, *United States Housing Act of 1936*, 330; Allie Freed, "Should the Administration's Housing Policy be Continued: Con," *Congressional Digest* 15(4) (April 1946): 120.

92. Schmidt, "Public versus Private," 347, 350; Senate Committee, *Slum and Low Rent Housing*, 130; House Committee, *United States Housing Authority*, 284; U.S. Chamber of Commerce Special Committee on Housing, "Should the Administration's Housing be Continued: Con," *Congressional Digest* 15 (4) (April 1936): 120.

93. Senate Committee, *Slum and Low-Rent Housing*, 131–133; Senate Committee, *United States Housing Act of 1936*, 111f, 330f, 333, 344, 346; Senate Committee, *United States Housing Authority*, 222ff.

94. Schmidt, "Public versus Private," 347; Senate Committee, *United States Housing Authority*, 222ff; Charles Lewis, "An Investment Approach to Housing," *Annals of the American Academy of Political and Social Science* 190 (March 1937): 18.

95. Schmidt, "Public versus Private" 345, 347; Lewis, "Investment Approach," 19; House Committee, *United States Housing Authority*, 223ff.

96. House Committee, *Slum and Low-Rent Housing*, 223ff; Senate Committee, *United States Housing Act of 1936*, 314, 329; House Committee, *United States Housing Authority*, 215ff, 223ff; Lewis, "Investment Approach," 18.

97. Senate Committee, *Slums and Low-Rent Housing*, 218f; Senate Committee, *United States Housing Act of 1936*, 299f; House Committee, *United States Housing Authority*, 223f, 249.

98. Ernest Fisher, "Housing Problems," *Quarterly Journal of Economics* 48 (1) (November 1933): 139–140; Schmidt, "Public versus Private," 348; House Committee, *United States Housing Authority*, 192; Senate Committee, *United States Housing Act of 1936*, 330, 346; Senate Committee, *United States Housing Authority*, 222f, 225f.

99. Herbert Nelson, "Urban Housing and Land Use," *Law and Contemporary Problems* 1 (2) (March 1934): 159; Freed, "Housing Policy," 121; House Committee, *United States Housing Authority*, 178, 247; Senate Committee, *Slums and Low-Rent Housing*, 215ff.

100. Christian Science Monitor, "Editorial" (15 February 1936) in *Congressional Digest* 15 (4) (April 1936): 125; Senate Committee, *United States Housing Act of 1936*, 111, 154, 156, 166, 193.

101. Ernest Fisher, "Housing Legislation and Housing Policy in the United States," *Michigan Law Review* 31 (3) (January 1933): 325; Senate Committee, *United States Housing Act of 1936*, 166, 315, 345; Hoben, "Realism," 85.

102. House Committee, *United States Housing Authority*, 175, 181, 182; Fisher, "Housing Problems," 137–8.

103. House Committee, *United States Housing Authority*, 175; Senate Committee, *United States Housing Act of 1936*, 304.

104. Schmidt, "Public versus Private," 350; House Committee, *United States Housing Authority*, 223ff; Senate Commit-

tee, *United States Housing Act of 1936*, 168.
105. James Ford, *Slums and Housing* (Cambridge, 1936), 840, 849.

Chapter Two

1. Gail Radford, *Modern Housing For America: Policy Struggles in the New Deal Era* (Chicago, 1996), 92–93.
2. Ford, *Slums and Housing*, 593; Joel Schwartz, *The New York Approach: Robert Moses, Urban Liberals and Redevelopment of the Inner City* (Columbus, 1993), 34.
3. Mabel Walker, *Urban Blight and Slums* (Cambridge, 1938), 319.
4. Milnarik, "American Dream," 205; Alfred Mayer, "Why Not Housing," 96; Alfred, *Municipal Housing*, 34; Schwartz, *New York Approach*, 40–41; Senate Committee, *United States Housing Authority*, 49ff.
5. Harold Ickes, "The Federal Housing Program: A Progress Report," *New Republic* 81 (1046) (19 December 1934): 157; Harold Ickes, "The Place of Housing in National Rehabilitation," *Journal of Land and Public Utility Economics* 11(2) (May 1935): 116; Harold Ickes, "In Defense of the PWA," *New Republic* 94 (1217) (30 March 1938): 214.
6. Alfred Fellheimer, "Planning American Standards for Low-Rent Housing," *American Architect* 14 (February 1935): 15, 18; Milnarik, "American Dream," 158.
7. Fellheimer "Standards," 16, 18; Milnarik, "American Dream," 252, 279.
8. Mayer, "Why Not Housing," 96; Richard Pommer, "The Architecture of Urban Housing in the United States in the Early 1930s," *Journal of the Society of Architectural Historians* 37 (4) (December 1978): 242, 243.
9. Lewis Mumford, "The Sky Line: The New Order," *The New Yorker* (26 February 1938): 209–212.
10. Mumford, "The New Housing," 136.
11. Nicholas Bloom, *Public Housing That Worked: New York in the Twentieth Century* (Philadelphia, 2008), 49.
12. Senate Committee, *United States Housing Act of 1936*, 58, 60.
13. Milnarik, "American Dream," 297–298; Ickes, "Place of Housing," 116; Joel Schwartz, "Tenant Unions in New York City's Low-Rent Housing, 1933–1949," *Journal of Urban History* 12 (4) (August 1986): 420–421.
14. Michael Straus and Talbot Wegg, *Housing Comes of Age* (New York, 1938), 152; Senate Committee, *United States Housing Authority*, 8ff; Gwendolyn Wright, *Building the Dream: A Social History of Housing in America* (New York, 1981), 226.
15. John Bauman, *Public Housing, Race and Renewal: Urban Planning in Philadelphia, 1920–1974* (Philadelphia, 1987), 49.
16. Bloom, *Housing That Worked*, 52; Rosalie Genevro, "Site Selection and the New York City Housing Authority, 1934–1039," *Journal of Urban History* 12 (4) (August 1986): 344.
17. House Committee, *United States Housing Authority*, 160; Senate Committee, *United States Housing Act of 1936*, 194; Senate Committee, *United States Housing Authority*, 170ff; Straus and Wegg, *Housing Comes of Age*, 166–7.
18. Harold Ickes, "The Housing Policy of the PWA," *Architectural Forum*, 40 (2) (February 1934): 92; Ickes, "Place of Housing," 111–113.
19. Senate Committee, *United States Housing Authority*, 8f, 71f; Schmidt, "Public versus Private," 345; Henry Churchill, "Begin Housing Now!" *The Nation* 138 (3580) (14 January 1934): 179.
20. Lewis Mumford, "Shortage of Dwellings and Direction," 71; Charles Ascher, "Federal Housing Symbols are Tiresome," *Public Opinion Quarterly* 1 (1) (January 1937): 111.
21. Mayer, "Housing Program Has Failed," 409; Carol Aronovici, "Housing the Poor: Mirage of Reality," *Law and Contemporary Problems* 1 (2) (March 1934): 155.
22. Mumford, "Shortage of Dwellings and Direction," 71; Mayer, "Housing Program Has Failed," 409; Mayer, "Practical Program," 403.
23. House Committee, *United States Housing Authority*, 43, 55–6, 63; Senate Committee, *United States Housing Authority*, 75ff.
24. Senate Committee, *United States Housing Authority*, 44.
25. Senate Committee, *Slum and Low-*

Rent Housing, 20ff, 180ff; Senate Committee, *United States Housing Authority*, 178.

26. S. 2392, 74th Cong., 1st sess. (13 March 1935).

27. H.R. 7399, 74th Cong., 1st sess. (10 April 1935).

28. S. 4424, 74th Cong., 2nd sess. (24 February 1936).

29. Public Law 837, 74th Cong., 2nd sess. (29 June 1936).

30. S. 1685, 75th Cong., 1st sess. (24 February 1937).

31. Joseph Huthmacher, *Senator Robert F. Wagner and the Rise of Urban Liberalism* (New York, 1971), 109, 113, 116, 153; Roger Biles, "Robert F. Wagner, Franklin D. Roosevelt and Social Welfare Legislation in the New Deal," *Presidential Studies Quarterly* 28 (1) (Winter 1998): 141, 146.

32. Senate Committee, *United States Housing Act of 1936*, 15–16.

33. Senate Committee, *United States Housing Act of 1936*, 15–16, 17; Timothy McDonnell, *The Wagner Housing Act: A Case Study in the Legislative Process* (Chicago, 1957), 135, 136; *Congressional Record*, 8077, 7989 (2 August 1937).

34. McDonnell, *Urban Liberalism*, 136; Senate Committee, *United States Housing Authority*, 107; *Congressional Record*, 7979 (2 August 1937).

35. *Congressional Record*, 7977, 7978, 7982, 7985 (2 August 1937); Senate Committee, *United States Housing Act of 1936*, 17.

36. McDonnell, *Urban Liberalism*, 136; *Congressional Record*, 8099 (3 August 1937); Senate Committee, *United States Housing Act of 1936*, 16.

37. *Congressional Record*, 8077, 8078 (3 August 1937); 8286–7 (5 August 1937).

38. Senate Committee, *United States Housing Authority*, 75ff, 139–40, 240.

39. Senate Committee, *United States Housing Authority*, 75ff; *Congressional Record*, 7969–70 (2 August 1937); 8369 (6 August 1937).

40. Senate Committee, *Slums and Low-Rent Housing*, 8; Senate Committee, *United States Housing Authority*, 315.

41. Senate Committee, *United States Housing Authority*, 140; *Congressional Record*, 8079 (3 August 1937).

42. *Congressional Record*, 8187 (4 August 1937), 8360 (6 August 1937), 9246 (18 August 1937); Senate Committee, *United States Housing Authority*, 20, 143.

43. *Congressional Record*, 8360 (6 August 1937); 9246–7 (18 August 1937).

44. House Committee, *United States Housing Authority*, 19; *Congressional Record*, 8083 (3 August 1937); 8197 (4 August 1937).

45. *Congressional Record*, 9236–7, 9254 (18 August 1937).

46. *Congressional Record*, 8079 (3 August 1937); 9237, 9252 (18 August 1937).

47. *Congressional Record*, 8288 (5 August 1937), 9249 (18 August 1937); 1982 (Appendix) (5 August 1937).

48. Public Law 75–412 (1 September 1937), 50 Stat. 888.

49. Catherine Bauer, "Now, at Last, Housing: the Meaning of the Wagner-Steagall Act," *New Republic* (8 September 1937): 119–121; Langdon Post, *The Challenge of Housing (New York, 1938)*, 201, 203; "False Friends of Housing," *New Republic* 92 (1185) (18 August 1937): 34–35.

Chapter Three

1. Ruth Weintraub and Rosalind Tough, "Federal Housing and World War II," *Journal of Land and Public Utility Economics* 18 (2) (May 1942): 157.

2. Weintraub and Tough, "Federal Housing," 158; Kristin Szylvian, "The Federal Housing Program During World War II," in *From Tenements to the Taylor Homes*, ed. John Bauman, Roger Biles, and Kristin Szylvian, 124 (University Park, 2000).

3. Szylvian, "Federal Housing Program," 128–129, 130–131.

4. Roger Biles, "Nathan Straus and the Failure of U.S. Public Housing, 1937–1942," *Historian* 53 (1) (Autumn 1990): 35, 36; Marriner Eccles to the President, memorandum (21 August 1937), *Federal Reserve Archive, Eccles Papers*, Box 7, Folder 2.

5. United States Housing Authority, *Annual Report for the Fiscal Year 1939* (Washington, 1940), 1.

6. Nathan Straus, "End the Slums," *Vital Speeches of the Day* 4 (6) (1 January 1938): 184.

7. USHA, *Annual Report 1939*, 5–6.

8. Straus, "End the Slums," 184; Nathan

Straus, *The Seven Myths of Housing* (New York, 1944), 102; D. Bradford Hunt, *Blueprint for Disaster: The Unraveling of Chicago Public Housing* (Chicago, 2009), 44–45.

9. Straus, *Seven Myths*, 103.

10. Senate Special Committee on Post-War Economic Policy and Planning, *Housing and Urban Redevelopment*, 79th Cong., 1st sess., 1755, 1978; Senate Committee on Banking and Currency, *General Housing Legislation*, 81st Cong., 1st sess. (February 1949), 236; National Association of Housing Officials, *Housing for the United States After the War* (1944), 7–8; Charles Abrams, *The Future of Housing* (New York, 1946), 270, 271–2.

11. Norman Strunk, "Low Cost Housing under the USHA Experiment," *Journal of Land and Public Utility Economics* 16 (1) (February 1940): 96–99.

12. Bloom, *Public Housing That Worked*, 39–40, 56–57; Pommer "Architecture of Urban Housing," 256.

13. Catherine Bauer, *A Citizen's Guide to Public Housing* (Poughkeepsie, 1940), 32, 40.

14. Lewis Mumford, "The Skyline: Versailles for the Millions," *The New Yorker* (17 February 1940): 42–44; Lewis Mumford, "The Skyline: Looking Forward, Looking Backward," *The New Yorker* (6 September 1941): 48.

15. Mumford, "Versailles," 42–44.

16. NAHO, *After The War*, 9; Robert Lasch, *Breaking the Building Blockade* (Chicago, 1946), 204, 205; Mary Simkhovitch, *Here Is God's Plenty: Reflections of American Social Advance* (New York, 1949), 46; Henry Churchill. *The City Is the People* (New York, 1945), 123; Abrams, *Future of Housing*, 371; Senate Committee, *General Housing Legislation*, 596.

17. Lasch, *Building Blockade*, 204–205.

18. Catherine Bauer, "Good Neighborhoods," *Annals of the American Academy of Political and Social Science*, 242 (1945): 111; Catherine Bauer, "What Are Our Goals? II: Freedom of Choice," *The Nation* (15 May 1948): 535–536.

19. House Committee on Banking and Currency, *Amendments of 1939 to the United States Housing Act*, 76th Cong., 1st sess. (1939), 70; Senate Committee, *Housing and Urban Redevelopment*, 1521; Hunt, *Unraveling*, 43–44.

20. USHA, *Annual Report 1939*, 8; House Committee, *Amendments of 1939*, 69; Genevro, "Site Selection," 348.

21. Straus, *Seven Myths*, 35.

22. Senate Committee, *Housing and Urban Redevelopment*, 1522; Lasch, *Building Blockade*, 74ff; Robert Fairbanks, *Making Better Citizens: Housing Reform and the Community Development Strategy in Cincinnati, 1890–1960* (Urbana, 1988), 116–117.

23. Richard Plunz, *A History of Housing in New York City* (New York, 1990), 240; Anthony Jackson, *A Place Called Home: A History of Low Cost Housing in Manhattan* (Cambridge, 1976), 232.

24. Alfred Rheinstein and Henry Pringle, "Why Slum Clearance May Fail," *Harpers* (October 1939): 523–524; Post, *Challenge of Housing*, 222, 224ff.

25. Carol Aronovici, *Housing the Masses* (New York, 1939), 25–26; Alfred Mayer, "Letter to the Editor," *New Republic* 98 (1261) (8 February 1939): 8–9.

26. USHA, *Annual Report 1939*, 2–3; Straus, "End the Slums," 183.

27. Straus, *Seven Myths*, 137; NAHO, *After the War*, xiii.

28. *Congressional Record*, 4809 (20 April 1949).

29. House Committee, *Amendments of 1939*, 63; Senate Committee, *General Housing Legislation*, 171; United States Housing Authority, *What the Housing Act Can Do for Your City* (Washington, 1938), 66; Edith Elmer Wood, "Letter to the Editor," *New York Times* (7 April 1940): 144.

30. Public Administration Service, *Housing and Welfare Officials Confer: A Summary of Discussion at the Joint Conference of Housing and Welfare Officials, Chicago May 11–13, 1939* (Chicago,) 1939, 14–15; Charles Abrams, "The Real Housing Issue," *The Nation* 149 (17) (21 October 1939): 440; John Ihlder, "The How and Why of Graded Rents," *Survey* 77 (5) (May 1941): 146; Nicholas Bloom and Matthew Lasner (eds.), *Affordable Housing in New York: The People, Places and Policies That Transformed a City* (Princeton, 2016), 101; *Congressional Record*, 4874 (21 April 1949).

31. Bloom, *Housing That Worked*, 82.

Notes—Chapter Three

32. Public Administration Service, *Officials Confer*, 11, 14, 15.

33. Public Administration Service, *Officials Confer*, iii, 15.

34. Public Administration Service, *Officials Confer*, 13; Catherine Bauer, "Low Rent Housing and Home Economics," *Journal of Home Economics* 31 (1) (January 1939): 15–16.

35. House Committee, *Amendments of 1939*, 12; Senate Committee, *Housing and Urban Redevelopment*, 1701, 1722, 1745, 1753; NAHO, *After the War*, 18.

36. Emanuel Stein, "The Objectives of Public Housing," *American Municipal Law Review* 7 (2) (July 1942): 125–127; Robert Marshall, "Slum Clearance: A Flight from Reality," *Forum and Century* 101 (2) (February 1939): 106.

37. Rheinstein, "Slum Clearance," 522; Edith Elmer Wood, "That 'One Third' of a Nation," *Survey Graphic* 29(2) (1 February 1940): 83.

38. Senate Committee, *General Housing Legislation*, 177; Edith Elmer Wood, *Introduction to Housing: Facts and Principles* (Washington, 1940), 119–120.

39. Rheinstein, "Slum Clearance," 521–522.

40. USHA, *Annual Report 1939*, 3; Hunt, *Unraveling*, 48.

41. Bauer, *Citizens Guide*, 52.

42. Public Administration Service, *Officials Confer*, 4–5; Lawrence Vale, *From the Puritans to the Projects: Public Housing and Public Neighbors* (Cambridge, 2000), 201–203; Fairbanks, *Cincinnati*, 108.

43. United Auto Workers-Congress of Industrial Organizations, *Memorandum on Post War Urban Housing* (Detroit, 1944), 58; Senate Committee, *General Housing Legislation*, 236.

44. Senate Committee, *Housing and Urban Redevelopment*, 1716–1717.

45. Stein, "Objectives," 121, 122, 124, 127.

46. Senate Committee, *Housing and Urban Redevelopment*, 1979–1981, 1984.

47. Beatrice Rosahn and Abraham Goldfield, *Housing Management: Principles and Practices* (New York, 1937), v–vi.

48. Senate Committee, *Housing and Urban Redevelopment*, 1751f; Bloom, *Housing That Worked*, 93–94, 95.

49. Dorothy Canfield, "I Visit a Housing Project," *Survey Graphic* 29 (2) (February 1, 1940): 89; Dorothy Rosenman, *A Million Homes a Year: Modern Housing for Every Income—the Problems and the Possibilities* (New York, 1945), 232; Hugh Carter, "How Shall We Manage Housing," *Social Service Review* 14(4) (December 1940): 726–728; Abrams, *Future of Housing*, 354.

50. Charles Abrams, *A Housing Program for America* (New York, 1946), 6.

51. Richard Davies, *Housing Reform During the Truman Administration* (Columbia, 1966), 22; Alexander Crosby, "Public Housing in the Doldrums," *New Republic* (1 May 1944): 596; Helen Fuller, "The Invisible Congress III: The Real Estate Lobby," *New Republic* (3 April 1944): 465.

52. Senate Committee, *Housing and Urban Redevelopment*, 2080–2081; Senate Committee, *General Housing Legislation*, 515ff.

53. Guy Greer and Alvin Hansen, *Urban Redevelopment and Housing: A Program for Post War* (Washington, 1941), 16, 20–21.

54. UAW, *Memorandum*; Congress of Industrial Organizations Department of Research and Education, *Good Shelter for Everyone* (February 1944); Textile Workers Union of America, *Towards a New Day* (1943); United Auto Workers, *Homes for Workers in Planned Communities* (1943).

55. Senate Committee, *Housing and Urban Redevelopment*, 1682.

56. Bauer, "Good Neighborhoods," 113–114.

57. Charles Abrams, "Housing and Politics," *Survey Graphic* 29(2) (1 February 1940): 91; Abrams, *Future of Housing*, 314; Charles Abrams, "The Politics of Housing II: A Plank in the Platform," *The Nation* (15 May 1948): 549.

58. Catherine Bauer, "Cities in Flux: A Challenge to the Postwar Planners," *The American Scholar* 13(1) (Winter 1943-44): 83; Abrams, *Future of Housing*, 216; Charles Abrams, *Revolution in Land* (New York, 1939), 283; Lewis Mumford, "What Are Our Goals I: Cities Fit to Live In," *The Nation* (15 May 1948): 531; Lasch, *Building Blockade*, passim.

59. Abrams, *Housing Program*, 26.

60. Nathan Straus, "Can We Do It? A Business Man's Prescription," *The Nation* (15 May 1948): 544–545; Abrams, *Future of Housing*, 185; Catherine Bauer, "The Middle Class Needs Houses, Too," *New Republic* (29 August 1949): 19.

61. Charles Abrams, "Homeless America III: A Workable Housing Program," *The Nation* (4 January 1947): 13; Straus, "Prescription," 544.

62. Senate Committee, *Housing and Urban Redevelopment*, 1567, 1569, 1572.

63. House Committee, *Amendments of 1939*, 71; Senate Committee, *Housing and Urban Redevelopment*, 1296; USHA, *What Housing Act Can Do*, 73ff.

64. NAHO, *After the War*, x, 16, 17; Senate Committee, *Housing and Urban Redevelopment*, 1689, 1700, 1744.

65. Abrams, *Housing Program*, 22–23; Abrams, *Revolution in Land*, 250.

66. Abrams, *Housing Program*, 28; Abrams, *Future of Housing*, 353–354, 361–362, 373.

67. Catherine Bauer, " Housing in the United States: Problems and Policy," *International Labor Review* 52 (1) (July 1945): 8, 9.

68. Bauer, "Middle Class," 18.

69. Abrams, *Revolution in Land*, 252; Abrams, *Housing Program*, 22; Senate Committee, *Housing and Urban Redevelopment*, 1737; Langdon Post, "Attainable Standards in Housing," *Annals of the American Academy of Political and Social Science* 199 (September 1938): 129; Bauer, "Middle Class," 18.

70. Senate Committee, *Housing and Urban Redevelopment*, 1919, 1933, 1934; Senate Committee, *General Housing Legislation*, 337, 387, 405, 569; Fuller, "The Invisible Congress," 464; Helen Fuller, "Stalled in the Lobby," *New Republic* (1 March 1948): 11.

71. Marshall, "Slum Clearance," 104; Senate Committee, *Housing and Urban Redevelopment*, 2063.

72. Senate Committee, *Housing and Urban Redevelopment*, 1603, 2016, 2080; Senate Committee, *General Housing Legislation*, 570.

73. Senate Committee, *Housing and Urban Redevelopment*, 1934, 2077, 2084.

74. Wayne McMillen, "Public Housing in Chicago," *Social Service Review* 20 (2) (June 1946): 164.

75. Samuel Zipp, *Manhattan Projects: The Rise and Fall of Urban Renewal in Cold War New York* (New York, 2010), 148–149, 150–151.

76. This and the following paragraphs are based on Lewis Mumford, "The Sky Line: Prefabricated Blight," *The New Yorker* (30 October 1948): 49–55; Lewis Mumford, "The Sky Line: Stuyvesant Town Revisited," *The New Yorker* (27 November 1948): 65–72.

77. Bauer, "Cities in Flux," 79–80; Bauer, "Good Neighborhoods," 112.

78. Abrams, *Future of Housing*, 322; Charles Abrams, "The Walls of Stuyvesant Town," *The Nation* (28 March 1945): 328.

79. Robert Moses, "Slums and City Planning," *The Atlantic* (January 1945); Abrams, *Future of Housing*, 290.

80. NAHO, *After the War*, 39; Senate Committee, *Housing and Urban Redevelopment*, 1558, 1560, 1689; Coleman Woodbury and Frederick Gutheim, *Rethinking Urban Development* (Chicago, 1949), 13.

81. UAW-CIO, *Memorandum*, 94; "Housing's White Knight," *Architectural Forum* (March 1946), 117, 119.

82. P.L. 171, 81st Cong., 1st sess. (15 July 1949).

83. Davies, *Housing Reform*, 23–24, 26, 33, 67f, 70, 111f; Leonard Freedman, *Public Housing: The Politics of Poverty* (New York, 1969), 19.

84. S. 1592, 79th Cong., 1st sess. (29 October 1945).

85. Hunt *Unraveling*, 188.

86. *Congressional Record*, 4876 (21 April 1949).

87. Mark Gelfand, A *Nation of Cities: The Federal Government and Urban America, 1933–1965* (New York, 1975), 129, 138.

88. Subcommittee on Housing and Urban Redevelopment, *Post War Housing: Report to the Special Committee on Postwar Economic Policy and Planning*, 79th Cong., 1st sess. (1 August 1945); Joint Committee on Housing, *Housing Study and Investigation: Final Majority Report*, 80th Cong., 2nd sess. (15 March 1948).

89. *Congressional Record*, 4837, 4838 (21 April 1949); Senate Committee, *Housing and Urban Redevelopment*, 1614.

90. *Congressional Record*, 4812 (20 April 1949); *Congressional Record*, 8134 (22 June 1949).

91. Senate Committee, *Housing and Urban Redevelopment*, 235.

92. Abrams, *Housing Program*, 29; Charles Abrams, "We Need a Better Housing Bill," *The Nation* (17 May 1947), 562–563; Abrams, "The Politics of Housing," 550.

93. Bauer, "Middle Class," 17–19; Bauer, "Freedom of Choice," 534; "Housing's White Knight," 119.

94. *Congressional Record*, 4799 (20 April 1949); *Congressional Record*, 8131, 8133 (22 June 1949).

95. Joint Committee on Housing, *Housing Study and Investigation: Minority Report*, 80th Cong., 2nd sess. (15 March 1948); *Congressional Record*, 4617 (14 April 1949); *Congressional Record*, 4874 (21 April 1949).

Chapter Four

1. Roger Biles, "Public Housing and the Postwar Urban Renaissance," in *From Tenements to the Taylor Homes*, ed. John Bauman, Roger Biles and Kristin Szlvian 145 (University Park, 2000); Davies, *Housing Reform*, 125f.

2. U.S. Housing and Home Finance Agency, *Views on Public Housing: Symposium of Letters Written at the Request of Norman P. Mason, U.S. Housing Administrator* (Washington, 1960), 153, 154.

3. Alvin Rabushka and William Weissert, *Caseworkers or Police? How Tenants See Public Housing* (Stanford, 1977), 6.

4. Michael Stone, "Housing and the Dynamics of U.S. Capitalism," in *Critical Perspectives on Housing*, ed. Rachel Bratt, Chester Hartman and Ann Meyerson, 51 (Philadelphia, 1986).

5. U.S. Housing and Home Finance Agency, *Views on Public Housing*, 153, 154.

6. William Grisby, "Housing Markets and Public Policy," in *Urban Renewal: The Record and the Controversy*, ed. James Wilson 39 (Cambridge, 1967); Chester Hartman, *Housing and Social Policy* (Englewood Cliffs, 1975), 10–11; Michael Stone, *Shelter Poverty: New Ideas on Housing Affordability* (Philadelphia, 1993), 91, 108, 109.

7. Harold Wolman, *Politics of Federal Housing* (New York, 1971), 52, 55.

8. Murray Meld, "Housing Snafu: Paradox or Portent," *The Nation* (28 September 1957): 192–193.

9. Donald Johnson and Kirk Porter, *National Party Platforms, 1940–1972* (Urbana, 1975), 432, 452, 476, 484, 534–535, 550, 587, 593, 617, 648, 660–661, 680, 721, 731, 750, 799, 868.

10. Davies, *Housing Reform*, 118f; Roger Mulvihill, "Problems in the Management of Public Housing," *Temple Law Review* 35 (1961–1962): 167.

11. D. Bradford Hunt, "How Did Public Housing Survive the 1950s," *Journal of Policy History* 17 (2) (2005): 199.

12. Hunt, "Survive," 201.

13. President's Advisory Committee on Government Housing Policies and Programs, *Government Housing Policies and Programs* (Washington, 1953), 1, 2, 13–14, 16, 260, 266.

14. House Committee on Banking and Currency, *Housing Act of 1954: Hearings on H.R. 7839* 83rd Cong., 2nd sess. (1954), 134–135, 141, 142, 147.

15. Roger Biles, *The Fate of Cities: Urban America and the Federal Government, 1945–2000* (Lawrence, 2011), 59; House Committee, *Housing Act of 1954*, 133, 149, 401.

16. Public Law 560, 83rd Cong., 2nd sess. (2 August 1954).

17. Public Law 1020, 84th Cong., 2nd sess. (7 August 1956); Public Law 103, 85th Cong., 1st sess. (11 July 1957); Public Law 86th Cong., 1st sess. (23 September 1959).

18. William Foley, "John F. Kennedy and the American City: The Urban Program of the New Frontier, 1961–1963." PhD. diss., Indiana University, 2005, 350.

19. Foley, "New Frontier," 94, 144, 150, 347, 348.

20. Elizabeth Drew, "The Long Trial of Public Housing," *The Reporter* (17 June 1965): 15, 17; Alexander von Hoffman, "Calling Upon the Genius of Private Enterprise: the Housing and Urban Development Act of 1968 and the Liberal Turn to Public-Private Partnerships," *Studies in American Political Development* 17 (October 2013): 174, 175–176, 184; Biles, *Fate of Cities*, 124, 125–127, 153–154.

Notes—Chapter Four

21. Senate Committee on Banking and Currency, *Housing Legislation of 1965*, 89th Cong., 1st sess. (1965), 48; House Committee on Banking and Currency, *Housing and Urban Development Act of 1965*, 89th Cong., 1st sess. (1965), 261.

22. President's Committee on Urban Housing, *A Decent Home: Report* (Washington, 1969), i, 1, 5.

23. Biles, *Fate of Cities*, 150; National Commission on Urban Problems, *Building the American City* (Washington, 1968), 119, 180, 192; Anthony Downs, "The Successes and Failures of Federal Housing Policy," *The Public Interest* 34 (Winter 1974): 132.

24. Downs, "Successes and Failures," 137, 138; Charles Orlebeke, "The Evolution of Low Income Housing Policy, 1949 to 1999," *Housing Policy Debate* 11(2) (2000): 501.

25. Richard Nixon, "Special Message to the Congress Proposing Legislation and Outlining Administration Actions to Deal with Federal Housing Policy," September 19, 1973. Online by Gerhard Peters and John T. Woolley, *The American Presidency Project*. http://www.presidency.ucsb.edu/ws/?pid=3968.

26. Nathaniel Keith, *Politics and the Housing Crisis Since 1930* (New York, 1973), 102; Don Parson, *Making a Better World: Public Housing, the Red Scare and the Direction of Modern Los Angeles* (Minneapolis, 2005), 90ff; Thomas Sugrue, "Crabgrass-Roots Politics: Race, Rights the Reaction Against Liberalism in the Urban North, 1940–1964," *Journal of American History* 82 (2) (September 1995): 568; Robert O. Self, *American Babylon: Race and the Struggle for Postwar Oakland* (Princeton, 2003), 73–74.

27. Sugrue, "Crabgrass Roots," 563, 567, 573ff.

28. Arnold Hirsch, *Making the Second Ghetto: Race and Housing in Chicago, 1940–1960* (Chicago, 1998), 53, 55, 179; Thomas Sugrue, *The Origins of the Urban Crisis: Race and Inequality in Postwar Detroit* (Princeton, 2005), 73.

29. Senate Committee on Banking And Currency, *Housing Legislation of 1960*, 86th Cong., 2nd sess., 248; Robert Taggart, *Low Income Housing: A Critique of Federal Aid* (Baltimore, 1970), 126.

30. Parson, *Better World*, 104, 188; Freedman, *Pubic Housing*, 53–54.

31. Harry Conn, "Housing; A Vanishing Vision IV: The Housing Movement in Retreat," *New Republic* (13 August 1951): 15–16; Jordan Luttrell, "The Public Housing Administration and Discrimination in Federally Assisted Low Rent Housing," *Michigan Law Review* 64 (5) (March 1966): 876 (note).

32. House Committee, *Housing Act of 1954: Hearings on H.R. 7839* 83rd Cong., 2nd sess., 271–273, 296–298; House Committee on Banking and Currency, *Slum Clearance and Related Housing Problems*, 85th Cong., 2nd sess. (1958), 112; Senate Committee, *Housing Legislation of 1960*, 1960, 267, 408; House Committee, *Housing and Urban Development*, 481ff.

33. Hunt, *Unraveling*, 135; Peter Marcuse, "Housing Policy and the Myth of the Benevolent State," in *Critical Perspectives on Housing*, ed. Rachel Bratt, Chester Hartman and Ann Meyerson, 254–255 (Philadelphia, 1986).

34. Martin Anderson, *The Federal Bulldozer: A Critical Analysis of Urban Renewal, 1949–1962* (Cambridge, 1964), x, 6, 67, 225, 226.

35. Anderson, *Federal Bulldozer*, 60ff; Chester Hartman, "The Limitations of Public Housing: Relocation Choices in a Working Class Community," *Journal of the American Institute of Planners* 29 (4) (November 1963): 283; Lawrence J. Vale, *Purging the Poorest: Public Housing and the Design Politics of Twice-Cleared Communities* (Chicago, 2103), 204, 213–214; Hunt, *Unraveling*, 79.

36. National Commission on Urban Problems, *Building the American City*, 194; Charles Abrams, *The City is the Frontier* (New York, 1965), 34; Wolf Von Eckardt, "Urban Renewal and the City I: Bulldozers and Bureaucrats," *New Republic* (14 September 1963): 17.

37. Hartman, "Relocation Choices," 284, 285, 289–290, 294, 295.

38. Chester Hartman and Greg Carr, "Housing Authorities Reconsidered," *Journal of the American Institute of Planners* 35 (1) (January 1969): 11, 12; John Bauman, "Public Housing: the Dreadful Saga of a Durable Policy," *Journal of Planning Liter-*

Notes—Chapter Four

ature 8 (4) (May 1994): 101; Hunt, *Unraveling*, 36.

39. Chester Hartman and Margaret Levi, "Public Housing Managers: An Appraisal," *Journal of the American Institute of Planners* 39 (2) (March 1973): 126.

40. Hartman and Carr, "Authorities Reconsidered," 15, 16.

41. Martin Meyerson and Edward Banfield, *Politics, Planning and the Public Interest* (New York, 1955), 25; Nicholas Bloom, "Myth #4: High Rise Public Housing Is Unmanageable," in *Public Housing Myths: Perception, Reality and Social Policy*, ed. Nicholas Bloom, Fritz Umbach, and Lawrence Vale, 91 (Ithaca, 2105); Bloom, *Housing That Worked*, 114, 126, 153–154.

42. Bloom, "Unmanageable," 93; Bloom, *Housing That Worked*, 125; Jackson, *Home*, 229, 255ff; John Clapp, "The Formation of Housing Policy in New York City, 1960–1970," *Policy Sciences* 7 (1) (March 1976): 84.

43. Zipp, *Manhattan Projects*, 261, 268.

44. Zipp, *Manhattan Projects*, 210, 211–212, 286, 287.

45. Clapp, "Housing Policy," 79, 80, 82, 84.

46. Zipp, *Manhattan Projects*, 204, 211.

47. Lewis Mumford, "The Sky Line: The Red Brick Beehives," *The New Yorker* (6 May 1950): 92, 93, 97; Lewis Mumford, "The Sky Line: The Great Good Place," *The New Yorker* (12 November 1949): 73, 78.

48. Lewis Mumford, "The Sky Line: The Gentle Art of Overcrowding," *The New Yorker* (20 May 1950): 79, 81, 82.

49. Jane Jacobs, *The Death and Life of Great American Cities* (New York, 1961), 30.

50. Jacobs, *Great American Cities*, 20, 215, 310.

51. Jacobs, *Great American Cities*, 17, 20, 21, 289, 310.

52. Jacobs, *Great American Cities*, 4, 272, 278, 325.

53. Lewis Mumford, "The Sky Line: Mother Jacobs' Home Remedies," *The New Yorker* (1 December 1962): 163, 167, 171, 178–179.

54. Herbert Gans, "The Death and Life of Great American Cities by Jane Jacobs," *Commentary* (1 February 1962).

55. McMillen, "Chicago," 154.

56. Vale, *Purging the Poorest*, 200; Meyerson and Banfield, *Public Interest*, 32, 33–34, 161,164ff, 207.

57. D. Bradford Hunt, "What Went Wrong with Public Housing in Chicago? A History of the Robert Taylor Homes," *Journal of the Illinois State Historical Society* 94 (1) (Spring 2001): 99, 194; Carl Condit, *Chicago 1930–1970: Building, Planning and Urban Technology* (Chicago, 1974), 158.

58. Alexander Von Hoffman, "Why They Built Pruitt-Igoe," in *From Tenements to the Taylor Homes*, ed. John Bauman, Roger Biles, and Kristin Szlivian, 185 (University Park, 2000); Roger Montgomery, "Pruitt-Igoe: Policy Failure or Societal Symptom," in *The Metropolitan Midwest: Policy Problems and Prospects for Change*, ed. Barry Checkoway and Carl Patton, 233–234 (Urbana, 1985).

59. Eugene Meehan, *Public Housing Policy: Convention Versus Reality* (New Brunswick, 1975), 35, 62; James Bailey, "The Case History of a Failure," *Architectural Forum* 123 (5) (1965), 22.

60. Eugene Meehan, "The Rise and Fall of Public Housing: Condemnation Without Trial," in *A Decent Home and Environment: Housing Urban America*, ed. Donald Phares, 3, 6 (Cambridge, 1977).

61. Robert Fisher, *Twenty Years of Public Housing: Economic Aspects of the Federal Program* (New York, 1959), 245.

62. Fisher, *Twenty Years*, 163.

63. Meehan, *Pubic Housing Policy*, 18; Fisher, *Twenty Years*, 158; House Appropriations Subcommittee, *Independent Offices Appropriations for 1952*, 82nd Cong., 1st sess. (March 1951), 1074–1075; House Committee, *Housing Act of 1954*, 148; Senate Committee on Banking and Currency, *Housing Act of 1958*, 85th Cong., 2nd sess. (1958), 156–157.

64. Hunt, *Unraveling*, 200; Lisa Peattie, "Public Housing: Urban Slums Under Public Management," in *Race, Change and Urban Society*, ed. Peter Orleans and William Ellis, 287 (Beverly Hills, 1971); Albert Walsh, "Is Public Housing Headed for a Fiscal Crisis," in *Housing and Economics: The American Dilemma*, ed. Michael Stegman, 284 (Cambridge, 1970).

65. Walsh, "Fiscal Crisis," 280–281, 282, 283; Fran deLeeuw, *Operating Costs in Public Housing: A Financial Crisis* (Washington, 1969), 12, 13, 22; C. Peter Rydell, *Factors Affecting Maintenance and Operating Costs in Federal Public Housing Projects* (New York, 1970), v.

66. Vale, *Purging*, 231; Hunt, *Unraveling*, 53, 193, 194.

67. Senate Committee, *Housing Act of 1958*, 149, 155, 548.

68. Fisher, *Twenty Years*, 42.

69. Meehan, *Public Housing Policy*, 60–61, 62, 125; Montgomery, "Pruitt-Igoe," 236–237.

70. Senate Committee, *Housing Legislation of 1960*, 258; Subcommittee on Housing, Senate Committee on Banking and Currency, *Housing and Community Development Legislation*, 88th Cong., 2nd sess. (February 1964), 325; Eugene Meehan, *The Quality of Federal Policy Making: Programmed Failure in Public Housing* (Columbia, 1979), 89.

71. R. Allen Hays, *The Federal Government and Urban Housing* (Albany, 2012), 131.

72. Anthony Downs, *Federal Housing Subsidies: How Are They Working* (Lexington, 1973), 46.

73. Rabushka and Weissert, *Caseworkers*, 30.

Chapter Five

1. Harrison Salisbury, *The Shook-up Generation* (New York, 1958), 74, 75.

2. Arnold Hirsch, "Searching for a 'Sound Negro Policy': A Racial Agenda for the Housing Acts of 1949 and 1954," *Housing Policy Debate* 11 (2) (2000): 394; Matthew Thall, "Design Visions and New Missions: The Origins of High-Rise Public Housing in the United States" (master's thesis, Massachusetts Institute of Technology, 1975), 55; Vale, *Puritans*, 243–244.

3. Albert Mayer, "Architecture as Total Community: The Challenge Ahead; Part 2: Public Housing as Community," *Architectural Record* (April 1964): 178; Catherine Bauer, "Clients for Housing: The Low Income Tenant. Does He Want Super-Tenements?" *Progressive Architecture* (May 1952): 63–64; Thall, "Design Visions," 47; Richard Muth, *Public Housing: An Economic Evaluation* (Washington, 1973), 13.

4. Jeanne Lowe, "Housing and Urban Change: Where Does Social Work Fit In," *The Social Service Review* 45 (1) (March 1971): 5.

5. Nathan Glazer, "Housing Policy and the Family," *Journal of Marriage and the Family* 29 (1) (February 1967): 154.

6. Ronald Jones, David Kaminsky and Michael Roanhouse, *Problems Affecting Low Rent Public Housing Projects: A Field Study* (Washington, 1979), x, 3, 6.

7. Fisher, *Twenty Years*, 237; Devereux Bowly, *The Poorhouse: Subsidized Housing in Chicago* (Carbondale, 2012), 57–58; Samuel Zipp, "The Roots and Routes of Urban Renewal," *Journal of Urban History* 39 (3) (May 2013): 381; Rachel Bratt, "Public Housing: The Controversy and Contribution," in *Critical Perspectives on Housing*, ed. Rachel Bratt, Chester Hartman, and Ann Meyerson, 344 (Philadelphia, 1986).

8. Abrams, *City Is the Frontier*, 32; Jacobs, *American Cities*, 261; Anthony Wallace, *Housing and Social Structure: A Preliminary Survey* (Philadelphia, 1952), 45, 76; Gerald Taube, *A Family Album: The Many Faces of Public Housing* (Boston, n.d.), 1, 16.

9. Salisbury, *Shook-Up Generation*, 81; Jacobs, *American Cities*, 57–58, 286; Senate Committee, *Housing Act of 1958*, 805.

10. Michael Harrington, *The Other America: Poverty in the United States* (New York, 1962) 140–145.

11. Herbert Gans, *The Urban Villagers: Group and Class in the Life of Italian-Americans* (New York, 1983), 13–14, 350, 351, 353.

12. Gans, *Urban Villagers*, 393.

13. Herbert Gans, "The Failure of Urban Renewal," *Commentary* (1 April 1965).

14. Von Hoffman, "Pruitt-Igoe," 181; Thall, "Design Visions," 6; Bauman, "Public Housing," 113; Vale, *Puritans*, 252; Bratt, "Public Housing," 344.

15. Thall, "Design Visions," 39, 44.

16. Zipp, *Manhattan Projects*, 288; Zipp, "Roots," 391; Bloom, *Housing That Worked*, 141; William Ledbetter, "Public Housing: A Social Experiment Seeks Acceptance," *Law and Contemporary Problems* 32 (3)

(Summer 1967): 521; Thall. "Design Visions," 43.

17. Vale, *Purging*, 218, 219; Condit, *Chicago*, 159.

18. Wallace, *Housing and Social Structure*, v, 1.

19. Von Hoffman, "Pruitt-Igoe," 185, 195–6,199; Hunt, *Unraveling*, 134.

20. Parson, *Better World*, 168; Senate Committee on Banking and Currency, *Housing Act of 1954*, 83rd Cong., 2nd sess. (March/April 1954), 298; Timothy Lombardo, "The Battle of Whitman Park: Race, Class and Public Housing in Philadelphia, 1956–1982," *Journal of Social History* 47 (2) (Winter 2013): 407; Clare Cooper, *Easter Hill Village; Some Social Implications of Design* (New York, 1975), 186.

21. Wallace, *Housing and Social Structure*, 60, 90, 94, 100.

22. Elizabeth Wood, "The Case for the Low Apartment," *Architectural Forum* (January 1952): 103, 114; Abrams, *City Is the Frontier*, 31; Bauer, "Super-Tenements?" 61–63.

23. National Commission on Urban Problems, *Building the American City*, 60, 124.

24. Public Law 90-448 (1 August 1968).

25. Zipp, *Manhattan Projects*, 291; Meyerson and Banfield, *Public Interest*, 211; Wallace, *Housing and Social Structure*, 26.

26. Karen Franck and Michael Mostoller, "From Courts to Open Space to Streets: Changes in the Site Design of U.S. Public Housing," *Journal of Architectural and Planning Research* 12 (3) (Autumn 1995): 190, 209.

27. Jacobs, *American Cities*, 15, 57–58, 215.

28. Wallace, *Housing and Social Structure*, 44; Elizabeth Wood, *The Balanced Neighborhood: A Study and Recommendations* (New York, 1960), 25; Lewis Mumford, "In Defense of the Neighborhood," *Town Planning Review* 24 (January 1954); Zipp, *Manhattan Projects*, 333.

29. Bloom, *Housing That Worked*, 136; Condit, *Chicago*, 152; Meehan, *Rise and Fall*, 9.

30. United States Public Housing Administration, *Low-Rent Public Housing: Planning, Design and Construction for Economy* (Washington, 1950), 1, 4–5; Fisher, *Twenty Years*, 141; Thall, "Design Visions," 50, 51, 52.

31. Bloom, *Housing That Worked*, 136; House Committee, *Slum Clearance and Related Housing Problems*, 148.

32. Fisher, *Twenty Years*, 61; House Subcommittee, *Independent Offices Appropriations for 1952*, 992; Abrams, *Frontier*, 31; Ledbetter, "Social Acceptance," 509; Daniel Seligman "Enduring Slums," in *The Exploding Metropolis*, ed. William Whyte, 126 (Berkeley, 1993); Irving Welfeld, "Toward a New Federal Housing Policy," *The Public Interest* (Spring 1970): 32.

33. Katherine Bristol, "The Pruitt-Igoe Myth," *Journal of Architectural Education* 44 (3) (May 1991): 165, 166.

34. Bloom, *Housing That Worked*, 184; Hunt, *Unraveling*, 156.

35. Harrington, *Other America*, 150.

36. Jacobs, *American Cities*, 42; Oscar Newman, *Defensible Space: Crime Prevention through Urban Design* (New York, 1972), 33.

37. Newman, *Defensible Space*, 24, 27, 51, 52, 53, 56, 78–79, 195.

38. Lee Rainwater, "Fear and the House as Haven in the Lower Class," *Journal of the American Institute of Planners* 32 (1) (January 1966): 30.

39. Newman, *Defensible Space*, 12, 19, 34, 38, 200.

40. Newman, *Defensible Space*, 1, 10–11, 12–13, 204.

41. Salisbury, *Shook-Up Generation*, 84.

42. "Worse Than Slums: Pubic Housing Is a Monument to the Welfare State," *Barron's* (27 July 1970): 2; Vale, *Puritans*, 265.

43. Salisbury, *Shook-Up Generation*, 75.

44. Harrington, *Other America*, 151.

45. Jacobs, *American Cities*, 76, 113.

46. Lee Rainwater, *Behind Ghetto Walls: Black Families in a Federal Slum* (New York, 1970), 20; J. S. Fuerst, "Public Housing in Chicago," in *Public Housing in Europe and America*, ed. J.S. Fuerst, 165 (London, 1974); Rabushka and Weissert, *Caseworkers*, 49; George Sternlieb and Bernard Indik, *The Ecology of Welfare: Housing and the Welfare Crisis in New York City* (New York, 1973), 122.

47. "Pruitt-Igoe: Survival in a Concrete

Ghetto," *Social Work* 12 (4) (October 1967): 9; Rainwater, "Fear," 30; Rainwater, *Behind Ghetto Walls*, 20.

48. Fritz Umbach, *The Last Neighborhood Cops: The Rise and Fall of Community Policing in New York Public Housing* (New Brunswick, 2011), 55, 64, 71, 73; Lowe, "Social Work," 13.

49. "Survival," 9; Umbach, *Neighborhood Cops*, 26, 28–29, 44, 196.

50. George Genung, "Public Housing: Success or Failure," *George Washington Law Review* 39 (1970–1971): 751; Hunt, "Robert Taylor," 112; Rabushka and Weissert, *Caseworkers*, 55ff.

51. Mayer, "Public Housing as Community," 170; William Moore, *The Vertical Ghetto: Everyday Life in an Urban Project* (New York, 1969), 218; W. Victor Rouse, *Crime in Public Housing: A Review of Major Issues and Selected Crime Reduction Strategies* (Washington, 1978), v, 1, 2.

52. John Farley, "Has Public Housing Gotten a Bum Rap: The Incidence of Crime in St. Louis Public Housing Developments," *Environment and Behavior* 14 (4) (July 1982): 465ff, 448–449.

53. Bloom, *Housing That Worked*, 193; Richard Bingham and Samuel Kirkpatrick, "Social Services for the Urban Poor: An Analysis of Public Housing Authorities in Large American Cities," *Social Service Review* 49 (1) (March 1975): 67ff.

54. Hunt, *Unraveling*, 160; Public Housing Administration, *Low Rent Public Housing*, 88; National Commission on Urban Problems, *Building the American City*, 127, 190.

55. Bloom, *Housing That Worked*, 143–144, 148.

56. Beatrice Friedman, *Better Housing for the Family* (New York, 1948), 38ff.

57. HHFA, *Views*, 55; Bailey, "Case History," 23; Wood, *Balanced Neighborhood*, 14.

58. HHFA, *Views*, 61; Zipp, *Manhattan Projects*, 304, 307; Bloom, *Housing That Worked*, 146; Alice Alexiou, *Jane Jacobs: Urban Visionary* (New Brunswick, 2006), 47.

59. Jacobs, *American Cities*, 71, 129–130, 132, 133, 312; Jane Jacobs, "The Missing Link in City Redevelopment," *Architectural Forum* (June 1956): 132, 133.

60. Newman, *Defensible Space*, 112.

61. Peattie, "Slums," 292–353; Ray Vicker, "Taxpayer Tenants—Problem Families Hike Public Housing Upkeep, Threaten New Slums," *Wall Street Journal* (10 April 1958).

62. Meehan, *Programmed Failure*, 94ff.

63. Salisbury, *Shook-Up Generation*, 85, 216; Vicker, "New Slums"; Al Hirshen and Vivian Brown, "Too Poor for Public Housing: Roger Starr's Poverty Preferences," *Social Policy* 3 (1) (1972): 29.

64. Newman, *Defensible Space*, 188; Hirshen and Brown, "Preferences," 29; Hartman and Levi, "Managers," 128.

65. United States Department of Housing and Urban Development, *National Housing Policy Review (Housing in the Seventies) Working Papers*, Vol. II (Washington, 1976), 1396, 1397, 1388; Rabushka and Weissert, *Caseworkers*, 42; Robert Sadacca, Suzanne Loux, Morton Isler and Margaret Duffy, *Management Performance in Public Housing* (Washington, 1974), 71.

66. Bloom, *Housing That Worked*, 182, 222; Bratt, "Public Housing," 344–345.

67. Bloom, *Housing That Worked*, 63, 181,182, 185.

68. Ledbetter, "Social Acceptance," 499.

69. Newman, *Defensible Space*, 22–24, 103, 189.

70. Glazer, "Housing Policy," 153.

71. Drayton Bryant, "The Next Twenty Years in Public Housing," *Social Work* 4 (2) (April 1959): 47; Ledbetter, "Social Acceptance," 498; Public Housing Administration, *Low Rent Public Housing*, 33–34.

72. Thall, "Design Visions," 49, 83, 87ff, 98, 103.

73. "What Architects Think About Public Housing," *Architectural Record* (July 1958): 183–186; Thall, "Design Visions," 108.

74. Pommer, "Architecture," 263; Zipp, *Manhattan Projects*, 325.

75. William Whyte, ed., *The Exploding Metropolis* (New York, 1993), 11; Robert Montgomery, "Comment on 'Fear and House as Haven in the Lower Class,'" *Journal of the American Institute of Planners* 32 (1) (January 1966): 33.

76. Catherine Bauer, "The Social Front of Modern Architecture in the 1930s," *Journal of the Society of Architectural Historians* 24 (1) (March 1965): 48, 49.

77. Bauer, "Social Front," 50–52.
78. Bowly, *Poorhouse*, 51; Wallace, *Housing and Social Structure*, 33; Rainwater, "Fear," 30; Friedman, *Better Housing*, 22, 34; Newman, *Defensible Space*, 106.
79. Rainwater, *Behind Ghetto Walls*, 11; HUD, *National Housing Policy Review Working Papers II*, 1388.
80. Umbach, *Neighborhood Cops*, 137–138.

Chapter Six

1. Stephanie Ventura and Christine Bachrach, "Nonmarital Childbearing in the United States, 1940–99," *National Vital Statistics Reports* 48 (16) (18 October 2000): 17; Gretchen Livingston, "Fewer than Half of U.S. Kids Today Live in a 'Traditional' Family," Pew Research Center (22 December 2014).
2. Christine Ross, Sheldon Danziger, and Eugene Smolensky, "The Level and Trend of Poverty in the United States, 1939–1979," *Demography* 24 (4) (November 1987): 597.
3. U.S. Department of Commerce, Bureau of the Census, *Statistical Abstract of the United States for 1970* (Washington, 1970), 297; U.S. Department of Commerce, Bureau of the Census, *Statistical Abstract of the United States for 1980* (Washington, 1980), 354; Michael Katz, *In the Shadow of the Poorhouse: A Social History of Welfare in America* (New York, 1996), 275.
4. Fisher, *Twenty Years*, n.p.; National Commission on Urban Problems, *Building the American City*, 115–116; Henry Aaron, *Shelter and Subsidies: Who Benefits from Federal Housing Policies* (Washington, 1972), 116.
5. Fisher, *Twenty Years*, n.p.; Aaron, *Shelter and Subsidies*, 116; U.S. Department of Commerce, *Statistical Abstract of the United States 1980*, 451; Rabhushka and Weissert, *Caseworkers*, 6–7.
6. Fisher, *Twenty Years*, 241; Meehan, *Public Housing Policy*, 129–130; HUD, *National Housing Policy Review Working Papers II*, 1389ff; Richard Scobie, *Problem Tenants in Public Housing: Who, Where and Why Are They?* (New York, 1975), 36–37; deLeeuw, *Operating Costs*, 20–22; Hartman, *Housing and Social Policy*, 13.
7. Zipp, *Manhattan Projects*, 305, 306.
8. Fisher, *Twenty Years*, n.p.; Aaron, *Shelter and Subsidies*, 117; Bowly, *The Poorhouse*, 68; Hunt, "Robert Taylor," 109; Bloom, *Housing That Worked*, 211; Sternlieb and Indik, *Ecology*, 71; Rabhushka and Weissert, *Caseworkers*, 7.
9. Fisher, *Twenty Years*, n.p.; HUD, *National Housing Policy Review Working Papers II*, 1387–88; deLeeuw, *Operating Costs*, 20–22; Bowly, *Poorhouse*, 113.
10. Rainwater, *Behind Ghetto Walls*, 10, 13–14.
11. A Scott Henderson, "Tarred with the Exceptional Image: Public Housing and Popular Discourse, 1950–1990," *American Studies* 36 (1) (Spring 1995): 41.
12. Lawrence Friedman, "Public Housing and the Poor: An Overview," *California Law Review* 54 (2) (May 1966): 646.
13. Grisby, "Housing Markets," 48; Scobie, *Problem Tenants*, 3; Alvin Schorr, *Slums and Insecurity: An Appraisal of the Effectiveness of Housing Policies in Helping Eliminate Poverty in the United States* (Washington, 1966), 110; H. Warren Dunham and Nathan Grundstein, "The Impact of a Confusion of Social Objectives on Public Housing: A Preliminary Analysis," *Marriage and Family Living* 17 (2) (May 1955): 110–111; J. S. Fuerst, "Hidden Successes of Public Housing," *The Nation* (12 November 1973): 494.
14. Meyerson and Banfield, *Public Interest*, 94–95; Vale, *Purging*, 90–91; Friedman, "Overview," 648.
15. Schorr, *Slums and Insecurity*, 110; Scobie, *Problem Tenants*, 3; HHFA, *Views*, 72.
16. Elizabeth Wood, *The Small Hard Core: The Housing of Problem Families in New York City* (New York, 1957), 1, 16, 19; HHFA, *Views*, 118; Vale, *Puritans*, 283; Fisher, *Twenty Years*, 173.
17. Fisher, *Twenty Years*, n.p.; Aaron, *Shelter and Subsidies*, 117.
18. Wallace, *Housing and Social Structure*, 66; Hartman, *Housing and Social Policy*, 127–128.
19. Taggart, *Low Income Housing*, 24.
20. Vale, *Puritans*, 258; Rhonda Williams, *The Politics of Public Housing: Black Women's Struggles Against Urban Inequality* (New York, 2004), 74; House Commit-

tee on Appropriations, *Independent Offices Appropriations for 1951*, 81st Cong., 2nd sess. (February 1950), 1960; House Committee on Appropriations, *Independent Offices Appropriations for 1953* 82nd Cong., 2nd sess. (January 1952), 1009.

21. Bloom, *Housing That Worked*, 212; Ledbetter, "Social Acceptance," 5056; National Commission on Urban Problems, *Building the American City*, 115–116.

22. House Committee, *Housing Act of 1954*, 401; Hartman, *Housing and Social Policy*, 116; Clapp, "New York City Housing Policy," 83; HHFA, *Views*, 25; Mulvihill, "Problems," 180–181.

23. HHFA, *Views*, 14, 69, 118, 158; Abrams, *Frontier*, 37; House Committee, *Housing Act of 1954*, 583.

24. Wood, *Balanced*, 10, 18–19, 20; Wallace, *Housing and Social Structure*, 50; Mayer, "Public Housing as Community," 175; Freedman, *Public Housing*, 108; Architectural Record, *Architects*, 185.

25. Meehan, *Public Housing Policy*, 135.

26. Harry Reynolds, "Public Housing and Social Values in an American City," *Social Service Review* 39 (2) (June 1965): 161–163.

27. Bloom, *Housing That Worked*, 176, 179; Vale, *Puritans*, 257.

28. Richard Scobie, *Problem Tenants*, 9–10; Umbach, *Neighborhood Cops*, 58, 109; J.S. Fuerst and Roy Petty, "Public Housing in the Courts: Pyrrhic Victories for the Poor," *The Urban Lawyer* 9 (3) (Summer 1977): 504, 505.

29. Bloom, *Housing That Worked*, 209; Sternlieb and Indik, *Ecology*, 56, 89.

30. Genung, "Success of Failure," 760–762.

31. Hirshen and Brown, "Preferences," 28, 32; Fisher, *Twenty Years*, 251; Scobie, *Problem Tenants*, 8; Schorr, *Slums and Insecurity*, 113.

32. Robert Ellickson, "Government Housing Assistance to the Poor," *Yale Law Journal* 76 (3) (January 1967): 51; Joel Steinberg, "Other Peoples' Battles, Our War," *Social Policy* (July/August 1973): 74; "The Dreary Deadlock of Public Housing—How to Break It," *Architectural Forum* 106 (6) (June 1957): 141, 232; Dunham and Grundstein, "Confusion," 109.

33. Wallace, *Housing and Social Structure*, 31, 54; Friedman, "Overview," 666; HHFA, *Views*, 137.

34. Friedman, "Overview," 666; Bloom, *Housing That Worked*, 175; Ledbetter, "Social Acceptance," 505, 522.

35. Fuerst and Petty, "Pyrrhic," 496, 497, 499.

36. Salisbury, *Shook-Up Generation*, 77, 78; Bloom, *Housing That Worked*, 177–178; Roger Starr, "Which of the Poor Shall Live in Public Housing," *The Public Interest* 23 (April 1971): 123.

37. Rainwater, *Behind Ghetto Walls*, 48; Lee Rainwater, "The Lessons of Pruitt-Igoe," *The Public Interest* (Summer 1967): 116, 120, 121.

38. Schorr, *Slums and Insecurity*, 41, 44, 55.

39. House Committee on Banking and Currency, *Housing Act of 1959*, 86th Cong., 1st sess. (January/February 1959), 129.

40. HHFA, *Views*, 39, 59–60; Whyte, *Exploding Metropolis*, 124–125.

41. Whyte, *Exploding Metropolis*, 113, 114; HHFA, *Views*, 136; Senate Committee on Banking and Currency, *Housing Act of 1959*, 86th Cong., 1st sess. (January 1959), 803.

42. Michael Harrington, "Slums, Old and New," *Commentary* 30 (August 1960): 119; Freedman, *Public Housing*, 111; Preston David, "The Human Dimension in Public Housing," *Social Work* 22 9 (1) (January 1964): 32.

43. National Commission on Urban Problems, *Building the American City*, 118; Harrington, *Other America*, 146; Peattie, "Slums Under Public Management," 290; Vicker, "New Slums"; J.S. Fuerst and Roy Petty, "High Rise Housing for Low Income Families," *The Public Interest* 103 (Spring 1991): 126.

44. HHFA, *Views*, 57, 136; Hartman and Carr, "Authorities Reconsidered," 15; Zetta Putter, "Social Work and Public Housing," *Social Work* 8 (4) (October 1963):100, 101–102.

45. Wood, *Hard Core*, 1, 3–4, 5; HHFA, *Views*, 120.

46. Anthony Downs, *Who Are the Urban Poor* (New York, 1968), 4; Starr, "Which," 117; Elizabeth Wood, "Social Welfare Planning," *Annals of the American Academy of*

Political and Social Science 352 (March 1964), 125.

47. Starr, "Which," 116, 117, 123–124.

48. Charles Willie and Janet Weinandy, "The Structure and Composition of 'Problem' and 'Stable' Families in a Low Income Population," *Marriage and Family Living* 25 (4) (November 1963): 446–447.

49. HHFA, *Views*, 15, 20, 127; Scobie, *Problem Tenants*, 28, 53–54, 58, 66; Rabushka and Weissert, *Caseworkers*, 72; Elton Smith, Laurence O'Toole and Beverly Burke, "Managing Public Housing: A Case Study of Myths and Realities," *State and Local Government Review* 16 (2) (Spring 1984): 76, 78–79, 80; Hirshen and Brown, "Preferences," 29.

50. Wood, *Hard Core*, 1; Wallace, *Housing and Social Structure*, 84–85; Roger Starr, "A Reply," *The Public Interest* 31 (Spring 1973): 131.

51. Hunt, *Unraveling*, 189; HHFA, *Views*, 55, 118; Putter, "Social Work and Public Housing," 96; Milnarik, "Federally Funded American Dream," 296.

52. HHFA, *Views*, 41, 55; Catherine Bauer, "Social Questions in Housing and Community Planning," *Journal of Social Issues* 7 (Spring 1951): 107, 112.

53. Hartman, *Politics*, 705; Schorr, *Slums and Insecurity*, 46, 50; National Commission on Urban Problems, *Building the American City*, 123.

54. Harrington, "Slums," 119; Whyte, *Exploding Metropolis*, 125; *Architectural Record*, "Architects," 184.

55. HHFA, *Views*, 120; Harrington, *Other America*, 150, 152–153; Jacobs, *American Cities*, 58, 68; Salisbury, *Shook-Up Generation*, 8–81.

56. Peattie, "Slums Under Public Management," 303; Putter, "Social Work and Public Housing," 97; Ledbetter, "Social Acceptance," 501.

57. Jacobs, *American Cities*, 15, 278, 400; Newman, *Defensible Space*, 107.

58. Rainwater, *Behind Ghetto Walls*, 409; HUD, *Housing in the Seventies*, 100–101; John Dean, "The Myths of Housing Reform," *American Sociological Review* 14 (2) (April 1949): 282–283, 288; Vicker, "New Slums."

59. Hartman, "Politics," 714; Senate Committee, *Housing Legislation of 1965*, 47–48; Freedman, *Public Housing*, 109; Mayer, "Public Housing as Community," 169.

60. Daniel Wilner, Rosabelle Walkley, Thomas Pinkerton and Matthew Tayback, *The Housing Environment and Family Life* (Baltimore, 1962), xix, 5, 23, 243–246, 248f.

61. Schorr, *Slums and Insecurity*, 11, 13, 14, 17, 23, 31.

62. Wallace, *Housing and Social Structure*, v, vi; Irving Rosow, "The Social Effects of the Physical Environment," *Journal of the American Institute of Planners* (1961): 129–131; Dean, "Myths," 284.

63. Wood, *Hard Core*, 2, 11; HHFA, *Views*, 116, 117, 119.

64. Scobie, *Problem Tenants*, 5.

65. Rainwater, "Pruitt-Igoe," 124.

66. Hartman and Carr, "Authorities Reconsidered," 15; Senate Committee, *Housing Act of 1958*, 154; House Committee, *Housing Act of 1959*, 129; Senate Committee, *Housing Legislation of 1960*, 251; House Committee, *Housing and Urban Development Act of 1965*, 202.

67. Rainwater, *Behind Ghetto Walls*, 100–101; David Whitaker, *Cabrini-Green in Words and Pictures* (Chicago, 2000), 24; Umbach, *Neighborhood Cops*, 126.

68. Rabushka and Weissert, *Caseworkers*, 40; Cooper, *Easter Hill*, 156, 187.

69. D. Bradford Hunt, "Myth #2: Modernist Architecture Failed Public Housing," in *Public Housing Myths: Perception Reality and Social Policy*, ed. Nicholas Bloom, Fritz Umbach and Lawrence Vale, 58 (Ithaca, 2015).

70. Schwartz, "Tenant Unions," 429, 430, 433–435.

71. Nick Juravich, "'We the Tenants': Resident Organizing in New York City's Public Housing, 1964–1978," *Journal of Urban History* 43 (3) (2017): 406–412.

72. Peter Marcuse, "Goals and Limitations: The Rise of Tenant Organizations," *The Nation* (19 July 1971): 51; Peter Dreier, "The Tenants Movement," in *Marxism and the Metropolis*, ed. William Tabb and Larry Sawyers, 257–258 (New York, 1984).

73. Michael Karp, "The St. Louis Rent Strike of 1969: Transforming Black Activism and American Low Income Housing," *Journal of Urban History* 40 (4) (2014):

648, 652, 654–655, 656–657; Harris David, "The Settlement of the Newark Public Housing Rent Strike: The Tenants Take Control," *Clearinghouse Review* 10 (1976–77): 103, 108.

Chapter Seven

1. Bauman, "Public Housing," 53; Spann, *Modern America*, 109.

2. Hunt, *Unraveling*, 206; Grisby, "Housing Markets," 33; Wolf Von Eckardt, "Urban Renewal and the City: Black Neck in a White Noose," *New Republic* (10 October 1963): 14; Fern Colborn, *The Neighborhood and Urban Renewal* (New York, 1963), 97–98; William Grimshaw, *Bitter Fruit: Black Politics and the Chicago Machine* (Chicago, 1992), 96; Douglas Massey and Nancy Denton, *American Apartheid: Segregation and the Making of the Underclass* (Cambridge, 1993), 47.

3. John M. Gries and James Ford, eds., *Negro Housing* (Washington, 1932), vii–viii, 114, 115.

4. Senate Committee, *Slum and Low-Rent Housing*, 208; Senate Committee, *United States Housing Act of 1936*, 16, 18–19.

5. Arnold Hirsch, "Choosing Segregation: Federal Housing Policy Between Shelley and Brown," in *From Tenements to the Taylor Homes*, ed. John Bauman, Roger Biles and Kristin Szlvian, 209 (University Park, 2000).

6. John Kirby, *Black Americans in the Roosevelt Era: Liberalism and Race* (Knoxville, 1980), 23; Modibo Coulibaly, Rodney Green and David James, *Segregation in Federally Subsidized Low Income Housing in the United States* (Westport, 1998), 63; Frank Ruechel, "Public Housing, Urban Poverty and Jim Crow: Techwood and University Homes in Atlanta," *Georgia Historical Quarterly* 81 (4) (Winter 1997): 927.

7. Kirby, *Black Americans*, 23.

8. George Wolf and Donald Shriver, "De Facto Segregation in Low-Rent Public Housing," *Urban Law Annual* 175 (1968): 180.

9. Ruechel, "Atlanta, 920, 929, 931–933; Stephen Meyer, *As Long as They Don't Move Next Door* (Lanham, 2000), 57.

10. Schwartz, *New York Approach*, 56.

11. Meyerson and Banfield, *Public Interest*, 121; Fairbanks, *Cincinnati*, 131; Robert Fairbanks, *For the City as Whole: Planning, Politics and the Public Interest in Dallas, Texas, 1900–1965* (Columbus, 1998), 152–153, 153–154; Williams, *Politics*, 35–36; Christopher Wye, "The New Deal and the Negro Community: Toward a Broader Conceptualization, " *Journal of American History* 59 (3) (December 1972): 629–631; Jennifer Donnelly, "Myth, Modernity and Modern Housing: The Development of Public Housing in Depression-Era Cleveland," *Traditional Dwellings and Settlements Review* 25 (1): 58.

12. *Congressional Record*, 4852 (21 April 1949); Davis McEntire, *Residence and Race: Final and Comprehensive Report to the Commission on Race and Housing* (Berkeley, 1960), 318: Coulibaly, *Segregation*, 80, 81, 83.

13. William Barnes, "A Battle for Washington: Ideology, Racism and Self-Interest in the Controversy over Public Housing," *Records of the Columbia Historical Society* 50 (1980): 455, 456, 470; Fairbanks, *Dallas*, 157–158, 162–163; Robert B. Fairbanks, "Public Housing for the City as a Whole: the Texas Experience, 1934–1955," *Southwestern Historical Quarterly* 3 (4) (April 2000): 419; Sugrue, *Origins*, 74.

14. John Bauman, "Safe and Sanitary Without the Costly Frills: The Evolution of Public Housing in Philadelphia, 1929–1941," *Pennsylvania Magazine of History and Biography* 101 (1) (1 January 1977): 125–126.

15. Bloom, *Housing That Worked*, 88, 89.

16. Hirsch, *Second Ghetto*, 217–218, 230.

17. Vale, *Purging*, 188, 210; Hirsch, *Second Ghetto*, 218.

18. Meyer, *Next Door*, 55–57; Wendell Pritchett, *Robert Clifton Weaver and the American City* (Chicago, 2008), 83–84; Walter Stafford, "Dilemmas of Civil Rights Groups in Developing Urban Strategies and Changes in American Federalism, 1931–1970," *Phylon* 37 (1) (First Quarter 1976): 65.

19. Robert Weaver, "Racial Policy in Public Housing," *Phylon* 1 (2) (Second Quarter 1940): 149–152, 155.

20. Weaver, "Racial Policy," 155, 156.
21. Robert Weaver, *The Negro Ghetto* (New York, 1948), 74, 75, 158, 165.
22. Weaver, *Negro Ghetto*, 187ff.
23. Weaver, *Negro Ghetto*, 75–76.
24. Weaver, *Negro Ghetto*, 311, 333–334.
25. Weaver, *Negro Ghetto*, 323, 324, 327–328, 330, 331, 337.
26. George Nesbit, "Relocating Negroes from Urban Slum Clearance Sites," *Land Economics* 25 (3) (August 1949): 278, 279ff.
27. Nesbit, "Relocating," 283.
28. Karen Dash, "Slum Clearance Farce," *The Nation* 142 (3691) (1 April 1936): 411–412.
29. Preston Smith, *Racial Democracy and the Black Metropolis* (Minneapolis, 2012), 32, 33, 36; Hirsch, *Second Ghetto*, 10–11, 15, 133.
30. Hirsch, *Second Ghetto*, 13.
31. Smith, *Racial Democracy*, 47ff, 52, 60–61; Sugrue, *Origins*, 66–71.
32. Joint Committee on Housing, *Housing in America: Its Present Status and Future Implications; A Factual Analysis of Testimony and Studies*, 80th Cong., 2nd sess. (1948), 13; Senate Committee, *Housing and Urban Redevelopment*, 1683; Judith Trolander, *Professionalism and Social Change: From the Settlement House Movement to Neighborhood Centers: 1886 to the Present* (New York, 1987), 80.
33. Bauer, "Good Neighborhoods," 106, 107; Catherine Bauer, "What Are Our Goals II," 535.
34. Bauer, "Freedom of Choice," 535; Bauer, "Middle Class," 19.
35. A. Scott Henderson, *Housing and the Democratic Ideal: The Life and Thought of Charles Abrams* (New York, 2000), 133; Abrams, "Stuyvesant Town," 328.
36. Henderson, *Abrams*, 128, 137.
37. Charles Abrams, "Will Interracial Housing Work," *The Nation* (2 August 1947): 122, 123; Charles Abrams, "Our Chance for Democratic Housing," *The Nation* (16 August 1947): 160–161.
38. Abrams, "Our Chance," 162.
39. Abrams, *Future of Housing*, 404.
40. Abrams, "Our Chance," 161; Schwartz, *New York Approach*, 165.
41. Abrams, "Our Chance," 161.
42. *Congressional Record*, 4851, 4853, 4854, 4855 (21 April 1949).
43. *Congressional Record*, 4850, 4852, 4855, 4856 (21 April 1949).
44. Meyer, *Next Door*, 85–86.
45. *Congressional Record*, 4876 (21 April 1949).
46. McEntire, *Residence and Race*, 318–319; Meyerson and Banfield, *Public Interest*, 246; Arnold Hirsch, "'Containment' on the Home Front: Race and Federal Housing Policy from the New Deal to the Cold War," *Journal of Urban History* 26 (2) (January 2000): 168, 178, 180.
47. Hirsch, "Searching," 425–426, 427; President's Advisory Committee, *Government Housing Policies and Programs*, 257.
48. Meyer, *Next Door*, 139.
49. Meyer, *Next Door*, 142.
50. Luttrell, "Public Housing Administration Discrimination," 879, 880.
51. Luttrell, "Public Housing Administration Discrimination," 880, 881–882, 886.
52. Fisher, *Twenty Years*, Table 14; Department of Housing and Urban Development, *Statistics Yearbook* (Washington, 1966), 264; HUD, *Statistical Yearbook* (Washington, 1974), 61; HUD, *Statistical Yearbook* (Washington, 1978), 220.
53. Adam Bickford and Douglas Massey, "Segregation in the Second Ghetto: Racial and Ethnic Segregation in American Public Housing, 1977," *Social Forces* 69 (4) (June 1991): 1018.
54. Bickford and Massey, "Segregation," 1024–1025.
55. Bloom, *Housing That Worked*, 170, 174–175.
56. Elizabeth Drew, "Long Trial," 16.
57. Hartman and Carr, "Authorities Reconsidered," 97–98.
58. John Bauman, "Row Housing as Public Housing: The Philadelphia Story, 1957–2013," *Pennsylvania Magazine of History and Biography* 138 (4) (October 2014): 431; Williams, *Politics*, 97.
59. Mark Barron, "Adequately Re-Housing Low Income Families: A Study of Class and Race in the Architecture of Public Housing: Marietta, Georgia, 1938–1941," *Perspectives in Vernacular Architecture* 11 (2004): 57, 60.
60. Mittie Olion Chandler, "Politics and the Development of Public Housing," in *Cleveland: A Metropolitan Reader*, ed. W. Dennis Keating, Norman Krumholz, and

David Perry, 236 (Kent, 1995); Sugrue, *Origins*, 86–87.

61. Williams, *Politics*, 105, 109–110; Vale, *Puritans*, 309–310.

62. Neil Kraus, *Race, Neighborhoods and Community Power: Buffalo Politics, 1934–1997* (Albany, 2000), 107–111.

63. See, among others, Hirsch, *Second Ghetto*; Meyerson and Banfield, *Public Interest*; Bowly, *Poorhouse*; Hunt, *Unraveling*.

64. Hirsch, *Second Ghetto*, 238–239; Bowly, *Poorhouse*, 74–75; Hunt *Unraveling*, 203.

65. Schwartz, *New York Approach*, 122; Bloom, *Housing That Worked*, 204–207.

66. Salisbury, *Shook-Up Generation*, 7; Roger Starr, "Housing the City's People," *Proceedings of the Academy of Political Science* 29 (4) (1969): 144.

67. Roberta Gold, *When Tenants Claimed the City: The Struggles for Citizenship in New York City Housing* (Urbana, 2014), 60; Bloom, *Housing That Worked*, 171, 173; Ledbetter, "Social Acceptance," 504; Luttrell, "Public Housing Administration Discrimination," 888; Bernard Roshco, "The Integration Problem and Public Housing," *New Leader* (4–11 July 1960): 10, 11, 12.

68. Roshco, "Integration Problem," 10–13.

69. Zipp, *Manhattan Projects*, 313–314.

70. Zipp, *Manhattan Projects*, 316–317.

71. *National Housing Policy Review Working Papers II*, 1388, 1410, 1413.

72. Friedman, "Overview," 644.

73. George Grier, "The Negro Ghettos and Federal Housing Policy," *Law and Contemporary Problems* 32 (3) (Summer 1967): 550.

74. Harrington, *Other America*, 143–144.

75. Friedman, "General Considerations," 362.

76. Senate Committee, *Housing Legislation of 1960*, 247.

77. Charles Abrams, *Forbidden Neighbors: A Study in Prejudice in Housing* (New York, 1955), 306, 309.

78. Abrams, *Forbidden Neighbors*, 310–314.

79. Abrams, *Forbidden Neighbors*, 247, 249, 313; Charles Abrams, "Slums, Ghettos and the GOP's Remedy," *The Reporter* 10 (10) (11 May 1954): 28–30; Charles Abrams, "The Segregation Threat to Housing," in *Two-Thirds of a Nation: A Housing Program*, ed. Nathan Straus, 232, 234 (New York, 1952).

80. Abrams, *Frontier*, 37, 274; Charles Abrams, "The Housing Problem and the Negro," *Daedalus* 95 (1) (Winter 1966): 73, 74.

81. Robert Weaver, "Integration in Public and Private Housing," *Annals of the American Academy of Political and Social Science* 304 (1) (March 1956): 86, 89.

82. Weaver, "Integration," 90; Robert Weaver, "Recent Developments in Urban Housing and their Implications for Minorities," *Phylon* 16 (3) (1955): 278, 279.

83. Weaver, "Integration," 86; Weaver, "Recent Developments," 281.

84. Von Eckardt, "Black Neck," 17; Mulvihill, "Problems," 175–177.

85. Fuerst and Petty, "Hidden Successes," 494, 495; J.S. Fuerst and Roy Petty, "The Quota Approach to Housing," *The Nation* (9 April 1977): 429, 431.

86. Victor, Navasky, "The Benevolent Housing Quota," *Howard Law Journal* 6 (30) (January 1960): 67; Wolf and Shriver, "De Facto Segregation," 181, 182.

87. Frank Horne, "Interracial Housing in the United States," *Phylon Quarterly* 19 (1) (First Quarter 1958): 15–16; J.S. Fuerst, "Public Housing in the United States," in *Public Housing in Europe and America*, ed. J.S. Fuerst, 160–161 (London, 1974); Wolf and Shriver, "De Facto Segregation," 185; James Hanlon, "Fair Housing Policy and the Abandonment of Public Housing Desegregation," *Housing Studies* 30 (1) (2015): 84ff.

88. Hirsch, "Searching," 411; Hirsch, "Containment," 175.

89. Horne, "Interracial," 17.

90. Hays, *Urban Housing*, 133; HUD, *Housing in the Seventies*, 102; Chandler, "Cleveland," 232.

91. Hunt, *Unraveling*, 242; Fuerst and Petty, "Bleak Housing in Chicago," 105.

92. Frederick Lazin, "The Failure of Federal Enforcement of Civil Rights Regulations in Public Housing, 1963–1971: The Co-option of a Federal Agency by its Local Constituency," *Policy Sciences*, 4 (3)

(September 1973): 272; R.J. Gilson, "Public Housing and Urban Policy: Gautreaux v. Chicago Housing Authority," *Yale Law Journal* 79 (March 1970): 717–718, 720; Fuerst and Petty, "Bleak Housing," 105.

93. Herbert Hill, "Demographic Change and Racial Ghettoes: The Crisis of American Cities," *Journal of Urban Law* 231 (44) (Winter 1966): 231, 242, 261, 262, 269, 270, 271.

94. Christopher Bonastia, *Knocking on the Door: The Federal Government's Attempt to Desegregate the Suburbs* (Princeton, 2006), 78; McEntire, *Residence and Race*, 320–321; Condit, *Chicago*, 152.

95. John McDonald, "Public Housing Construction and the Cities: 1937–1967," *Urban Studies Research* (2011): 9–10; Ira Goldstein and William Yancey, "Public Housing Projects, Blacks and Public Policy: The Historical Etiology of Public Housing in Philadelphia," in *Housing Desegregation and Federal Policy*, ed. John Goering, 282–283 (Chapel Hill, 1986).

96. Gans, "Urban Renewal"; Von Eckardt, "Black Neck," 14.

97. Gans, "Urban Renewal."

98. Frances Fox Piven and Richard Cloward, "Desegregating Housing: Who Pays for the Reformers' Ideal," *New Republic* (17 December 1966): 18–19.

99. Piven and Cloward, "Desegregating Housing," 22.

Chapter Eight

1. Rabushka and Weissert, *Caseworkers*, xvi.

2. Rabushka and Weissert, *Caseworkers*, xii, 46ff; HUD, *National Housing Policy Review Working Papers II*, 1384, 1387, 1389; Rainwater, *Behind Ghetto Walls*, 11.

3. National Commission on Urban Problems, *Building the American City*, 118; Taggart, *Low Income Housing*, 24–25.

4. Zipp, *Manhattan Projects*, 264; A. Scott Henderson, ""Exceptional Image," 33, 40; Lawrence Friedman, "Government and Slum Housing: Some General Considerations," *Law and Contemporary Problems* 32 (2) (Spring 1967): 362; Rachel Bratt, "Public Housing," 344.

5. Vale, *Puritans*, 284; Rabushka and Weissert, *Caseworkers*, xv.

6. Fuerst, "Hidden Successes," 496; Chester Hartman, "The Politics of Housing," *Dissent* 14 (6) (1 November 1967): 709; Newman, *Defensible Space*, 105; Bingham and Kirkpatrick, "Social Services," 65–66.

7. Friedman, "Overview," 652–653; Rabushka and Weissert, *Caseworkers*, 83; "Worse Than Slums."

8. HUD, *National Housing Policy Review Working Papers II*, 1435–1436.

9. Dean, "Myths of Housing Reform," 282–288.

10. Catherine Bauer, "The Dreary Deadlock of Public Housing," *Architectural Forum* 106 (5)(May 1957): 140, 219, 221.

11. Bauer, "Dreary Deadlock," 219.

12. Bauer, "Dreary Deadlock," 142, 221.

13. Bauer, "Dreary Deadlock," 219.

14. "How to Break It," 218.

15. "How to Break It," passim.

16. "How to Break It," 141, 222, 224.

17. HHFA, *Views*, 55.

18. "How to Break It," 141, 218.

19. House Committee, *General Housing Legislation, 1960*, 355–361; Abrams, *Frontier*, 36, 38–39, 257–258, 266, 267.

20. Schorr, "Poor," 240.

21. Hartman and Carr, "Authorities Reconsidered," 18.

22. Jacobs, *Great American Cities*, 394f.

23. Jacobs, *Great American Cities*, 271, 288.

24. "How to Break It," 141, 218; Friedman, "Overview," 663–664; Aaron, *Shelter*, 108.

25. Bauer, "Social Questions," 114; Bauer, "Dreary Deadlock," 221.

26. Glazer, "Housing Policy," 152, 153.

27. Glazer, "Housing Policy," 154.

28. Glazer, "Housing Policy," 141, 142, 163.

29. Glazer, "Housing Policy," 143, 144.

30. Glazer, "Housing Policy," 141, 142, 145.

31. Jewel Bellush and Murray Hausknecht, "Public Housing; The Context of Failure," in *Urban Renewal: People, Politics and Planning*, ed. Jewel Bellush and Murray Hausknecht, 455 (New York, 1967); Arthur P. Solomon, *Housing the Urban Poor: A Critical Evaluation of Federal Housing Policy* (Cambridge, 1974), 20–22; HHFA, *Views*, 117.

32. Aaron, *Shelter*, 109; Alvin Schorr, "How the Poor Are Housed," in *Urban Housing*, ed. William Wheaton, Grace Milgram, and Mary Meyerson, 235 (New York, 1966).

33. Leon Keyserling, *Progress or Poverty: The U.S. at a Crossroads* (Washington, 1964), 35–36; Rainwater, "Pruitt-Igoe," 125; Solomon, *Housing the Urban Poor*, 22.

34. Genung," Success of Failure," 734; Meehan, *Programmed Failure*, 19.

35. Bauer, "Dreary Deadlock," 140; Mayer, "Public Housing as Community," 169.

36. Bauer, "Social Questions," 113; Bellush and Hausknecht, "Failure," 455; Rabushka and Weissert, *Caseworkers*, xvi.

37. Welfeld, *New Policy*, 36–37; Meehan, "Rise and Fall," 17; HHFA, *Views*, 50; Henderson, *Abrams*, 200.

38. Catherine Bauer, "Housing, Planning and Public Policy," *Marriage and Family Living* 17 (2) (May 1955): 101; Bauer, "Dreary Deadlock," 140–141; Hartman, "Politics," 709–710; Salisbury, *Shook-Up Generation*, 75.

39. Bauer, "Dreary Deadlock," 141–142; Bauer, "Social Questions," 114.

40. Bellush and Hausknecht, "Failure," 452–454; Freidman, "General Considerations," 360, 361; Friedman, "Overview," 649.

41. National Commission on Urban Problems, *Building the American City*, 129, 130.

42. United States Department of Housing and Urban Development, *Housing in the Seventies: A Report of the National Housing Policy Review* (Washington, 1974), 123.

43. HUD, *Housing in the Seventies*, 5–6, 89–90, 126–127.

44. HUD, *Housing in the Seventies*, 88, 101, 181.

45. HUD, *Housing in the Seventies*, 101.

46. HUD, *Housing in the Seventies*, 95, 196.

47. HUD, *Housing in the Seventies*, 95.

Bibliography

Government Documents

Eccles, Marriner, to the President, memorandum, 21 August 1937. *Federal Reserve Archive, Eccles Papers.* Box 7, Folder 2.

Home Owners Loan Corporation. *Residential Security Map and Area Descriptions.* Hartford, CT, 1937.

National Commission on Urban Problems. *Building the American City.* Washington, 1968.

Nixon, Richard. "Special Message to the Congress Proposing Legislation and Outlining Administration Actions to Deal with Federal Housing Policy." September 19, 1973. Online by Gerhard Peters and John T. Woolley, *The American Presidency Project.* http://www.presidency.ucsb.edu/ws/?pid=3968.

President's Advisory Committee on Government Housing Policies and Programs. *Government Housing Policies and Programs.* Washington, D.C., 1953.

President's Committee on Urban Housing. *A Decent Home: Report.* Washington, 1969.

President's Conference on Home Building and Home Ownership. *Housing Objectives and Programs.* Edited by John M. Gries and James Ford. Washington, 1932.

_____. *Negro Housing.* Edited by John M. Gries and James Ford. Washington, 1932.

_____. *Slums Large-Scale Housing and Decentralization.* Edited by John M. Gries and James Ford. Washington, 1932.

United States Congress. *Congressional Record.* 1937, 1949. Washington, D.C.

Bills

United States Congress. House. 7399, 74th Cong., 1st sess., 10 April 1935.

United States Congress. Senate. 2392, 74th Cong., 1st sess., 13 March 1935.

_____. 4424, 74th Cong., 2nd sess., 24 February 1936.

_____. 1685, 75th Cong., 1st sess., 24 February 1937.

_____. 1592, 79th Congress, 1st sess., 29 October 1945.

Hearings

United States Congress. House. Committee on Appropriations. *Independent Offices Appropriations for 1951.* 81st Cong., 2nd sess., February 1950.

_____. *Independent Offices Appropriations for 1952.* 82nd Cong., 1st sess., March 1951.

_____. *Independent Offices Appropriations for 1953.* 82nd Cong., 2nd sess., January 1952.

_____. Committee on Banking and Currency. *Amendments of 1939 to the United States Housing Act.* 76th Cong., 1st sess., 1939.

_____. *General Housing Legislation.* 86th Cong., 2nd sess., 1960.

_____. *Housing Act of 1954: Hearings on H.R. 7839.* 83rd Cong., 2nd sess., 1954.

_____. *Housing Act of 1959.* 86th Cong., 1st sess., 1959.

_____. *Housing Act of 1959.* 86th Cong., 1st sess., January/February 1959.

_____. *Housing and Urban Development Act of 1965*. 89th Cong., 1st sess., 1965.

_____. *Slum Clearance and Related Housing Problems*. 85th Cong., 2nd sess., 1958.

_____. Committee on Education and Labor. *To Create a United States Housing Authority*. 75th Cong., 1st sess., 1937.

United States Congress. Senate. Committee on Banking and Currency. *General Housing Legislation*, 81st Cong., 1st sess., 1949.

_____. *Housing Act of 1954*. 83rd Cong., 2nd sess., March/April 1954.

_____. *Housing Act of 1958*. 85th Cong., 2nd sess., 1958.

_____. *Housing Act of 1959*. 86th Cong., 1st sess., January 1959.

_____. *Housing Legislation of 1960*. 86th Cong., 2nd sess., 1960.

_____. *Housing Legislation of 1965*. 89th Cong., 1st sess., 1965.

_____. Committee on Education and Labor. *Slum and Low-Rent Public Housing; Hearings on S. 2392*. 74th Cong., 1st sess., 1935.

_____. *To Create a United States Housing Authority*. 75th Cong., 1st sess., 1937.

_____. *United States Housing Act of 1936*. 74th Cong., 2nd sess., 1936.

_____. Special Committee on Post-War Economic Policy and Planning. *Housing and Urban Redevelopment*, 79th Cong., 1st sess., 1945.

_____. Subcommittee on Housing. *Housing and Community Development Legislation*. 88th Cong., 2nd sess., February 1964.

Reports

United States Congress. Senate. Joint Committee on Housing. *Housing in America: Its Present Status and Future Implications; A Factual Analysis of Testimony and Studies*. 80th Cong., 2nd sess., 1948.

_____. *Housing Study and Investigation: Final Majority Report*, 80th Cong., 2nd sess., 15 March 1948.

_____. Joint Committee on Housing. *Housing Study and Investigation: Minority Report*, 80th Cong., 2nd sess., 15 March 1948.

_____. Special Committee on Post War Economic Policy and Planning: Subcommittee on Housing and Urban Redevelopment. *Post War Housing: Report to the Special Committee on Postwar Economic Policy and Planning*. 79th Cong., 1st sess., 1 August 1945.

United States Department of Commerce, Bureau of the Census. *Statistical Abstract of the United States for 1970*. Washington, 1970.

_____. *Statistical Abstract of the United States for 1980*. Washington, 1980.

United States Department of Housing and Urban Development. *Housing in the Seventies: A Report of the National Housing Policy Review*. Washington, 1974.

_____. *National Housing Policy Review (Housing in the Seventies) Working Papers*, Vol. II. Washington, 1976.

_____. *Statistics Yearbook*. Washington, 1966.

_____. *Statistical Yearbook*. Washington, 1974.

_____. *Statistical Yearbook*. Washington, 1978.

United States Housing and Home Finance Agency. *Views on Public Housing: Symposium of Letters Written at the Request of Norman P. Mason, U.S. Housing Administrator*. Washington, 1960.

United States Housing Authority. *Annual Report for the Fiscal Year 1939*. Washington, 1940.

_____. *What the Housing Act Can Do for Your City*. Washington, 1938.

United States Public Housing Administration. *Low-Rent Public Housing: Planning, Design and Construction for Economy*. Washington, 1950.

Contemporaneous Sources

Aaron, Henry. *Shelter and Subsidies: Who Benefits from Federal Housing Policies*. Washington, 1972.

Abrams, Charles. *The City Is the Frontier*. New York, 1965.

_____. *Forbidden Neighbors: A Study in Prejudice in Housing*. New York, 1955.

_____. *The Future of Housing*. New York, 1946.

_____. "Homeless America III: A Workable Housing Program." *Nation* (4 January 1947): 13–16.

____. "Housing and Politics." *Survey Graphic* 29 (2) (1 February 1940): 91.
____. "The Housing Problem and the Negro." *Daedalus* 95 (1) (Winter 1966): 64–76.
____. *A Housing Program for America*. New York, 1946.
____. "Our Chance for Democratic Housing." *Nation* (16 August 1947): 160–162.
____. "The Politics of Housing II: A Plank in the Platform." *Nation* (15 May 1948): 548–551.
____. "The Real Housing Issue." *Nation* 149 (17) (21 October 1939): 439–441.
____. *Revolution in Land*. New York, 1939.
____. "The Segregation Threat to Housing." In *Two-Thirds of a Nation: A Housing Program*, edited by Nathan Straus. New York, 1952.
____. "Slums, Ghettos and the GOP's Remedy." *The Reporter* 10 (10) (11 May 1954): 27–30.
____. "The Walls of Stuyvesant Town." *Nation* (28 March 1945): 328–330.
____. "We Need a Better Housing Bill." *Nation* (17 May 1947): 562–3.
____. "Will Interracial Housing Work." *Nation* (2 August 1947): 122–124.
Anderson, Martin. *The Federal Bulldozer: A Critical Analysis of Urban Renewal, 1949–1962*. Cambridge, 1964.
Alfred, Helen. *Municipal Housing*. New York, 1932.
Aronovici, Carol. *Housing the Masses*. New York, 1939.
____. "Housing the Poor: Mirage or Reality," *Law and Contemporary Problems* 1 (2) (March 1934): 148–157.
Ascher, Charles. "Federal Housing Symbols are Tiresome." *Public Opinion Quarterly* 1 (1) (January 1937): 110–112.
____. "The Housing Authority and the Housed." *Law and Contemporary Problems* 1 (2) (March 1934): 250–256.
Bailey, James. "The Case History of a Failure." *Architectural Forum* 123 (5) (1965): 22–25.
Bauer, Catherine. "Cities in Flux: A Challenge to the Postwar Planners." *The American Scholar* 13 (1) (Winter 1943–44): 70–84.
____. *A Citizen's Guide to Public Housing*. Poughkeepsie, 1940.
____. "Clients for Housing: The Low Income Tenant. Does He Want Super-Tenements?" *Progressive Architecture* (May 1952): 61–64.
____. "The Dreary Deadlock of Public Housing." *Architectural Forum* 106 (5) (May 1957): 140–142, 219, 221.
____. "Good Neighborhoods." *Annals of the American Academy of Political and Social Science* 242 (1945): 104–115.
____. "Housing in the United States: Problems and Policy." *International Labor Review* 52 (1) (July 1945): 1–28.
____. "Housing, Planning and Public Policy." *Marriage and Family Living* 17 (2) (May 1955): 101–102.
____. "Individualism and Housing." *Nation* (10 February 1932): 173.
____. "Low Rent Housing and Home Economics." *Journal of Home Economics* 31 (1) (January 1939): 14–18.
____. "The Middle Class Needs Houses, Too." *New Republic* (29 August 1949): 17–20.
____. *Modern Housing*. New York, 1934.
____. "Now, at Last, Housing: the Meaning of the Wagner-Steagall Act." *New Republic* (8 September 1937): 119–121.
____. "Slums Aren't Necessary." *American Mercury* 31 (123) (31 March 1934): 296–305.
____. "The Social Front of Modern Architecture in the 1930s." *Journal of the Society of Architectural Historians* 24 (1) (March 1965): 48–52.
____. "Social Questions in Housing and Community Planning." *Journal of Social Issues* 7 (Spring 1951): 1–34.
____. "What Are Our Goals? II: Freedom of Choice." *Nation* (15 May 1948): 535–537.
Bingham, Richard, and Samuel Kirkpatrick. "Social Services for the Urban Poor: An Analysis of Public Housing Authorities in Large American Cities." *Social Service Review* 49 (1) (March 1975): 64–78.
Bryant, Drayton. "The Next Twenty Years in Public Housing." *Social Work* 4 (2) (April 1959): 46–54.
Canfield, Dorothy. "I Visit a Housing Project." *Survey Graphic* 29 (2) (1 February 1940): 89.
Carter, Hugh. "How Shall We Manage Housing. " *Social Service Review* 14 (4) (December 1940): 723–729.

Churchill, Henry. "Begin Housing Now!" *Nation* 138 (3580) (14 January 1934): 178–179.

———. *The City Is the People.* New York, 1945.

Clapp, John. "The Formation of Housing Policy in New York City, 1960–1970." *Policy Sciences* 7 (1) (March 1976): 77–91.

Colborn, Fern. *The Neighborhood and Urban Renewal.* New York, 1963.

Condit, Carl. *Chicago 1930–1970: Building, Planning and Urban Technology.* Chicago, 1974.

Congress of Industrial Organizations: Department of Research and Education. *Good Shelter for Everyone* (February 1944).

Conn, Harry. "Housing; A Vanishing Vision IV: The Housing Movement in Retreat." *New Republic* (13 August 1951): 15–16.

Cooper, Clare. *Easter Hill Village: Some Social Implications of Design.* New York, 1975.

Crosby, Alexander. "Public Housing in the Doldrums." *New Republic* (1 May 1944): 595–596.

Dash, Karen. "Slum Clearance Farce." *Nation* 142 (3691) (1 April 1936): 410–412.

David, Harris. "The Settlement of the Newark Public Housing Rent Strike: The Tenants Take Control." *Clearinghouse Review* 10 (1976–77): 103–110.

David, Preston. "The Human Dimension in Public Housing." 9 (1) (January 1964): 29–37.

Dean, John. "The Myths of Housing Reform." *American Sociological Review* 14 (2) (April 1949): 281–288.

deLeeuw, Fran. *Operating Costs in Public Housing: A Financial Crisis.* Washington, 1969.

Downs, Anthony. *Federal Housing Subsidies: How are they Working.* Lexington, 1973.

———. "The Successes and Failures of Federal Housing Policy." *The Public Interest* 34 (Winter 1974): 124–144.

———. *Who Are the Urban Poor.* New York, 1968.

"The Dreary Deadlock of Public Housing: How to Break It." *Architectural Forum* 106 (6) (June 1957): 139–141, 218, 222, 224, 226, 228, 230, 232.

Drew, Elizabeth. "The Long Trial of Public Housing." *The Reporter* (17 June 1965): 15–18.

Dunham, H. Warren, and Nathan Grundstein. "The Impact of a Confusion of Social Objectives on Public Housing: A Preliminary Analysis." *Marriage and Family Living* 17 (2) (May 1955): 103–112.

"Editorial." *Christian Science Monitor* (15 February 1936). In *Congressional Digest* 15 (4) (April 1936): 125.

Ellickson, Robert. "Government Housing Assistance to the Poor." *Yale Law Journal* 76 (3) (January 1967): 508–544.

"False Friends of Housing." *New Republic* 92 (1185) (18 August 1937): 34–35.

Farley, John. "Has Public Housing Gotten a Bum Rap: The Incidence of Crime in St. Louis Public Housing Developments." *Environment and Behavior* 14 (4) (July 1982): 443–477.

Fellheimer, Alfred. "Planning American Standards for Low-Rent Housing." *American Architect* 14 (February 1935): 12–28.

Fisher, Ernest. "Housing Legislation and Housing Policy in the United States." *Michigan Law Review*, 31 (3) (January 1933): 320–345.

———. "Housing Problems." *Quarterly Journal of Economics* 48 (1) (November 1933): 129–149.

Fisher, Robert. *Twenty Years of Public Housing: Economic Aspects of the Federal Program.* New York, 1959.

Ford, James. *Slums and Housing.* Cambridge, 1936.

Freed, Allie. "Should the Administration's Housing Policy be Continued: Con." *Congressional Digest* 15 (4) (April 1946): 120–122.

Freedman, Leonard. *Public Housing: The Politics of Poverty.* New York, 1969.

Friedman, Beatrice. *Better Housing for the Family.* New York, 1948.

Friedman, Lawrence. "Government and Slum Housing: Some General Considerations." *Law and Contemporary Problems* 32 (2) (Spring 1967): 357–370.

———. "Public Housing and the Poor: An Overview." *California Law Review* 54 (2) (May 1966): 642–669.

Fuerst, J. S. "Hidden Successes of Public

Housing." *Nation* (12 November 1973): 493–496.

———. "Public Housing in Chicago." In *Public Housing in Europe and America*, edited by J.S. Fuerst. London, 1974.

———. "Public Housing in the United States." In *Public Housing in Europe and America*, edited by J.S. Fuerst. London, 1974.

Fuerst, J.S., and Roy Petty. "Bleak Housing in Chicago." *The Public Interest* 53 (Summer 1978): 103–110.

———. "High Rise Housing for Low Income Families." *The Public Interest* 103 (Spring 1991): 118–130.

———. "Public Housing in the Courts: Pyrrhic Victories for the Poor." *The Urban Lawyer* 9 (3) (Summer 1977): 496–513.

———. "The Quota Approach to Housing." *Nation* (9 April 1977): 428–431.

Fuller, Helen. "The Invisible Congress III: The Real Estate Lobby." *New Republic* (3 April 1944): 463–466.

———. "Stalled in the Lobby." *New Republic* (1 March 1948): 11–14.

Gans, Herbert. "The Death and Life of Great American Cities by Jane Jacobs." *Commentary* (1 February 1962): n.p.

———. The Failure of Urban Renewal," *Commentary* (1 April 1965): n.p.

———. *The Urban Villagers: Group and Class in the Life of Italian-Americans*. New York, 1983.

Genung, George. "Public Housing: Success or Failure." *George Washington Law Review* 39 (1970–71): 734–763.

Gilson, R.J. "Public Housing and Urban Policy: Gautreaux v. Chicago Housing Authority." *Yale Law Journal* 79 (March 1970): 712–729.

Glazer, Nathan. "Housing Policy and the Family." *Journal of Marriage and the Family* 29 (1) (February 1967): 140–163.

Goldfield, Abraham. *The Diary of a Housing Manager*. New York, 1938.

Greer, Guy, and Alvin Hansen. *Urban Redevelopment and Housing: A Program for Post War*. Washington, 1941.

Grier, George. "The Negro Ghettos and Federal Housing Policy." *Law and Contemporary Problems* 32 (3) (Summer 1967): 550–560.

Grisby, William. "Housing Markets and Public Policy." In *Urban Renewal: The Record and the Controversy*, edited by James Wilson. Cambridge, 1967.

Hanlon, James. "Fair Housing Policy and the Abandonment of Public Housing Desegregation." *Housing Studies* 30 (1) (2015): 78–99.

Harrington, Michael. *The Other America: Poverty in the United States*. New York, 1962.

———. "Slums, Old and New." *Commentary* 30 (August 1960): 118–119.

Hartman, Chester. *Housing and Social Policy*. Englewood Cliffs, 1975.

———. "The Limitations of Public Housing: Relocation Choices in a Working Class Community." *Journal of the American Institute of Planners* 29 (4) (November 1963): 283–296.

———. "The Politics of Housing." *Dissent* 14 (6) (1 November 1967): 701–714.

Hartman, Chester, and Greg Carr. "Housing Authorities Reconsidered." *Journal of the American Institute of Planners* 35 (1) (January 1969): 10–21.

Hartman, Chester, and Margaret Levi. "Public Housing Managers: An Appraisal." *Journal of the American Institute of Planners* 39 (2) (March 1973): 125–137.

Hill, Herbert. "Demographic Change and Racial Ghettoes: The Crisis of American Cities." *Journal of Urban Law* 231 (44) (Winter 1966): 231–285.

Hirshen, Al, and Vivian Brown. "Too Poor for Public Housing: Roger Starr's Poverty Preferences." *Social Policy* 3 (1) (1972): 28–32.

Hoben, Edmond. "Realism versus Real Estate in Housing." *Journal of Land and Public Utility Economics*, 12 (1) (February 1935): 82–85.

Horne, Frank. "Interracial Housing in the United States." *Phylon Quarterly* 19 (1) (First Quarter 1958): 13–20.

"Housing's White Knight." *Architectural Forum* (March 1946): 116–119, 146–150.

Ickes, Harold. "In Defense of the PWA." *New Republic* 94 (1217) (30 March 1938): 213–215.

———. "The Federal Housing Program: A Progress Report." *New Republic* 81 (1046) (19 December 1934): 155–157.

_____. "The Housing Policy of the PWA." *Architectural Forum* 40 (2) (February 1934): 92.

_____. "The Place of Housing in National Rehabilitation." *Journal of Land and Public Utility Economics* 11(2) (May 1935): 109–116.

Ihlder, John. "The How and Why of Graded Rents." *Survey* 77 (5) (May 1941): 145–147.

Jacobs, Jane. *The Death and Life of Great American Cities*. New York, 1961.

_____. "The Missing Link in City Redevelopment." *Architectural Forum* (June 1956): 132–133.

Johnson, Donald, and Kirk Porter, *National Party Platforms, 1940–1972*. Urbana, 1975.

Jones, Ronald, David Kaminsky, and Michael Roanhouse. *Problems Affecting Low Rent Public Housing Projects: A Field Study*. Washington, 1979.

Keith, Nathaniel. *Politics and the Housing Crisis since 1930*. New York, 1973.

Keyserling, Leon. *Progress or Poverty: The U.S. at a Crossroads*. Washington, 1964.

Lasch, Robert. *Breaking the Building Blockade*. Chicago, 1946.

Lazin, Frederick. "The Failure of Federal Enforcement of Civil Rights Regulations in Public Housing, 1963–1971: The Co-Option of a Federal Agency by its Local Constituency." *Policy Sciences* 4 (3) (September 1973): 263–273.

Ledbetter, William. "Public Housing: A Social Experiment Seeks Acceptance." *Law and Contemporary Problems* 32 (3) (Summer 1967): 490–527.

Leven, Maurice, Harold Moulton, and Clark Warburton. *America's Capacity to Consume*. Washington, 1934.

Lewis, Charles. "An Investment Approach to Housing." *Annals of the American Academy of Political and Social Science* 190 (March 1937): 17–23.

Lowe, Jeanne. "Housing and Urban Change: Where Does Social Work Fit In." *The Social Service Review* 45 (1) (March 1971): 1–16.

Luttrell, Jordan. "The Public Housing Administration and Discrimination in Federally Assisted Low Rent Housing." *Michigan Law Review* 64 (5) (March 1966): 871–890.

Marshall, Robert. "Slum Clearance: A Flight from Reality." *Forum and Century* 101 (2) (February 1939): 103–107.

Mayer, Albert. "Architecture as Total Community: The Challenge Ahead; Part 2: Public Housing as Community." *Architectural Record* (April 1964): 169–178.

_____. "Can We Have a Housing Program? I." *Nation* 141 (3666) (9 October 1935): 400–402.

_____. "Housing: A Call to Action." *Nation* 138 (3589) (18 April 1934): 435–436.

_____. "Letter to the Editor." *New Republic* 98 (1261) (8 February 1939): 8–9.

_____. "New Homes for a New Deal I: Slum Clearance, but How?" *New Republic* 78 (1002): (14 February 1934): 7–9.

_____. "A Practical Housing Program," *Nation* 141 (3667) (16 October 1935): 432–434.

_____. "Why the Housing Program Has Failed." *Nation* (3588) (11 April 1934): 408–409.

_____. "Why Not Housing." *New Republic* 78 (1002) (4 September 1935): 96–98.

Mayer, Albert, Henry Wright, and Lewis Mumford. "New Homes for a New Deal IV: A Concrete Program." *New Republic* 78 (1005) (7 March 1934): 91–94.

McEntire, Davis. *Residence and Race: Final and Comprehensive Report to the Commission on Race and Housing*. Berkeley, 1960.

McMillen, Wayne. "Public Housing in Chicago." *Social Service Review* 20 (2) (June 1946): 150–164.

Meehan, Eugene. *Public Housing Policy: Convention Versus Reality*. New Brunswick, 1975.

_____. *The Quality of Federal Policy Making: Programmed Failure in Public Housing*. Columbia, 1979.

_____. "The Rise and Fall of Public Housing: Condemnation Without Trial." In *A Decent Home and Environment: Housing Urban America*, edited by Donald Phares. Cambridge, 1977.

Meld, Murray. "Housing Snafu: Paradox or Portent." *Nation* (28 September 1957): n.p.

Meyerson, Martin, and Edward Banfield. *Politics, Planning and the Public Interest*. New York, 1955.

Montgomery, Roger. "Comment on 'Fear

and House as Haven in the Lower Class.'" *Journal of the American Institute of Planners* 32 (1) (January 1966): 31–37.

_____. "Pruitt-Igoe: Policy Failure or Societal Symptom." In *The Metropolitan Midwest: Policy Problems and Prospects for Change*, edited by Barry Checkoway and Carl Patton. Urbana, 1985.

Moore, William. *The Vertical Ghetto: Everyday Life in an Urban Project*. New York: 1969.

Moses, Robert. "Slums and City Planning." *The Atlantic* (January 1945): n.p.

Mulvihill, Roger. "Problems in the Management of Public Housing." *Temple Law Review* 35 (1961–1962): 163–194.

Mumford, Lewis. "The Chance for Civilized Housing." *New Republic* 64 (824) (17 September 1930): 115–117.

_____. *The Culture of Cities*. New York, 1938.

_____. "Housing versus Ownership." *New Republic* 69 (889) (16 December 1931): 122–123.

_____. "In Defense of the Neighborhood," *Town Planning Review* 24 (January 1954). Reprinted in *Urban Housing*, edited by William Wheaton, Grace Milgram and Mary Meyerson. New York, 1966.

_____. "New Homes for a New Deal III: The Shortage of Dwellings and Direction." *New Republic* 78 (1004) (28 February 1934): 69–72.

_____. "The Plan of New York II." *New Republic* (22 June 1932): 146–154.

_____. "The Sky Line: The Gentle Art of Overcrowding." *New Yorker* (20 May 1950): 79–83.

_____. "The Sky Line: The Great Good Place." *New Yorker* (12 November 1949): 73–78.

_____. "The Skyline: Looking Forward, Looking Backward." *New Yorker* (6 September 1941): 47–49.

_____. "The Sky Line: Mother Jacobs' Home Remedies." *New Yorker* (1 December 1962): 148–179.

_____. "The Sky Line: The New Housing." *New Yorker* (7 December 1935): 134–136.

_____. "The Sky Line: The New Order." *New Yorker* (26 February 1938). Reprinted in *Sidewalk Critic: Lewis Munford's Writing on New York*, edited by Robert Wojtowicz. New York, 1998.

_____. "The Sky Line: Prefabricated Blight." *New Yorker* (30 October 1948): 49–55.

_____. "The Sky Line: The Red Brick Beehives." *New Yorker* (6 May 1950): 92–98.

_____. "The Sky Line: Stuyvesant Town Revisited." *New Yorker* (27 November 1948): 65–72.

_____. "The Skyline: Versailles for the Millions." *New Yorker* (17 February 1940): 42–44.

_____. "What are Our Goals? I: Cities Fit to Live." *Nation* (15 May 1948): 520–522.

_____. "What Prevents Good Housing?" *New Republic* 67 (866) (8 July 1931).

Muth, Richard. *Public Housing: An Economic Evaluation*. Washington, 1973.

National Association of Housing Officials. *Housing for the United States After the War*. 1944.

_____. *A Housing Program for the United States*. Chicago, 1934.

Navasky, Victor. "The Benevolent Housing Quota." *Howard Law Journal* 6 (30) (January 1960): 30–68.

Nelson, Herbert. "Urban Housing and Land Use." *Law and Contemporary Problems* 1 (2) (March 1934): 158–167.

Nesbit, George. "Relocating Negroes from Urban Slum Clearance Sites." *Land Economics* 25 (3) (August 1949): 275–288.

Newman, Oscar. *Defensible Space: Crime Prevention through Urban Design*. New York, 1972.

Peattie, Lisa. "Public Housing: Urban Slums Under Public Management." In *Race, Change and Urban Society*, edited by Peter Orleans and William Ellis. Beverly Hills, 1971.

Perry, Clarence. "The Neighborhood Unit." *Regional Plan of New York and Its Environs* 7 (1) (1929): 21–140.

Phares, Donald. *A Decent Home and Environment: Housing Urban America*. Cambridge, 1977.

Piven, Frances Fox, and Richard Cloward. "Desegregating Housing: Who Pays for the Reformers' Ideal." *New Republic* (17 December 1966): 17–22.

Post, Langdon. "Attainable Standards in Housing." *Annals of the American Academy of Political and Social Science* 199 (September 1938): 128–132.

_____. *The Challenge of Housing*. New York, 1938.

———. "How Not to Plan Public Housing." *Nation* 144 (13) (27 May 1937): 344–346.

"Pruitt-Igoe: Survival in a Concrete Ghetto." *Social Work* 12 (4) (October 1967): 3–13.

Public Administration Service. *Housing and Welfare Officials Confer: A Summary of Discussions at the Joint Conference of Housing and Welfare Officials, Chicago, 11–13 May 1939*. Chicago, 1939.

———. *A Housing Program for the United States: A Report Prepared for the National Association of Housing Officials*. Chicago, 1935.

Putter, Zetta. "Social Work and Public Housing." *Social Work* 8 (4) (October 1963): 95–103.

Rabushka, Alvin, and William Weissert, *Caseworkers or Police? How Tenants See Public Housing*. Stanford, 1977.

Rainwater, Lee. *Behind Ghetto Walls: Black Families in a Federal Slum*. New York, 1970.

———. "Fear and the House as Haven in the Lower Class." *Journal of the American Institute of Planners* 32 (1) (January 1966): 23–31.

———. "The Lessons of Pruitt-Igoe." *The Public Interest* (Summer 1967): 116–126.

Reynolds, Harry. "Public Housing and Social Values in an American City." *Social Service Review* 39 (2) (June 1965): 57–164.

Rheinstein, Alfred, and Henry Pringle. "Why Slum Clearance May Fail." *Harpers* (October 1939): 520–526.

Robbins, Ira. "Methods of Holding Residential Property." *Annals of the American Academy of Political and Social Science* 190 (March 1937): 109–119.

Rosahn, Beatrice, and Abraham Goldfield. *Housing Management: Principles and Practices*. New York, 1937.

Rosenman, Dorothy. *A Million Homes a Year: Modern Housing for Every Income—the Problems and the Possibilities*. New York, 1945.

Roshco, Bernard. "The Integration Problem and Public Housing. " *New Leader* (4–11 July 1960): 10–13.

Rosow, Irving "The Social Effects of the Physical Environment." *Journal of the American Institute of Planners* (1961): 127–133.

Rouse, W. Victor. *Crime in Public Housing: A Review of Major Issues and Selected Crime Reduction Strategies*. Washington, 1978.

Rydell, C. Peter. *Factors Affecting Maintenance and Operating Costs in Federal Public Housing Projects*. New York, 1970.

Sadacca, Robert, Suzanne Loux, Morton Isler, and Margaret Duffy. *Management Performance in Public Housing*. Washington, 1974.

Salisbury, Harrison. *The Shook-up Generation*. New York, 1958.

Schorr, Alvin. "How the Poor Are Housed." In *Urban Housing*, edited by William Wheaton, Grace Milgram, and Mary Meyerson. New York, 1966.

———. *Slums and Insecurity: An Appraisal of the Effectiveness of Housing Policies in Helping Eliminate Poverty in the United States*. Washington, 1966.

Schmidt, Walter. "Private versus Public Enterprise in Housing." *Journal of Land and Public Utility Economics* 11 (4) (November 1935): 342–351.

Scobie, Richard S. *Problem Tenants in Public Housing: Who, Where and Why Are They?* New York, 1975.

Seligman, Daniel. "The Enduring Slums." In *The Exploding Metropolis*, edited by William Whyte. Berkeley, 1993.

Simkhovitch, Mary. *Here Is God's Plenty: Reflections of American Social Advance*. New York, 1949.

Smith, Elton, Laurence O'Toole, and Beverly Burke, "Managing Public Housing: A Case Study of Myths and Realities." *State and Local Government Review* 16 (2) (Spring 1984): 75–83.

Solomon, Arthur P. *Housing the Urban Poor: A Critical Evaluation of Federal Housing Policy*. Cambridge, 1974.

Stapp, Peyton. *Urban Housing: A Summary of Real Property Inventories Conducted as Work Projects, 1934–36*. Washington, 1938.

Stafford, Walter. "Dilemmas of Civil Rights Groups in Developing Urban Strategies and Changes in American Federalism, 1931–1970." *Phylon* 37 (1) (First Quarter 1976): 59–72.

Starr, Roger. "Housing the City's People." *Proceedings of the Academy of Political Science* 29 (4) (1969): 133–147.

———. "A Reply." *The Public Interest* 31 (Spring 1973): 130–144.

———. "Which of the Poor Shall Live in Public Housing." *The Public Interest* 23 (April 1971): 116–124.

Stein, Emanuel. "The Objectives of Public Housing." *American Municipal Law Review* 7 (2) (July 1942): 121–127.

Steinberg, Joel. "Other Peoples' Battles, Our War." *Social Policy* (July/August 1973): 71–75.

Sternlieb, George, and Bernard Indik. *The Ecology of Welfare: Housing and the Welfare Crisis in New York City.* New York, 1973.

Straus, Michael, and Talbot Wegg. *Housing Comes of Age.* New York, 1938.

Straus, Nathan. "Can We Do It? A Business Man's Prescription." *Nation* (15 May 1948): 544–545.

———. "End the Slums." *Vital Speeches of the Day*, 4 (6) (1 January 1938): 182–184.

———. *The Seven Myths of Housing.* New York, 1944.

Strunk, Norman. "Low Cost Housing under the USHA Experiment." *Journal of Land and Public Utility Economics* 16 (1) (February 1940): 96–99.

Taggart, Robert. *Low Income Housing: A Critique of Federal Aid.* Baltimore, 1970.

Taube, Gerald. *A Family Album: The Many Faces of Public Housing.* Boston, n.d.

Textile Workers Union of America. *Towards a New Day.* 1943.

Thall, Matthew. "Design Visions and New Missions: The Origins of High-Rise Public Housing in the United States." Master's thesis, Massachusetts Institute of Technology, 1975.

United Auto Workers. *Homes for Workers in Planned Communities.* 1943.

———. *Memorandum on Post War Urban Housing.* Detroit, 1944.

Vicker, Ray. "Taxpayer Tenants—Problem Families Hike Public Housing Upkeep, Threaten New Slums." *Wall Street Journal* (10 April 1958).

Vinton, Warren Jay. "A Survey of Approaches to the Housing Problem." *Annals of the American Academy of Political and Social Science* 190 (March 1937): 7–16.

Von Eckardt, Wolf. "Urban Renewal and the City: Black Neck in a White Noose." *New Republic* (10 October 1963): 14–17.

———. "Urban Renewal and the City I: Bulldozers and Bureaucrats." *New Republic* (14 September 1963): 15–19.

Walker, Mabel. *Urban Blight and Slums.* Cambridge, 1938.

Wallace, Anthony. *Housing and Social Structure: A Preliminary Survey.* Philadelphia, 1952.

Walsh, Albert. "Is Public Housing Headed for a Fiscal Crisis." In *Housing and Economics: The American Dilemma*, edited by Michael Stegman. Cambridge, 1970.

Watson, Frank. *Housing Problems and Possibilities in the United States.* New York, 1935.

Weaver, Robert. "Integration in Public and Private Housing." *Annals of the American Academy of Political and Social Science* 304 (1) (March 1956): 86–97.

———. *The Negro Ghetto.* New York, 1948.

———. "Racial Policy in Public Housing." *Phylon* 1 (2) (Second Quarter 1940): 149–156, 161.

———. "Recent Developments in Urban Housing and their Implications for Minorities." *Phylon* 16 (3) (1955): 275–282.

Weintraub, Ruth, and Rosalind Tough. "Federal Housing and World War II." *Journal of Land and Public Utility Economics* 18 (2) (May 1942): 155–162.

Welfeld, Irving. "Toward a New Federal Housing Policy." *The Public Interest* (Spring 1970): 31–43.

"What Architects Think About Public Housing." *Architectural Record* (July 1958): 183–186.

Whyte, William. *The Exploding Metropolis.* New York, 1993.

Willie, Charles, and Janet Weinandy, "The Structure and Composition of 'Problem' and 'Stable' Families in a Low Income Population." *Marriage and Family Living* 25 (4) (November 1963): 439–447.

Wilner, Daniel, Rosabelle Walkley, Thomas Pinkerton, and Matthew Tayback. *The Housing Environment and Family Life.* Baltimore, 1962.

Wolf, George and Donald Shriver, "De Facto Segregation in Low-Rent Public Housing." *Urban Law Annual* 175 (1968): 174–195.

Wolman, Harold. *Politics of Federal Housing*. New York, 1971.
Wood, Edith Elmer. "A Century of the Housing Problem." *Law and Contemporary Problems* 1(2) (March 1934): 137–147.
_____. "The Costs of Bad Housing." *Annals of the American Academy of Political and Social Science* 190 (March 1937): 145–150.
_____. *Introduction to Housing: Facts and Principles*. Washington, 1940.
_____. "Letter to the Editor." *New York Times* (7 April 1940): 144.
_____. *Recent Trends in American Housing*. New York, 1931.
_____. "The Statistics of Room Congestion: Purpose and Technique." *Journal of the American Statistical Association* 23 (163) (September 1928): 263–273.
_____. "That 'One Third' of a Nation." *Survey Graphic* 29 (2) (1 February 1940): 83.
Wood, Elizabeth. *The Balanced Neighborhood: A Study and Recommendations*. New York, 1960.
_____. "The Case for the Low Apartment." *Architectural Forum* (January 1952): 103, 114–117.
_____. "Social Welfare Planning." *Annals of the American Academy of Political and Social Science* 352 (March 1964): 119–128.
_____. *The Small Hard Core: The Housing of Problem Families in New York City*. New York, 1957.
Woodbury, Coleman. "Integrating Private and Public Enterprise in Housing," *Annals of the American Academy of Political and Social Science* 190 (March 1937): 162–175.
Woodbury, Coleman, and Frederick Gutheim. *Rethinking Urban Development*. Chicago, 1949.
"Worse Than Slums: Public Housing Is a Monument to the Welfare State." *Barron's* (27 July 1970).
Wright, Henry. "New Homes for a New Deal II: Abolishing Slums Forever." *New Republic* 78 (1003) (21 February 1934): 41–44.
_____. *Rehousing Urban America*. New York, 1935.

Secondary Works

Alexiou, Alice. *Jane Jacobs: Urban Visionary*. New Brunswick, 2006.
Barnes, William. "A Battle for Washington: Ideology, Racism and Self-Interest in the Controversy over Public Housing." *Records of the Columbia Historical Society* 50 (1980): 452–483.
Barron, Mark. "Adequately Re-Housing Low Income Families: A Study of Class and Race in the Architecture of Public Housing: Marietta, Georgia, 1938–1941." *Perspectives in Vernacular Architecture* 11 (2004): 54–70.
Bauman, John. *Public Housing, Race and Renewal: Urban Planning in Philadelphia, 1920–1974*. Philadelphia, 1987.
_____. "Public Housing: The Dreadful Saga of a Durable Policy." *Journal of Planning Literature* 8 (4) (May 1994): 347–361.
_____. "Row Housing as Public Housing: The Philadelphia Story, 1957–2013." *Pennsylvania Magazine of History and Biography* 138 (4) (October 2014): 425–456.
_____. "Safe and Sanitary Without the Costly Frills: The Evolution of Public Housing in Philadelphia, 1929–1941." *Pennsylvania Magazine of History and Biography* 101 (1) (1 January 1977): 114–128.
Bellush, Jewel, and Murray Hausknecht, "Public Housing; The Context of Failure." In *Urban Renewal: People, Politics and Planning*, edited by Jewel Bellush and Murray Hausknecht. New York, 1967.
Bickford, Adam and Douglas Massey, "Segregation in the Second Ghetto: Racial and Ethnic Segregation in American Public Housing, 1977." *Social Forces* 69 (4) (June 1991): 1011–1036.
Biles, Roger. *The Fate of Cities: Urban America and the Federal Government, 1945–2000*. Lawrence, 2011.
_____. "Nathan Straus and the Failure of U.S. Public Housing, 1937–1942." *Historian* 53(1) (Autumn 1990): 33–46.
_____. "Public Housing and the Postwar Urban Renaissance." In *From Tenements to the Taylor Homes*, edited by John Bauman, Roger Biles and Kristin M. Szlvian. University Park, 2000.

_____. "Robert F. Wagner, Franklin D. Roosevelt and Social Welfare Legislation in the New Deal." *Presidential Studies Quarterly* 28 (1) (Winter 1998): 139–152.

Bloom, Nicholas. "Myth #4: High Rise Public Housing is Unmanageable." In *Public Housing Myths: Perception, Reality and Social Policy*, edited by Nicholas Bloom, Fritz Umbach, and Lawrence Vale. Ithaca, 2105.

_____. *Public Housing that Worked: New York in the Twentieth Century*. Philadelphia, 2008.

Bloom, Nicholas, and Matthew Lasner, eds. *Affordable Housing in New York: The People, Places and Policies that Transformed a City*. Princeton, 2016.

Bonastia, Christopher. *Knocking on the Door: The Federal Government's Attempt to Desegregate the Suburbs*. Princeton, 2006.

Bowly, Devereux. *The Poorhouse: Subsidized Housing in Chicago*. Carbondale, 2012.

Bratt, Rachel. "Public Housing: The Controversy and Contribution." In *Critical Perspectives on Housing*, edited by Rachel Bratt, Chester Hartman, and Ann Meyerson. Philadelphia, 1986.

Bristol, Katherine. "The Pruitt-Igoe Myth." *Journal of Architectural Education* 44 (3) (May 1991): 163–171.

Chandler, Mittie Olion. "Politics and the Development of Public Housing. " In *Cleveland: A Metropolitan Reader*, edited by W. Dennis Keating, Norman Krumholz, and David Perry. Kent, 1995.

Coulibaly, Modibo, Rodney Green, and David James. *Segregation in Federally Subsidized Low Income Housing in the United States*. Westport, 1998.

Davies, Richard. *Housing Reform During the Truman Administration*. Columbia, 1966.

Day, Jared. *Urban Castles: Tenement Housing and Landlord Activism in New York City, 1890–1943*. New York, 1999.

Donnelly, Jennifer. "Myth, Modernity and Mass Housing: the Development of Public Housing in Depression-Era Cleveland," *Traditional Dwellings and Settlements Review* 25 (1) (2013): 55–68.

Dreier, Peter. "The Tenants Movement." In *Marxism and the Metropolis*, edited by William Tabb and Larry Sawyers. New York, 1984.

Fairbanks, Robert. *For the City as Whole: Planning, Politics and the Public Interest in Dallas, Texas, 1900–1965*. Columbus, 1998.

_____. *Making Better Citizens: Housing Reform and the Community Development Strategy in Cincinnati, 1890–1960*. Urbana, 1988.

_____. "Public Housing for the City as a Whole: the Texas Experience, 1934–1955." *Southwestern Historical Quarterly* 3 (4) (April 2000): 403–424.

Foley, William. "John F. Kennedy and the American City: The Urban Program of the New Frontier, 1961–1963." PhD. Diss. Indiana University, 2005.

Franck, Karen, and Michael Mostoller. "From Courts to Open Space to Streets: Changes in the Site Design of U.S. Public Housing." *Journal of Architectural and Planning Research* 12 (3) (Autumn 1995): 186–220.

Gelfand, Mark. A *Nation of Cities: The Federal Government and Urban America, 1933–1965*. New York, 1975.

Genevro, Rosalie. "Site Selection and the New York City Housing Authority, 1934–1039." *Journal of Urban History* 12 (4) (August 1986): 344–352.

Greer, James. "The Home Owners Loan Corporation and the Development of the Residential Security Maps." *Journal of Urban History* 39 (2) (March 2013): 275–296.

Grimshaw, William. *Bitter Fruit: Black Politics and the Chicago Machine*. Chicago, 1992.

Gold, Roberta. *When Tenants Claimed the City: The Struggles for Citizenship in New York City Housing*. Urbana, 2014.

Goldstein, Ira, and William Yancey. "Public Housing Projects, Blacks and Public Policy: the Historical Etiology of Public Housing in Philadelphia." In *Housing Desegregation and Federal Policy*, edited by John Goering. Chapel Hill, 1986.

Hanlon, James. "Fair Housing Policy and the Abandonment of Public Housing Desegregation." *Housing Studies* 30 (1) (2015): 78–99.

Hays, R. Allen. *The Federal Government and Urban Housing*. Albany, 2012.

Henderson, A. Scott. *Housing and the Democratic Ideal: The Life and Thought of Charles Abrams*. New York, 2000.

———. "'Tarred with the Exceptional Image': Pubic Housing and Popular Discourse, 1950–1990." *American Studies* 36 (1) (Spring 1995): 31–52.

Hirsch, Arnold. "Choosing Segregation: Federal Housing Policy Between Shelley and Brown." In *From Tenements to the Taylor Homes*, edited by John Bauman, Roger Biles, and Kristin M. Szlvian. University Park, 2000.

———. "'Containment' on the Home Front: Race and Federal Housing Policy from the New Deal to the Cold War." *Journal of Urban History* 26 (2) (January 2000): 158–189.

———. *Making the Second Ghetto: Race and Housing in Chicago, 1940–1960*. Chicago, 1998.

———. "Searching for a 'Sound Negro Policy': A Racial Agenda for the Housing Acts of 1949 and 1954." *Housing Policy Debate* 11 (2) (2000): 393–441.

Hunt, D. Bradford. *Blueprint for Disaster: The Unraveling of Chicago Public Housing*. Chicago, 2009.

———. "How Did Public Housing Survive the 1950s." *Journal of Policy History* 17 (2) (2005): 193–216.

———. "Myth #2: Modernist Architecture Failed Public Housing." In *Public Housing Myths: Perception, Reality and Social Policy*, edited by Nicholas D. Bloom, Fritz Umbach and Lawrence J. Vale. Ithaca, 2015.

———. "What Went Wrong with Public Housing in Chicago? A History of the Robert Taylor Homes." *Journal of the Illinois State Historical Society* 94 (1) (Spring 2001): 96–123.

Huthmacher, Joseph. *Senator Robert F. Wagner and the Rise of Urban Liberalism*. New York, 1971.

Jackson, Anthony. *A Place Called Home: A History of Low Cost Housing in Manhattan*. Cambridge, 1976.

Juravich, Nick. "'We the Tenants': Resident Organizing in New York City's Public Housing, 1964–1978." *Journal of Urban History* 43 (3) (2017): 400–420.

Karp, Michael. "The St. Louis Rent Strike of 1969: Transforming Black Activism and American Low Income Housing." *Journal of Urban History* 40 (4) (2014): 648–670.

Katz, Michael. *In the Shadow of the Poorhouse: A Social History of Welfare in America*. New York: 1996.

Kirby, John. *Black Americans in the Roosevelt Era: Liberalism and Race*. Knoxville, 1980.

Kraus, Neil. *Race, Neighborhoods and Community Power: Buffalo Politics, 1934–1997*. Albany, 2000.

Livingston, Gretchen. "Fewer than Half of U.S. Kids Today Live in a 'Traditional' Family." *Pew Research Center*. http://www.pewresearch.org/fact-tank/2014/12/22/less-than-half-of-u-s-kids-today-live-in-a-traditional-family/ (22 December 2014).

Lombardo, Timothy. "The Battle of Whitman Park: Race, Class and Public Housing in Philadelphia, 1956–1982." *Journal of Social History* 47 (2) (Winter 2013): 410–428.

Marcuse, Peter. "Housing Policy and the Myth of the Benevolent State." In *Critical Perspectives on Housing*, edited by Rachel Bratt, Chester Hartman, and Ann Meyerson. Philadelphia, 1986.

———. "Goals and Limitations: The Rise of Tenant Organizations." *Nation* (19 July 1971): 50–53.

Massey, Douglas, and Nancy Denton. *American Apartheid: Segregation and the Making of the Underclass*. Cambridge, 1993.

McDonald, John. "Public Housing Construction and the Cities: 1937–1967." *Urban Studies Research* (2011): 1–12.

McDonnell, Timothy. *The Wagner Housing Act: A Case Study in the Legislative Process*. Chicago, 1957.

Meyer, Stephen. *As Long as They Don't Move Next Door*. Lanham, 2000.

Milnarik, Elizabeth. "The Federally Funded American Dream: Public Housing as an Engine for Social Improvement, 1933–1937," Ph.D. Diss. University of Virginia, 2009.

Montgomery, Roger. "Pruitt-Igoe: Policy Failure or Societal Symptom." In *The Metropolitan Midwest: Policy Problems* and Prospects for Change, edited by Barry Checkoway and Carl Patton. Urbana, 1985.

Oberlander, H. Peter, and Eva Newbrun. Houser: The Life and Work of Catherine Houser. Vancouver, 1999.

Orlebeke, Charles. "The Evolution of Low Income Housing Policy, 1949 to 1999." Housing Policy Debate 11 (2) (2000): 489–520.

Parson, Don. Making a Better World: Public Housing, the Red Scare and the Direction of Modern Los Angeles. Minneapolis, 2005.

Plunz, Richard. A History of Housing in New York City. New York, 1990.

Pommer, Richard. "The Architecture of Urban Housing in the United States in the Early 1930s." Journal of the Society of Architectural Historians 37 (4) (December 1978): 235–264.

Pritchett, Wendell. Robert Clifton Weaver and the American City. Chicago, 2008.

Rabushka, Alvin, and William Weissert. Caseworkers or Police? How Tenants See Public Housing. Stanford, 1977.

Radford, Gail. Modern Housing For America: Policy Struggles in the New Deal Era. Chicago, 1996.

Ross, Christine, Sheldon Danzinger, and Eugene Smolensky, "The Level and Trend of Poverty in the United States, 1939–1979." Demography 24 (4) (November 1987): 587–600.

Ruechel, Frank. "Public Housing, Urban Poverty and Jim Crow: Techwood and University Homes in Atlanta." Georgia Historical Quarterly 81 (4) (Winter 1997): 915–937.

Schwartz, Joel. The New York Approach: Robert Moses, Urban Liberals and Redevelopment of the Inner City. Columbus, 1993.

_____. "Tenant Unions in New York City's Low-Rent Housing, 1933–1949." Journal of Urban History 12 (4) (August 1986): 414–443.

Self, Robert O. American Babylon: Race and the Struggle for Postwar Oakland. Princeton, 2003.

Smith, Preston. Racial Democracy and the Black Metropolis. Minneapolis, 2012.

Spann, Edward K. Designing Modern America: The Regional Planning Association of America and its Members. Columbus, 1996.

Stone, Michael. "Housing and the Dynamics of U.S. Capitalism." In Critical Perspectives on Housing, edited by Rachel Bratt, Chester Hartman, and Ann Meyerson. Philadelphia, 1986.

_____. Shelter Poverty: New Ideas on Housing Affordability. Philadelphia, 1993.

Sugrue, Thomas. "Crabgrass-Roots Politics: Race, Rights the Reaction Against Liberalism in the Urban North, 1940–1964." Journal of American History 82 (2) (September 1995): 551–578.

_____. The Origins of the Urban Crisis: Race and Inequality in Postwar Detroit. Princeton, 2005.

Szylvian, Kristin. "The Federal Housing Program During World War II." In From Tenements to the Taylor Homes, edited by John Bauman, Roger Biles, and Kristin Szylvian. University Park, 2000.

Trolander, Judith. Professionalism and Social Change: From the Settlement House Movement to Neighborhood Centers: 1886 to the Present. New York, 1987.

Umbach, Fritz. The Last Neighborhood Cops: The Rise and Fall of Community Policing in New York Public Housing. New Brunswick, 2011.

Vale, Lawrence J. From the Puritans to the Projects: Public Housing and Public Neighbors. Cambridge, 2000.

_____. Purging the Poorest: Public Housing and the Design Politics of Twice-Cleared Communities. Chicago, 2013.

Ventura, Stephanie, and Christine Bachrach. "Non-Marital Childbearing in the United States, 1940–99." National Vital Statistics Reports 48 (16) (18 October 2000): 1–38.

von Hoffman, Alexander. "Calling Upon the Genius of Private Enterprise: the Housing and Urban Development Act of 1968 and the Liberal Turn to Public-Private Partnerships." Studies in American Political Development 17 (October 2013): 165–194.

_____. "The End of the Dream: The Political Struggle of America's Public Housers." Journal of Planning History 4 (3) (August 2003): 222–253.

_____. "Why They Built Pruitt-Igoe." In From Tenements to the Taylor Homes, edited by John Bauman, Roger Biles, and Kristin Szylvian. University Park, 2000.

Whitaker, David. *Cabrini-Green in Words and Pictures*. Chicago, 2000.

Williams, Rhonda. *The Politics of Public Housing: Black Women's Struggles Against Urban Inequality*. New York, 2004.

Wright, Gwendolyn. *Building the Dream: A Social History of Housing in America*. New York, 1981.

Wye, Christopher. "The New Deal and the Negro Community: Toward a Broader Conceptualization." *Journal of American History* 59 (3) (December 1972): 621–639.

Zipp, Samuel. *Manhattan Projects: The Rise and Fall of Urban Renewal in Cold War New York*. New York, 2010.

——. "The Roots and Routes of Urban Renewal." *Journal of Urban History* 39 (3) (May 2013): 366–391.

Index

Aaron, Henry 228, 230
Abrams, Charles 68, 80, 83, 84, 86, 87, 92, 98, 135, 140, 144, 167, 198, 201, 212, 226, 232, 235, 243
Addams, Jane 43, 48, 81, 190, 192
Advisory Committee on Government Housing Policies and Programs 105–107, 127, 201
Aid for Families with Dependent Children (AFDC) 160, 162
Alabama 52, 61, 98, 105, 199
Alaska 95
Alfred, Helen 26, 28, 44
Allen, Leo 99
Amalgamated Clothing Workers 6
American Association of Social Workers 26, 114
American Association of University Women 12
American Civil Liberties Union 201, 216
American Federation of Labor (AFL) 24, 25, 94, 114
American Federation of Labor-Congress of Industrial Organizations (AFL-CIO) 114
American Friends Service Committee 183, 201
American Labor Party 182
American Public Health Association 143
Americans for Democratic Action 114, 226
America's Capacity to Consume 27
Anderson, Martin 115
Architectural Forum 121, 139
Arkansas 52
Aronovici, Carol 72
Association of Neighborhood Workers 53

Astoria (New York City) 17
Atlanta 65, 116, 139, 189, 190
Atlanta Housing Authority 189
Atlanta University 189

Baltimore 33, 105, 166, 179, 182, 185, 190, 203–205
Baltimore Housing Authority 190, 204, 205
Banfield, Edward 118, 123, 133
Banks v Housing Authority of San Francisco 202, 214
Barron's 147
Bauer, Catherine 21–25, 33, 40, 45, 54, 62, 64, 70, 75, 77, 83, 84, 87, 88, 92, 94, 99, 105, 122, 133, 140, 141, 156, 157, 176, 197, 198, 200, 215, 224–226, 228, 231, 232, 234, 235, 238, 240, 242, 243
Behind Ghetto Walls 171
Better Housing League 80
Blandford, John 65, 86
Bodfish, Morton 35, 38, 39
Bohn, Ernest 28, 65
Boston 2, 26, 78, 103, 115, 116, 128, 129, 133, 136, 137, 147, 149, 150, 152, 161, 166, 168, 175, 185, 204, 205, 223, 229
Boston Housing Authority 128, 129, 133, 168, 175, 176, 205, 223
Boston University 26
Bricker, John 99
Bridgeport (Connecticut) 17
Bronx 17, 65, 72, 89, 119, 207
Bronx Borough Taxpayers League 35
Brooke, Edward 130
Brookings Institution 27
Brooklyn 17, 18, 83, 119, 132, 148, 207, 211

Index

Buffalo 167, 205
Buffalo Housing Authority 205
Byrd, Harry 57, 60

Cabrini-Green Homes 181
Cabrini Homes 138, 181, 192, 195
Cain, Harry 99
California 112, 113, 139, 202
Camden (New Jersey) 17
Canfield, Dorothy 80
Carl Mackley Houses 45
Carnahan, Frank 36
Carter, Hugh 80
Caseworkers or Police 221
Chicago 2, 10, 17, 43, 48, 74, 77, 81, 113, 116, 117, 123, 124, 127, 128, 133, 135, 138–141, 143, 145, 147–149, 152, 157, 161, 162, 164, 165, 170, 180–183, 185, 186, 188, 190–192, 195–197, 203, 205–207, 210, 211, 214–217, 22, 223, 242
Chicago City Council 196
Chicago Daily News 210
Chicago Housing Authority 74, 81, 82, 117, 123, 124, 127, 128, 138, 140, 149, 164, 170, 182, 190, 192, 193, 197, 203, 206, 214, 216, 217
Chicago Tenants Union 183
Children of Sanchez 229
Christian Science Monitor 147
Churchill, Henry 50, 69, 92
Cincinnati 71, 78, 79, 190
Cincinnati Metropolitan Housing Authority 71, 79, 190
City Affairs Committee, Subcommittee on Housing 26
City Housing Corporation 6
City Planning Commission (New York City) 118, 120
Civil Rights Act of 1964 202, 214, 215, 216
Civil Rights Commission 208
Civil Works Administration 8
Clark, Joseph 113, 181, 212
Clark, Kenneth 179
Cleveland 10, 28, 32, 105, 161, 185, 186, 190, 205, 216
Cleveland Housing Authority 105, 205, 216
Cloward, Richard 219
Cole, Albert 105, 106, 127
Colean, Miles 172
Columbia University 12, 26
Columbus (Ohio) 194
Committee for Economic Recovery 39
Communist Party 19, 53, 182
Congress of Industrial Organizations (CIO) 82, 83, 94, 112, 114, 182, 197

Cook County (Illinois) Department of Public Welfare 43
Corona (New York City) 207
Cox, Edward 99

Dale, Richard 206
Dallas 113, 186, 190, 191, 203, 204, 222
Dallas Housing Authority 190
Darst, Joseph 139
Dash, Karen 196
Dayton 215
Dean, John 180, 224
The Death and Life of Great American Cities 121
Defensible Space 146
Delaware County (Pennsylvania) 11
Delinquency Areas 14
Democrats 27, 57, 61, 80, 94, 101, 104, 107, 113, 131, 199, 200, 231, 238
Department of Health, Education and Welfare (HEW) 169, 172, 181, 227
Department of Housing and Urban Development (HUD) 111, 127, 134, 141, 149, 150, 153, 169, 176, 202, 203, 209, 214, 216, 221, 233, 234
Department of the Interior 3, 4, 29, 42, 53, 188
Detroit 17, 65, 112, 113, 165, 186, 191, 196, 197, 203–205, 216
Detroit Housing Authority 204
The Diary of a Housing Manager 31
Dickerson, Earl 197
District of Columbia 74, 166, 191
Douglas, Paul 97, 110, 200
Downs, Anthony 130
Drew, Elizabeth 203

East Harlem (New York City) 69, 122, 136, 151, 152, 161, 178, 207, 209
East River Houses 69, 71, 138, 209
Easter Hill Village 139
Eccles, Marriner 65
Eckers, Frederick 89
Edelman, John 24, 25
Egan, John Taylor 127, 143
Eisenhower, Dwight 102, 105, 107, 108, 128, 143, 181, 201, 212, 226
Ellenbogen, Henry 53, 54
Ellender, Allen 94
Elmer, Manuel 8
England 13
The Exploding Metropolis 172

Fair Housing Act of 1968 202
The Federal Bulldozer 115
Federal Home Loan Bank Board 25

Index

Federal Housing Administration (FHA) 11, 17, 52, 56, 68, 191, 215
Federal Public Housing Authority 64
Federal Works Agency 64
First Houses 29, 46, 47, 135
Fish, Hamilton 60
Fisher, Ernest 39
Flatbush (New York City) 17
Foley, Raymond 97, 200
Forbidden Neighbors 212
Ford, Henry 65
Ford, James 39
Forest Hills (New York City) 207
Fort Greene Houses 132, 137, 152, 153, 154
Fort Worth 165, 203, 222
France 13
Frankfurt (Germany) 22, 23
Freed, Allie 36, 39
French, Frederick 43
Fresh Meadows (New York City) 120
Friedman, Beatrice 151
Friedman, Lawrence 163, 211, 223
Fuerst, James S. 170, 214

Gans, Herbert 122, 123, 136, 137, 218, 219
Gautreaux, Dorothy 216
Geddes, Patrick 21, 121
George, Walter 60
George-Healey Act 55
George Washington Carver Houses 161, 209
Georgia Tech 189
Germany 13, 22
Ginsburg, Horace 46
Ginsburg, Mitchell 169
Glazer, Nathan 134, 155, 228, 229, 230
Goldfield, Abraham 31, 32, 48, 79
Gore, Albert 66, 144
Great Britain 28, 39, 56, 126
Green, William 24, 25
Greenwich House 26
Greenwich Village 26, 83, 121
Greer, Guy 82
Grimm, Peter 50

Hackett, Horatio 51
Hansen, Alvin 82
Harlem 49, 52, 89, 119, 183, 198, 209, 212
Harlem River Houses 29, 46, 50, 190
Harrington, Michael 136, 145, 147, 148, 173, 177, 211
Hartman, Chester 115, 116, 177, 179, 223, 232

Hill, Herbert 217
Hill, Octavia 34, 79
Hill Creek Houses 49
Hillside Homes 31, 65
Home Owners Loan Corporation 10, 11, 112, 158
Hoover, Herbert 3, 5, 16
Horne, Frank 215
Housing Act of 1934 17, 42, 52, 131, 238
Housing Act of 1937 1, 42, 43, 61, 64, 65, 67, 70, 73, 80, 83, 85–87, 93–99, 131, 187, 193, 232, 237, 238, 242
Housing Act of 1949 64, 94–99, 101, 104, 106–109, 112, 115, 117, 118, 123, 126, 131–133, 165, 178, 193, 197, 199–202, 215, 216, 220, 224, 226, 238
Housing Act of 1954 107, 114, 201
Housing Act of 1961 168
Housing Act of 1965 109
Housing Act of 1969 130
Housing and Community Development Act of 1974 112
Housing and Home Finance Agency 65, 73, 97, 105, 108, 133, 172, 181, 200, 215, 226
Housing and Urban Development Act of 1968 109, 141
Housing Authority of San Francisco 202, 214
Housing Division 44, 45, 50, 51, 53, 179
Housing Environment and Family Life 179
Housing Management 79
The Housing of the Unskilled Wage Earner 12
"A Housing Program for the United States" 33
Housing Study Guild 16
Houston 113, 186, 191
"How the Federal Government Builds Ghettos" 217
Howard, Ebenezer 121
Howard Law Journal 214

Ickes, Howard 29, 42, 43, 44, 48, 49–51, 65, 117, 188, 189
Illinois Wesleyan 123
Independent Offices Appropriations Act 105
Inter-Project Council 182

Jacob Riis Houses 140
Jacobs, Jane 121–123, 135, 136, 142, 145, 148, 152, 177, 178, 228
Jane Addams Houses 48, 81, 190
Johnson, Lyndon 102, 104, 109–111, 181, 203

Johnson, Reginald 188
Joint Committee on Housing 97, 99, 197

Kaiser, Edgar 110
Kansas 42
Kansas City 204, 222
Kean, William 206
Kennedy, John 102, 104, 108, 201, 202
Kerner, Otto 110, 223
Keynes, John Maynard 82
Keyserling, Leon 54, 108, 230
King, Martin Luther, Jr. 206
Klutznick, Philip 85
Knickerbocker Village 42, 43, 53
Kohn, Robert 42, 151
Ku Klux Klan 215

Labor Housing Conference 24, 53
LaGuardia, Fiorello 27, 29, 44, 78
Lamont, Robert 3, 187
Lanham, Fritz 65
Lasker, Loula 50
Lavanburg, Fred 31, 32, 53
Lavanburg Homes 31, 53
League of Mothers Clubs 53
Le Corbusier 91, 121, 156, 241
Lewis, Oscar 173, 229
Lincoln Center 120
Lindsay, John 207
Little Italy 192
Long Island City 17
Loop (Chicago) 124
Los Angeles 113,, 139, 161, 185, 194
Louisville 43, 214
Lower East Side (New York City) 17, 22, 29, 31, 42, 43, 46, 53, 72, 119, 120, 148, 207, 282
Lower East Side Housing Conference 53
Lurie, Ellen 151, 170, 209

Madden, Ray 98
Manhattan 20, 27, 43, 71, 89, 90–92, 119–121, 241
Marietta, Georgia 204
Marquette, Bleeker 76
Massachusetts 26, 57, 130
Mayer, Alfred 16–20, 44, 45, 51, 71, 72, 92, 133, 142, 149, 167, 179, 231, 24
McCarthy, Joseph 94, 99
McDonald, Stewart 52
McGuire, Maria 108
Meany, George 110
Meehan, Eugene 125, 143, 231
Merrion, Joseph 81
Metropolitan Life Insurance Company 6, 72, 89, 90–92, 198

Meyer, Agnes 170, 173
Meyerson, Martin 118, 123, 133, 141
Michigan 94, 107
Minneapolis 161
Mitchell, Clarence 215
Mobilization for Youth 168
Modern Housing 21
Moore, William 149
Moscow 132
Moses, Robert 91, 92, 119–121, 198, 206
Mumford, Lewis 16–21, 25, 26, 46, 50, 52, 69, 84, 90–92, 120–122, 140–142, 151, 176, 178, 185, 226, 240, 242
"The Myths of Housing Reform" 224

Nassau County (New York) 11
The Nation 16, 104, 196
National Advisory Commission on Civil Disorders 110, 223
National Association for the Advancement of Colored People (NAACP) 188, 193, 200, 201, 215–218
National Association of Home Builders 81, 105
National Association of Housing and Redevelopment Officials 129, 173, 180
National Association of Housing Associations 76, 86
National Association of Housing Officials 31, 32, 34, 68, 73, 82, 86, 93, 114
National Association of Real Estate Boards 35, 81, 83
National Commission on Urban Problems 110, 141, 151, 160, 166, 173, 178, 222, 223, 233
National Committee Against Discrimination in Housing 114, 201, 217
National Committee on Housing 80
National Council of Catholic Charities 26, 28, 114
National Council of Negro Women 200
National Federation of Settlements (and Neighborhood Centers) 21, 133, 173, 197
National Housing Agency 64, 86
National Housing Conference 104, 114, 128, 130
National Housing Law Project 169
National Housing Policy Review 161, 221
National Industrial Recovery Act 42, 43, 56
National Lumber Dealers Association 36
National Negro Council 206
National Public Housing Conference 25–27, 53, 68, 76, 82, 86, 93, 94, 98

National Tenants Organization 169, 183
National Urban League 188, 201
National Women's Trade Union League 26
Nelson, Herbert 35, 38
Nesbit, George 195, 196
New Deal 10, 23, 42, 57, 80, 82, 92, 100, 125, 131, 228, 238
New Jersey 6, 16, 17
New Masses 16
New Orleans 165
New Republic 16, 62
New York City 2, 8–11, 14–17, 20, 22, 26, 27, 29, 31, 35–38, 42–46, 50, 52, 53, 55, 62, 65, 68, 69, 71, 72, 74, 76–78, 89–82, 117–119, 120, 121, 125, 127, 134, 135, 137–139, 140–144, 147–154, 157, 158, 162, 165–169, 171, 174, 175, 180–183, 185, 188, 190–192, 195, 198, 202, 203, 206–209, 212, 213, 219, 222, 229, 230, 242
New York City Housing Authority 29, 46–48, 65, 68, 69, 71, 72, 74, 77, 79, 83, 118, 125, 133, 134, 143, 145, 148–151, 153, 154, 162, 166, 168, 169, 171, 183, 190, 192, 194, 207–209
New York Housing Board 20, 26
New York Life Insurance Company 120
New York State 26, 65, 108, 120
New York State Committee on Discrimination in Housing 120
New York Times 46, 50, 132, 147
The New Yorker 16, 46
Newark 183, 223
Newman, Oscar 145–147, 149, 152–155, 157, 158, 178
Niebuhr, Reinhold 148
Nixon, Richard 1, 101, 102, 111, 112, 130, 202, 233, 238

Oakland 112, 181
Oakman, Charles 107
O'Grady, Monsignor John 28, 33, 42, 79, 108, 136
Open Communities Initiative 111
Operation Breakthrough 111
The Other America 136

Palmer, Charles 65
Park Avenue 20, 22, 46
Parkchester 72, 89, 154, 155
Peattie, Lisa 152
Pennsylvania 24, 53, 113, 121, 181
Pennsylvania Federation of Labor 24
Perry, Clarence 4, 5, 31, 125
Peter Cooper Village 89

Philadelphia 2, 12, 17, 24, 45, 48, 71, 117, 135, 137–140, 165, 185, 186, 191, 192, 204, 212, 218
Philadelphia Housing Authority 48, 49, 138, 140, 204
Phoenix 186
Pink, Louis 26, 29
Pittsburgh 8, 148, 162, 185
Piven, Frances 219
Polikoff, Alexander 216
Politics, Planning and the Public Interest 123
Post, Langdon 33, 46, 62, 72
President's Committee on Urban Housing 110
President's Conference on Home Building and Home Ownership 3–7, 12, 39, 187, 188
Pruitt-Igoe 111, 124–126, 129, 137, 139, 142–146, 148, 149, 152, 156, 157, 162, 163, 171, 181, 203, 221–224, 242
Public Housing Administration 64, 70, 71, 85, 96, 101, 102, 105, 107, 108, 117, 124, 127, 133, 137, 139, 143, 144, 150, 152, 155–157, 165, 166, 172, 195, 201, 202
Public Housing Authority 96
The Public Interest 217
Public Works Administration 29, 42–46, 48–53, 55, 57–59, 66–69, 71, 74, 87, 88, 108, 110, 113, 120, 134, 139, 188–190, 194
Puerto Rico 12, 173

Queens (New York City) 16–18, 119, 120, 183, 207
Queensbridge Houses 68, 69, 71, 195
Queensbridge Tenants League 183

Rabushka, Alvin 148, 153, 176, 221, 231
Radburn (New Jersey) 6, 16, 17, 185
Radcliffe 26
Rainwater, Lee 146, 148, 157, 163, 171, 175, 178, 181, 230
Real Estate Board of New York 35
Recent Trends in American Housing 12
Reconstruction Finance Corporation 42, 43, 56
Red Hook Houses 68, 69, 71, 195
Regional Planning Association of America 16, 21, 45
Republicans 27, 80, 94, 101, 104, 113, 199
Resettlement Administration 10, 88
Residential Security Maps 10
Residents Advisory Council 183

Index

Reuther, Walter 110
Rheinstein, Alfred 72, 74, 76, 151
Richmond (California) 139
Riverton Houses 89, 198
Robbins, Ira 26, 167
Robert Taylor Homes 124, 137, 139, 162, 182, 203, 211, 222, 223
Rockefeller Foundation 32, 121
Romney, George 111, 202
Roosevelt, Eleanor 26
Roosevelt, Franklin 8, 18, 42, 42, 57, 61, 62, 64–66, 80, 82, 94, 104, 189, 238
Rosahn, Beatrice 79
Rosenman, Dorothy 80
Roshco, Bernard 208
Rosow, Irving 180
Rouse, James 105

St. Louis 2, 10, 17, 11, 123–126, 129, 130, 137–139, 145, 147, 149, 150, 152, 153, 161–163, 167, 182, 183, 185, 203, 204, 222, 223
St. Louis Housing Authority 124, 129, 139, 145, 152, 156, 183
Salisbury, Harrison 132, 136, 145, 147, 148, 152, 153, 171, 177, 207, 232
San Antonio Housing Authority 109
San Diego 186
San Francisco 149, 202, 214
Schmidt, Walter 35–37, 50
Schorr, Alvin 169, 177, 179, 230
Scobie, Richard 175, 176
Seattle 74, 194
Section 8 112
Seligman, Daniel 172, 177
Shannon v. United States Department of Housing and Urban Development 216
Shaw, Clifford 14
Shelley v Kramer 201
Shelter Poverty 103
Shishkin, Boris 114
The Shook-Up Generation 132, 147
The Skyline 16
Slums and Housing 39
Slums and Insecurity 172, 179
Slusser, Charles 144
Simkhovitch, Mary Kingsbury 26, 29, 33, 48, 69, 179, 192, 235, 242, 243
Simkhovitch, Vladimir 26
The Small Hard Core 174
Smith, Al 55
Social Security 83, 162
Social Service Exchange 32
South Side (Chicago) 124, 186, 196, 197, 217
Soviet Union 15

Sparkman, John 98, 105, 199
Special Committee on Post War Planning 94
Stamford (Connecticut) 164
Starr, Roger 174–176, 207
Staten Island (New York City) 119, 207
Steagall, Henry 61
Stein, Clarence 16, 26, 31, 121, 142
Stein, Emanuel 78
Stone, Michael 103
Stonorov, Oscar 24, 45
Straus, Nathan 31, 65–67, 70–72, 75, 84–86, 95, 143, 193
Stuyvesant Town 89, 90–92, 140, 154, 158, 198
Subcommittee on Housing and Urban Redevelopment, Special Committee on Post War Planning 94, 97
Sunnyside Gardens 6, 8, 16, 17, 91, 142

Taft, Robert 71, 84, 94, 95, 97, 98, 105, 200
Taylor, Robert 197
Teamsters 183
Techwood Homes 65, 189
Tenants Council 53
Texas 65, 114
Textile Workers 82
Thomas, Norman 26, 27
Thomas, R.J. 83
Truman, Harry 84, 94, 101, 102, 104, 105, 108, 127, 143, 155, 242
Twin Cities 162
Tydings, Millard 60

Unemployed Councils 19
Union Settlement Association 151, 152, 162, 209
United Auto Workers (UAW) 65, 82, 83, 93, 197
United States Attorney General 182, 183
United States Building and Loan League 35
United States Chamber of Commerce 35, 36
United States Children's Bureau 13
United States Housing Authority (USHA) 49, 54, 61, 64–77, 82, 85–88, 95, 108, 191, 193, 194
United States Savings and Loan League 68, 105
University Homes 189, 190
University of Berlin 26
University of Michigan 123
Unwin, Raymond 121

Urban Institute 153
The Urban Villagers 136

Vassar 21
Vertical Ghetto 149
Vicker, Ray 173
Vienna 15, 30

Wagner, Robert 26, 53–57, 59–61, 94, 95, 97
Wagner, Robert, Jr. 119
Wald, Lillian 31
Walker, Jimmy 27
Wall Street Journal 152, 173
Wallace, Anthony 135, 140–142, 165, 170, 176, 179
Wallace, Henry 182, 242
Walsh, David 57–61, 63
Washington (state) 99
Washington, D.C. 24, 44, 69, 81, 82, 85, 89, 97, 123, 143, 155, 161, 162, 183, 203, 206, 231
Washington Post 170
Washington Square 121
Watson, Frank 30
Weaver, Robert 108, 109, 179, 188, 193–195, 200, 201, 213
Weissert, William 148, 153, 176, 221, 231
West End (Boston) 115, 116, 136, 137
West Side (New York City) 120
West Village (New York City) 121

Westchester County (New York) 11, 104
Wheaton, William 226
Whelan, Ralph 147, 148
"Which of the Poor Shall Live in Public Housing" 174
White, Walter 188, 193
Whyte, William 172
Williams, J.W. 25
Williamsburg (New York City) 49, 190, 211
Williamsburg Houses 29, 46, 49, 69, 76, 190, 211
Willow Run (Michigan) 65
Wilmington (Delaware) 148, 153, 162, 176, 221
Wilmington Housing Authority 176, 221
Wisconsin 94
Wolcott, Jesse 94, 107
Wood, Edith Elmer 12–16, 20, 26, 27, 33, 48, 73, 76, 85, 103, 126, 179, 215, 238
Wood, Elizabeth 123, 124, 138, 140, 142, 143, 151, 164, 174, 176, 177, 180, 192, 206, 214, 223, 226, 230
Woodbury, Coleman 31, 173
Works Progress Administration 8
Wright, Henry 16–20

Yale Law Journal 216
Yamasaki, Minoru 139, 156
Young, Whitney, Jr. 110

www.ingramcontent.com/pod-product-compliance
Lightning Source LLC
Chambersburg PA
CBHW021348300426
44114CB00012B/1131